SHREDS OF MATTER

RE-MAPPING THE TRANSNATIONAL

A Dartmouth Series in American Studies

SERIES EDITOR
Donald E. Pease
Avalon Foundation Chair of Humanities
Founding Director of the Futures of American Studies Institute
Dartmouth College

The emergence of Transnational American Studies in the wake of the Cold War marks the most significant reconfiguration of American Studies since its inception. The shock waves generated by a newly globalized world order demanded an understanding of America's embeddedness within global and local processes rather than scholarly reaffirmations of its splendid isolation. The series Re-Mapping the Transnational seeks to foster the cross-national dialogues needed to sustain the vitality of this emergent field. To advance a truly comparativist understanding of this scholarly endeavor, Dartmouth College Press welcomes monographs from scholars both inside and outside the United States.

For a complete list of books available in this series, see www.upne.com.

Julius Greve, *Shreds of Matter: Cormac McCarthy and the Concept of Nature*
Elisabeth Ceppi, *Invisible Masters: Gender, Race, and the Economy of Service in Early New England*
Yael Ben-zvi, *Native Land Talk: Indigenous and Arrivant Rights Theories and the US Settler State*
Joanne Chassot, *Ghosts of the African Diaspora: Re-Visioning History, Memory, and Identity*
Samuele F. S. Pardini, *In the Name of the Mother: Italian Americans, African Americans, and Modernity from Booker T. Washington to Bruce Springsteen*
Sonja Schillings, *Enemies of All Humankind: Fictions of Legitimate Violence*
Günter H. Lenz, edited by Reinhard Isensee, Klaus J. Milich, Donald E. Pease, John Carlos Rowe, *A Critical History of the New American Studies, 1970–1990*
Helmbrecht Breinig, *Hemispheric Imaginations: North American Fictions of Latin America*
Jimmy Fazzino, *World Beats: Beat Generation Writing and the Worlding of U.S. Literature*
Zachary McCleod Hutchins, editor, *Community without Consent: New Perspectives on the Stamp Act*
Kate A. Baldwin, *The Racial Imaginary of the Cold War Kitchen: From Sokol'niki Park to Chicago's South Side*

JULIUS GREVE

SHREDS OF MATTER

Cormac McCarthy and the Concept of Nature

DARTMOUTH COLLEGE PRESS
HANOVER, NEW HAMPSHIRE

Dartmouth College Press
An imprint of University Press of New England
www.upne.com

Manufactured in the United States of America
Typeset in Sabon and Scala Sans Pro by Integrated Publishing Solutions

Library of Congress Cataloging-in-Publication Data
available upon request

Hardcover ISBN: 978-1-5126-0339-2
Paperback ISBN: 978-1-5126-0340-8
Ebook ISBN: 978-1-5126-0341-5

5 4 3 2 1

To my parents

CONTENTS

ACKNOWLEDGMENTS

In the context of the idea, composition, and eventual publication of this book, trying to thank everyone who directly or indirectly, wittingly or not, helped along the way seems to be a difficult, if not impossible, task. However, a situation like this—which is itself a little bit like unpacking an obscure quotation by one's favorite author—always provides at least a few signposts or helpful markers that ought to display the main individuals and institutions that made possible the realization of the given project.

It is because this study of Cormac McCarthy's concept of nature is based on my doctoral thesis, accepted by and defended at the Faculty of Arts and Humanities of the University of Cologne, Germany, in 2016, that I want to start by thanking my two supervisors, Hanjo Berressem and Bernd Herzogenrath, for their support and inspiration, during as well as prior to the conception and composition of *Shreds of Matter*. My time at the University of Cologne, first as a student and then as a lecturer and research associate, has been a defining stage of my life, and their enthusiasm for all things American, literary, and philosophical have made a lasting impact on me. I will always be grateful for that. I also want to express my gratitude to Leyla Haferkamp and Dan O'Hara for many invaluable seminar sessions—for instance, on the American Renaissance, violence in American literature, and the history of criticism. After these sessions the initial frustration about one's own lack of knowledge regularly turned into a freshly renewed excitement about the intricacies of literary history and/or French theory. (Dan is also the person who introduced me to McCarthy's work.)

I want to thank my former fellow students and colleagues at the University of Cologne who, over the years, helped me shape some of the ideas to be found in this book, including Jasmin Herrmann, Eleana Vaja, Moritz Ingwersen, Kelly Kawar, and Sebastian Goth. In this context, I want to mention that the German Academic Scholarship Foundation (Studienstiftung des deutschen Volkes) generously funded my doctoral research on McCarthy from 2013 until 2016, for which I am immensely grateful.

Special thanks go to those colleagues and friends outside of the Cologne campus with whom I discussed the themes of this book: Christopher John Müller, Rick Wallach, David Holloway, Peter Josyph, Steven Frye, Louise

Jillett, Patrick O'Connor, Markus Wierschem, James Dorson, Sascha Pöhlmann, Ian Buchanan, Marcelo Svirsky, Martin Butler, and Florian Zappe. I am deeply indebted, in particular, to Rocco Gangle, Paul Sheehan, Stacey Peebles, and Chris Eagle, who read and edited large parts of the manuscript of this book, provided helpful suggestions, and generally aided me in conceptualizing what it is that makes McCarthy's fiction so uniquely beautiful and disturbing at the same time.

Parts of my following contributions to criticism on McCarthy appear in the introduction; chapters 1, 3, 4, and 5; and the conclusion of this book: "'Another Kind of Clay': On *Blood Meridian*'s Okenian Philosophy of Nature," *Cormac McCarthy Journal* 13, no. 1 (2015): 27–53; and "'Cloaca Maxima': Conceptualizing Matter in Cormac McCarthy's Southern Fiction," in *Philosophical Approaches to Cormac McCarthy: Beyond Reckoning*, edited by Chris Eagle (New York: Routledge, 2017), 5–32. I am grateful to Penn State University Press and to Routledge, respectively, for their kind permission to reuse some of that material. In that regard, I also want to extend my gratitude both to Katie Salzmann, the lead archivist at the treasure trove of an archive that contains the Cormac McCarthy Papers in the Wittliff Collections, Alkek Library, at Texas State University, San Marcos, and to Amanda Urban on behalf of McCarthy himself, for granting me permission to quote from small portions of the unpublished notes and typescripts to be found there.

Furthermore, I would like to thank everyone involved at Dartmouth College Press and the University Press of New England—in particular, Donald E. Pease, the series editor; Richard Pult, its acquisitions editor, for taking an interest in this project; and Jeanne Ferris, for her amazingly rigorous job of copyediting the manuscript. The fact that the present book is part of Re-Mapping the Transnational, a great book series in American studies, is something that makes me feel proud. Indeed, I am deeply honored to be among the authors who have contributed to this series.

Outside academia, I am grateful for the patience of the following friends, who endured my fascination with—and sometimes were even eager to discuss—literature, philosophy, and the particular conception of nature that connects the two in complex and exciting ways: Malin Nagel, Jasmin Reisdorf, Dominik Schmitz, Jörn Unterburger, Dierk Peters, Philip Stade, and Constantin Krahmer.

I want to thank my extended family—particularly my parents and siblings, Evelyn Constien-Winkelmann, Hans-Ludwig Greve, Charlotte Greve, Anneke de Rudder, Karsten Winkelmann, Johann Greve, Luise Greve, Alma Greve, Matthias Winkelmann, and Stephan Winkelmann—for supporting me, each in his or her own special way, throughout all these years. Finally, my profoundest thanks go to Hanna Riggert for her unconditional love, emotional support, and unending patience. I depend on all three of those incomparable gifts—and more.

ABBREVIATIONS

While the majority of sources for references will be indicated by endnotes, Cormac McCarthy's published works will be cited by abbreviations that are in common use in the scholarship about him. In addition, I have abbreviated the specific titles of the volumes in the following German edition of Friedrich Schelling's entire works in the endnotes: Friedrich W. J. Schelling, *Schellings sämmtliche Werke*, ed. Karl Friedrich August Schelling, 14 vols. (Stuttgart: J. G. Cotta'scher Verlag, 1856–61). The abbreviations used in those cases—*SW* I–XIV, respectively—correspond to the manner in which this edition is cited in Schelling studies.

The abbreviations for McCarthy's works are as follows:

TOK	*The Orchard Keeper*
OD	*Outer Dark*
COG	*Child of God*
S	*Suttree*
BM	*Blood Meridian*
PH	*All the Pretty Horses*
TC	*The Crossing*
CP	*Cities of the Plain*
NC	*No Country for Old Men*
TR	*The Road*
TSL	*The Sunset Limited*
KP	"The Kekulé Problem"

SHREDS OF MATTER

INTRODUCTION: CORMAC MCCARTHY'S CONCEPT OF NATURE

Perhaps in the world's destruction it would be possible at last to see how it was made. Oceans, mountains. The ponderous counterspectacle of things ceasing to be. The sweeping waste, hydroptic and coldly secular. —Cormac McCarthy, *The Road*

Anything whose conditions simply cannot be given in nature, must be absolutely impossible. —Friedrich W. J. Schelling, *System of Transcendental Idealism*

SINCE THEIR EMERGENCE on the horizon of American literature, Cormac McCarthy's novels have taken up a discussion that can be traced back to American and German nineteenth-century literary and philosophical circles. It is the kind of literary prose exemplified in the passage quoted above from *The Road*, originally published in 2006, that signals McCarthy's engagement with that discussion and that sets him apart from other writers of his generation, who are either less interested in it or have taken up a different stance toward it. To distill the topic of this discussion into a single question —"What is nature?"—at once overly simplifies the issue at hand and drives home its most important point: especially in literature, there is a certain difficulty in the practice of determining that which determines—*nature*—rather than determining the nature or the disposition of an object that is thereby determined. Even so, it is the guiding hypothesis of this book that the metaphysical question "What is nature?" is the most adequate one to ask with regard to McCarthy's fictions. This is so above all because it is the central question that these fictions themselves strive to "answer"—albeit in literary, rather than philosophical, terms.

To rephrase the problem involved in the literary response to that metaphysical question, it is important to note that an American author such as McCarthy, who has been writing novels about American life in the Southeast, the Southwest, and the US-Mexican borderlands since the 1960s, would at first glance be described as doing just that—writing *about* the disposition *of* that life. An effect of the way in which the notions of "disposition" and "nature" are defined and used in language is the construction of multiple versions of the very conception of these notions both in literature and in life: there are often innumerable instances at hand of the particular nature of some thing (as in "the nature of racial politics," "the nature of the Civil War," and "the nature of the frontier," for example), while an inquiry into what it is that effectuates the disposition seems lacking. In contrast, it is the claim of this study that the entirety of McCarthy's novelistic work can be interpreted as precisely this latter kind of inquiry. Since his first novel, *The Orchard Keeper* (1965), until *The Sunset Limited* (2006),[1] McCarthy has not merely depicted American life in the South, nor has he just given literary testimony about the landscapes and cityscapes of Tennessee, Texas, or New Mexico—although he has also done that. McCarthy's prose poses, by literary means, a question that is normally developed and examined in philosophy: "What is nature?" It is this distinctive practice of writing that this book examines: McCarthy's narrative *evocation of* a given object that is thus determined, like a city or a dialect in it, and the necessarily related *speculation about* what it is that makes the determination possible. For instance, the way in which his novel *Suttree* (1979) describes the distinct features of Knoxville, Tennessee, in the 1950s includes statements, produces plotlines, and gives rise to a style of writing prose that delineates the author's concept of nature itself, outside of the particular context of the narrative. Yet it is important to recognize that this delineation is not meant as a reflection or representation of a particular idea about nature. To make use of a by now common turn of phrase to be found, above all, in the French philosophy of the past few decades, we might say that McCarthy's novels "think" the question concerning nature's identity, albeit in a different formal and generic register to that of philosophy.

This might seem a difficult if not impossible procedure, in part because the word "nature" already has so many connotations. Indeed, *nature* is one of the most used and misused of all concepts in human forms of inquiry—artistic, aesthetic, scientific, political, and philosophical—in the sense that the discourse on it more often than not takes nature's identity as a given that does not have to be explained. This givenness is premised on the belief that we all know what nature is. For example, nature is often characterized as the "green" part of the globe that should be preserved and fought for by means of political activism. It is conceived of as the opposite of culture and therefore the domain in which human beings are not alienated from themselves, one image of which has been the paradisiacal garden, as Leo Marx explains in *The Machine in the Garden: Technology and the Pastoral Ideal in America* (1964). Nature, as Marx and others have shown, is often characterized as a place of refuge. It is a place of retreat from the commodification of human technologies and the self-destructive behavior of human beings. Furthermore, the word "nature" has, for better or worse, been used synonymously with the word "essence," which is why for a long time during the twentieth century cultural studies have stigmatized the concept of nature. Lastly, of course, nature is the material object of inquiry (the subject matter) of physics, chemistry, biology, and other natural sciences.

This latter connotation of "nature" in particular leads us to make an assumption that will be supported during the specific analyses of this book but that needs to be stated clearly at this point: for McCarthy, nature is always material. His interest in the factors that make the material world what it is, his desire "to see how it was made," is not restricted merely to the perspectives of the narrators in *The Road* or McCarthy's earlier novels. For decades, the writer has been a fellow of the Santa Fe Institute, in New Mexico, which is an independent research institution addressing disciplines from physics to the social sciences and specializing in the dynamics of computational, biological, and social systems, as a quick look at their website indicates. In addition to McCarthy's affiliation with the institute, another circumstance shows his awareness of that part of the world that is not shaped just by the cultural significations of human beings but also by the ways in which deep geological time functions. What I mean is the frequency with which he uses a clearly scientific diction in his novels. As Dana Phillips puts it, McCarthy has a characteristically "forensic manner" of describing particular settings or moods.[2]

This realist tone, however, is generally counterbalanced by the mythical depth of McCarthy's work, and as many scholars have remarked, it is this tension between lyrical mythography and stark realism that defines the unique character of McCarthy's storytelling techniques. Criticism on his work has repeatedly emphasized either the mythical and religious features of his writing or its materialist and scientifically informed aspects.[3] As an illustration of the kinds of commonly cited passages that, for the former camp of interpreters, attest to this reading of McCarthy as a Southern mythographer, consider the ending of *The Crossing* (1994), in which Billy, the protagonist of the novel, laments his state of loneliness: "After a while he sat in the road. He took off his hat and placed it on the tarmac before him and he bowed his head and held his face in his hands and wept. He sat there for a long time and after a while the east did gray and after a while the right and godmade sun did rise, once again, for all and without distinction" (*TC*, 426).

This ending seems "both devastating and strangely hopeful," in Edwin Arnold's words[4]—an assessment that holds for a whole array of passages that show McCarthy's characters struggling with their lives and in conflict with the plans that God supposedly has for them. To borrow a phrase from Raymond Williams, there is a certain "structure of feeling"[5] to McCarthy's work that is probably best described by words such as "sorrow," "despair," and "distress"; yet the same structure gives rise to "grace," "hope," and "beatitude." Importantly, both tendencies are often present simultaneously although to varying degrees, and for the narrator, the protagonists, and the reader, McCarthy's mixture of these tendencies is essential. This affective mixture is also reflected on the level of content. Thus, in *The Road*, "all things of grace and beauty such that one holds them to one's heart have a common provenance in pain. Their birth in grief and ashes" (*TR*, 54). *Starting from grief, arriving at grace*: this is not only the ethical and aesthetic but also the stylistic formula that is projected by the religiously inscribed facet of McCarthy's fiction. However, that facet does not justify the exaggerated claim that a humanist ethics is at the heart of McCarthy's project, as some scholars have argued. In fact, the present book is intended to disprove the generally ethicist grounding of McCarthy's work to underline his engagement with the concept of nature. While there is indeed an ethical angle to his fiction, that angle is insufficient to serve as a general critical framework and should instead be regarded as one factor among others in a more inclusive approach, grounded in nature.

Turning to the stark realism of McCarthy's novels, and those who have discerned a more sober worldview in his writing, akin to literary naturalism, once again it needs to be said that there are understandable reasons for such an interpretation, especially if we consider the abundant passages in his fiction that describe death, decay, and acts of violence. While his 1985 novel *Blood Meridian, Or the Evening Redness in the West* may be the most prominent example of this materialist worldview, which it combines with an aestheticization of processes of destruction, McCarthy's mastery of the uncannily forensic diction mentioned above starts with *The Orchard Keeper* and is used repeatedly in novels such as *Outer Dark* (1968) or *No Country for Old Men* (2005), to name but a few. For instance, consider how the narrator describes the death of Kenneth Rattner, the father of John Wesley Rattner, one of the main characters in *The Orchard Keeper*. The man who kills Rattner is another protagonist named Marion Sylder, a small-time bootlegger in the East Tennessee mountains during Prohibition, which is the setting of McCarthy's first novel. After Rattner snuck into Sylder's car at the parking lot of a roadside bar in Atlanta, Georgia, Sylder reluctantly agreed to let the hitchhiker go with him toward Maryville, Tennessee. But when Sylder tries to repair a flat tire on their northbound journey, he finds himself being attacked by his passenger with the jack. Arguably, this scene neatly exemplifies McCarthy's stark realism: "The man looked down at him, and in the gradual suffusion of light gathered and held between the gloss of the car's enamel and the paling road dust he saw terror carved and molded on that face like a physical deformity" (*TOK*, 38).

This image of the beginning of Sylder and Rattner's mortal combat points to McCarthy's vision of an all-encompassing materiality when he writes in well-nigh medicinal language of a "suffusion" that is to be found not merely on the bruised flesh of the two fighters, but also in the colors of the adumbrated landscape, the road, and the car at dawn. The whole physical continuum is somehow involved in the scene of the fight. The "detached"[6] and naturalistic description of how Sylder strangles the hitchhiker is even more emblematic of this kind of vision:

> He . . . bore down upon the man's neck with all his weight and strength. The boneless-looking face twitched a few times but other than that showed no change of expression, only the same rubbery look of fear, speechless and uncomprehending, which Sylder felt was not his doing either but the everyday look of the man. And the jaw kept coming down not on any detectable hinges but like a mass of offal, some obscene waste matter uncongealing and collapsing in slow folds over the web of his hand. (*TOK*, 39)

Rattner's death is just one of many violent scenes depicted in McCarthy's oeuvre, but it suffices to identify an important element in the author's stance—an element already spelled out in the epigraph above from *The Road*, whose narrator muses that maybe "in the world's destruction it would be possible at last to see how it was made" (*TR*, 274). The depiction of Rattner's death implies not only that nature is fundamentally composed of matter, but also that the way of getting to know the inner workings of nature, of intuiting the course of its schemes and dynamics and its modes of creation, is paradoxically to witness its processes of destruction. It is in this sense that the death of a given character, like Rattner, is not only necessary *after the fact* for the plot of the novel to be what it is. According to McCarthy's poetics, such a death is also necessary to inquire into nature's identity, by literary means.

As I mentioned at the outset of this introduction, McCarthy's standpoint vis-à-vis the question "What is nature?" is situated in the thick of arguments about the connections between the national and the natural, and between the organic and the mechanical, which date back to early nineteenth-century debates on both sides of the Atlantic. In fact, the concept of nature, from that time until today, has been important to the making of American culture *tout court*. It has been a defining factor in the development of the literary and philosophic imagination manifested in the United States, to the point where the latter has been called "Nature's Nation."[7] Yet where is the connection, mentioned above, to the concept's version that one can find in German philosophical circles especially in the first half of that same century, the time when Ralph Waldo Emerson, Henry David Thoreau, and Walt Whit man (the first major American thinkers and poets after the Declaration of Independence) came to define the young nation according to their own perception of the environment? What is the thoroughly transnational component that characterizes the inquiry into nature's identity, into the nature of nature? For one thing, transcendentalism in America and idealism and Romanticism in Germany were fundamentally post-Kantian movements of thought and artistic practice, and the question about nature was asked by adherents of both movements to define the perspective and place of humans with respect to their particular national and social circumstance, as well as to the environment in which human life occurred.[8]

Due to their grimness and pessimistic character, the fictions of McCarthy are not entirely commensurate with Romantic ideas and forms of the worship of nature to be found in the transcendentalist poetry of Whitman or Emerson, nor with the Romantic image of the artist-subject sensually immersed in nature. However, McCarthy's prose asks the question "What is nature?" in ways that equally sets it apart from those works with which it is contemporaneous: modernist and postmodernist modes of narration. Nor do his novels fit entirely into the respective registers of the two remaining prevalent styles of writing, to be located historically within the "American Renaissance" and "the Pound Era,"—namely, realism and naturalism.[9] Although much scholarly work has categorized McCarthy's novels in one or more of these camps, I contend that while making use of each of the preceding literary techniques, McCarthy's style of narration does not belong wholly to any one camp and instead forges a poetics yet to be named. Especially the divergence from literary postmodernism, the dominant form of aesthetic production at the time of McCarthy's early career as a novelist, needs to be addressed. It is the task of the present book to give an account of this divergence in terms of literary history and to develop a new framework to examine the kinds of answers to the question at stake offered by McCarthy in his novels.

Since the transcendentalist initiation, or rather substantiation, of American intellectual history and, in parallel, the idealist development of Germany's post-Kantian era (that is, from the beginning of the nineteenth century onward) there have been many answers to the question concerning nature—so many, in fact, that it would be nearly impossible to discuss all of them at length in these introductory remarks (or, for that matter, in a single book). It would, moreover, detract from the primary concern of this book, which is the novelistic work of McCarthy. And yet the concept of nature indexes the kinds of ontological and epistemological presuppositions of authors of fiction and philosophy alike, especially in the cultural practices of "Nature's Nation." Therefore, the identification of McCarthy's fictional and narrative expressions of a specific set of ideological presumptions, in the sense of the generation of ideas, necessitates a partial tracing of the concept of nature from transcendentalism to the literary and philosophical present. Furthermore, to explain the connection established here between the American and the German trajectories in answering the question "What is nature?," it must be specified which philosophical strand exactly is meant when referring to German idealism vis-à-vis McCarthy in the first place. Indeed, a specific notion of nature is meant here, and a particular philosophical context within which nature and its concept are to be understood. The philosopher of nature Friedrich W. J. Schelling complains in his *Philosophical Investigations into the Essence of Human Freedom* (1809) that "the entire new European philosophy since its beginning (with Descartes) has the common defect that nature is not available for it and that it lacks a living ground"[10]—a complaint that has a peculiar resonance with the poetics of McCarthy's books, as I explain below.

Schelling's complaint is strikingly polemical and seems at first unjustified, given the explicit interest in and sophisticated examinations of contemporary findings and experimental results in the natural sciences on the part of modern European philosophers, be they Cartesian, post-Cartesian, or otherwise. In other words, it is at least barely believable if not outrageous to contend that nature was of no concern at all for modern philosophers until the treatises of Schelling. Incredible as it may sound, his denunciatory comments have recently been repeated in the name of Schelling's *Naturphilosophie* itself by the philosopher Iain Hamilton Grant, who asserts that Schelling's diagnosis of 1809 remains valid to this day, in spite of two hundred intervening years of distinct research programs directly concerned with investigations of the metaphysical question at hand.[11] It seems that both Schelling and, by extension, Grant, who is arguably the former's heir in terms of the promotion of the philosophy of nature today, are not referring in their denunciation of rival systems to all the numerous concepts of nature that exist, but to a specific one. It is, in fact (and unsurprisingly so), the *Schellingian* concept of nature, and the those of his colleagues, students, and followers, that the present book makes use of with regard to McCarthy's poetics. This is because McCarthy's position within the American literature of his time—meaning the 1960s and onward—is curiously similar to that of Schelling's in terms of their answers to the question "What is nature?" and the consequences of those authors' answers in their disciplines of fiction and philosophy.

Around the beginning of the nineteenth century, Schelling terms his philosophy of nature a "speculative physics," thereby likening it to the cultural practice of the natural sciences in his time. Simultaneously, he ascribes to it an explicitly imaginative, that is to say, nonempirical, or rather superempirical, characteristic called "speculation." This terminology recalls the way in which I have described McCarthy's works above—namely, as mixtures of both a highly poetic and, at times, religious sensibility, and an increasingly forensic detachment with regard to the characters and landscapes described. But the parallel between Schelling's speculative physics and McCarthy's realist mythographics does not end here. Contrary to his eventually rival thinkers, Johann G. Fichte and Georg W. F. Hegel, Schelling viewed the issue of ethics within philosophy as secondary at best and ruinous at worst, compared to the advantages of *Naturphilosophie*—which for him meant ontology (the science of being), first and foremost. Likewise, McCarthy has been less concerned with the political upheavals and various social movements in America during his writing career than other writers of the same generation such as Thomas Pynchon, Don DeLillo, or Michael Herr, to name but a few.[12] Similar to the late Schelling's philosophies of mythology and revelation that were diametrically opposed to the social and historical turn in German thought around the 1840s and the predominant concern with political questions, McCarthy's novels are replete with references to Greek mythology and biblical passages, evoking a sense of universalism and the absolute that is counterbalanced by the regionalism of his work: an element of locality and care for particular details persist throughout his oeuvre. Regarding the postmodernist narrative techniques that echoed the linguistic turn and the corresponding paradigm of social and cultural construction in the humanities, McCarthy's storytelling is at odds with the fashion of his time in his usage of archaic language as well as his incorporation of mythical references that are devoid of any hint of irony. Nor does this kind of storytelling merely repeat the modernist gesture of reconstructing the lost center of modernity with recourse to myth and formal experimentation, as in the seminal outputs of James Joyce, T. S. Eliot, or William Faulkner—even though McCarthy is certainly aware of that tradition, as can be witnessed especially in his early fiction that is set in the southeastern United States.

McCarthy's novelistic work can, and perhaps should, be understood along the lines of the Schellingian philosophy of nature, broadly conceived. What does this similarity consist of? McCarthy's novels "think" ontological questions, and in particular that of nature, but in fictional rather than strictly philosophical terms. In Schelling's case, *Naturphilosophie* states that it is *nature itself philosophizing* that is the issue in the practice of the philosophy of nature, rather than philosophizing about *what nature might be*. The name of that practice already signifies the precise meaning and functioning of Schelling's conception of *Naturphilosophie* as a "science *of* nature [*Wissenschaft* der *Natur*]" instead of a "science *about* nature [*Wissenschaft* von der *Natur*]."[13] Schelling's practice of a generalized science, then, is less a discourse on a specific object than the object itself reflecting on and dictating its own elementary character in scientific terms, in this way having an agential character of its own. This prepositional peculiarity, in fact, represents a core issue of the present book. As much as Schelling's *Naturphilosophie* is not a philosophy about nature but simply an activity of the latter, something of which nature itself is capable, McCarthy's "literature *of* nature" is not to be conceived of as a narrative discourse that merely depicts nature but as a practice that is performed by nature itself to gain reiterative traction on itself. As Nick Land writes, "thought is a function of the real, something that matter can do."[14] Along these lines, I hold that McCarthy's project is to think nature by literary means, or, in other words, *to present nature as thinking itself in literature.*

But what does that mean in the context of McCarthy's fiction if not directly tapping into nature—and reality, for that matter—that is seemingly uninhibited, in a clichéd version of Romanticism, and reminiscent of Emerson's "transparent eye-ball"?[15] How does McCarthy's literary practice present "nature itself," and how can this hypothesized self-presentation of nature be delineated in literary criticism, given that "reality has an essence that fiction cannot subsume" and that "whatever the level of representation, reality is invariantly the referent of discourse," as Bertrand Westphal has put it?[16] Deferring the answers to these questions to a later point, I have to concede that the interpretation and usage of Schelling's philosophy in the present book is channeled mainly through Iain Grant's reading of it. His recent promotion of a return to the question of nature and his refusal to read Schelling's main contributions to philosophy either as precursory to dialectical materialism and Lacanian psychoanalysis or simply as systematic reflections on the problem of human freedom alone set him apart from the main strands of Schelling studies. In particular, his claim that the philosophy of nature remains the sole continuous element in Schelling's overall philosophy is provocatively unique in the context of scholarship on this German idealist thinker.[17] Grant's work stands—perhaps together with that of Reza Negarestani and Ray Brassier—as the most intriguing option within the contemporary philosophical movement called "speculative realism," itself a transnational phenomenon with representatives in such cities as Los Angeles, Paris, Beirut, and Bristol. The four initiators of a new option in today's debates on metaphysics, epistemology, and aesthetics—Graham Harman, Quentin Meillassoux, Brassier, and Grant, who are more of a cluster of like-minded thinkers in the vast and heterogeneous network of philosophical discourse than an outspoken school of thought—have each taken measures in their respective projects against the antirealist consensus in the continental philosophy of the past fifty-odd years that spawned much of postmodern theory and fiction, in its most extreme form delving into what might be termed linguistic solipsism. As Ursula Heise puts it, "literary critics during this period took a fresh look at questions of representation, textuality, narrative, identity, subjectivity, and historical discourse from a fundamentally skeptical perspective that emphasized the multiple disjunctures between forms of representation and the realities they purported to refer to."[18] The philosophical discussion of ontological realism versus antirealism—the belief that there is or is not, respectively, a mind-independent reality that is indifferent to the culturally and linguistically mediated perception of human beings and their individual perspectives—was either regarded as irrelevant or as simply beside the point or a false problem. In fact, this presumed irrelevance applied to ontological questions in general, with issues regarding the proliferation of knowledge championed over those regarding the characterization of being. The nonhuman realities of the natural realm were seen to be first of all constructions in and of the transcendental apparatus, the human mind that perceived them. They were viewed as secondary cognitive, social, cultural, and historical constructs compared to the primary "tool kit" unique to humankind that performed the construction, the consciousness that fabricated the relations between persons and things in the world: "'Nature' in postmodern thought [was] by default culturized, semiotic nature . . . connected mainly with the theories of Michel Foucault, Jacques Lacan, Jacques Derrida, and Judith Butler."[19] Foucauldian discourse analysis concerned with the historical proliferation of cultural texts and power, Lacan's theory of the subject in psychoanalysis, Derrida's deconstructive readings of the signifier's dissemination in the language of philosophy, and Butler's theory about the cultural performativity of gendered identities all either avoided the concept of nature or dismantled it as derivative of the perceptual faculties of human beings, their sense and intellect. In this way, nature was commonly depicted "as a retro-effect of culture,"[20] and the major theoretical frameworks continued to endorse the main thrust of Kant's critical philosophy that shackled the metaphysical inventions of dogmatism by emphasizing the analysis of how the world can be known, not of what might actually be there to be known.

Contrary to some scholars who see McCarthy's work as congruent with this culture-centered approach to literary practice, I hold that while McCarthy's fiction is well versed in the specificities of its subject matter (such as a particular dialect spoken by the characters or social rituals performed by a community), novels such as *The Orchard Keeper* or *The Crossing* do not reflect on nature as a cultural construction or a "retro-effect" of the latter. To put it in a language that postmodern literary theorists might perhaps denounce as naïve and outmoded, McCarthy's pathos, as projected and expressed in his narratives, seems "real" and "sincere." It is not part of a postmodern strategy that is intended to debunk the very idea of "the authentic." Instead, McCarthy contemplates metaphysical questions about nature's identity and its inner workings in both scientifically and religiously informed ways—a fact that aligns him much more to the nature-philosophical tenets of speculative realism than to those strands of poststructuralism that emphasize the inevitability of cultural inscription. In McCarthy's hands Derrida's statement that "there is nothing outside the text" becomes the axiom that there is nothing outside of nature.[21] Or, in the words of Schelling quoted above, "anything whose conditions simply cannot be given in nature, must be absolutely impossible."[22]

Moreover, if this all-encompassing nature is essentially material without ignoring the reality of the spiritual, it must be conceived of as both independent of and belonging to the humanity that perceives it and generates its concept. Indeed, the notion of an existence that temporally and ontologically precedes its partial capture in human consciousness, or its bodily formation in states of aggregation, is a trope one finds in McCarthy's novels on the levels of both form and content from *The Orchard Keeper* all the way to *The Sunset Limited*. In fact, the narrators in these novels allude to a particular notion of matter, a site of productivity before its manifestation as, and crystallization into, ideas and bodies in the world. In Grant's reconstruction of the Schellingian philosophy of nature, speculative physics entails a "physics of the idea"[23] *and* the empirical natural sciences (physics, chemistry, and biology)—two areas of research, both of which are said to determine the aggregates of bodies and ideas via modeling and experimentation. As we have seen above, this conception of matter as force, eventually resulting in ideas or bodies in the world, is present in numerous scenes in McCarthy's novels, at moments that are mystical or spiritual and also materially inscribed. According to the stance evoked in these scenes, matter can be alluded to only in speculation, but it cannot be fully contained in the conscious thought that thinks it. There is always an excess of its features outside the borders of its concept. It is material, yet not necessarily corporeal since it cannot be grasped by any of the senses: it cannot be seen, touched, heard, tasted, or smelled, even if its thought may hint at some of these forms of sense. "The ultimate 'ground,' then," in Grant's Schellingian account, as in McCarthy's narratives, "is a certain becoming that is less a ground than the shifting sands of reality. . . . In other words, the absolute is thinkable, but cannot be apprehended directly through the things of the world."[24]

Bearing in mind the phrase that McCarthy's fictions *think* in the way in which the verb is used here, and assuming that this primordial materiality cannot be sensed but thought, consider the following example from *The*

Orchard Keeper. At the end of the first part of the novel, the narrative of which spans the years between the First and the Second World Wars, there is a brief description of the burning of an inn, a place usually frequented by Marion Sylder. The passage starts with a conventionally sober description of the facts: "The Green Fly Inn burned on December twenty-first of 1936 and a good crowd gathered in spite of the cold and the late hour" (*TOK*, 47). After an elaborate account of the gradual collapse of the building's scaffolding, the passage ends with the following paragraph: "There it continued to burn, generating such heat that the hoard of glass beneath it ran molten and fused in a single sheet, shaped in ripples and flutings, encysted with crisp and blackened rubble, murrhined with bottlecaps. It is there yet, the last remnant of that landmark, flowing down the sharp fold of the valley like some imponderable archeological phenomenon" (48).

The poetic act of pondering an otherwise "imponderable archeological phenomenon" like, in this case, the fluidity of the disintegrated glass "molten and fused in a single sheet" is repeated again and again in this novel, a making visible of material nature in thought—that is, the literary imagination—rather than on a canvas. What is remarkable is that other than Emerson's vision of becoming one with nature as the direct experience of divinity, McCarthy's descriptions of the "imponderable" (*TOK*, 48) seem to be connected with acts of destruction—as if "in the world's destruction it would be possible at last to see how it was made" (*TR*, 274), to recall one of the epigraphs above. The detailed and often detached renderings of violent acts, such as the burning, dismantling, or shattering of bodies and objects, as well as their decay and decomposition, always seem to be accompanied by sentences that point toward a realm from which these bodies are generated. This realm, however, is not a transcendent kingdom foreclosed to worldly affairs; that is, it is not exactly consistent with the images and preconceived ideas of transcendence that today's literary and cultural studies often ascribe to the term. As McCarthy continues, "the ponderous counterspectacle of things ceasing to be" results in "sweeping waste, hydroptic and coldly secular" (274). What is at stake here is a demise that is "coldly secular," a demise in which the ideas and bodies of the world are immanent, as it is but one facet in the conglomeration of forces that is nature.

In spite of all the stark realism of coldness and secularity, however, there is a question that needs to be addressed: What is the precise meaning of the frequent references to God and the religious motifs in McCarthy's oeuvre, which includes a whole array of passages that makes it seem susceptible to a naïve spiritualism? In the Schellingian philosophy of nature, the claim is that nature cannot be divine or transcendent—in the sense in which the latter term has often been ridiculed—since it is the single site of and horizon for things, objects, subjects, bodies, and ideas to exist in the first place, including the idea of God, of a divine being. As we saw above, Schelling's concept does not allow for an outside of nature or of the production of forces, but certainly there is an outside of thought, sense, and other finite modes of being in the world. In other words, the idea of the divine, like any other idea, might be in nature, but nature is not in the divine. Nature encompasses both the absolute or infinite *and* the relative and finite. There is no reciprocity between the two terms of the natural and the divine. They simply cannot be sides of the same equation, since this would make *Naturphilosophie* a crude breed of phenomenology, in which consciousness is that of nature and nature that of consciousness. By the same token, what is sometimes called immanence means just this aspect of nature, its "maximized extensity," or the impossibility of anything at all being beyond the natural realm.[25] The reasoning, which views every single entity according to nature as the production and agglomeration of forces, is, in fact, the philosophy of nature or "speculative physics," as Schelling called his theoretical practice interchangeably. Furthermore, this philosophical (and, in McCarthy's case, narrative) speculation can be understood as the act of nature thinking itself, the self-construction of matter by conceptual means, or *autopoiesis* (discussed in chapters 2 and 3).

If there is a certain amorphous character to this notion of matter that is theoretically related to psychoanalytically determined notions of formlessness, that is the case only as long as we allow for the subtraction of any grounding aspirations with respect to the affective or ethical pretext inherent to Freudian and post-Freudian versions of psychology. The Kristevan account of the abject, for instance, functions against the backdrop of a culture for which notions of abjection are necessary "primers."[26] They are the "other" of the superego on a polar scale of ideological inscription.[27] The nonethical depictions of the disintegration of corpses in McCarthy's Southern novels, in contrast, are fully in keeping with Schelling's account of endlessly generative deviations from the dynamism or flux of potencies themselves, "an infinite dissociation into ever new products."[28] This kind of deviation is not to be understood here as the overly negative concept that might be associated with it in cultural terms. "To deviate" is not merely to enter into the dynamics of social stigmatization but rather describes the activity of the finite product or object with regard to its infinite production or manufacture, in ontological terms. Expressed positively, the genesis of forms in the world—*morphogenesis*—becomes coextensive with the excess of matter at the margins of either its concepts or its bodies, which are necessarily departing from their cause and in turn becoming the ground for ever new organisms and phenomena. I will argue that the dissociative potencies inherent in the differentiation of the formless into distinct forms and phenomena are present in crucial passages throughout McCarthy's oeuvre and that, accordingly, the decomposition of nature's products results in decay as an ontological concept that is narratively elaborated from the start of McCarthy's career.

Furthermore, the relationships between those bodies that are endowed with life and those that are not indicate the ways in which a single body reacts to its social, cultural, or ecological surroundings. Negarestani's concept of "ontological decay"[29] and his recasting of the Jungian term *nigredo* (the practice of facing the "shadow" of one's personality) in nature-philosophical terms seem useful for an analysis of this fundamental condition. This is because not only is there a basic affinity between Jungian psychology and McCarthy's work, as others have noted, but also because the notion of decay as nature's method of proliferation, diversification, and multiplication is congruent with the vision of nature to be found both in McCarthy's writing and in Schellingianism (by which I mean Schelling's work and that of his followers in the nineteenth-century developments of *Naturphilosophie*—chief among them Lorenz Oken, who will become the main theoretical anchor point in chapter 4). Two questions are posed at this point: What is the finitude of bodies or forms measured against their territory within nature? And how can we determine the relationship between subtraction and construction in the simultaneous processes of creativity and decay in nature? These are the basic issues that are negotiated in McCarthy's Southern novels, above all in *Child of God*. They are issues, moreover, whose metaphysical character aligns them with McCarthy's novel about his alter ego Cornelius Suttree and with yet another more formal and stylistic aspect concerning the literary depiction of the amorphous and the putrid among nature's forms.

Suttree—McCarthy's most autobiographical novel,[30] reflecting his time in Knoxville, Tennessee—is no exception in terms of the depiction of nature's character. It combines scenes of "a dreamy tranquility" (*S*, 196), which connotes the protagonist's rugged daily life on a houseboat, with those situations that present processes of decaying "shreds of matter" (96) both human and nonhuman, organic and inorganic, borne on the Tennessee River—the all-encompassing image of fluidity, aptly called "Cloaca Maxima" (13).

Regarding the level of form, the ornamental language of *Suttree* has been a crucial topic of the critical response within McCarthy scholarship, but it is the erudite characterization of Knoxville from Suttree's point of view that has led to comparisons of the novel to Joyce's *Ulysses* and its portrait of modern Ireland's capital, Dublin, in critical studies of McCarthy's fourth novel.[31] Furthermore, McCarthy openly hints at the tradition, in which he moves about stylistically in his text, by given his characters names such as

Ulysses and Joyce.[32] However, the connection between McCarthy's novel and a modernist text such as *Ulysses* should not just be understood as an easy way to categorize the novel as a late modernist work of art. The link between the two could also be comprehended as a literary form of recycling much like the decomposition of organic bodies in nature, in accord with Schelling's doctrine of the impossibility of anything outside the latter's processes. As John Elder has argued, literary texts can be regarded as "fermentations" of what has been written before, as the echoes of a tradition antecedent to them. Furthermore, the syntheses of those decaying bodies that were once separate, in culture as well as in organic ecology and inorganic cosmology, "create new life in a composting, fermentive pattern."[33] This "bacteriological sense of culture"[34] corresponds with McCarthy's hybridization of an eclectic array of literary sources, periods, and styles, all of which will be addressed in chapters 1 and 2.

Like earlier work, then, *Suttree* as a thinking work of art is, among other things, the presentation of a certain dialectic established between subtraction and construction, between composition as a creative process and decomposition as a building process shorn of any form of intentional creativity. According to Negarestani, "decay builds without creation" and "introduces power to the misadventures of matter. But it is 'entities as beings' which *narrate* the adventures of decay as a cosmic odyssey between themselves."[35] As the analysis of *Suttree* in chapter 3 will show, we can identify characters like Suttree or his fellow ex-convict Gene Harrogate as these "entities as beings" that move through the debris of Knoxville's subculture of the homeless, depraved, and drunkards; that make their way through bars, brothels, and tunnels of the city's sewage system among fecal slime and rats—once again, a particular setting, a precise *locality* that paradoxically seems necessary to render explicit themes that are much more universal. Like the dialectic between subtraction and construction, those between the particular and the universal and between American life and the human condition in general are crucial elements in McCarthy's narrative strategy not only in his early fiction but also in his Western novels.[36]

Blood Meridian deals with the violent history of a band of scalp hunters who, in the middle of the nineteenth century, roam the Southwestern desert, the region near the border between the United States and Mexico. Often regarded as a revisionist Western that debunks the ideology of manifest destiny, *Blood Meridian* covers a range of topics associated with nineteenth-century America. Reminiscent of figures from McCarthy's Southern novels, characters like the nameless kid and his fellow gang members, led by John Joel Glanton and Judge Holden, who combines the traits of a warlord, a scientist, and a prophet in one person, seem for the most part to lack affective faculties. When they decimate Indian villages and commit other hideous crimes, they remain indifferent. But the faces of the people they pass also remain "without expression" (BM, 84), like the soldiers whom the kid joins before meeting Glanton's gang. This nonaffective and expressionless posture of McCarthy's characters does not just occur in *Blood Meridian* but is a stylistic trademark of his entire oeuvre, albeit to differing degrees. It is one of the ingredients that make for what will be termed the *narrative continuity* that is typical of McCarthy's prose work as a whole. It must be readily noted however, that this nonaffective attitude is counteracted by the social bonds between the protagonist and his friends in *Suttree*, the nascent heroism in the Border Trilogy, and the courage of the boy and his father in *The Road*. I will argue that Schelling's philosophy of nature can give an adequate account of these oppositional forces.

As any reader of *Blood Meridian* will notice, the theme of warfare is central to an understanding of the novel. Rooted in a philosophical tradition that goes back to Heraclitus, as numerous scholars have noted,[37] the judge—who is one of the most important characters in *Blood Meridian* and also one of the most violent figures in American fiction—gives a speech on what he takes to be "the nature of war" (BM, 249). In front of his fellow scalp hunters and slayers of American Indians, the judge claims the following: "It makes no difference what men think of war. . . . War endures. As well ask men what they think of stone. War was always there. Before man was, war waited for him. . . . That is the way it was and will be. That way and not some other way" (248). War, understood as the explication of antecedent nature itself, can therefore not be circumvented or avoided by humankind. Both war and nature are thus conceived as the subjects for which individual men and women are merely accidental objects compelled to put up with the harsh reality of—in McCarthy's case—the American deserts and borderlands that point toward "a time before nomenclature was and each was all" (172). Thus, the account of war in *Blood Meridian* is the result of a very different poetics from the one that is evident in Thomas Pynchon's *Gravity's Rainbow* (1973) and its depiction of the Second World War, as well as in Michael Herr's account of the Vietnam War in *Dispatches* (1977). While these two works have been described as prime examples of literary postmodernism, McCarthy's fictions seem to imply, and consequently write, an alternative history driven in part by nature-philosophical premises that rely on the rejection of what could be termed "human exceptionalism." *Blood Meridian*'s objective is less a fictional critique of American imperialism and its ideologies than the development of a theory of nature, expressed in narrative terms.

In spite of the thoroughly transnational context in which I regard McCarthy's philosophically engaged narratives, it is crucially important at this point to note the aspect of *locality*. In forging his "theory," which really is a counterhistory of that written by allegedly privileged humankind, McCarthy places this alternative version of both the factual and the fictional past in a distinctly American milieu. Similar to *Blood Meridian*'s territories, where "death seem[s] the most prevalent feature of the landscape" (*BM*, 48), the "darkening land, the world to come" (*PH*, 306) at the end of *All the Pretty Horses* (1992), for instance, wrests the aspect of promise and salvation from the old Puritan antagonism between the elect and the preterite and leaves only the latter to read and make sense of the world's events. There is "human suffering *without* redemption"[38] in McCarthy's prose. This bleak discrepancy from the first white settlers' Manichean and Protestant doctrine seems to allow McCarthy and his readers to make a paradoxical decision prior to any writing or reading of his books. For McCarthy, surveying or even discerning both the human condition and that of the world at large can be illustrated artistically only from the point of view of fiction set in America. Thus, both the deep rootedness of his works in the tradition of myths like the American Adam and Puritan cultures and discourses of the Wild West and the rendering of the particular dictions of the Southern states and the US-Mexican borderlands appear to be the ground on which, paradoxically, a speculative vision of the world is pitted against the belief in human sovereignty over the world of things and processes. In other words, US regionalism or—to use a more politically charged term in a slightly modified way—American exceptionalism provides McCarthy's narratives with the necessary source material to vitiate the human exceptionalism, the anthropocentrism of postmodernity that at least tacitly lays claim to a primal correlation between the human mind and the world, and a kind of law-giving human perception that in the last analysis rules the latter.[39] It is this "formal" American exceptionalism that makes possible the author's nature-philosophical dialogue with the likes of Schelling and Oken. The regional—and, by extension, the national—becomes the condition of possibility for a transnational re-mapping of the concept of nature across literary and philosophical cultures and their boundaries.

The present study consequently argues that a somewhat "speculative" reading of McCarthy can make sense only if this aspect of speculation is extended beyond the connotation of the word that implies merely the "specular image" of the human subject, or the (necessarily limited) vision of women and men in society—a connotation that can be traced back to the early French psychoanalytic theory of Lacan and his followers. Part of what I hope to achieve by using the terms "speculation" or "the speculative" is a characterization of McCarthy's work as what Vereen Bell termed "a critique of our culture's anthropocentrism."[40] Put simply, specularity is not speculation.

Instead of the problem of intuiting the phenomena of nature through the senses of characters like Lester Ballard in *Child of God* or the kid in *Blood Meridian*, McCarthy's work is concerned with the task of narratively thinking the dark materiality underlying all appearances. It points toward the indifferent universality of this "dark matter" while itself being entangled in the local human and nonhuman histories of East Tennessee, the Southwest, and Mexico. Expressed in Faulknerian language, McCarthy's poetics are "speculative beyond any staring."[41] Nevertheless, allusions to the usage of nature's resources as a means to achieve human ends, otherwise known as Prometheanism, and, in opposition to that, to what the French philosopher Pierre Hadot has called "the Orphic attitude,"[42] which is characterized by a reverence for nature's potency, are combined to various degrees in McCarthy's novels. Therefore, and contrary to a number of influential readings in the ecocritical tradition, McCarthy's fictions are not to be seen as straightforward rebuttals of a human-centered worldview in the name of life—that is, as subversions of logocentrism from the perspective of bio- or ecocentrism. Instead, his narratives are to be understood as auto-descriptions of nature's potencies, in which both reason and life figure as merely local phenomena.

Like some of the characters from McCarthy's Tennessee period, in *The Crossing* (1994), the protagonist Billy is very close to the realm of animals, and at the beginning of the narrative his main companion is not a horse but a she-wolf for whom he cares deeply—a plotline that is reminiscent of Jack London's seminal naturalist novels *The Call of the Wild* (1903) and *White Fang* (1906).[43] *The Crossing* is not exceptional in terms of McCarthy's overall thematic emphasis on nature's indifference and autonomy vis-à-vis human perception. Yet especially in regard to this novel, it is worth recalling the tensions between McCarthy's portrayals of grief and grace in the world. The poetic rendering of nature's basic carelessness has a high aesthetic value for the author. As many critics have noted, it is the most gruesome actions, happenings, and sceneries in McCarthy's novels that are crafted most beautifully.[44] Accordingly, in *The Crossing*, nature is "at once terrible and of a great beauty, like flowers that feed on flesh" (*TC*, 127).

This tradition is continued in McCarthy's later works, like *No Country for Old Men* (2005), a neo-Western detective story that negotiates the intertwined issues of chance and choice as well as the outcomes of the latter and the conditions of the former—all of which are also central aspects of Schelling's *Philosophical Investigations into the Essence of Human Freedom*. The less-ornamental style of *No Country for Old Men* is also used in *The Road* (2006) and *The Sunset Limited* (2006), and McCarthy's variation in terms of genre goes hand in hand once more with the continuing narrative version of nature-philosophical concerns so prevalent in his previous works. In *The*

Road, the detached storytelling I noted above is that of a father and son in relation to the American wasteland through which they wander, trying to survive and hide from the pillaging gangs that move through the same landscape. There is a certain disconnect between the human characters and their nonhuman surroundings that is unique in this novel. The engagement consists of the arguably epistemological merit of the novel concerning the problem of facing that increasingly life-threatening environment and, connected to this, the issue of admitting one's finality as a human being, a living body in a universe that is devoid of any sense of care for its temporary inhabitants.

This manifest verdict of humanity as lost in an alien world composed of ashes finds its parallel in the bleak worldview of White, the suicidal professor in *The Sunset Limited*, and both novels that ask and speculate about such existential questions as the following: Is life worth living in the face of death and despair? How can one maintain the possibility of hope and the sense of community when one's living conditions become increasingly unbearable? Is it better to have faith or knowledge, especially when one is confronting life-threatening conditions? Does one choose freely between either looking backward or focusing on the future in such a situation, or is the environment responsible for one's preference for one of these alternatives? In addressing these types of questions, *The Road* and *The Sunset Limited* may come closer to ethical concerns than McCarthy's earlier works do. Yet once again, ethics, here, like any other concept in nature, is not an idea that is constitutive of the latter all by itself (even if a universe that includes ethically thinking minds certainly differs from a hypothetical one that does not). Like the idea of God, ethical or moral concerns in the human realm have no exact correlative in the nonhuman one, while both are part of nature as the system of partially self-contemplating and wholly dynamic forces.[45]

Like all of McCarthy's novels, then, both *The Road* and *The Sunset Limited* are intricately speculative attempts to think, by means of narrative fiction, the "imponderable archeological phenomenon" (*TOK*, 48) that is nature. It is the dark ground of all appearances that might be revealed, according to McCarthy's narrators, in the "ponderous counterspectacle of things ceasing to be. The sweeping waste, hydroptic and coldly secular" (*TR*, 274). Instead of the image of the Emersonian "transparent eye-ball,"[46] therefore, McCarthy's image of thinking nature is that of a black sheet of molten glass, as in *The Orchard Keeper*, spreading over an assortment of abandoned objects in a roadside ditch; objects that will disintegrate in turn, like so many "shreds of matter" (*S*, 96) giving rise to ever-new formations.

THIS STUDY OF MCCARTHY'S fiction is not structured according to the order of the novels' publication, from *The Orchard Keeper* to *The Sunset Limited*, or in terms of a supposed chronology of these tales' historical settings. Instead it is thematically organized, due to the abovementioned narrative continuity of the novels. I have assembled the novels in each of the remaining chapters with respect to their relationship to a topic that is essential to McCarthy's vision of literary practice: his narrative rendition of nature and its concept. The reason for this slightly unorthodox structure is that although McCarthy's work is indeed divided in the successive phases that other scholars have outlined in their interpretations—the Tennessean period, the Western period, crime fiction, and postapocalyptic fiction—in the context of the present discussion it makes more sense to structure his oeuvre thematically. This is because the kernel of his concept of nature does not change in the course of his career; only the geographical and historical settings of his novels do. In other words, the narrative continuity that is the hallmark of his fiction is most effectively rendered intelligible by the structure employed in chapters 1–6 and their thematic groupings: the conceptual supervenience of ethics upon ontology; the narrative construction of a physiocentric, rather than an ecocentric, perspective; the literary and ontological exploration of decay and decomposition; the logics of antecedence and war; the relation between the notions of indifference and identity; and the mythographical traditions of Orphism and Prometheanism.

The first two chapters differ slightly from the later ones in that they are designed to facilitate what could be called a premeditative theoretical survey of, or macroperspective on, the literary and philosophical backdrop against which McCarthy's concept of nature is forged. These chapters elaborate in detail the major theoretical underpinnings of the present interpretation of McCarthy's work from the perspective of a philosophy of nature, inspired predominantly by Schelling and Oken, but also by the recent theoretical frameworks of geocriticism and speculative realism.[47] Chapter 1 will touch upon the issue of regionalism as a narrative strategy in McCarthy's fiction and the ways in which it makes possible his participation in the transnational and transhistorical debate on what a speculative kind of metaphysics—and literature—concerned with nature's processes might look like. In connection with the issue of regionalism as a narrative strategy, I will discuss the question of periodization, especially in regard to McCarthy's relationship to the postmodern mode of narration and his ingenious sampling of various literary styles from the past two hundred years of American literature. I will do so, moreover, by highlighting the advantages and drawbacks of reading McCarthy from a strictly ecocritical perspective, or from that of environmental criticism. In chapter 2, I suggest using Schellingian *Naturphilosophie* as a possible corrective vis-à-vis the ethical inclinations of the former, a move that will entail, among other things, the construction of a new theory of "writing nature "in contrast to the long American tradition of "nature writing." Concluding the more theoretical part of the book, which also includes analyses from a macro-level or survey-like perspective, chapter 2 explicates the main tenets of the theory developed predominantly out of the works of Schelling, Oken, Negarestani, Brassier, and Grant to engage in a new reading of McCarthy's prose.

In an initial micro-level approach to McCarthy's literary conception of nature's identity, chapter 3 deals with *The Orchard Keeper*, *Child of God*, and *Suttree*—the works that most outspokenly deal with the notion of decay (biophysical, social, and moral) in their narratives and that thereby contain specific treatments of what in Schellingian terms might be called the natural dialectic between composition and decomposition. What Land has termed "geotrauma"[48] will taken into account and used to depict the literary characters from McCarthy's Southern period and show how their violent lives are somehow grounded in the violent dispositions of their East Tennessean environs. Furthermore, the concept of *nigredo* will be elaborated and linked to the notion of *katabasis*, the exploration of subterranean depths. Chapter 4 provides a new reading of *Blood Meridian*'s main question—namely, whether or not human beings are "another kind of clay" (*BM*, 5)—and subsequently addresses the theological consequences of McCarthy's answer to this question in terms of the notion of the void in the second volume of the Border Trilogy, *The Crossing*. The chapter traces a hitherto unrecognized but fully fledged Okenian philosophy of nature that underlies the metaphysical stance of these novels, apart from the Schellingianism that is consistent throughout McCarthy's work and that I take to be harmonious with Oken's *Naturphilosophie*. Although the relation between nature's identity and its indifference is an important one in all of McCarthy's works, this relation is mainly foregrounded in chapter 5, which analyzes it in all its Cormackian connotations, as these are expressed most vividly in *Outer Dark*, *All the Pretty Horses*, and *Cities of the Plain*. This chapter demonstrates the many levels of the concept of indifference in McCarthy and how it is entwined in his work with a specific theory of identity, a literary practice of ethology (in the tradition of American naturalists like Jack London and Stephen Crane), and a specifically nonmimetic conception of storytelling that I will define as *narrative extainment*, as opposed to representational containment. Chapter 6 takes a slightly different methodological perspective in the sense that it reframes some of the arguments developed in earlier chapters in mythographical terms and thus adds a new theoretical dimension to the central problems elaborated in chapters 1 and 2. This last chapter delineates McCarthy's indebtedness to both the Orphic and Promethean traditions in Western literary, philosophical, and scientific culture in selective readings of

Blood Meridian, *No Country for Old Men*, *All the Pretty Horses*, *The Road*, and *The Sunset Limited*.

Proceeding in this manner, this book tries to clarify the ways in which the thematic developments of McCarthy's fictions are cyclical and do not follow a linear progression. In keeping with Schelling's notion of time as an unceasing flow of the past that projects itself into the present and toward the future, McCarthy's prose returns to its beginnings in a constant process of renewal and recapitulation. That is to say, the narrative continuity of McCarthy's prose throughout his oeuvre is in line with the persistence of speculating about nature's identity.

[1]

"TRAILING THE CORD": LITERARY DESCENT AND THE ETHOS OF ECOLOGY

He felt his heart pumping down there under the palm of his hand. Who tells it so? Could a whole man not author his own death with a thought? Shut down the ventricle like the closing of an eye? —Cormac McCarthy, *Suttree*

Regrounding culture in the natural world involves a descent.
—John Elder, *Imagining the Earth*

TO STATE THAT Cormac McCarthy's work is immersed in the materiality of the world seems hardly to present a thesis and almost to reiterate a truism. Perhaps the scholars who emphasize McCarthy's interest in material culture and, above all, nature do not just follow one of the many ways of reading his work. Rather, the notion of materiality may be what divides scholars into various factions—gnostics, ethicists, materialists, and especially environmentalists, to name but a few of the most prevalent ones that explicitly address McCarthy's notion of matter, his concept of nature. From Leo Daugherty to Petra Mundik, critics have analyzed McCarthy's focus on the religious tradition of gnosis, weighing in on the evil nature of matter, as opposed to the pneumatic spirit that manifests itself in the human capacity to think and contemplate a given problem—the immaterial goodness that is also called "the lingering scent of divinity" in *The Sunset Limited* (13).[1] Along similar lines, critics like Edwin Arnold and Lydia Cooper have foregrounded the question of ethics vis-à-vis McCarthy's depictions of the grim realities of material being, respectively emphasizing "the possibility of grace and redemption even in the darkest of his tales" and theorizing an "ethics of empathy" that supposedly permeates the depictions of literary "characters [who] nevertheless exist in a naturalistic world."[2] Dana Phillips, Vereen Bell, and others have argued that McCarthy's narratives employ an almost scientific diction, a characteristically "forensic manner" of describing particular settings or moods, so that "the world seems to draw even language into itself to lay claim to a higher priority"—the priority of the material.[3] Lastly, readings provided by scholars like Andrew Keller Estes and K. Wesley Berry home in on McCarthy's engagement with environmental issues and his ostensible ascription of "intrinsic rights" to the natural world, meaning here the regional and global ecosphere.[4]

All of these approaches suggest that the material world is a central issue in McCarthy's narratives, even if, according to some of these readings, this issue is central only insofar as it is a means to a certain end. In the gnostic accounts, for instance, the evil nature of matter is secondary to—or, rather, in the service of—the self-revelation of the human spirit, in moral terms. McCarthy's characters endure the archonic law—the *nomos* of externality—only to care for, or by means of, what remains intrinsically and eternally divine. As Mundik notes, many forms of gnosticism "taught that the *pneuma* was eternal and could never truly be destroyed."[5] This is so with the divine spirit that inheres in the kid of *Blood Meridian*, for example. Along these lines, Cooper's acknowledgment of McCarthy's naturalism notwithstanding, her suggestion that the supposed ideal of "human communion" is a general ethos capable of grounding McCarthy's poetics as a whole actually entails the conceptual priority of moral notions over those of nature—that is to say, materiality.[6] It results in the supervenience of the concept of nature upon that of morality. Both gnosticist and ethicist accounts of McCarthy's narrative conceptualization of matter seem to treat it merely as *a material*, as something that is malleable during the spiritual becoming of the *pneuma*, and according to the virtue of empathetic behavior. In parallel, the notion of materiality becomes mere subject matter, used to refer to the virtues but also the cruelty of humanity's being in the world. Discussions of McCarthy from the materialist perspective tend to be grounded either in the dialectical materialist philosophies of human praxis, together with a downright rejection of religious symbolism, or in the existential reasoning that traces "a kind of moral ecology."[7] In contrast, ecocritical interpretations use the terms "nature" and "the environment" synonymously, which results in an ethico-aesthetic determination of the ontological question at stake—namely, "What is nature?"

Despite these caveats about the diverse analyses of this key issue in McCarthy, they nevertheless lead us to several questions that might seem naïve at first, but that are actually indispensable at this point: Exactly what concept of matter are we dealing with, when we are dealing with the importance of materiality in McCarthy's fiction? Which concept of nature can be discerned in his novels, given their explicit emphasis on questions about the interdependency of humans and their environment; the bond between human and nonhuman beings such as animals, plants, and other phenomena supposedly endowed with life; and the genesis of forms of life that come from a realm "beyond the world of men" (TOK, 222)? Is the reality of the material world coterminous with *corpo*reality in McCarthy's narratives, or does his understanding of nature's identity exceed the body as its main constituent?

This chapter follows a threefold line of argument: First, I explore the way in which McCarthy's twist on the regionalist poetics of American literature renders possible both a synthesis or integration of a scientific and materialist interpretation of McCarthy's worlds, and a spiritual and religious reading. McCarthy achieves such a metaphysical integration via a literary methodology that I describe as "descendentalism."[8] Second, I delineate McCarthy's literary descent insofar as his evocation of nearly all major periods of American literature since Ralph Waldo Emerson constitutes the performative formulation of his own concept of nature: one of the ways, in fact, in which his fiction "answers" the question concerning nature's identity and thereby contributes to transnational cultures of literary and philosophical speculation. Third, I discuss at length the question of whether an ecocritical perspective on McCarthy's concept of nature does justice to its expansiveness. This is an issue that has already been addressed by arguing that equating nature and environment produces too narrow a framework to account for McCarthy's world-affirming *and* world-negating poetics.

My new take on McCarthy and the history of concepts of nature seeks to create a theoretical framework that would be appropriate for McCarthy's fiction and its capability of presenting nature as it is writing itself in literature. The present approach seeks to construct a point of view that would adequately account for his evident fascination with the idea that word and world are to be placed on one and the same footing. From the local to the absolute, from descent to tragedy, and from the laconic to the excessive, McCarthy re-maps transnational cultures of literary and philosophical expression in terms of nature's complexity.

WHAT, THEN, OF MCCARTHY'S regionalist heritage, his fascination with the American locale? This issue is central in any consideration of his fiction, and not just with respect to his conception of natural processes. It points to a downright peculiar coincidence, not common in the history of literary criticism: the emphasis that McCarthy's narratives put on the particular localities in which they take place is the one topic on which most members of the Cormackian community of exegetes seem to agree. If anything, McCarthy's storytelling depends on being site-specific. However, why this might be so and what the function of this trait is ought to be explained.

Starting from *The Orchard Keeper* and continuing through the 2011 adaptation for cinema of *The Sunset Limited* and McCarthy's screenplay for *The Counselor* (2013), what is most important in his conception of the writer's task is the accumulation of knowledge about the regions in which the events to be imagined and described will take place. Thus, as the first monograph on McCarthy notes, his "first four novels . . . convey to us vividly . . . the specific whole ecology and spirit of a region."[9] The human experience is embedded in the places and situations in which it takes place, and it seems important that, in the case of McCarthy, this experience is above all an American one. As Berry argues, with respect to the novels set in Appalachia, McCarthy is "focusing on the details of the land—the surface features and landforms, the vegetation covering it, and the human structures built upon it,"[10] instead of telling stories that unfold in Malta; London, England; or Nordhausen, Germany, as Thomas Pynchon has done. McCarthy's literary imagination is steeped in the American scenery of the Southeast and Southwest, and, like Walker Evans's photographs and James Agee's writings in *Let Us Now Praise Famous Men*, it constantly affirms its local points of departure.[11] In terms of content, McCarthy seems to present small American lives on the micro level in preference to the categories and figures of those larger literary canvases that navigate across nations and centuries. It is because his fiction's site- and time-specificity—that is, *the realm of the particular*—are among the rare points on which critics seem to agree that this aspect appears to be its defining feature.[12]

Yet if we acknowledge that the places of the individual plots in his novels—from Eastern Tennessee's forests and mountains to the Southwestern prairies and the region of the US-Mexican border, from peach orchard to postapocalyptic waste, and from the solitude of the desert to that of the human mind—are vital to any understanding of their plots, then the question becomes *in what sense* the emphasis on locality in McCarthy's fiction is to be interpreted. Is regionalism—the narrator's explicit acknowledgment of the particular place and time from and about which a plot or story is constructed—an explicit end in itself, or is it a means to an end? Is the homage his texts pay to the Smoky Mountains, the poverty-stricken parts of Knoxville, the Sonora desert, or the Rio Grande Valley intended to simply romanticize these sites, or is it meant to fulfill a purpose within a narrative schema as well as appealing to the reader's aesthetic (that is to say, affective) appreciation? The present book argues strongly in favor of the latter. As others have proclaimed, McCarthy's often bleak renderings of American life in mainly rural areas are balanced by the metaphysically and sometimes even religiously inclined passages for which his storytelling is equally famous, and the latter coincides with the former.[13] Rather than affirming any kind of antimetaphysical attitude in the author's narrative technique, however, the void of bleak materiality appears to be the actual condition of possibility for McCarthy's contemplation of all things metaphysical. The particular and local fates and situations of American life are the possible foundation for more universal and global scenarios, for macro-histories and their transnational tendencies. Put differently, regionalism can be understood here as a literary strategy used to pose questions of an order that transcends the bounds of single lives. Locality is the starting point for delving into a more speculative realm, reiterating the genesis of an all-encompassing nature, recapitulating traces of cosmogenesis (sometimes implicitly, at other times explicitly), and thus transcending the national boundaries of literary and philosophical culture.[14]

The twofold notion of transcendence notwithstanding, McCarthy's strategy of the local does not accord with what Robert Tally Jr., in his work on Edgar Allan Poe, describes as the American "rhetoric of ascent."[15] For Tally, this "ascendental" worldview includes the Puritans' belief that they were a chosen people, the well-known trope of manifest destiny and American progress, and the outlining of a "heavenward" or generally "upward mobility" as it "animates the discourse of the 'inevitable' ascension of the nation to the top of the global hierarchy in a geopolitical, sometimes also military and economic, organization of the world system."[16] Conversely, the rhetoric employed by McCarthy is more akin to a "downward mobility," as he constantly reflects on the shadowy depths of his characters' personalities, their past, and the future in which they will go back to where they have come from in the first place, which is not heaven but, literally, the earth. In fact, this mobility is captured by a term that is normally taken to denote the mapping of global and local spaces: McCarthy's narrative negotiation of his characters' downward path works according to a logic of the earth—*geology*. Regionalism, then, is key to enabling us to ask the kind of speculative questions that Cornelius Suttree, the protagonist of McCarthy's fourth novel poses. While lying in a hospital bed, where he is recovering from a delirious fever caught on his sojourn through the Smoky Mountains, Suttree wonders: "Could a whole man not author his own death with a thought? Shut down the ventricle like the closing of an eye?" (*S*, 295).

Thus, the passage from the specific to the general, from the empirical to the speculative, and from the national to the transnational is a transcendence downward, if it is transcendent at all.[17] McCarthy's strategy of the regional is *descendental*, perhaps similar if not identical to the way in which Tally describes Poe's poetics. In clarifying the latter's conception of subversive literature as an "almost geological" activity rather than an "oppositional political project" in the all-too-familiar vein of many postmodernist writers and critics, Tally states: "In contrast to the rhetoric of ascent, Poe formulates a poetics of descent, which operates as a critique of all things lofty. It is a mode by which to 'take things down,' to bring the highfalutin conceits back down to the level of the street or even lower, to plunge such grand ideals into the muck and mire of material culture."[18]

It is true that McCarthy's literary practice can be regarded as a perpetual survey of all things material in the American context, whereby "matter" is literally understood as "muck and mire," not as in phrases like "the political matters of protest culture" or as in book titles such as Judith Butler's *Bodies That Matter*. This shying away from presenting his conception of materiality in political terms reflects the somewhat antisocial invective that defines McCarthy's literary strategy on the level of content: the conceptual transition from the details of Southern culture in the United States to more classic, universal themes such as the time and experience of one's own death, the value of a life, and the accessibility of what lies beyond the perceptually accessible phenomena of sense is made possible by a tendency to be earthward bound, which is why so many of the novels' narrators' speculations are set within or near caves or cave-like structures, such as the hearth onto which Lester Ballard climbs when his house has burned down (*COG*, 100), or the cave into which he crawls at the end of the second part of *Child of God*, when we read that some of his "possessions lay about in the grotto where chance had arranged them" (125). Given the poetic nature of McCarthy's diction in this short novel, it is safe to say that his use of a word like "chance" is not accidental. In contrast to saying that Ballard's belongings were merely placed randomly or chaotically, the use of "chance" evokes a whole range of significations.[19] This is because the verb "arrange" connotes an intentional quality different from random spatial distribution. To arrange something means to give it shape and form. The way that Ballard's small camp in the dark (which is flooded shortly afterward) is described seems to require a mention of chance: even though he might have placed his "mattress . . . in a pile of brush with the stuffed animals upon it and his other few possessions" (*COG*, 125) in an Appalachian "grotto," it is still chance—understood in an ontological sense still to be determined—that has really made possible the arrangement of these belongings.

The emphasis on the local, then, is the prerequisite for raising these metaphysically inclined questions and for pursuing them. McCarthy's basic and somewhat paradoxical premise is that it is only in the American context that a writer of fiction can speculate on "how the world was sentient to its core and secret and black beyond men's imagining and that its nature did not reside in what could be seen or not seen" (*TC*, 283), as a blind Mexican intimates to a companion in a story Billy Parham is told on his journey through the borderlands in *The Crossing*. To ask the question concerning nature's identity, we must start from the immediate environs of the American experience, and the writer's task is understood to be a descent into both the blurred yet static realities of the past and the distinct yet open possibilities of the future. One of McCarthy's chief idiosyncrasies is to capitalize on a certain artistic version of American exceptionalism to lay bare and debunk a particular worldview that privileges the human aspect of nature ontologically. In contrast to John Cant, who interprets McCarthy's fiction as "a critique of American Exceptionalism in particular and Western gnosis in general,"[20] I argue that the novels make use of an exceptionally American perspective to contemplate what it means to be human in a world that resists humanity's attempts to change it. McCarthy's literary method is to reorient the vector of ascension toward its opposite and thereby to combine literary speculation and a concept of nature grounded in the physicality of the latter.[21]

McCarthy's uniqueness as a writer notwithstanding, regionalism (both as a strategy and as an end in itself) has a long history in American literature. And McCarthy—the lifelong researcher in every intellectual field possible between quantum physics and the quest narrative—is certainly aware of this very tradition.[22] The tendency of American literature and culture in general to express a certain reverence for the specific regions and landscapes of the United States is a motif that has been present ever since the inception of US intellectual life by seminal transcendentalists like Emerson, Margaret Fuller, Henry David Thoreau, and Walt Whitman.[23] For instance, Emerson's first essay, "Nature" (1836), as well as "The Method of Nature" (1841) and "Man the Reformer" (1841), developed a metaphysical theory with aspirations to have universal purchase, while clearly being connected to the environment and newly established nation in the context of which they were written. "Nature" famously begins by distancing the American context from that of its colonialist fathers, with Emerson lamenting that many of his compatriots still oriented themselves culturally toward Europe.[24] "Our age is retrospective," Emerson claims. "It writes biographies, histories, and criticism." He suggests Americans should instead recognize that "the sun shines to-day also" and that they should live in the present, urging "let us demand our own works and laws and worship."[25] He then turns from the questions of his nation's collective identity and every individual's part in this collective to the environment within which the ascension of the souls of the young nation's citizens ought to take place. He justifies this move by proposing that "every man's condition is a solution in hieroglyphic to those inquiries he would put. He acts it as life, before he apprehends it as truth. In like manner, nature is already, in its forms and tendencies, describing its own design."[26] This means that to know the identity of this new type of individual that is the American, one has to determine how nature's "design" is to be deciphered.[27] In the remainder of his essay, Emerson examines the following question: "to what end is nature?"[28] In contrast to McCarthy, for whom the issue is not merely the end but the means of nature, Emerson strives "to find a theory of nature" to understand the exceptionality of the American soul and determine how man should conduct himself, how an ethical practice could and should be maintained that pertains to society and ecology in the United States in general and in New England in particular. "All science has one aim, namely, to find a theory of nature,"[29] Emerson claims, yet a few pages before he concludes his argument he returns to his claim that cultural mannerisms that look backward (that is, toward European ways of life) are still too prevalent in America. Americans need to turn toward their environment if they intend to forge a new and thriving nation. "At present, man applies to nature but half his force. He works on the world with his understanding alone," instead of immersing himself in "the miracles of enthusiasm"[30] about the environment that has been given to him. Man subordinates the physical via analysis, instead of affectively engaging with it and "becom[ing] a transparent eye-ball" with "the currents of Universal Being circulat[ing] through" him, Emerson writes, as he imagines the ideal reconciliation between humanity and the realm of nature, or what he calls the "plantations of God."[31]

Emerson's idealization of the sensual encounter between the American people with their natural surroundings testifies to his ascendental poetics. To experience the divine, one must feel one's individual environment—this is one meaning of Emerson's championing of "self-reliance" as one of the highest goals of human conduct.[32] According to Emerson, any theorization of nature must serve the transvaluation of ethical practices, irrespective of the universal aspiration of that theory. The concept of nature ought to be ethically prescribed, whether it seeks to aspire to universality or not. "The one condition coupled with the gift of truth is its use," and "the only way unto nature is to enact our best insight," Emerson writes in "The Method of Nature."[33] This form of practicism—that is, the prioritization of practicability in metaphysical considerations—reveals that in Emerson the "ends of nature" are the pleasure and well-being of humankind. However, they are only thus insofar as the sole reason of this worship of nature is to provide Emerson's argumentative means to social and cultural reform in the first place.[34] For Emerson, all inquiry into the question concerning nature's identity is instrumental for the imagining and eventual making of a distinctly American society. The emancipation of the latter from its European ancestors and their mores hinges on and is "organically linked" to the acknowledgment of the natural American habitat.[35]

Even if we set aside the rather obvious difference between a fiction writer, on the one hand, and an essayist and poet, on the other, we can see that McCarthy's perspective is diametrically opposed to that of Emerson with regard to the categories of means and ends and their distribution among the authors' respective areas of research, natural organization and cultural reform. While it is clear that there are certainly and necessarily a plethora of sensual encounters between McCarthy's fictional characters and their surroundings, it is less certain that these encounters are described to engage in an ethics of reform and reconstruction. McCarthy's view that novel writing may "encompass all the various disciplines and interests of humanity"[36] is related to and perhaps even alludes to Emerson's estimation that "all science has one aim, namely, to find a theory of nature."[37] Yet Emerson's goal in finding such a theory is to create an American identity, ascending from the natural (read: *organic*) environment to the national (read: *inorganic*) working through of cultural values, whereas McCarthy moves from delineating American identities to the ecological environment and then to the inorganic foundation of that environment by way of metaphysical, and sometimes outspokenly religious, speculation. His perspective on the quest for a theory of nature is one of grounding and descent, rather than uplifting and ascent. McCarthy's fiction does not address questions such as "to what end is nature?"[38] Rather, his narratives point to the complexity of the means by which nature exists and can be said to exist, and this other kind of reflection is made possible by the use of regionalism as a narrative strategy.

Like Emerson's essays, Thoreau's *Walden* (1854) started from the literality of the New England region, more specifically at Walden Pond in a forest nearby Concord, Massachusetts. Thoreau used the framework of describing his immediate environs to arrive at an answer to the question "What is nature?" He states in the book's penultimate chapter that "there is nothing inorganic" that may be part of nature's processes and that "the earth is all alive,"[39] an example of the vitalist stance of much of American writing during that period. In *Walden* we also find an early mixture of the two uses of regionalism mentioned above, as a strategy and as an objective. Thoreau's chosen habitat at the pond becomes the empirical laboratory he uses to build his speculative theory of nature. "The phenomena of the year take place every day in a pond on a small scale," Thoreau reasons,[40] and this is why his observations may be projected onto a larger scale. Thoreau's "intensified sensitivity to seasonal microphenomena"[41] allows him to think about "the biggest pond"—that is, *nature*. This passage from the particular to the universal works much like McCarthy's rendering of life in the Southern regions of the United States that from the beginning of his career have been the prerequisite for his formulating statements that transcend these regions—or, rather, McCarthy's depictions are to be understood as expressions of a nature that comes to know itself by narrative means.[42] From both Thoreau's and McCarthy's point of view, to forge a concept of the universal schemes of nature, literature must repeat a finite number of instances of nature's phenomena and in this forging reproduce the phenomenality of nature that is thereby culturally expressed.[43]

Yet the notion of regionalism denotes far more than the worship of nature that the transcendentalists practiced. In literary prose, it also includes the tradition of using local color, a technique of which Mark Twain a seminal representative and that McCarthy uses in every piece of fiction he has published since 1965 (with the possible exception of *The Road*).[44] Indeed, a Twainian use of local color and the depiction of regional customs; themes like cutting family ties in favor of leading an adventurous and sometimes solitary life, in which the protagonist ponders moral questions; and the frequent use of racialized and therefore controversial vocabulary are evident not only in *Suttree*, as other critics have remarked.[45] For instance, Steven Frye identifies this technique in the narrative sequences of *No Country for Old Men*, where Sheriff Ed Tom Bell contemplates what it means to face criminality on a daily basis, how the US-Mexican borderlands have changed over the years, as well as his marriage, among other things: "Mark Twain and the local color tradition come immediately to mind, not just in the use of dialect but in the artful and witty turn of phrase, the folk wisdom, and the pointed impact of the language of reflection."[46] This observation is especially apposite since Bell's narrative, like *Huckleberry Finn* (1884), is written in the first person—a rarity in McCarthy's work. Most of his novels are told primarily in the third person, ethologically describing the actions of his characters from a distance, however minimal. Nevertheless, it is not only in Bell's contemplations and in the first-person monologues of *Suttree*'s protagonists that we find exceptions to McCarthy's usual procedure of alternating versions of a third-person narrator, omniscient, detached, or engaged. In *Child of God*, unnamed country people recount tales about Ballard's past, such as how he once hit a boy from the neighborhood in the face (COG, 18–19) and how seemingly little affected he was after his father committed suicide, similar to the other country folk: "I don't know. They say he never was right after his daddy killed hisself. They was just the one boy. The mother had run off. . . . Me and Cecil Edwards was the ones cut him down. He come in the store and told it like you'd tell it was rainin out. We went out there and walked in the barn. . . . We just cut him down, let him fall in the floor. Just like cutting down meat" (22).

However, local color is not confined to first-person passages in McCarthy, as it is in William Faulkner's *As I Lay Dying* (1930). Except for only a few instances, whenever there is direct speech in McCarthy it is presented in a regional accent. In *Blood Meridian*, the narrator does not use the vernacular of the nineteenth-century borderlands, but a highly poetic and oftentimes archaic diction, as has been noted by most critics of the novel. The majority of its characters, though, speak in the manner of the time and place in which the novel is set—akin to the mode of literary realism—as can be seen paradigmatically in the dialogue between the kid and the hermit in chapter 3 of the novel.

Even before *Blood Meridian* or *Child of God*, the motif of locality assumes its realist role on the first page of *The Orchard Keeper* in the memorable Southern scene that is the novel's prologue. It features three men—two white, one black—cutting logs of a tree into sizable pieces before they come to the stump, which has grown around parts of an iron fence that threatens to ruin the saw they are using before they finish their job. With caution the older white man examines the situation and then calls the other two over:

> *The young man came over to see. Here, said the man, look sideways here. See? He looked. All the way up here? he said. Yep, the man said. He took hold of the twisted wrought-iron, the mangled fragment of the fence, and shook it. It didn't shake. It's growed all through the tree, the man said. We cain't cut no more on it. Damned old elum's bad enough on a saw.*
>
> *The Negro was nodding his head. Yessa, he said. It most sholy has. Growed all up in that tree.* (TOK, 3)

This scene is a good point to start considering different ways of reading McCarthy's take on the relationships and spaces of interaction between organic and inorganic things and processes in the world, on the one hand, and, on the other hand, the narrative means he uses to navigate the metaphysical questions entailed by these relations and spaces. As Jay Ellis and Erik Hage observe, McCarthy's formulation suggests a certain agency on the part of the fence—it has "*growed all through the tree*" instead of the tree's growing around it.[47] This detail suggests the main focus of both the scene and the whole novel: in what sense can literature show the ways in which the organic and the inorganic are fused in their commonality, which is nature?[48] Among all cultural habitats of the human species, it is the cemetery that is the prime example of "descendental" contemplation—the prime example also in literary Romanticism of *memento mori*, the human subject's awareness of its finitude. In this case, however, it is much more: the prologue to *The Orchard Keeper* sets the tone for the ensuing narrative and establishes McCarthy's signature technique generally, whereby the dialect of a particular region in the American Southeast colors the metaphysical statement that implies a certain agency, a certain residue of natural force in the inorganic material of the graveyard fence. In other words, even this short glimpse into the first few paragraphs of McCarthy's initial major prose work demonstrates how an apparently realistically depicted dialogue gives rise to the more speculative questions that haunt all of McCarthy's novels from that point on.

McCarthy's inclination to start from the matter-of-fact reality of the American experience and eventually address the imaginative realm of the human and nonhuman conditions, as given in nature, is consistent throughout his novelistic work. As I have mentioned above, this consistent inclination has created two camps in McCarthy scholarship. Those in one camp focus on his narrative starting point of human actuality, the cultural and historical bases of the novels, and thus explore the realist dimension of his fictions. Those in the other camp home in on McCarthy's speculations—philosophical, religious, or otherwise. Among the diverse ways of reading McCarthy vis-à-vis his concept of nature, then, I suggest a division with gnostics and ethicists on the one hand and materialists and ecocritical scholars on the other hand. As will become clear, I navigate between the two factions to integrate them along the lines of a *nature-philosophical synthesis* that is compatible (but not isomorphic) with accounts of environmental criticism. The most accurate interpretations have also leaned toward such a synthesis, which is further evidence that an account that combines science and spiritualism, or a "realism concerning Ideas,"[49] is the proper way of seriously coming to terms with McCarthy's poetics.[50]

For example, in *Reading the World: Cormac McCarthy's Tennessee Period* (2009), Dianne Luce emphasizes both McCarthy's bleak realism and his religiously inflected mythography. Her interpretation is also related to an abovementioned issue in his work—gnosticism. I want to examine this issue more closely as it tends to neglect the regionalism of McCarthy's work and thus seemingly contradicts my claim above that one of the few things on which scholars agree is that his fiction depends on being site-specific.

In a 1992 article, "Gravers False and True: *Blood Meridian* as Gnostic Tragedy," Daugherty was the first to examine this crucial mystical direction in McCarthy's work. This article showed how McCarthy's prose could be characterized in terms of gnosticism and mysticism.[51] Daugherty starts his argument by stating that although the origins of gnostic thought are still subject to some debate, "it is generally agreed that it came about as yet another answer to the question, How is it that the world is experienced as so very evil and that so many people's central response to it is alienation?"[52] The problem of evil is indeed perpetually present in the world of Judge Holden, and it is safe to say that it is a problem that is addressed in the entirety of McCarthy's work, to varying degrees. Among the views held by the gnostics, "evil was simply everything that *is*, with the exception of the bits of spirit emprisoned here."[53] In other words, the realm of finitude—that is, of corporeality—within the world is evil, while the ideational part of it is inherently good. In the Manichean version of gnosticism, which is what Daugherty mostly discusses, the problem of evil is linked to an irresolvable war within the world, a "cosmic drama which pits spirit against matter, light against darkness, and the alien god (and the alien pneumatic spirit within sleeping humankind) against the archons."[54] Lesser deities called archons, who are responsible for the creation of sin on earth, exist together with "the Gnostic god, being totally not of this world," and therefore alien; a god who "generates no *nomos*, no law, for either nature or human activity. The law, instead, is that of the archons, and justice is theirs as well."[55] This alien deity is not part of human law or customs; it is the alien and nevertheless divine spark, "the spirit imprisoned within matter . . . called *pneuma*," which is the inherently good part of the world.[56] It manifests itself in the human capacity to think and to contemplate a problem. As Shane Schimpf explains, the universe exists and perpetuates itself by "dividing from itself via an internal will to self-understanding," as seen in varieties of gnosticism and their cosmologies—a conception also known as *gnosis*, which denotes this particular form of thinking.[57] Consequently, the ontologization of war via the conception of an unending conflict between the two polarities of the archonic and the transcendent, or the *nomos* and the *logos*, applies to the philosophy of war imagined by Judge Holden. In the gnosticism of Jacob Boehme, a sixteenth-century German mystic, theologian, and philosopher whose work greatly influenced German idealism in the nineteenth century, "*war is the ultimate cause of unity*";[58] it is "at last a forcing of the unity of existence. War is god" (*BM*, 249).

It would be wrong, then, to state that a mainly gnostic account of McCarthy's fiction is reductionist in that it downplays the attention his narratives pay to the importance of materiality, because the unification and subsequent synthesis of conflicting and conflicted elements in the world on all levels of organization and intensity are precisely what determine the experiential limits of McCarthy's literary figures. This is true of Ballard, whose whole life appears to be characterized by cosmic pain. Even though he is certainly not as intelligent a character as Suttree, and even though his alienation from the *nomos* of Sevierville differs in many ways from that of Suttree's alienation in Knoxville, the two men certainly have comparable psychological conflicts. In *Child of God*, Ballard sees "two hawks couple and drop, their wings upswept. . . . He did not know how hawks mated but he knew that all things fought" (*COG*, 160). This is also a lesson learned by the protagonist of *Suttree* who leaves Knoxville at the end of the novel as his neighborhood is transformed by government trucks: "new roads being laid over McAnally, over the ruins, the shelled facades and walls standing in crazed shapes" (*S*, 463).

Judging from novels as different as *Child of God* and *No Country for Old Men*, McCarthy has taken notice of human alienation in the world, a psychological and bodily form of alienation from the material world that is both outside and inside of the human self. Some scholars might consider this a rather general grounding for a critical account of McCarthy's work, yet it is crucial for any understanding of the latter. Psychological and bodily alienation, considered from the point of view of gnosticism, displays an immanent world of sin that is transcended only by a divine spark within humanity. In *The Sunset Limited* Black calls this spark "the lingering scent of divinity" (*TSL*, 13). What may be fruitful for an examination of the gnostic metaphysics debated in the largely theological discussion between the two characters in *The Sunset Limited*, Black and White, appears less satisfying for readings of other major narratives by McCarthy that are firmly grounded in their places and spaces.

In contrast to Daugherty and Mundik, Luce explicates the ways in which McCarthy alludes to gnostic elements of viewing that world of sin by using regionalism as a narrative strategy.[59] In her treatment of *Suttree*, for example, Luce writes, "the novel suggests that Suttree's family, America's colonizers and empire-builders, and humanity in general are not far removed from their feral beginnings and on a metaphoric level are avatars of the archontic powers."[60] The human animal is doomed to repeat the deeds of its forebears at the same time that it retains the godlike motivation to acquire more knowledge about its alienated position in the cosmos. In other words, the human animal is capable of creating its own world while being bound to the instinctual realm of sense. In addition, it seems important that it is specifically "*America's* colonizers"[61] that simultaneously represent the gnostic transcendence of humanity and its immanent predation. The present study employs a similar interpretation of McCarthy's fiction, even though Luce's tracing of the philosophical aspects in his narratives (gnostic, Platonist, mystic, and ecocritical) is augmented here by the Schellingian and Okenian philosophies of nature.

In opposition to Daugherty, Luce, and other critics who have noted the spiritual aspects of McCarthy's fiction, Phillips's materialist reading emphasizes the importance of the author's phrases that portray characters who are "without expression" (*BM*, 84) even when they confront the most appalling sights. There are innumerable scenes throughout McCarthy's work in which people are "looking" at their surroundings "with no expression at all" (*TC*, 244), and the nonaffective stance evoked in such scenes is all the more significant for its inexpressiveness—that is, it may be read in allegorical terms. Phillips formulates this approach quite forcefully: "Salvation history, which understands the natural world and man's travails in it as symbols of the spirit, has long since been played out, as the ruined, eroded, and buzzard-draped mission churches in *Blood Meridian* suggest. Only natural history, which regards neither nature nor man as symbolic, is left."[62] This investigation of *Blood Meridian*'s dependence on and connectedness to material history is on point in its rigorous and insightful analysis of the novel's aestheticization of a nature that is indifferent to humankind and the rest of its flora and fauna—that is, *a nature indifferent to itself*. However, it strikes me as curious that Phillips's reading is convincing in its emphasis on the importance of natural history for McCarthy, while it fails to make adequate sense of the irreducibly spiritual aspect of nature in his fiction.

As I have been arguing, regionalism is a crucial element in McCarthy's narratives from *The Orchard Keeper* until the present. I have also claimed that there is a polar divide in the scholarly literature on McCarthy between the historical and the mythological, the material and the spiritual (in particular, when comes to the issue of locality). However, there are many variations and divergences even within these "two polar metaphysical strands."[63] Also, it is certainly difficult to distinguish between, say, materialists and spiritualists when discussing the scholarship on any given contemporary author: there is always the risk of oversimplification in using concepts such as that of a polar divide.[64] If by materialism we mean a view that sees a corporeal basis for every phenomenon in the world, and if by spiritualism we mean a view that sees a divine spirit as the basis for these phenomena, it seems clear that there are materialist and spiritualist tendencies in many different interpretations of McCarthy's work, rather than two distinct factions of interpreters.[65] Yet it also becomes clear that there is an increasing differentiation among the readings of his work, with topics that seem as incompatible as the religious quest narrative and literature's link to the notion of entropy that originated in thermodynamics and information theory.[66]

Consequently, for the purpose of the present argument, it does indeed make sense to speak of two factions, since even though many scholars combine both tendencies to varying degrees, the issue of regionalism is always approached and discussed from a certain position that is either predominantly materialist or spiritualist. In other words, the question concerning the regional seems to be the linchpin for any critic's approach to McCarthy. The position one takes regarding his novels clearly depends to a certain extent on whether one sees their rootedness in social, cultural, and historical contexts as an end in itself, or as a means to an end within narratives that have a metaphysical scope. I opt for the second alternative and thereby in contrast to gnostic, ethicist, materialist, and environmental readings, I see McCarthy's concept of nature as primary. I want to qualify this decision by adding that his novels do not merely depict the hardships of the homeless in 1950s Knoxville and its environs (as is the case in *Suttree*) or the cultural landscape of 1960s Appalachia and its social deviants (as is the case in *Child of God*), although they also indubitably do that. Rather, they are novels that somehow depend on these particular surroundings to formulate speculations that transcend the bounds of cultural particularity. For example, *Child of God* can be described as a fictionalization of historically verifiable murder cases—namely, those of James Blevins and Ed Gein, as Luce has shown.[67] But it is precisely this violent setting that serves as the defining condition of possibility for its narrator's contemplation of "some strange underground force" in one of Ballard's caves that is mysteriously related to the motion within the pools of "water rushing off into the darkness before him, *descending* from pool to pool in stone cups of its own devising" (*COG*, 126, emphasis added). It is almost as if the distinctly American environment of those poor and tragic lives is an intentional constraint: similar to the ways in which twentieth-century experimental fiction has employed self-imposed syntactical prohibitions when it comes to using only certain letters or words to achieve a particular effect. Along these lines, McCarthy's narrative strategy can be described as a stylistic experiment insofar as he transposes the logic of the originally political notion of American exceptionalism into the structure of his poetics.

Furthermore, McCarthy's literary transcendence of cultural particulars on a philosophical level is grounded in the same way that his narratives are bound by their regionalist character. In contrast to Phillips's view, the present reading allows for notions of the transcendent with regard to McCarthy's fiction. However, it is a transcendence downward, not upward, that takes place in his novels; it is descendental, not ascendental. One of the reasons for this claim is the importance of materiality in the narrative "theory of nature" that McCarthy constructs throughout his oeuvre on his quest for an "idea of creation," to use Emerson's terms once again.[68]And although McCarthy is not a philosopher in the sense of writing about philosophical questions according to the norms of the discipline, for him literature can "encompass all the various disciplines and interests of humanity."[69] In his case, the relevant disciplines would certainly include philosophy and science, bearing in mind both his well-documented interest in Plato and his long fellowship at the Santa Fe Institute in New Mexico.[70]

I suggest that even the theological underpinnings of McCarthy's fiction can be grounded in a concept of nature, and that an "ethics of empathy" is surpassed by the ontological status of nature in his work. What this means is that the ways in which the spiritual element features in the novels have nothing to do with any "discourse of the 'inevitable' ascension of the nation to the top of the global hierarchy,"[71] as Tally describes the form of human transcendence that was ideologically fused with the religious piety of nineteenth-century Americans, who feared for their status as a people chosen by

God. Although Cooper does not endorse such an ascendental rhetoric per se, she nevertheless sees the ideal of "human communion"[72] as a general ethos capable of grounding McCarthy's poetics. She thereby implies that it is from a high moral ground that McCarthy creates his concept of nature, whereas it is from *Suttree*'s highly poetic image of a "formless macule of plasm trapped in a vapor drop" (*S*, 430) that he derives his understanding of ethical conduct and normative structure. Thus, the literary characters and the narrators that describe them possess a downward mobility—meaning that to investigate an ostensibly human form of transcendence has its origin in what is nonhuman.[73]

Furthermore, many spiritualist readings of McCarthy neglect the notion that his ethico-aesthetic formula—*starting from grief, arriving at grace*—coincides with the importance accorded to the realm of nature in his fictional worlds. Frye's expression of that formula replaces the words "grief" and "grace" with "horror" and "beauty," when he suggests that *Blood Meridian* is "a novel of incomparable beauty derived from the raw matter of incomparable horror."[74] In terms of natural history, the juxtaposition of these four terms and their respective succession in the way intended by Frye results in an image in which the notions of grief and horror that precede those of grace and beauty have to count as the nonhuman realm that exists before the human. The indifferent horror of nature is oblivious to the grace of "human communion"—a grace that is one with the strictures of norms and values—yet the latter is "derived from the raw matter of" the former. In McCarthy's fiction, acts of empathy (despite being irreducibly cultural practices) are natural in the final analysis. In terms of narrative time, however (that is, according to the logic of McCarthy's strategy of regionalism, used as a way to address that which transcends the regional), the alignment of the four notions results in grace and beauty preceding grief and horror, and the human realm existing before the nonhuman. This is exactly what is meant by downward mobility, or descendental transcendence, at the level of narration: the literary investigation into the raw materiality of that which is nonliterary must proceed from the particular to the universal.

On closer examination, then, it turns out that the ostensible agreement in the scholarship on the importance of site-specificity in McCarthy's fiction leads to a parting of the ways between materialist and spiritualist interpretations. Whereas one faction of critics only implicitly acknowledges the crucial aspect of the particular regions depicted in the novels, for the other faction this aspect licenses a dismissal of any symbolism or speculation whatsoever.

AFTER THE THEMATIC COMPLEX regarding the tensions in McCarthy's fiction between a contemporary version of mythography and a historically grounded realism, and between the places of rural America and the spaces of transnational speculation, the second issue to be addressed is even more contentious: the problem of periodization. The question concerning McCarthy's style and its context, however, is multifaceted—first, given the time during which he published the bulk of his novels; second, due to the singular use of language in them; and third, because of the relationship these two aspects have with the content of his works and their themes.

One way of determining the literary period of a fiction writer is to simply inquire into the historical circumstances of his or her novels' publication. For instance, McCarthy's first three novels, *The Orchard Keeper*, *Outer Dark*, and *Child of God*, were published from the mid-1960s to the early 1970s, at a time of public upheaval and cultural unrest in the United States and elsewhere on the globe. It was "the era of American history defined by the military involvement in Vietnam," as Vince Brewton notes.[75] For Brewton, it is also *Suttree* and *Blood Meridian* that reflect this long and tumultuous moment in the second half of the twentieth century, "while the novels of the Border Trilogy" somehow represent the "cultural landscape of America beginning in the 1980s, a landscape best evoked by the Reagan presidency and the Gulf War with Iraq."[76] These kinds of historicist correspondences that literary critics find between the cultural artifacts of a given period and the major events that give shape to the latter are sometimes highly informative, but they can also be misleading. Cultural artifacts are evidently products of their time, as the materialist approaches to McCarthy attest, but they must always be more than that if they are to count as aesthetic objects. Moreover, the discernment of a given novel's literary period always has to do with the kind of diction that predominates in that text; it has to do with how both the historical context of the novel and its diction relate to the themes it depicts in terms of plot, atmosphere, and character. It is at this point that especially the reader who is keen to follow Fredric Jameson's advice to "always historicize"[77] faces a rather difficult situation when she confronts McCarthy's oeuvre. This is because the individual readings that constitute the scholarship on McCarthy have already managed to ascribe *nearly every single style in American literary history* to the formal inventions and thematic directions McCarthy has deployed in his narratives. In a situation in which each literary period from transcendentalism to the present has been considered to be an influence on the writing process of a particular author, it becomes very hard to determine the context in which readers are to see his work.

Certainly, one possible objection here is that it is not really important how one categorizes a particular novel in historical terms. On the contrary, some critics might say, all great literature should be able to rise above its historical context and thus remain readable hundreds of years after its publication. In other words, great works of literature, like all great works of art, are timeless. Yet there are several reasons why the supposed greatness of McCarthy's fiction does not warrant any kind of ahistorical bias on the part of the reader. As many scholars have demonstrated, it is essential to account in some way for the author's interest in every kind of the world's historical dynamics, including the specificities of regional turns of phrase, the conception of progress and regress in the evolution of science, and the ideology of manifest destiny. Furthermore, it should strike any scholar of McCarthy as noteworthy that the author's works have been compared to each literary period in American literature from transcendentalism to post-postmodernism (in more or less convincing interpretations, respectively). The fact that it is possible to thoroughly argue that his novels are transcendentalist, Romanticist, realist, naturalist, modernist, late modernist, postmodernist, or post-postmodernist is reason enough to ponder this situation as a second, and much more complex, difference between the perspectives on McCarthy's work. Similar to the synthetic perspective taken up with respect to McCarthy's use of regionalism as a narrative strategy to contribute to metaphysical questions vis-à-vis nature's identity, in the context of periodization it is imperative both to affirm every contextualization of McCarthy's work according to the poetic parameters of styles from transcendentalism onward, and to negate their critical authority or definitive role in his singular achievement as an author of literary fiction.

I have already alluded to the transcendentalist heritage of McCarthy with respect to Emerson and Thoreau and their regionalist forms of writing. McCarthy scholars have repeatedly connected his work to that of both transcendentalists, sometimes to contrast their poetics with his and sometimes to note McCarthy's transcendentalist roots.[78] Furthermore, traces of Romanticism and its two main literary types, gothic fiction and the historical romance, can be found in McCarthy's style. The works of James Fenimore Cooper, Poe, Nathaniel Hawthorne, and especially Herman Melville resonate to varying degrees with McCarthy's work, as scholars have rightfully pointed out.[79] For instance, Frye writes about *The Crossing*, "In the broadest sense, the novel employs the formal features of the American historical romance through a character distinctly human but configured as mythic through his heroic action and his tragic encounter with a changing world."[80] Together with the depiction of "landscape [as] imbued with sublime resonance" and the metaphysical concern with the spiritual dispositions of nature, these are core "features of the romance tradition."[81] Moreover, the general lack of introspection on the part of McCarthy's characters is not merely an idiosyncratic feature of his prose but instead dramatizes seemingly timeless themes like heroism and moral integrity by using the characters as examplars.[82] However, Cant writes that "neither realism nor naturalism is of particular relevance to McCarthy"[83]—a claim that is highly controversial, given that other scholars have demonstrated the myriad ways in which McCarthy has been influenced by the narratives and respective worldviews of just these two literary movements. As with transcendentalism and Romanticism, then, there are traits of literary realism and naturalism in McCarthy's prose, again to varying degrees and across the novels.[84]

Consider the language used for the birth scene at the beginning of *Outer Dark*, directly after Culla has come back from a short walk near the cabin in the forest. I am quoting the passage at length to show how the narrative's unflinching treatment of violence is not always coded in Romantic symbolism, as is the case in Hawthorne or Melville, but instead makes for what has been described as McCarthy's forensic objectivism:

> When he went in again she had crawled or fallen from the bed and lay in the floor clutching the bedstead. He did think she had died, lying there looking up with eyes that held nothing at all. Then her body convulsed and she screamed. He struggled with her, lifting her to the bed again. The head had broken through in a pumping welter of blood. He knelt in the bed with one knee, holding her. With his own hand he brought it free, the scrawny body trailing the cord in anneloid writhing down the bloodslimed covers, a beet-colored creature that looked to him like a skinned squirrel. He pinched the mucus from its face. It didn't move. (*OD*, 14)

McCarthy's literary realism is not psychological in the Jamesian sense.[85] Considering the repeated attention McCarthy's narratives—especially the Southern works—pay to social ills, his realism is more akin to works of fiction like Rebecca Harding Davis's *Life in the Iron Mills* (1861).[86] However, McCarthy's style, which uses a sober and seemingly indifferent manner to describe scenes like the child's birth at the beginning of *Outer Dark*, can also be read in a naturalist framework. This is not just because the imagery used in the description of the newborn—namely, that of a "skinned squirrel" (*OD*, 14)—recalls the gruesome accounts of human life at the mercy of (its) nature in the novels of Frank Norris, Jack London, and other early twentieth-century naturalists. It is also because McCarthy's habit of likening his human characters to animals is a classic trait of literary naturalism, and one of the clearest indicators of the influence that Darwinian biology had on its adherents in America.[87]

Another key component here, along the lines of what Mark Seltzer has termed "the naturalist aesthetic doctrines of determinism and degeneration,"[88] is the very specific role of violence in the naturalist novel. This is a factor that in London's work, for instance, illuminates the close relationship between the human animal and the members of other species of fauna. "Violence is the explicit manifestation of the conflict inherent in natural systems, and it is a counterpoint to cosmic optimism"[89] of the sort one finds in the ascendental poetics of Emerson and others. This aspect of McCarthy's fiction demonstrates that in American literature, it is not only Romanticism but also naturalism that differs from the optimism of the transcendentalists and realism's character psychologies. Both Romanticism and naturalism waver between optimism and pessimism, on the one hand, and, on the other hand, between "progress (as evolution)" and "recapitulation (as devolution)."[90]

In addition to the influence of nineteenth-century (and early twentieth-century) American literature on McCarthy's work, scholars have recognized a modernist trait in his style of writing. Above all, Faulkner has had a very strong influence on McCarthy's prose, as many have noted. Jonathan Yardley, the *Washington Post* book critic, once wrote that "McCarthy is perhaps the closest we have to a genuine heir to the Faulknerian tradition,"[91] but it could also be argued that Faulkner's experimental novels come closest to being predecessors of McCarthy's in employing regionalism as a narrative strategy and not as an end in itself. McCarthy's work has also been compared to other seminal writers of the modernist period, including James Joyce, Flannery O'Connor, and James Agee.[92] In spite of the arguments to be made for this stylistic lineage, like the preceding periods, modernism is insufficient to describe McCarthy's literary idiosyncrasies.

Perhaps the greatest controversy in the periodizing of McCarthy's work is whether or not it has been influenced by (or is indeed part and parcel of) postmodernism, the literary practice contemporaneous with the majority of his novels. In spite of the large number of critics who believe that McCarthy's fiction is historically, stylistically, and thematically postmodern, I argue that this periodization is the most unsatisfactory of all, as regards its aspiration to sufficiently account for the singularity of his style.[93] However, I also disagree with the attempt to frame *The Road* in terms of a "post-postmodern" style.[94] In any case, postmodernism's obsession with the fundamentally textual fabrication of the world somehow prevents any form of research into nonhuman nature that does not have recourse to its cultural construction, which makes it a difficult framework to use for coming to terms with the metaphysics evoked by McCarthy. As Bertrand Westphal has also argued, this situation is in many ways due to Jacques Derrida's famous proviso that "*there is nothing outside of the text* [there is no outside-text; *il n'y a pas de hors-texte*]"[95]—or rather, it is due to those academics who transformed this epistemological statement into an ontological one. According to my reading, it is the dimension of *nature*'s identity, as opposed to the formation of cultural identities, that differentiates McCarthy's fiction from the work of his contemporaries such as Pynchon, John Barth, and Paul Auster.[96]

In the course of this argument I will show that McCarthy's relation—or, rather, lack thereof—to the tendencies in fiction and the academic trends in the humanities during the past fifty years sets him apart from his fellow fiction writers. His usage of archaic diction (somewhere between somber contemplation and sober description) and his treatment of classical themes in literature (including life's and death's respective valences, human techniques of dealing with fear and loss, physical and psychic pain, and the role of violence in the establishment of cultural norms) are characterized not by a dismissal of grand narratives but by their reformulation in terms of a distinct metaphysics of nature.[97] It is not satisfactory to call McCarthy's work postmodern. Nor is it appropriate to call it "post-postmodern,"[98] just because it does not entirely fit into either of the preceding periods and styles from Brown's *Edgar Huntly* (1799) to Pynchon's *Mason & Dixon* (1997). Linda Woodson argues that McCarthy's postapocalyptic narrative reflects the postmodern assumption that language is foundational for the establishment of one's experiential horizon in social interaction (in *The Road*, between father and son).[99] Yet she states that the narrative takes an "essentialist" stance regarding the capacity of language to express what lies outside of it—namely, a kind of immediacy that is both nonlinguistic and tied to a specific ethos, the "essence of living authentically" and communally: "*The Road* demonstrates that it is possible to tell a story of what is best in humans as reflective of all that can be described as a positive force in the natural world. In that sense it becomes an affirmation, an expectancy."[100] However, it is difficult to see in what sense this essentialist pointing toward a nonlinguistic realm of ethics is linked to a form of writing that makes it particularly predestined to be called post-postmodern, a term that had already been used in 2004 in connection to David Foster Wallace's writing.[101] While *The Road* is unique in McCarthy's work in depicting a loving relationship between a father and son, and (unlike the majority of McCarthy's previous novels) in focusing on ethics throughout its plot, it is still in keeping with his larger project of using narrative means to answer the question concerning nature's identity. Moreover, Woodson's claim that *The Road* presents a view of language as being capable of intuiting a non- or prelinguistic realm makes an innovative point about the novel, but to tie the conception of this realm back to an affirmative ethics of "living authentically"[102] misses a vital opportunity to connect McCarthy's poetic diction in general, and the idea of intuiting a realm outside of language by means of that diction in particular, to the principal space that ontologically speaking is independent of what is told about it—*nature*.

Above all, it is the strong investment in the conception of nature by means of narrative that separates McCarthy's poetics from those of many of his contemporaries, including Don DeLillo, Auster, and Wallace. It might be said that if a writer like DeLillo is thinking through the network of the American cultural and political climate before and after the assassination of President John F. Kennedy in a novel such as *Libra* (1988), based on the lives of the assassin Lee Harvey Oswald and the archivist Nicholas Branch, McCarthy's *Blood Meridian*, published three years earlier, is a thought experiment that renders visible the meshes of natural process, based on the historical lives of scalp hunters like John Joel Glanton. While DeLillo's project is remarkable, it differs from McCarthy's insofar as it does not have the same kind of philosophical background to the narrative. *Libra* is a poetic tale about how the process of reading defines the human condition, while *Blood Meridian* is a swan song for the ascendental rhetoric that American intellectual history is founded upon. In terms of the post-Kantian philosophy of nature that serves as one of the crucial intellectual backbones to McCarthy's project as a whole, DeLillo works according to the narrative strictures of the transcendental apparatus that sees nonhuman nature merely "as a retro-effect of culture,"[103] while McCarthy examines almost naïvely the identity of natural process as *absolute* in the Schellingian sense, detecting the dynamics of perpetual inscription and re-inscription in matter itself.[104] This can be seen as early as in *Child of God*. In a passage that is curiously reminiscent of the penultimate chapter of Thoreau's *Walden*, called "Spring," McCarthy writes: "In the spring or warmer weather when the snow thaws in the woods the tracks of winter reappear on slender pedestals and the snow reveals *in palimpsest* old buried wanderings, struggles, scenes of death. Tales of winter brought to light again like time turned back upon itself" (*COG*, 130, emphasis added).

This image of disintegrating snow is metaphorically rich in many ways. From the perspective of a naïve historicism that would simply focus on the year in which the book containing that image was published (1973), one might be led to conclude, in a Derridean manner, that this is simply a passage that shows how McCarthy extends the intricacies of language beyond the realm of textual signification to the domain of nature—or, rather, how he uses the culturally constructed concept of nature and the ontological ramifications of its discourse to refer back to the epistemological complexity involved in human memory, as it is written and overwritten "in palimpsest."[105] But that would again collapse the question "What is nature?" into its premeditated dismissal in the form of a renewed claim that anything nonhuman in nature is really just a projection of what our transcendental apparatus is capable of imagining. It would disregard McCarthy's attention to those processes of nature that go beyond the notion of such a projection, while in the last instance, they can be said to give rise to it.

I will come back to this passage about a natural palimpsest below. At this point of the argument it mainly serves to illustrate the preliminary solution to the problem of McCarthy's periodization. The numerous tracings of transcendentalist, Romanticist, realist, naturalist, modernist, postmodernist, and post-postmodernist influences, traits, or "tracks" in his work notwithstanding, it seems that it is still too early to categorize McCarthy according to existing generic labels or styles.

While McCarthy's prose is highly eclectic in that his "books are made out of books,"[106] as he once conceded in passing to one of his few interviewers, it is probably too early to make any definitive statement along the lines of "McCarthy combines a mythographical affinity with formally novelistic experiments that recall Joyce and Faulkner, which makes him a late modernist by default" or "McCarthy's novels were published roughly at the same time as Pynchon's, which automatically designates both authors as postmodernists, irrespective of their poetics." Rather, McCarthy's eclecticism can be read as a performative representation of his concept of nature. For McCarthy, it seems, literature is a self-organizing and, by extension, self-composting process, in the sense in which John Elder describes T. S. Eliot's and Gary Snyder's poetry in his study *Imagining the Earth: Poetry and the Vision of Nature* (1985). The present study repudiates every periodization of McCarthy's work that limits it to a specific style and simultaneously affirms his oeuvre's relationship to each and every period discussed. This is because McCarthy's yet-to-be-defined style is chiefly distinguished by the kinds of inscriptions and re-inscriptions in it of the mostly American literary traditions that precede it. In other words, McCarthy appears to cross-fertilize the entirety of American literature since Brown and Emerson, and by doing so, he invents a style that is entirely his own, using narrative means to answer the question "What is nature?" In this performative act that is less self-reflexive than auto-generative—meaning that the reference of the literary work to itself is more a pointing to its being a process of recounting past literary styles and periods than to its being a work of fiction—McCarthy somehow equates the idea of literature to the concept of nature. There is a similarity, his fiction suggests, between natural objects and literary ones, in that both kinds of objects depend on that process in which the acts of *recounting* and *composting* become one and the same.

The question remains, how is the transition possible between the theory of nature underlying McCarthy's fiction at the level of content and its stylistic representation (or, rather, repetition) at the level of form? This question is a reformulation of the problematic that is posed by the projection of biological and ecological dynamics—what is often understood, in fact, by the term "nature" in ecocriticism—onto those of literary culture. In other words, how can we reframe the realm of the cultural within that of organic nature? Elder writes:

> Regrounding culture in the natural world involves a descent. *Decay* . . . derives after all from *cadere*, to fall. The decay of old systems both allows and necessitates fresh attention to the soil's process of regeneration. Tradition becomes a landscape of human meaning, continually paced off on the ancient renewing earth. . . . But from the vantage of space, earth itself becomes a radiant particular of decay—a crystal, a seed. Poetry and science, nature and culture, all are included within such an oscillation. In the mutual surrender of process and particular, there is a model for human assent. Reconciliation takes the form of alternation: observation and imagination, left foot and right, a person finds the wholeness of a world flickering through time and space.[107]

This lengthy quote demonstrates both the advantages and the shortcomings of Elder's take on the reintegration of human culture into nonhuman nature. On the one hand, he provides the starting point for the positive evaluation of decay in McCarthy's novels, in contrast to the Kristevan theory of abjection and the concept of decay developed therein. In Schellingian parlance, it is as much the science of nature (*Naturwissenschaft*) as it is the literature of nature (*Naturliteratur*) that is part of the same "oscillation." On the other hand, the problem with Elder's account lies in his concept of nature itself, as it somehow excludes its inorganic aspect, while constructing a nature that is viewed as "whole" and complete merely because it is phenomenologically so. Like other ecocritics, Elder conceives of nature as a self-sufficient and solely organic whole in his "project of reconciliation,"[108] instead of acknowledging the always irresolvable difference between product and productivity in natural dynamics. This difference is "the incomprehensible base of reality in things, the indivisible remainder, that which with the greatest exertion cannot be resolved in understanding but rather remains eternally in the ground," as Friedrich W. J. Schelling writes in his *Freedom* essay.[109] While the conceptual scaffolding of Elder's characterization of literature initially works descendentally rather than ascendentally, the orientation of his reading toward a reconciliation between the human realm and that of organic nature means that its critical edge never takes full shape. The idea of reconciliation—an exaggerated version of the Orphic attitude that exclusively dictates a reverence for the environment and prescribes the worship of what Alfred North Whitehead once called "nature alive"[110]—is indeed indicative of one of the problems of many recent approaches in McCarthy scholarship of an ecocritical bent. This is not to say that ecocritical or ecocentric approaches are to be dismissed in general. On the contrary, those are highly valuable frameworks for investigating the work of writers who are outspokenly concerned with the well-being of our global ecosystem. In the case of criticism on McCarthy, however, it is hard to see how the author would join forces with the many strands of literary ecology as well as the ethical focus of the environmental humanities on a rhetoric of preservation and humanistic self-empowerment.

IN HIS 2007 REVIEW for the *Guardian*, George Monbiot writes about McCarthy's novel *The Road* that it "is the most important environmental book ever written."[111] This is just one statement among many that aligns McCarthy's fiction with ecologically invested forms of literature that often go by the name of "nature writing," collectively represented by Thoreau, Snyder, Annie Dillard, Edward Abbey, and others. However, the question is whether or not McCarthy should be seen as a novelist whose work is steeped in the discourses of what Lawrence Buell has called "the environmental imagination" and what Timothy Morton has termed "the ecological thought."[112] More precisely, I am interested in the question of how the tradition of ecocriticism might explain McCarthy's concept of nature. Clearly, there are many variants of "the environmental imagination," a type of thinking that is inextricably linked to or directed toward the well-being of our surroundings, and scholars have been inventing many terms to distinguish their particular brands and understandings of this kind of thinking. The most prevalent subcategories are deep ecology, literary ecology, ecocriticism, environmental criticism, ecofeminism, ecocentrism, biocentrism, and bioregionalism. Also, there is an entire history of the movement that started with environmental questions about the interpretation of cultural objects in a way that sometimes ran counter to the insights of other fields that were already influenced by poststructuralism—a history that includes "phenomenological approaches," "literary Darwinism," and the inquiries of "ecopoststructuralists."[113] To refer to these nuanced forms of enquiry I will use the broadest and most encompassing of terms—"ecocentrism"—because its name implies the fundamental premise common to all of them—namely, the primacy of an ethical relationship to the environment. "Ecocentrism preaches the virtues of reverence, humility, responsibility, and care; . . . it demands a code of behavior that seeks permanence and stability based upon ecological principles of diversity and homeostasis," Timothy O'Riordan writes in his seminal monograph *Environmentalism* (1976).[114]

However, it is important to note a number of things here, chief among them the fact that ecocentrism is not so much a critical practice as it is a certain attitude toward a specific object of inquiry, the environment, that is often equated with nature. It seems initially wrong, therefore, to say that ecocentrism is the most encompassing term of these categories, simply because it denotes not a specific practice but a general viewpoint that condemns the exploitation and commodification of our planet, or the commercialization of its supposedly natural resources. Upon closer inspection, however, this ostensible misconception of "ecocentrism" as an umbrella term turns out to be not so much a misconception as a strategic characterization that serves my argument vis-à-vis the relation between McCarthy's poetics and the question of ecological awareness. The ethical orientation of the major environmentally aware forms of criticism and theory is their main feature, which is why it makes sense to assess the specific kinds of critique from this perspective. It is because this umbrella term refers to the ideological motivation behind each of the critical methodologies it has brought about it that it is treated as such a term in the present context. As Bryan Moore states, "ecocentrism" is in fact "short for the theory of *eco-centered ethics*"[115]—an ethics according to which everything outside of humanity's purview has a certain worth of its own and should not be misused, either practically or conceptually. Similar to what Bell and other scholars have said about McCarthy, then, "to be ecocentric is to hold a conscious opposition to anthropocentrism,"[116] to refuse to make judgments that take only human interests into account. The question of whether or not anthropocentrism is to be defined ontologically or epistemologically, both in environmental forms of criticism and McCarthy's fiction, remains to be answered.

I will first delineate the particularities of ecocentrism and the critical practices it has spawned, while focusing on the ways in which these practices regularly conflate the terms "environment" and "nature" or define the latter in terms of the former. Second, I will mount a critique of some scholars who home in on McCarthy's alleged ecocentrism against the backdrop of that very conflation. It will become apparent that while the use of ecology in literary studies is a valuable first step toward accounting for the outside of the text, in the case of McCarthy it impedes the search for his fiction's answer to the question of what is without the fictional and yet gives rise to it. In other words, while McCarthy does make use of poetic images that allude to the ecosphere, I argue that his concept of nature goes beyond the ecological. McCarthy's fiction refers to a nature that includes but is not coextensive with the environment. Despite the frequency of his narrators' affirmations of ecological tranquility, natural process does not depend on being ecological, while the world as an ecosystem depends on nature's potencies to maintain its existence. To be clear, this is not so much an attempt to downplay the role of the environment in the global dynamics of natural process as it is a recalibration of ecocentrism's authoritative reach with respect to the conception of nature as an ontological given—meaning that reality in which concepts come to exist in the first place.

Before I outline the extent to which the notion of ecocentrism can be said to figure as the ethical basis of ecocriticism, environmental criticism, and related forms of cultural and literary inquiry, as well as of political, artistic, and philosophical practice, it is crucial to acknowledge that not all of the terms in the list of subcategories above denote a specific practice. Biocentrism, for instance, is seemingly on a par with ecocentrism in representing a certain attitude or ethical worldview, rather than a field within literary criticism.[117] Yet an ethics based on life as a foundational concept is, by necessity, integrated into an ethics based on the environment of living systems. What seems crucial, nonetheless, is the emphasis put on an account of the environment that relies on a certain taxonomy of just and unjust forms of human activity and expression—an ethics, therefore, of an antagonistic relation to political, epistemological, and ontological points of view that do not concern themselves with the problematization of the relationships between humanity and its organic and inorganic environment, between the human and the nonhuman, and between literature and its outside. Biocentrism is embedded in ecocentrism in the sense that living systems, people, animals, and objects are parts of whole ecosystems. The objectives of the two categories to speak *in the name of* their respective foundational concepts (meaning, life and the environment) work in the same manner because they are intertwined. This is why a discourse like ecocriticism implements the objectives of both ecocentrism and biocentrism.

In my quotation of O'Riordan's definition of "the theory of *eco-centered ethics*,"[118] I omitted a section located between the list of "virtues" and the idea of "a code of behavior" that examines the possibility of a reconciliation with the environment, a temporary "stability" or harmony between the two polarities of the human and the nonhuman. O'Riordan writes that this form of ethics "argues for low impact technology (but it is not antitechnological)" and that "it decries bigness and impersonality in all forms (but especially in the city)."[119] In his seminal work *The Environmental Imagination* (1995), Buell discusses O'Riordan's definition of ecocentrism. He largely agrees with that definition, yet he wants to change two aspects of it: "I propose two amendments: (1) that ecocentrism may in fact be antitechnological, and (2) that it need not adhere to a dogma of homeostasis."[120] What is crucial here is that the perspective assumed in a cultural discourse centered on the first syllable of "*Oecologie*"—a term "coined by Darwinian biologist Ernst Haeckel in 1866," which "derives from the Greek 'οικοσ' (oikos; house, household, also dwelling place, family) and 'λογοσ' (logos; word, language, language of reason)"[121]—that this discourse from its inception placed ethics at the starting point of each of its critical variants. Whether one would endorse or oppose the importance of homeostasis (the equilibrium of given ecosystems), it is still the case that ecocentric and biocentric forms of critique are intended to protect and preserve the aspect of *givenness* in any such system. The discourse of nature's household (ecology) and the criticism of all things in the world inclined to disturb the domestic peace (ecocriticism) seem to be dealing less with the ways in which that household can be said to have come about, ontologically speaking, than with the kinds of ethical parameters according to which the plethora of systems, organisms, bodies, and things that are in the world can be sheltered from any disturbance of their particular being—the most pressing and persistent of all disturbances certainly being climate change. Ecology qua discourse on and of nature's household dictates *the primacy of ethics*, not ontology, irrespective of the emphasis put on corporeality, materiality, or nonhuman agency.[122]

Ecocentrism thus is the basis for the discursive promotion of an empathetic viewpoint regarding one's environment, including its organic and inorganic realms.[123] This is precisely how a certain form of humanism coincides with ecocentrism—namely, a humanism of the sort we encountered in Cooper's account of an "ethics of empathy," involving the ideal of "human communion"[124] that supposedly undergirds McCarthy's poetics. This coincidence is indexed by the question of rights, since notions like empathy, compassion, solidarity, and charity imply that the subject matter at hand (the ecosphere or the human) is worth fighting for. "Central to ecocriticism is the view that wild nature exists, first of all, for its own 'reasons,' independent of humans," and there is an "intrinsic significance, independent of human utility."[125] While McCarthy's narratives tap into this discursive field centered on the worth of the natural that is relentlessly being exploited by humanity, the ethos of ecocentrism is still not enough to account for the complexity of his concept of nature, since the latter does not just revere the communion of all that exists in the world but also includes speculations on an ethics of carelessness and expressionless indifference that is equally part of nature.[126] McCarthy's ecological reverence is made possible only by means of an undercurrent of violence—more often than not, within a context of deviation from cultural norms—in the specific passages where it is expressed. In *Child of God*, for instance, we read of the necrophiliac Lester Ballard hiking through the woods: "Old woods and deep. At one time in the world there were woods that no one owned and these were like them" (*COG*, 119). Certainly, from the perspective of deep ecology, this is an endorsement of "the intrinsic value of nature"[127] by narrative means. Yet the fact that it is a murderer and social deviant whose path leads through this seemingly untouched and thus paradisiacal forest runs counter to the author's channeling of deep ecology's central proviso—one it shares with later forms of environmentally invested kinds of cultural critique.

Although ecocritics were more careful in their use of the language of preservation, conservation, and reconciliation than the deep ecologists, in the wake of poststructuralist philosophies and postmodern methodologies scholars such as Max Oelschlaeger, Kate Soper, and David Mazel still took ethics, instead of ontology, to be the main driving force of environmental criticism.[128] In her important study *What Is Nature?* (1995), Soper acknowledges the critiques of Judith Butler and others who, for instance, have noted the sexual politics and gender-specific normativities at work in the connotations of the very notion of "the natural."[129] Yet, later in the book she writes that "it is . . . one thing to argue that eco-politics must attend to culturalist criticisms of naturalist rhetoric; it is another to suppose that everything has been said about nature once we have remarked on its 'textuality' and its continually shifting signifier."[130] Thus, while Soper takes into account the difficulties inherent in prevailing practices of "naturalist rhetoric," she is right to point out that embedding nature in a textual fabric, together with its concomitant obviation of the possibility of a metaphysics of nature, gets us only so far in advancing environmental criticism as a political discourse: "In short, it is not language that has a hole in its ozone layer; and the 'real' thing continues to be polluted and degraded even as we refine our deconstructive insights at the level of the signifier."[131] Faced with a choice between a naïve form of cultural ecology that treats the environment as a substantial entity that somehow transcends all of its expressions and ascriptions, and a poststructuralist approach that relativizes the materiality of the environment in terms of the discursive operations that are caused by it, Mazel is much more interested in the latter option in *American Literary Environmentalism* (2000). Nature and environment become nearly synonymous, again, when Mazel avows that poststructuralist concepts such as Michel Foucault's *dispositif* question what he calls "the ontological priority of the environment (*or of nature, the wilderness, or 'the ecology'*)."[132]

Two years before Mazel's discussion of what environmental criticism should look like, Cheryll Glotfelty had defined it in very general terms as "the study of the relationship between literature and the physical environment."[133] This straightforward characterization points to an aspect of ecocriticism and its concept of nature as environment that I mentioned above—the result of a conceptual equalization of "nature" and "the environment," this aspect is the understanding of both as extended and minimally organic space *tout court*. Glotfelty writes: "Analogous efforts in ecocriticism study how nature is represented in literature. Again, consciousness raising results when stereotypes are identified—Eden, Arcadia, virgin land, miasmal swamp, savage wilderness—and when absences are noticed: where *is* the natural world in this text? But nature per se is not the only focus of ecocritical studies of representation. Other topics include the frontier, animals, cities, specific geographical regions, rivers, mountains, deserts, Indians, technology, garbage, and the body."[134]

For the purposes of my overall argument regarding McCarthy, what is important in this statement is not so much that ecocriticism extends beyond the question concerning the identity (or, indeed, the nature) of "nature per se," but that both the environment and nature are depicted here in spatial terms. Nature is that which gives existence—that is to say, life—to the world. One question thus appears to be how literature represents that which lies outside of it as extended or actual space. I will demonstrate below how this approach is aligned with Westphal's notion of geocriticism, which broadens the inquiry of ecological spaces to include the world's forms of spatiality as such, resulting in what Tally has called "*literary cartography.*"[135]

Seemingly paraphrasing Glotfelty's definition, Greg Garrard claims that "the widest definition of the subject of ecocriticism is the study of the relationship of the human and the non-human, throughout human cultural history and entailing critical analysis of the term 'human' itself."[136] This passage constitutes one of the most useful delineations of ecocriticism as a critical methodology in the light of my argument, one reason of which is its downplaying of ethical imperatives and its implication of an ecocentric ontology—even though Garrard also concedes that "ecocriticism is an avowedly political mode of analysis."[137] The relationship he describes between "the human and the non-human," which could also be applied to the technological and the antitechnological, can be traced back to the divisions Samuel Taylor Coleridge made between fancy and the imagination and between the mechanical and the organic.[138] Like the supposed divide between the realms of the organic and the inorganic, "a current consensus among the otherwise very heterogeneous group of ecocritics is the realization that nature and culture can no longer be viewed as separate entities," Maureen Devine and Christa Grewe-Volpp state.[139] What is interesting about this remark is not just the fact that one of the current objectives of ecocriticism is the synthesis of the natural and the cultural, but also the way in which nature is again identified as the environment per se and not used as the encompassing term that is apparent in Schellingian *Naturphilosophie*. "Nature" in all of these ecocritical inflections remains a pre- or antitechnological concept of *the given*—the notion of a realm whose manipulation and consequential exploitation should be restricted both practically and theoretically.[140]

The majority of environmental critics, then, equate their respective concepts of nature and the ecosphere, or at least integrate one into the other, often viewing spatiality as a feature common to both. However, Morton—who is a scholar of Romanticism, ecocriticism, and also speculative realism—takes a different approach to the question of nature's place within ecocritical discourse. Instead of placing the notions of the environment and nature on the same footing, his aim is to replace the latter with the former. It should not come as a surprise that the motivation for this argument is rooted in the author's ethical approach to the question of what an ecocentric standpoint should look like. As Morton writes on the first page of *Ecology without Nature* (2007), "the very idea of 'nature' which so many hold dear will have to wither away in an 'ecological' state of human society. Strange as it may sound, the idea of nature is getting in the way of properly ecological forms of culture, philosophy, politics, and art."[141] From Morton's point of view, the main problem of ecocriticism is its continued reliance on some form of "nature" as a conceptual linchpin. Many scholars seem to regard this notion as indispensable to legitimize "a 'green' moral and political agenda,"[142] raise awareness of climate change, and critique those who are determined to sabotage that consciousness within society. Curiously, Morton argues that the idea of nature has accumulated so much baggage that it works against the political goals of environmentally aware thinking, or what he calls "the ecological thought."[143] But exactly what kind of baggage does he mean?

"'Nature' fails to serve ecology well," Morton writes. "I shall sometimes use capital N to highlight its 'unnatural' qualities, namely (but not limited to), hierarchy, authority, harmony, purity, neutrality, and mystery. Ecology can do without a concept of a something, a thing of some kind, 'over yonder,' called Nature."[144] It strikes me as symptomatic of the early trajectory of a given field of research, generally, and of ecocentric discourse, in particular, that the features deemed "unnatural" by Morton already were critical aspects of the kinds of deep ecology practiced previously and dismissed by environmentalist scholars who started to adopt poststructuralist methodologies. In effect, Morton criticizes the concept of nature in a way similar to that of William Cronon, who once dismissed the delusional idealization of the American wilderness as "as the standard against which actual landscapes are measured."[145] Yet the fact that Morton is still claiming to detect these characteristics in the mere usage of the word "nature" within environmental discourse, regardless of its eventual reevaluation and revision, shows the extent to which his intervention into that discourse is intended to repudiate even the poststructuralist recoding of the concept. Certainly, the rejection of any ostensibly essentialist features of a "nature" that would consequently lead to social oppression is not only appropriate, but even necessary. Yet that rejection points toward the ethicist root of Morton's project in eradicating "the natural" from ecological discourse. Nature's alleged "purity" and "hierarchy" are salient aspects of the baggage Morton ascribes to it.[146] However, it is not enough to just get rid of a concept within a given approach to cultural analysis—in this case, removing nature from environmental criticism—and project onto that concept all the ways in which that kind of analysis has been abused. In other words, the demonized form of nature very quickly reveals itself as an easy target—a straw man that Morton needs to attack to put forward his own notion of "*the mesh*," which really is just another word for "interconnectedness."[147]

It is not exactly true that the ideologically motivated misuse of nature in certain normative parameters with respect to sexuality, gender, race, or class, for instance, is by default aligned with the concept of nature in ecological discourse. Nature is not necessarily naturalization: the mere positing of a concept of nature does not have to result in the marginalization of any kind of behavior or group of people that one would henceforth characterize as unnatural. It is essential to note here that it is the very definition of nature as an entity, "a something, a thing of some kind" that leads to the misuse of the concept, or what Morton himself dismisses as the thinking of nature "as a reified thing."[148] The problem is that in the way he is trying to remove nature from ecology, he is negatively *affirming* the very features of nature that he tries to repudiate. By refusing to reinscribe "nature" along the lines of what he instead prefers to call "the mesh," he feeds into the concept he set out to eradicate. In other words, even though nature as a concept has been misused socially and politically (a fate shared by the concept of ecology), this does not mean that the concept itself should be discarded once and for all. It is much more fruitful to reconceive of nature in terms of an absolute process that is impossible to tie to *any* kind of feature—in the sense in which the Schellingian theorization of nature's identity refuses to ascribe any particular features or dispositions to nature except that it gives rise to particularity as such.

Morton's approach links him tightly to the ethicist's inhibition of ontological investigation that is evident in the main strands of ecocriticism. Morton argues that "to have ecology, we must give up Nature. But since we have been addicted to Nature for so long, giving up will be painful. Giving up a fantasy is harder than giving up a reality."[149] I am not saying that instead of an account of "ecology without nature" one should opt for a concept of "nature without ecology."[150] Yet especially in light of my overall argument regarding the tendency within McCarthy scholarship to categorize his fiction as ecologically invested, I argue that the dismissal of nature on the ground that it has been misused in the past to ostracize minority groups, for instance, is not valid in the context of determining the ontological underpinnings of McCarthy's fiction. Reversing Morton's statements about this context, I hold that by "giving up" nature—which, as a topic, exceeds McCarthy's focus on environmental awareness—one is not ridding oneself of a "fantasy" but of the narrative delineation of "reality." The wholesale replacement of the natural with green politics in McCarthy comes at the price of simplifying a highly complex ontological undercurrent in his fiction, which may very well include a nascent literary environmentalism but which would transcend such an ethical position.[151] Among other things, it is McCarthy's closeness to the poetics of the American naturalists that distances him from a belief in the ethical origination of natural processes. Like Stephen Crane's idea of a cosmos that, in the last analysis, cannot be obliged to take notice of the normativity constructed by human communities, McCarthy views nature's indifference and fundamental contingency as the basis of its disposition to be what it is.[152] Even besides this issue of McCarthy's narrative investigation into nature's identity, the formal separation of nature from the ecosphere seems to constitute the clearest confirmation of the ethical bias toward ontological questions in certain strands of ecocentrism.

Thus, in lieu of its ideological instrumentalization in terms of the false depiction of minority groups or alternative ways of living as unnatural, retaining nature as a valid concept within ecological thinking could (and should) entail the thesis of the veritable impossibility of the unnatural as a concept, in accord with Schelling's proviso that "anything whose conditions simply cannot be given in nature, must be absolutely impossible."[153] Beyond McCarthy, such a concept of nature would, in all likelihood, turn out to be more progressive than the negative ascription and imagination of a conception such as "the natural," since the latter's obverse would no longer be thinkable. If nature as a concept remains part of political discourse, ecological thinking would do well to not let those opposed to the gathering of facts of climate change be in charge of the decision concerning what is "natural" and what is not. Nor should the discourse on what the concept of nature might signify be exclusively in the hands of those who do not, in fact, critically reflect on the process of signification *within natural processes*, to begin with.

Regarding the practical as well as the theoretical implementations of the kinds of approaches to cultural objects, political situations, economic agendas, and philosophical positions from O'Riordan to Morton, it is safe to say that ecocriticism is informed largely by the foundational terms of both biocentrism and ecocentrism—namely, of the living and the environmental—sometimes including a concept of nature, and sometimes not. This is why, in its questioning of the relationship between single individuals and their collective surroundings, ecocriticism "aims to contribute to the development of appropriate moral, ethical and political stances towards that relation," as Nick Heffernan and David A. Bragg argue.[154] With respect to McCarthy's poetics, therefore, the ethicist's call for empathy within artistic practice and its discourses and the cultural criticism of the natural eliminate any descendentalism with regard to the question of nature's identity.

In reflecting on the relationship between McCarthy and environmental criticism, one inevitably returns to issues that were implicit in the discussions above of the influence of Emerson and Thoreau on his fiction. That is, as first-wave ecocriticism mainly dealt with the nature writing of these seminal figures of the American Renaissance, to speak about a transcendentalist McCarthy necessitates a discussion of his relationship to ecocritical matters: to examine his ostensible alignment with literary ecology explicates what is prefigured in the consideration of his transcendentalist heritage. The issue of McCarthy's relationship to "literature as cultural ecology"[155] also recalls the poetic image on the first page of *The Orchard Keeper*. In the scene, three men are trying to cut through a tree on the grounds of a cemetery. As it turns out, their task is more difficult than they first expected because of a "*twisted wrought-iron . . . fence*" that is "*growed all through the tree*" (TOK, 3). As I noted above, this scene not only alludes to McCarthy's understanding of the interaction between the organic and inorganic realms of the world (so central to ecocritical themes), but it also reveals the descendental poetics of his narratives. After all, the first scene in the first novel of the author's long career takes place in a cemetery. Along these lines, many critics have examined McCarthy's relation to literature's ecological dimension, arriving at different conclusions that reflect back on the themes discussed above—namely, the polarities of materialism and spiritualism and the problem of periodizing McCarthy. The fact that the majority of those scholars who are invested in the debates concerning McCarthy's regionalism, who are aware of his tendency to include both religious and scientific references in his work, and who have ascribed various and sometimes mutually exclusive periods and styles to his narratives are also arguing about whether or not he is an ecologically aware writer (that is, whether his novels' depictions of the natural world should be described as ecocentric or not) is further testament to the interconnections of these sets of issues.

Consider, for instance, Natalie Grant's argument that in spite of the close proximity of *The Orchard Keeper*'s characters to their mostly organic environment, it would be an overstatement to say that they are at one with nature: "despite their embeddedness in the vividly described rural environs, in the last analysis, the characters in McCarthy's novel at best co-exist uneasily with the natural world."[156] Like many scholars, Grant uses the word "nature" here interchangeably with the word "environs," which I argue does not sufficiently account for the vast range of natural processes described by McCarthy. This is also the case in David Holloway's reading, despite its admirable subtleties. Like others before and after him, Holloway discusses a passage in *Blood Meridian* that has come to be known among scholars by the term "optical democracy," which is a phrase in the passage that supposedly indicates McCarthy's ecocentrism. The phrase represents "a strange equality" among all kinds of bodies and things in the Southwestern desert lands, "that terrain" in which "no one thing nor spider nor stone nor blade of grass could put forth claim to precedence" (*BM*, 247). What is at stake here is the notion of an equality between all natural phenomena from humans to the tiniest grain of dust: "The very clarity of these articles belied their familiarity, for the eye predicates the whole on some feature or part and here was nothing more luminous than another and nothing more enshadowed and in the optical democracy of such landscapes all preference is made whimsical and a man and a rock become endowed with unguessed kinships" (ibid.). According to Holloway, McCarthy's prose delineates a whole worldview, as "optical democracy first of all means looking at landscape, and then writing about landscape, in such a way that any anthropocentric assumption of human primacy over the natural world is rejected."[157] Reminiscent of Moore's definition of an ecologically oriented ethics, McCarthy's rendering of a commonality of all things in existence—whether they are humans, animals, plants, or rocks—represents a thoroughly antianthropocentric stance. In effect, McCarthy seems to consciously perform a kind of ecocriticism, yet in the form of a narrative that is fictional rather than theoretical. Holloway goes on to argue that "if optical democracy is an ecocritical style that displaces human order from its privileged position at the center of the universe, then it is also necessarily a style that refutes the idea of directed hermeneutic activity in the world."[158] For Holloway, this activity is the hubristic belief of humanity in its capacity "to 'know' nature, to explain it, map it, or in whatever other way expropriate the world at large by motivated acts of will or rational intelligence."[159] This argument recalls the postmodern critique of grand narratives and of the Enlightenment trust in reason, the transcendental apparatus unique to the human animal. In fact, any assessment of McCarthy's relationship to corporeal nature seems to be premised on this criticism of humankind's exploitation of the living soil, be it in Appalachia or in the Southwestern United States. Moreover, this assessment of McCarthy's alleged refusal of grand narratives suggests that the ethico-aesthetic fervor of *optical democracy* is cut from the same cloth as those passages in Whitman's *Leaves of Grass* (1855) that put ethnicities, human bodies, flora, and fauna on the same footing. Like Whitman's, McCarthy's "democratic vista" seems ecological through and through.[160]

Arnold not only sees McCarthy's engagement with the environment's inherent value in the second volume of the Border Trilogy but also argues that

"McCarthy suggests a biocentric view of nature"—a stance that Arnold links to the spiritualism of McCarthy's work as a whole.[161] Similarly, Berry argues that McCarthy's narratives evoke "a vision of ecological holocaust, as if the collapse of the earth as we know it lurks in the near future—a devastation spurred by our fossil-fuel-driven, hurry-up economy of fire."[162] To be sure, this view has since been supported by *The Road*, which, according to Monbiot, "exposes the one terrible fact to which our technological hubris blinds us: our dependence on biological production remains absolute."[163] However, Berry's and Monbiot's claims and their condemnation of the continuously increasing exploitation of our planet in the service of human greed also shed light on the correlated issues of the conceptual conflation of the natural with the environmental, and the supervenience of ontology upon ethics in ecocritical discourse. The objective of raising consciousness via literary and cultural criticism is never primarily to ask what comes to exist but to ask how what exists should exist, so that the relationships between all bodies and things in the world can be ethically determined.[164]

I am certainly not arguing here that McCarthy is in any way oblivious to the dangers of global warming caused to a considerable degree by the technological and economical penetration of the ecosphere and by the ruthlessness of humankind. Nor am I simply disapproving of those scholars who have taken an ecocritical approach in investigating the concept of nature in McCarthy's work—in fact, that approach in the scholarship is the main forerunner of the present investigation. Rather, I claim that a concept of nature that is principally grounded in the ethical desire to fight the abuse of the environment depicted in McCarthy's prose and to cherish that environment's value falls short of what McCarthy's novels recognize as natural. The concept of "nature as environment" simply reduces the question concerning the identity of natural processes to a question of right or value and, in the last analysis, of a compassion toward the human self that is projected onto the realm of ecology—that which surrounds the human individual and constitutes its experiential context.[165]

Georg Guillemin provides an account that is an important example of the ultimately ethical approach to McCarthy's conception of natural processes. Proposing a stylistic, as well as a topical, triangulation in McCarthy's prose, consisting of "melancholy mood, allegorical style, and pastoral theme," Guillemin discusses McCarthy's entire novelistic oeuvre until 2004, the year of his monograph's publication—interestingly excepting *Suttree* from the main part of his book since "it stands out and therefore contains few nature scenes that would validate a pastoral reading."[166] "Nature" here signifies extended organic space, which is arguably just one among many aspects of McCarthy's conception of nature. Echoing other commentators on the ecocentric theme of *optical democracy* before and after him, Guillemin states, "It is precisely this equanimity [between the phenomena of the world] that conditions the pastoral vision of McCarthy."[167] Whereas the present study holds that this vision casts nature as an agglomeration of processes that are coextensive neither with the material extent of the environment, nor with the diversity and creativity of life, Guillemin situates McCarthy's trademark parables within the framework of biocentrism.[168] Arguing along similar lines, Willard Greenwood homes in on the ethical underpinnings of *The Road*, stressing the increasingly malevolent effect of humanity's greedy use of its technological resources to exploit its natural ones: "McCarthy's novel reflects the belief that the strength of human influence on the natural world has become unsettlingly apparent. The extreme bleakness of *The Road* is a cautionary tale about environmental degradation. It is also a clear reminder of McCarthy's pessimistic philosophy about human destiny"—which, according to Greenwood, correlates humanity's inclination to self-destruct with the decline of ecological homeostasis.[169]

Estes's *Cormac McCarthy and the Writing of American Spaces* (2013) provides the most emblematic of ecocritical accounts to date. His interpretations of McCarthy's novels from *Blood Meridian* to *The Road* proclaim the author's alleged investment in the "intrinsic rights"[170] of nature conceived of as environment. Estes reads these "within the context of a debate on the nature of U.S. spaces"[171] from utopian (read: *pastoral*) and dystopian (read: *antipastoral*) perspectives, respectively. For him, the key passages in these novels can be interpreted as "hintings at a way out of this debate" or sublimations, "as in the Hegelian re-working of the notion of dialectic involving thesis, antithesis and synthesis."[172] The rudimentary conceptualization of this clichéd version of Hegelianism aside, what exactly is meant by these provisional solutions to the discussions of the meaning of America's spaces?

Echoing Berry and Guillemin, Estes writes of McCarthy's transcendentalist heritage that "there is a continuity . . . between the ideas of space in these texts of our tradition and the wilderness aesthetic one finds in McCarthy novels."[173] As has become standard practice in ecocriticism, Estes conceptualizes a force contrary to this tradition of the wild—namely, the Enlightenment and the very idea of "human progress."[174] He posits the existence of two opposed standpoints regarding the relationship of humanity to its environment: the anthropocentric stance and the biocentric one. This opposition immediately recalls the one between the technological intrusion into the givenness of nature and the homeostatic essence of the latter. Estes regards it as coterminous with that of natural utopia versus dystopia, which for him is established by the discursive practices of figures as diverse and historically far apart as Amerigo Vespucci, Frederick Jackson Turner, and

Buell. The concept that ought to formally resolve these dualisms is what Estes calls "the synthesis of biocentric maps."[175] Following Guillemin, Estes identifies the *optical democracy* passage as one of the primary examples of such "maps" in McCarthy's oeuvre. He even connects this passage—for him at once a mapping in the broadest sense of the term, and a literary "map" in poetic diction—to Emerson's image of the "transparent eye-ball," stating that the "narrator renders the desert wilderness a sacred place where perspective is likewise dissolved."[176] It is a place that establishes "a strange equality" (*BM*, 247) among all kinds of perspective, given that the dissolution of all possible angles on a phenomenon like the Southwestern desert is also their amplification, resulting in the pluralism that is *optical democracy*.

The question remains, however, why this plurality of viewpoints should necessarily be bound to a biocentrism, an ethos based on the notion of a vital and self-sufficient ecosphere. Here is another of Estes's examples of a "biocentric map," which he detects in the epilogue of *Cities of the Plain*. Right before the end of the narrative, a foster family has taken up Billy Parham in old age. The passage in the text that Estes cites has the narrator describe the surface of Billy's hand during a conversation between the old man and Betty, the mother of the family. This map is "patterned onto living flesh"[177] rather than laid out on the desert floor, as in *Blood Meridian*: "She patted his hand. Gnarled, ropescarred, speckled from the sun and the years of it. The ropy veins that bound them to his heart. There was a map enough for men to read. There God's plenty of signs and wonders to make a landscape. To make a world. She rose to go" (*CP*, 291). It is understandable that Estes chooses this passage to carry home his argument that the standpoint in so many of McCarthy's novels corresponds to a vitalist ethics with respect to the American environment. The passage does indeed contain an image of how the character's experience is inscribed into his living body and likened to the "re-sacralization"[178] of America's spaces. These few yet meaningful sentences are indubitably important, placed at the very ending of the Border Trilogy and right before the "Dedication." However, two objections immediately arise: the first concerns a syntactical intricacy in the second sentence of McCarthy's text, whereas the second has to do with how Estes makes use of the passage within his overall argument.

As concerns the first caveat, the sentence—"Gnarled, ropescarred, speckled from the sun and the years of it"—can certainly be read in the context of a biocentric interpretation that champions McCarthy's emphasis on lived experience and the traces it leaves: the signs of life, as they are etched into the bodies of the living. It seems almost imperative to read the passage in this manner, followed as it is by the mention of "ropy veins that bound them to his heart"—with "them" referring to the years of Billy's life, the amount of experience he has amassed in his wanderings and border crossings. Yet what "it" in the earlier sentence refers to is unclear, since it could either be Billy's hand or "the sun." If one opts for the first alternative (which seems appropriate at first sight) Estes's interpretation pertains: the hand described as "speckled from the sun and the years of [the hand itself]" metonymically signifies the amount of lived experience as it shows on Billy's skin. Yet if one opts for the second alternative (which is not at all obvious, but semantically suggestive), the hand is, in fact, "speckled from the sun and [the years of the sun itself]." According to this reading, "them" in the following sentence refers to those "years" that are not Billy's but the sun's. It seems that only when these temporal units are "bound to his heart"—to Billy's individuality as a living being—is Estes's claim actually warranted, which is that McCarthy's "biocentric maps offer a view of nature as something dynamic" in which humankind is but one part among many.[179] However, this brings us to the second objection. Although Estes is at great pains to condemn all anthropocentrism, repeatedly stating how important the notion of a living ecosystem is to McCarthy, the biocentric map on the last pages of *Cities of the Plain* is centered on a human being, Billy. Estes does not focus on how McCarthy's language subtly links this character to a natural phenomenon that is so central and constant a feature of his fiction: *the sun*. Moreover, to state that biocentric maps point to nature's dynamism and to simultaneously claim that they "offer better ways of seeing and dealing with the environment"[180] is begging the question, since it remains unclear what exactly is meant by nature if it is not coterminous with the environment in the novels at hand. But if these two terms are coterminous, it becomes increasingly difficult to explain the spiritualist aspect of McCarthy's poetics in any way except by projecting human rights and dignity onto the sphere of ecology—that is, by replacing anthropocentrism by anthropomorphism.[181]

Until now, the ethos of ecocentrism—including any kind of vitalist ecology—seems to have won out over a properly ontological investigation of McCarthy's concept of nature. My diagnosis of the ecocritical approach to McCarthy posits that while being an important first step toward an account of his depictions of the world and its ecocultural landscapes, it cannot come to terms with his concept of nature itself. Taking my cue here from Anthony Paul Smith, who states that despite its claims to the contrary, "ecology's object is not nature as such, but the ecosystem," and that "the ecosystem reveals aspects or occasions of nature, but is not nature itself,"[182] I will examine the ways in which geocriticism; speculative realism; and, above all, *Naturphilosophie* can go beyond the bounds of ecological thought—without, however, negating the insights of the latter—to grasp the specificity of McCarthy's narrative answer to the question, "What is nature?"

[2]

"SHREDS OF MATTER": PHYSIOCENTRISM AND TRANSNATIONAL SPECULATION

Because what can be touched falls into dust there can be no mistaking these things for the real. At best they are only tracings of where the real has been. Perhaps they are not even that. Perhaps they are no more than obstacles to be negotiated in the ultimate sightlessness of the world. —Cormac McCarthy, *The Crossing*

If thought is put into a direct relation with the earth, what is a philosophy of geology where the genitive is not inverted, but is the product of geological formations themselves? —Iain Hamilton Grant, "The Chemistry of Darkness"

IN AN IMPORTANT ESSAY on *Blood Meridian*, Dana Phillips writes: "Human beings and the natural world do not figure as antagonists. . . . They are instead parts of the same continuum and are consistently described by McCarthy as such."[1] In this chapter, I seek to describe this "continuum" populated by the human and nonhuman elements of nature. I will explain in detail the major theoretical underpinnings of the critiques mounted against the major ways of reading McCarthy's concept of nature mentioned in the previous chapter—namely, the ethicist, gnosticist, materialist, and ecocritical approaches. My criticism is substantiated by the presuppositions of philosophies of nature from the nineteenth century to the present, including those of Friedrich W. J. Schelling, Lorenz Oken, and, to a lesser extent, Gilles Deleuze. I will also make use (albeit negatively) of Bertrand Westphal's notion of geocriticism and, more importantly, the work of Iain Grant, Reza Negarestani, Nick Land, and Ray Brassier—all of whom have been influenced, to varying degrees, by the two *Naturphilosophen* Schelling and Oken, and the French metaphysician Deleuze.[2]

Similar to the structure of chapter 1, the argument in this chapter unfolds in three steps. First, I characterize geocriticism as the recommencement of the ecocritical enterprise without the latter's ethical imperative of reconciliation and preservation, substituting for this motivation a renewed emphasis on space or spatiality. Geocriticism, as promoted above all by Westphal, traces literary renderings of real spaces and places without somehow writing *in the name of* these sites. Thus, it seems to offer an alternative to ecocritical readings of McCarthy's prose; it makes possible an analysis of McCarthy's descriptions of place, without overemphasizing the projection of human dignity onto that place.[3] In other words, a return to material reality in the work of McCarthy can be properly examined via geocriticism without premising that return on any bio- or ecocentrism whatsoever. In fact, some critics of McCarthy have already argued along those lines, as I will show in this chapter.

Second, a critical analysis of the most recent developments in continental philosophy (namely, speculative realism and the resurgent interests in materiality and ontology) provides yet another context for both McCarthy's work and today's geocritical endeavors. This analysis contributes to the discussion of some of the philosophical shortcomings of Westphal's notion of *geocritique* in general, and its concept of matter in particular, based as it is on a Deleuzian ontology of difference.[4] This ontology also serves as the backdrop against which many speculative realists have constructed their philosophical standpoints. I will focus on those theorists whose accounts are most fruitful in the context of McCarthy's narrative speculations that give rise to the concept of nature—namely, Negarestani, Brassier, and especially Grant.

Third, as the most crucial feature of the approach taken in the present study, I describe the intricacies of Schellingian and Okenian theories concerning nature's decay; the dynamics of its origin; its (point of) indifference; and, above all, its material character. Furthermore, I will revisit the question of in what sense literary culture can and should be integrated into corporeal nature, indicated by John Elder's theory of literature as a cross-fertilizing process. The ideas developed in these sections, then, will give rise to the conception of *a physiocentric continuum*, the contours of which McCarthy demarcates in every one of his novels.

GEOCRITICISM IS NOT so much a newly developed critical practice in literary studies as it is a synthesis of many approaches to narrative art, including postmodernism, postcolonialism, poststructuralism, social geography, geology, and many more. I have argued that this synthesis can be seen as continuous with ecocriticism, yet there is a basic difference in emphasis between the two approaches: if most representatives of ecocriticism are interested in the spaces of ecology, geocriticism focuses on the ecologies of space—encompassing discussions of literary representations of actual spaces and places in the world as well as contemplations on the notion of space itself.[5] Indeed, the notion of space is the premise with which geocritical practice begins.

At the beginning of *Geocriticism: Real and Fictional Spaces* (2007), Westphal spells out the most basic aspects of his novel approach to literary and cultural objects he sets out to define: "What do we mean by *space*? A priori, space is a concept that encompasses the universe; it is oriented toward the infinitely large or reduced to the infinitely small, which is itself infinitely or infinitesimally vast. . . . However, I will focus on the visible areas, which themselves are quite resistant to definition."[6] "Space," construed as "a concept that encompasses the universe," plays a role very similar to those of the environment or the ecosphere in ecocriticism. It is, in other words, a foundational concept, a theme that gives direction to the various forms of cultural analysis. Furthermore, Westphal specifies that it is the world's actual or real spaces and places that interest him, localities that are depicted by narrative works of art such as novels, films, poems, and short stories.

This view is a starting point for the present argument—namely, that rather than focusing mainly on the ways in which literature depicts a given place, such as a city, geocriticism is much more concerned with how and why the city gives rise to a whole array of texts and cultural representations of that place. Westphal calls this the "*multifocalization* of views on a given referential space."[7] This "*chief characteristic* of geocriticism"[8] (the gathering of information on a city, landscape, or region) thus multiplies the literary data, much like the collecting of empirical evidence in the descriptive sciences whose most valuable results seemingly depend on the amount and pertinence of the data. This is not to say that Westphal's theory is associated with any form of naïve positivism. Indeed, he concedes from the start that his approach "is situated in the labyrinthine space of the postmodern,"[9] which he means both historically and methodologically. Rather, as I show below, the multifocal approach is one aspect of geocriticism that shows Westphal's determination to escape the linguistic shackles that literary theory and practice imposed in the second half of the twentieth century—the idea that if one writes about a certain place in the world, all that one does, in a sense, is write about the practice of writing itself.

This aspect of multifocalization cannot be of any particular help in the context of the present thesis on McCarthy, which among other things is a monofocalized perspective on "a given referential space." It is centered on the Southeast and Southwest of the United States and is restricted to a single author's engagement with that space. However, Westphal's delineation of geocriticism still points in a direction that is relevant for the determination of McCarthy's engagement in the debate concerning nature's identity. This has to do with Westphal's championing of the term "referentiality," a term that many structuralist and poststructuralist approaches to literature have cast aside in favor of the linguistic intricacies of the signifier and the signified.[10] Put differently, since at least 1967, when Michel Foucault wrote "Of Other Spaces," the emphasis on space has not been a novelty in literary criticism and cultural theory, and Westphal's contribution lies in his use of the concept of referentiality as a guiding principle for his approach. "In literature as in other mimetic arts," he claims, "almost all studies of space tend to limit representation to a field in which the real *in itself* is set aside."[11] Geocriticism is concerned with how places that are real give rise to their literary depictions, which in turn have an effect on these places in terms of their public images, or the interpretations of what they are. Indeed, in addition to multifocalization, referentiality is one of the three principles of geocriticism that Westphal lists as representative concepts for his methodology. He notes that this spatial approach toward cultural objects comprises "three fundamental concepts: *spatiotemporality* (no spatial analysis may avoid temporal concerns); *transgressivity* (no representation is stable; on the contrary, as in Deleuze's deterritorialization process, permanent fluidity is the characteristic of representations and, consequently, of identities); and *referentiality* (any representation is linked with the referential world)."[12]

Westphal's notion of geocriticism is important for my argument concerning McCarthy's narrative speculations on nature's identity, because the formalization of the three core principles of spatiotemporality, transgressivity, and referentiality are convenient and even suggestive insofar as, at first sight, they succinctly describe how a new delineation of McCarthy's concept of nature might be achieved. Assuming that for McCarthy the external world may not be exhaustively described by the notion of the environment in ecocritical discourse, it would still be the case that it is a spatiotemporal expanse, irrespective of its being organic or inorganic, and also regardless of its "intrinsic rights."[13] Moreover, transgression or transgressivity is a well-established theme in the scholarship on McCarthy—understandably so, given the passages that contain violent and socially deviant behavior in such novels as *Outer Dark*, *Child of God*, and *Blood Meridian*, to name but a few. Referentiality is, once again, a core element, since Westphal is determined to examine the interactions between real and fictional kinds of space, as the subtitle of *Geocriticism* makes clear. Yet I also want to note the tradition within which Westphal places the threefold foundation of his theory—namely, *phenomenology*. According to him, "phenomenology separates the *Lebenswelt* . . . , which is the locus of intentional activities of man (and woman), from the *Umwelt*, which is the framework within which these activities are accomplished. . . . If the *Umwelt* is the realm of simple existence," meaning the spatiotemporal frame of human interaction, "the *Mitwelt* requires action, or rather interaction, which gives meaning to the existence of the individual."[14] This latter meaningful existence, then, is the *Lebenswelt*, or realm of lived experience. Directly after Westphal's summary of a number of phenomenological accounts inside and outside of literary criticism that make use of the relationship between *Umwelt*, *Lebenswelt*, and *Mitwelt*, he claims that "in fact, the study of this relationship motivates the entire project of geocriticism."[15] I take this statement as an admission to argue that Westphal replaces these phenomenological categories with his three principles of spatiotemporality (replacing *Umwelt*), transgressivity (replacing *Mitwelt*), and referentiality (replacing *Lebenswelt*).

A number of scholars have approached McCarthy's fiction from a vaguely geocritical angle without describing their readings in those terms—which is only to be expected, given the eclectic nature of the geocritical discourse and the understanding of geocritical practice as the study of spatiality.[16] In other words, in discussing McCarthy's rendering of space in his narratives it is difficult not to frame one's argument in terms that are very much akin to spatial studies of literature. It is not at all surprising that McCarthy's novels would provoke readings of this kind, since McCarthy is an author famous for his rendering of landscapes: deserts, mountains, forests, and the cityscape of Knoxville.[17]

Although there is a variety of quasi-geocritical accounts of McCarthy's work, I am mostly interested in a particular strand of them that is based on the metaphysical premises of Deleuze's writings and that therefore can allow us to segue into a nature-philosophical examination of McCarthy's narratives. Importantly, Deleuze's philosophical works (many coauthored by Félix Guattari) are at once ontological and ethical.

For Steven Shaviro, "*Blood Meridian* is a book . . . not of heights and depths, nor of origins and endings, but of restless incessant horizontal movements: nomadic wanderings, topographical displacements, variations of weather, skirmishes in the desert. There is only war, there is only the dance"[18]—this latter anaphoric remark referring to the judge's talent as a killer (which he demonstrates throughout the novel) and his skill as a dancer and musician (which McCarthy showcases toward the end of the novel, just before the epilogue). In mystifying phrases, the narrator conveys the quasi-immortal state that is ascribed to Holden, a disposition that is linked to the way he excels on the dance floor of the tavern: "He wafts his hat and the lunar dome of his skull passes palely under the lamps and he swings about and takes possession of one of the fiddles and he pirouettes and makes a pass, two passes, dancing and fiddling at once. His feet are light and nimble. He never sleeps. He says that he will never die" (*BM*, 335). Shaviro capitalizes on the Dionysian "hymns of violence" in the novel that are recapitulated in the hilarity of this last image of Holden dancing in the tavern.[19] But his discussion of *Blood Meridian* also focuses on the metaphysical implications of the desert scenery in the main body of the novel. The argument homes in on a refusal of depth and pathos on the part of the narrative voice. Shaviro consequently likens the novel's epistemology to Deleuze and Guattari's notion of "smooth space"[20] from *A Thousand Plateaus* (1980)—a notion that Westphal refers to again and again in *Geocriticism*. But what is the disposition of this type of space? And why should its "open topography" exclude "organicist metaphors of growth and decay," as Shaviro posits?[21]

Arguably, the key source text for Shaviro's reading is chapter 14 of Deleuze and Guattari's book, as they correlate the conceptual pair of "smooth space and striated space" with what the authors term "nomad space and sedentary space."[22] Westphal glosses this juxtaposition by adding a third pair of opposites, "heterogeneous and homogeneous space,"[23] which is helpful in the present attempt to get at the ethico-aesthetic objective behind Shaviro's emphasis on smooth space. Deleuze and Guattari are quick to point out that while the nomadic and the sedentary indeed constitute an oppositional polarity:

> The two spaces in fact exist only in mixtures: smooth space is constantly being translated, transversed into a striated space; striated space is constantly being reversed, returned to a smooth space. In the first case, one organizes even the desert; in the second, the desert gains and grows; and the two can happen simultaneously. But the de facto mixes do not preclude a de jure, or abstract, distinction between the two spaces.[24]

It is easy to see how Deleuze and Guattari's text prompted Shaviro's interpretation of *Blood Meridian*, given their distinction between two conceptions of space throughout their book. Although much has been said about these conceptions in *A Thousand Plateaus* and other works by Deleuze and Guattari, I want to focus on two issues in the short passage I just quoted that are especially suggestive with regard to the present argument.[25] The first of these is the fact that Deleuze and Guattari choose "the desert" as one of the exemplary spaces to explain both the intertwined nature of stratification and the history of Western cartography and the nomadic disposition of the subversion of any normative rigidity associated with sedentary forms of life. The desert is the initial space that dramatizes the reciprocity between the two orders of the sedentary and the nomadic, although afterward Deleuze and Guattari champion "the sea [as] the archetype of smooth space" but "also [as] the archetype of all striations of smooth space."[26]

The second issue that is of interest here is the difference made between a "de facto" unification and a "de jure" separation of terms. This distinction complicates the relationship between the nomadic and the sedentary insofar as the de facto perspective is itself grounded in the pragmatics of lived experience and, consequently, of *lived space*, while the de jure perspective already focuses on analysis and separation and, consequently, is oriented toward the space of abstract cartography. The synthesis of smooth and striated is already accounted for in terms of the former kind of spatial arrangement, while the abstract separation of the two is accounted for in terms of judgment. Unsurprisingly, the central figure in McCarthy's novel that embodies the stratification of the Western world, the cartography of the desert, and the indifference toward individual life is Judge Holden—even though (despite his title) he is not wholly defined by the de jure perspective. As Westphal glosses Deleuze and Guattari's terminology, "*striated space* . . . is the space occupied by the state apparatus," whereas smooth space is that of the heterogeneous subversion of that apparatus; it "unfolds between points, between points that can connect as many lines as one chooses. Virtually open to infinity, it arranges all the minutes of each individual's life."[27] Thus, Holden is both the ruthless cartographer and the most nomadic of all scalp hunters; his unparalleled force of individuality is without bounds since his behavior makes any attempt to define his disposition ridiculous.

Westphal is right to point out that it is this latter type of spatiality that Deleuze and Guattari prefer, in ethical terms.[28] They promote the de facto pragmatics of lived experience rather than the sedentary type of organization in their theory of space. As with many French philosophers of their generation, they cherish *the heterogeneous* for its opposition to logical and normative strictures that are indifferent to the conditions of the living. Openness thus becomes equivalent to a moral standard, because it is the unfixed and mobile kind of subjectivity that is preferable to the alleged stasis of rationality—one reason for the interpenetration of ontological and ethical questions in the work of Deleuze and Guattari and that of their contemporaries. Consequently, returning to the passage from *A Thousand Plateaus*, I argue that the conceptual pair of the smooth and the striated has three, rather than two, dimensions: ontological (the de facto mixture of both types of space), epistemological (the de jure separation in terms of service to the discernment of their oppositional character), and ethical (the supervenience of rigidity and homogeneity upon openness and heterogeneity).

Along these lines, Brian Evenson argues that this existential condition of what Shaviro terms "orphanhood"[29] is applicable to the majority of McCarthy's narratives, with their "characters living on the fringes of society: renegades, lone wolves, outcasts, self-imposed exiles, foreigners, wanderers, killers."[30] For Evenson, therefore, it is nomadic space rather than sedentary life that McCarthy's literary characters prefer. It is true that, as a rule of thumb, families in McCarthy's novels are dysfunctional and much of his characters' behavior and states of mind is connected to that fact—be it Culla Holme's guilt because of his incestuous relationship with Rinthy in *Outer Dark*, Suttree's fear of death in McCarthy's fourth novel, or the motherless kid in *Blood Meridian* who runs away from home at fourteen. In addition to the conceptual pair of smooth and striated space, Evenson relies on Deleuze and Guattari's notion of nomadology, claiming that "we might call the judge a nomadologist, a theorizer of nomadism, for it is he and only he who utters justifications for the violence of war . . . and who philosophizes upon the nomadism of the gang."[31]

But what exactly is the connection between war and the group structure and social dynamics of the scalp hunters? Nomadology is synonymous with what Deleuze and Guattari also term "nomad science"—a concept complementary to the "royal science" of the state apparatus.[32] Again, as in the dichotomy of smooth and striated spaces, it is the pragmatics of nomadology that permits variation and heterogeneity, whereas the "royal science" is anchored in all that is supposedly rigid, abstract, and more often than not separated from the realities of lived experience. Deleuze and Guattari use the thematic domains of war and the history of mathematics to clarify their concept: the bands of warriors in nomadic societies and certain forms of topology are the models they employ to account for nomadology,[33] rather than the strategies of rulers in historic battles or the degree of exactness in subdisciplines of mathematical logic like set theory. For example, they write that "the State is perpetually producing and reproducing ideal circles, but a war machine is necessary to make something round."[34] The image of the ideal geometrical form and the practicability of this form in a site- and time-specific context are helpful in showing that—as with the juxtaposition of the de facto mixed spatiality and the de jure separation of the smooth and the striated—the decisions of a given state apparatus are correlated with the brotherhood of a group of warriors. To use an important concept from Deleuze's early period, there is a "reciprocal determination" that correlates a state apparatus like that of Mexico in the middle of the nineteenth century with bands of scalp hunters like the one led by the judge and Glanton.[35]

This reciprocity, then, is key to understanding the distribution of different kinds of spaces in McCarthy, as both Shaviro's and Evenson's readings point out. Deleuze and Guattari's terminology is helpful here, and it illustrates that there is already a quasi-geocritical angle in the scholarship on McCarthy's works. The ethically inscribed focus on heterogeneity and movement—on a kind of motion that is essentially directionless, "without aim or destination, without departure or arrival"[36]—is congruent with Westphal's second foundational principle of geocriticism, transgressivity.[37] It is this principle that, phenomenologically speaking, refers to the domain of social interaction, of the *Mitwelt*. Evenson's characterization of the judge as a nomadologist ignores the logic of reciprocity at the heart of Deleuze and Guattari's work. While the group of scalp hunters can be said to exist according to a nomadological regime, it is Judge Holden in particular who (although he is anything but sedentary) embodies the mathematical model of a royal science in his open hostility toward everything he notes and depicts in his ledger. For the moment, it suffices to point out that McCarthy's fiction indeed lends itself to readings inspired by Deleuze and Guattari's theory of space in *A Thousand Plateaus* and related works, but this theory is not aligned with the minimal dimension of the ethical in McCarthy fiction, and the concept of matter implied in that theory does not wholly coincide with McCarthy's notion of material nature.

In his analyses of *The Orchard Keeper*, *Outer Dark*, *Child of God*, and *The Crossing*, Alan Bourassa traces the ways in which the nonhuman world intersects with the human realm. According to him, Deleuze's concept of the event provides a helpful theoretical tool for seeing how McCarthy's narratives are exemplary of and yet dependent on what Bourassa terms "the event of the human."[38] He writes, "there is something ghostly about what haunts McCarthy's narratives, something, like the strangers in *Outer Dark*, 'spectral, palpable as stone' [OD 239]. This is what I mean by the event."[39] Taken out of context, this statement could give the impression that Bourassa merely delineates the gothic sentiment of impending doom that certainly permeates McCarthy's prose. However, to make use of a Cormackian phrasing here, in its very palpability the event both is sensibly intuited and remains ineffable. Very similar to what happens in the spatial regimen of nomad science, the event is foreclosed to intelligibility and, therefore, cannot be apprehended.

Explicitly following Deleuze's *The Logic of Sense* (1969), Bourassa construes the event, first, as immeasurable and insubstantial. Second, the event is neither the act of giving form to a specific content by means of signification, nor is it the content of that activity. In other words, the event is not the ascription of meaning, nor is it the meaning that is thereby generated. However, it is necessarily linked to the practice of this semantic process. Third, Bourassa holds that while the event is effectuated by the interconnection and interaction of bodies in the spatiotemporal setting of the world, it is not wholly determined by it. It is not time- or site-specific, yet it is determinate nonetheless. In linguistic terms, it is "expressed as the infinitive verb," so according to this logic, the event somehow precedes its expression but is also the particular outcome of the latter.[40] In terms of this logic, Bourassa defines the Deleuzian "event of the human" in McCarthy's narrative as that which is functionally expressed by the characters in their respective actions, but it is also the precondition of these characters that connects them with the nonhuman realm of the world. If Bourassa regards "the event as the opposite of narrative,"[41] he does so only to think through the way in which the specific layers of meaning inherent in the behavior of McCarthy's characters are both possible in the first place and, in turn, give rise to their condition by embodying the latter, or by "*actualizing*" it.[42] Bourassa's challenge here is to think through this notion of the event not as a term that transcends McCarthy's narrative but, conversely, as the immanent expression of that narrative. However, it is important to bear in mind that it is the latter that, according to Bourassa, is made possible only on condition of this event. A good example of the way in which McCarthy's characters embody the human qua event is the character of Rinthy in *Outer Dark*, because in her search for her abandoned child she "is pure flight; it is as if the movement precedes her and she lives to embody it."[43]

All of this brings us back to the ways in which smooth space and the concept of nomadology in Shaviro and Evenson are not only ontologically and epistemologically defined, but also ethically determined. The specific character of the event in Bourassa's Deleuzian interpretation of McCarthy is likewise based on an ethical principle—namely, of the simultaneous impossibility to apprehend it and the need to embody it, so that it might come to pass in the first place. The conception of the infinite nature of the event (and also of smooth space) reveals its existential dependence on lived experience (since the event has to be actualized for it to exist at all), but it also shows its theoretical grounding in the plea for the heterogeneous, open, and unfixed that is so characteristic of French theory in the second half of the twentieth century and, by extension, of Westphal's account of a geocritical practice. I want to mention again the second principle of that practice, transgressivity, which posits that in the spatiotemporal orientations of human beings "no representation is stable"; that, instead, "permanent fluidity is the characteristic of representations and, consequently, of identities."[44] Bourassa's reading is very much in accordance with this argument, when he defines the human qua event as a process that is immanent, yet forever unstable. Something like the human is evoked in McCarthy's world, but so that it can be what it is, it is irredeemably connected to the nonhuman world of nature. The human disposition of logical thinking, of the tendency to abstract from the world—as with the "ideal circles" of "royal" geometry that are dependent on the embodiment of the idea of "roundness"[45]—is founded upon the nonhumanity that is nature. As Bourassa rightly argues, however, McCarthy's fiction shows that it is not enough to construct an allegedly deep relationship between literary characters and their ecological surroundings, as ecocritical accounts of McCarthy's prose would have it: "The human, to reveal its nonhuman roots, cannot simply be placed in a natural setting, but there must be something that lays the human out on the same plane as nature, and, by 'nature,' I mean events, singular points, disasters, pure happenings unconnected to personal meaning. The human must enter into a nonhuman becoming."[46]

This, then, is what lies at the heart of Bourassa's application of Deleuzian philosophy to McCarthy's fiction: a combination of three terms—namely. "the human," "the nonhuman," and "corporeal nature"—whereby the event of the human is precisely the embodiment of specific actions by McCarthy's characters that define what it means to be human. The event is also the resonance between the two terms "the human" and "the nonhuman," set in the spatiotemporal realm of nature. This is why Bourassa can claim that a novel like *The Orchard Keeper* "is not a human narrative, but rather the story of the becoming nonhuman of the human. That is the event of the novel: to become nonhuman, and as with all events, it is not located in a specific present, but presides over all the movements of the novel. And it is in the language of the novel that the series of human and nonhuman resonate."[47]

This last passage reveals the concept of nature inherent to these quasi-geocritical accounts of McCarthy's work. Whereas the concept importantly does without the ethical inscription of nature as environment, it is the delineation of nature understood as the fundamentally heterogeneous space of embodiment that reveals a different kind of ethics. This ethics, though, is still incompatible with McCarthy's conception of nature's identity. Although Westphal's conception of geocriticism entails a valuable critique of the ethos of natural homeostasis in the movement that preceded geocriticism, his approach in many ways falls prey to what Iain Grant criticizes in *Philosophies of Nature after Schelling* (2006) as the prolongation of the ethicist and anthropocentric orientation in many post-Kantian philosophies and, by the same token, in the major tenets of poststructuralist thought. While a geologically oriented criticism (*geocritique*) is certainly preferable to any ecologically engaged analysis of McCarthy's work, it is the notions of the geological, the spatial, and the material that need to be reassessed and transformed vis-à-vis the concept of nature to be found in McCarthy's narratives. Whereas this book certainly depends on the conceptual labor that has resulted in the essential principles of geocritical practice (spatiotemporality, transgressivity, and referentiality), it is the twin influences of speculative realism and the contemporary revival and reconstruction of nineteenth-century *Naturphilosophie* that serve as a corrective to a variety of important philosophical notions deployed in any geocritical practice, including space, time, and matter. This line of reasoning will ultimately make progress toward an adequate theoretical framework for coming to terms—in a more nuanced way than the spiritualist, materialist, and ecocritical accounts—with how McCarthy's fiction asks the question "What is nature?" by narrative means.

TO START WITH speculative realism, it is instructive to note the origin of that term. It was the name for a workshop that took place on April 27, 2007, at Goldsmiths, University of London. The workshop featured four speakers, all of whom would become the main initiators of a trend that seems to have identified key problems in the hitherto leading paradigm of literary and cultural theory known as poststructuralism. These speakers—Brassier, Grant, Graham Harman, and Quentin Meillassoux—had at that point in their career published their first major books.[48] In retrospect, it seems that what brought their rather diverse projects together was their mutual understanding that somehow the goals and procedures of their poststructuralist progenitors, such as Jean-François Lyotard, Jacques Derrida, Foucault, and even Deleuze, had to be questioned. It is instructive to consider the description of the workshop in an announcement of it, which began by claiming the following:

> Contemporary 'continental' philosophy often prides itself on having overcome the age-old metaphysical battles between realism and idealism. Subject-object dualism, whose repudiation has turned into a conditioned reflex of contemporary theory, has supposedly been destroyed by the critique of representation and supplanted by various ways of thinking the fundamental correlation between thought and world.[49]

What is clear is that even though the workshop's participants were—and some still are—in the process of outlining rather than consolidating their philosophical projects and respective positions, their accounts were definitely intended to rebut some of the most crucial trends in poststructuralist philosophy, including the condemnation of so-called bad words such as metaphysics (by Derrida) or representation (by Deleuze and Lyotard).[50] Regardless of the differences between the standpoints of Brassier, Grant, Meillassoux, and Harman, it is safe to say that they were trying to erect something in opposition to "the subjectivistic and anthropocentric foundations of much of 'continental philosophy.'"[51] They agreed that there was a common thread in these attempts, and it was Meillassoux who created the critical term for this underlying structure: "correlationism."[52] This is the belief in the impossibility of rendering the human mind and the world that surrounds it as two separately conceivable entities. The notion seems to adequately describe the consensus of most scholars that expressed a human-centered—if antihumanist—view of things in literary and cultural studies, as well as other domains of inquiry. It demarcates a particular form of anthropocentrism that saw the relationship between humanity and world as the crucial object of scrutiny, whatever the topic at hand—much like the fiction of some of McCarthy's contemporaries. In its most extreme form, the correlationist attitude resulted in a cultural constructivism that denied the ontological primacy of natural processes and even deduced the latter from the normative inscription of particular human cultures.

It is particularly fitting that in the first pages of *After Finitude* (2006), Meillassoux would cite the lasting impact of phenomenology on continental thought—an influence that extends to Westphal's outline of geocriticism, as I have shown above. According to Meillassoux, the essential correlation in phenomenology is that between consciousness and world, with Edmund Husserl setting the stage at the beginning of the twentieth century for postmodernism's correlationist agenda. According to Husserl, "the existence of a Nature *cannot* be the condition for the existence of consciousness, since Nature itself turns out to be a correlate of consciousness: Nature *is* only as being constituted in regular concatenations of consciousness."[53] Consequently, it is legitimate to say that the four speculative realists wanted to criticize the common phenomenologically informed stance in critical theory that had, for a substantial amount of time, affirmed the primacy of the correlation between consciousness and the object of consciousness—that is, between thinking and being, "thought and world," or, as Husserl termed it, "Nature" and the "regular concatenations of consciousness."

On these grounds, the connection to the issues I discussed in chapter 1 becomes apparent. First, McCarthy's strategy of regionalism conceived of as a literary strategy places itself squarely in the midst of the debate concerning the corporeal and ideational realms of nature, and the dynamics of their relation. By extension, the speculative realist discussion at Goldsmiths sheds a new light on the chasm between the materialist and spiritualist readings of McCarthy, since Meillassoux's notion of correlationism arguably would entail that both polarities within the secondary literature on McCarthy contain both correlationist and anticorrelationist tendencies. Second, keeping in mind the difficulty of contextualizing McCarthy's fiction in terms of literary history and the glaring inability until now to account adequately for "McCarthy's refusal to accept the postmodern condition"[54]—meaning the undisputed correlation between Husserlian consciousness and nature—speculative realism seems to be an appealing development.[55] Third, environmental criticism has already been influenced by a particular tenet of speculative realism via Timothy Morton's contributions to the field—which include concepts like the mesh, among others. Yet before we can connect a few carefully chosen concepts and ideas that resulted from the Goldsmiths workshop and that followed its philosophical innovations to Westphal's literary theory, it is important to historicize the inception of speculative realism and the return to ontological reflection in critical theory. Such a historicization must include an examination of speculative realism's ostensible originality.

All four of the original speculative realists—of the four, only Harman continues to use the term as a description of his theoretical position (apart from the increasingly untenable notion of "object-oriented philosophy" or "object-oriented ontology")—have some relation, either directly or indirectly, with three figures in continental philosophy who paved the way for speculative realism and the resurgence of ontology. This unlikely trio of thinkers consists of Deleuze, Alain Badiou, and Slavoj Žižek. At the risk of oversimplification, their work and legacies can be situated historically and thematically between poststructuralism's solipsistic obsession with linguistic and cultural construction and the metaphysical inquiry into the nature of a mind-independent reality, which really is the most basic concern of today's speculative philosophies. The writings of these three constitute the path from cultural constructivism to speculative realism, though I acknowledge that none of them fits neatly into either the former or the latter philosophical position.[56]

These three philosophers, then, can be seen as precursors to the current resurgence of speculative philosophy. While Brassier has translated some of Badiou's writings and endorses a few of his ideas, Meillassoux has been a student of Badiou and promotes the same kind of mathematized ontology as does his former mentor—that is, Cantorian and post-Cantorian set theory.[57] Both Brassier and Meillassoux are followers of the rationalist tradition in philosophy, although the former is far more reliant than the latter on the cognitive sciences, chemistry, and biology. In effect, Meillassoux elaborates a decidedly mechanistic conception of matter in a well-nigh Cartesian vein. By comparison, Grant's connection to the so-called "hard" sciences is different in a number of aspects, and Harman's project is not at all geared toward a new convergence between ontology and scientific discourse.[58]

Finally, it must be noted that the interdisciplinary research program of cybernetics as conceived by the neurophilosophers Humberto Maturana and Francisco Varela and their idea of self-organization (in addition to the discourses of mathematics, quantum physics, the cognitive sciences, chemistry, and biology) have informed the scientific unconscious of speculative realism. This can be seen most readily in the work of Grant and his former teacher, Nick Land. The resulting constellation is also confirmed by the fact that Grant's intellectual formation, even more than that of Brassier, has been defined crucially by the work of Deleuze (most likely via Land)—especially in Grant's new interpretation and re-reading of German idealism in general, and of Schelling's philosophy in particular.[59] The Deleuzian impetus of combining conceptual potentialities with the nonconceptual ones of the earth in pursuit of a "geology of morals" rather than a genealogy seems indicative of both the methodological driving force behind Grant's account and the mark of a rival thinker in the construction of a new philosophy of nature.[60] From Grant's perspective, Deleuze's project, which he and Guattari christened "geophilosophy," is the most sophisticated of contemporary endeavors in terms of reconsidering nature as a philosophical problem to be dealt with—contrary to Badiou's repeated attempts to expel nature altogether from the realm of philosophy.[61] In this sense, Grant's critique of Deleuze's account should both be regarded as an expansion of that project's nature-oriented inquiry and be understood as a rectification of its particular objectives.

In the same way, it can be said that Westphal's notion of geocriticism is the template for the present study to use in developing an appropriate theoretical framework for analyzing McCarthy's fiction and the conception of nature's identity to be found therein. What this means is that Grant's critical remarks, which mainly concern Deleuze's (and Guattari's) notion of matter, are equally applicable to Westphal's literary theory because geocriticism's chief philosophical influence is, in fact, geophilosophy, Deleuze and Guattari's last collaborative project. It is a discourse whose "genitive is not inverted"[62]—meaning a discourse premised on a supposed geology of philosophy—but is based, instead, on the fact that its theoretical enterprise is part and parcel of its subject matter, the earth—one of the largest macroscopic formations of nature to be part of philosophical discourse. It is in this sense, finally, that both the individual concept of the geological and the particular body that is placed on the earth have a specific relation to the latter. This relation is very similar—if not identical—to the one portrayed in a question raised in the introduction of the present study, concerning McCarthy's *Child of God*: What is the finitude of bodies or forms measured against their territory within nature? However, if ideas are conceived of as finite phenomena with respect to nature's infinity in the same way that bodies are susceptible to what Schelling called the "infinite dissociation into ever new products,"[63] this question might even be simplified for the purposes of my argument in the following manner: What is the relation between the concept and its territory?

Grant's response to this question, and his account of a foundational "naturephilosophy"[64] in the Schellingian tradition, broadly speaking, can be seen as a supplement to Deleuze's geophilosophy. Grant hails Deleuze for his persistent attempts to engage with the concept of nature from *Difference and Repetition* (1968) to his last essay "Immanence: A Life" (1995), yet he criticizes certain aspects of the solutions Deleuze offered. While for both Deleuze and Grant "thought is put into a direct relation with the earth,"[65] and while for both the anthropocentric and logocentric strands of twentieth-century philosophy are as untenable as the subordination of geology to philosophy and of the territory to the concept, how far their respective accounts differ must be clarified. Doing so within the present inquiry into McCarthy's concept of nature will permit a better recasting of Westphal's project for an analysis of McCarthy's fiction—one that can adequately account for that concept of nature. Accordingly, what follows is a short comparison of Grant's and Deleuze's specific standpoints regarding the geophilosophical project, and, by extension, that of *Naturphilosophie*.

Deleuze's first major work, *Difference and Repetition*, which presented his own philosophy rather than philosophical portraits of other thinkers, begins with the proposal to "embrace all the concepts of nature and freedom,"[66] thereby reiterating the Kantian division between determined materiality and determinable ideality. For Deleuze, this division does not merely separate two types of concepts per se but two domains that work according to two different conditions (even if they are eventually connected through the substrate of immanence—a concept he takes from Spinoza, as I will show below). For Deleuze, the "concepts of Nature . . . are not in Nature but in the mind which contemplates it or observes it, and represents it to itself. That is why it is said that Nature is alienated mind or alienated concept, opposed to itself."[67] While "Nature is alienated mind"—meaning that it is originally confused and "always in something else"—concepts of freedom are those of the emergence of newness, "always hidden among the remains of an old order and the first fruits of a new."[68] In other words, the negative ascription of nature and the corresponding degrees of freedom (meaning the exclusion of both domains inspired by Kantian transcendental philosophy) provide the basis both for Deleuze's definition of matter and, somewhat paradoxically, for the possibility of overcoming this apparently insurmountable gulf between mind and world—or what Fichte, the post-Kantian philosopher par excellence, defined as intellect and thing . . . between which there is no bridge."[69] In fact, Deleuze's account of matter is inherently connected to the realignment of the two domains of nature and freedom, but at the cost of any ethical asymmetry between the two.

Two questions arise at this point: What is matter for Deleuze? And which concept provides the necessary resources to simultaneously harmonize the realms of nature and freedom and keep them separate? A short answer to the first question would be that Deleuze's concept of matter is that of forces that must be extended in space and time as bodies. For him, there is no materiality that is not also a somatic formation of material force.[70] As elaborated in Bourassa's Deleuzian reading of McCarthy's fiction, it is the notion of the event that clarifies the necessity of materiality's incarnation, or its actualization, to be what it is.[71] After all, it is the condition of material extension that is the event, but this extension is also the event's realization in the first place: *matter needs to be actualized, or it is not material at all.* This definition is repeatedly elaborated in alternating circumstances throughout Deleuze's work and in his collaborations with Guattari, and it is crucially linked to a notion

I mentioned above that is intended to address the Fichtean insuperability of "intellect and thing"—the notion of "reciprocal determination," also called "reciprocal presupposition" or "mutual solidarity."[72]

Actual bodies and virtual ideas are correlated terms from *Difference and Repetition* to "Immanence: A Life," even if this correlation occurs in various guises and has different names. It is so crucial for both Deleuze's ethics and his ontology that it can be termed foundational in the sense given above. The grounding of thought in the body of the earth, evident in the nascent form of geophilosophy provided by *Difference and Repetition*, already corresponds to the domain of freedom as the site for this operation: "The fact is that to ground is to determine the indeterminate," and although matter is indeterminate, it "is already informed," molded, and coextensive with its intensive counterpart.[73] Therefore, there is no question of an ontological priority between being and thinking, actual and virtual, or territory and concept; instead, there is a primal correspondence or incessantly established harmony. Deleuze writes: "The actual and the virtual co-exist, and enter into a tight circuit," while "pure virtuality . . . is the strict correlative of the actual."[74] The closeness of the link between both terms, to the point of there being no difference between them (or, in Schellingian terminology, to the "point of indifference"), seems to suggest a version of geophilosophy whose genitive can indeed be inverted, as the virtual perception of materiality is coterminous with the actual materiality of perception, while both are constituted at the same time. Deleuze's overtly strongly panpsychist formulation of this correlation is the following: "Every body, every thing, thinks and is a thought to the extent that, reduced to its intensive reasons, it expresses an Idea the actualisation of which it determines."[75]

It is still unclear how the natural domain of bodies and the psychic domain of freedom can be simultaneously harmonized and kept separate. Grant's assessment of Deleuze's account of nature as somatically based seems both accurate and informative in this respect. Deleuze and Guattari's first collaboration, in *Anti-Oedipus* (1972), offers the notion of the "body without organs" as a mediator of some sort: "The body without organs is the matter that always fills space to the given degrees of intensity," and it is "the immobile motor, . . . the immanent substance, in the most Spinozist sense of the word."[76] In the already mentioned follow-up tome *A Thousand Plateaus*, the conditions of possibility for the thinking of nature remain based on an ultimately bodily level, since despite the nominal severance of all organisms from nature, the metaphysical foundation for every other notion is still a body whose names vary (including the "body without organs," the "planomenon," the "plane of consistency," and the "plane of composition"[77] (or that of immanence): "This body without organs is permeated by unformed, unstable matters, by flows in all directions, by free intensities or nomadic singularities, by mad or transitory particles."[78] The foundational concept, sporadically bridging the incommensurable gap between "intellect and thing," or meaning and being, is that "upon which everything is given"[79]—a body as the basis for the two domains of nature and freedom, which (despite their reciprocal presupposition, or perhaps because of it) remain separate.

This situation is no different from that in *What Is Philosophy?* (1991). In that book, the proper name of geological thinking (geophilosophy) appears as the title of a whole chapter. Yet even before that chapter, Deleuze and Guattari write: "The plane of immanence has two facets as Thought and as Nature, as *Nous* and as *Physis*."[80] This passage reveals once again both their understanding of nature as body and the somatic grounding of this understanding of nature as "alienated mind or alienated concept, opposed to itself."[81] What is more, recalling the earlier discussion of nomadology and royal science, related to Evenson's reading of McCarthy, it is in chapter 4 of *What Is Philosophy?* that one finds the ethical categorization of the place of nature as a concept within Deleuze and Guattari's theoretical apparatus, as it hinges on a preference for one specific science over another—the one being more invested in heterogeneity (that is, nomadology) and the other allegedly being divested of all heterogeneity (royal science), even though this distinction is only de jure and does not apply to a de facto situation.

In a passage that describes the geopolitical circumstance of the rise of Western philosophy, Deleuze and Guattari write: "Philosophy appears as a result of contingency rather than necessity, as a result of an ambiance or milieu rather than an origin, of a becoming rather than a history, of a geography rather than a historiography, of *a grace rather than a nature*."[82] To be sure, this is not a discussion of the philosophy of nature in particular, but a rendering of the material conditions of philosophy in general. Yet the phrasing here is important: like the time- and site-specific rendering of McCarthy's fiction by what I have termed the materialist camp of scholars, Deleuze and Guattari, in poststructuralist fashion, reject the concept of "origin" in favor of the "milieu" and subsequently contrast "geography" and "grace" in like manner with "historiography" and "nature." This way, the two aspects of the plane of immanence—*Nous* and *Physis*—are recast in ethical terms that characterize the side of natural history as a nondynamic undertaking separate from the heterogeneous geophilosophical practice grounded in the concept of immanence, rather than the supposed transcendence of historical determinism: "Geography wrests history from the cult of necessity in order to stress the irreducibility of contingency."[83] The question arises as to why a supposedly determined nature has to be different in kind from a contingent form of what Deleuze and Guattari call "grace"—which, in turn, could be defined as a being that is free from both cultural and biophysical shackles: "History today still designates only the set of conditions, however recent they may be, from which one turns away in order to become, that is to say, in order to create something new."[84] Where does this leave the concept of nature, which Deleuze and Guattari cast on the side of historiography rather than geography? What is nature, or rather, what becomes of nature conceptually, if it is opposed to the grace of the earth and to the creation of the new?

As Grant sees it, the severance of freedom from determination, of becoming from history, and of grace from nature undermines nature's capabilities and its generative powers. For him, the premise that "thought [be] put into a direct relation with the earth"[85] cannot be supported by a two-world metaphysics partially unified by "the immanent substance,"[86] since the positing of "an insuperable gulf between nature and freedom . . . is precisely a means to allow the causality of freedom to perforate inanimate nature and animal inertia."[87] The manipulation of nature's ostensible fixity by the order of free living beings would then result in a mere projection of the latter's qualities onto the dispositions of the former—very similar to the projection of inherent rights onto the environment in ecocritical discourse.[88] Conversely, the task of geophilosophy, understood as a subdiscipline of the philosophy of nature, is to show that rather than depending on either its bodily constitution or its substrate-dependent capture on the plane of immanence, "nature is its own analyst."[89] Geophilosophy means that "finding room in nature for freedom extends an ontology grounded on the former"[90] rather than grounding the two realms of nature and thought upon the body or plane of immanence. In Schelling's words, "we would think nature in its freedom as it develops along all possible trajectories,"[91] independent of the actualization of nature's productivity in bodies (or ideas). Therefore, matter is not what it is just as soon as it appears in its somatic formation. Matter is productivity itself, the capability for bodies to be realized and the reason for freedom to be thought. For Grant, there is a dynamic of bodies dependent on that of forces, just as there is a "physics of the Idea."[92]

Grant's reconstruction of Schellingian naturephilosophy insists on the ontological priority of being to thinking, rejecting their reciprocal constitution as conceptualized by the Kantian division of nature and thought. Just as "matter is not a substrate but a product" (namely, of nature's productivity realized in forces and of the idea's retroaction via the philosophy of nature), "intelligence is a phenomenon of force" and not the obverse of the somatic domain.[93] Consequently, two logics respond to the question concerning the concept's relationship to its territory. The first logic is that of reciprocal presupposition, endorsed by all three of the Deleuzian readings of McCarthy's work that I have discussed (and possibly also by the majority of the ecocritical approaches to McCarthy). The second logic is what Grant has called the "antecedence criterion," according to which the idea "that ground may not be substantial does not mean that it cedes priority with respect to the grounded, which is [neither] the totality of the actual."[94] This means that both ideas and bodies, or concepts and objects, are fully actual as products, while their antecedent productivity exceeds their ontological status, which is posterior to that production as ground. Conversely, reciprocity requires there to be a strict equivalence between the orders of nature and freedom, an equivalence that lies in their mutual exclusion in general as well as their particular determination. According to this account, although philosophy and geology are not "the same," the proposition that "the philosophy at hand is that of geology" is synonymous with saying "the geology under examination is that of philosophy." In other words, the genitive *is* inverted in the Deleuzian combination of thought and earth in that the philosophy of geology becomes identical with the geology of philosophy. Moreover, the same logic applies to the relationship between concept and territory: while the concept is always territorially grounded, (that is, time- and site-specific), the territory is grounded in the concept, solely with respect to the idea.

It is worth noting at this point that in the context of McCarthy's vision of nature as a process that is ontologically prior to any of its products, the logic of reciprocal determination simply does not hold, in spite of Shaviro's, Evenson's, and Bourassa's nuanced readings. The reason why this reciprocal logic becomes problematic is the following: if my interpretation of McCarthy's conception of natural process is correct (namely, that there is an ontological priority between being and meaning in his narratives), then it cannot be the case that for him the proposition "the literature at hand is that of nature" is ontologically coterminous with saying "the nature under examination is that of literature." If nature is antecedent with respect to its human perception (as I have been arguing it is, according to the concept of nature suggested throughout McCarthy's oeuvre), then it is impossible to invert the genitive of the "literature of nature" in the same way, as this inversion is incomprehensible from the position of Schellingian *Naturphilosophie*.

One component is missing still, however: the quality of the foundational element or ground that unites both sides of the Kantian equation in the Deleuzo-Guattarian account of geophilosophy and, by the same token, in Westphal's geocriticism. As the somatically inscribed plane of immanence unites its "two facets as Thought and as Nature,"[95] it does so only on the basis of being alive or "a life," as Deleuze's last essay, "Immanence: A Life" has it. Yet already in *A Thousand Plateaus* it is "a fixed plane of life upon which everything stirs, slows down or accelerates."[96] Thus, the ascription of organic features to the realm of the inorganic is instigated by the absolutization of an "immanent life" that is "indefinite," accompanied by an overt reference to Fichte's conceptualization of "*a life*, no longer dependent on a Being or submitted to an Act [but] an absolute immediate consciousness."[97] A life is therefore posited as independent of both the "Being" of bodies in nature, and the "Act[s]" of the understanding in reason and morality, while it is the necessary prerequisite of both.

The difference between the two logics of reciprocity and antecedence as possible solutions to the Kantian division of nature and freedom, then, are related to the question of whether one agrees with a vitalist thesis going all the way down to the tiniest elements of both domains (a doctrine also known as hylozoism), as Deleuze does in following Fichte, or whether one makes freedom a very complex expression of nature itself, without having recourse to an "immanent substance" of life, as Grant proposes in reiterating Schelling.[98] Grant writes: "It is precisely in its attachment to the vital instance that attempts at a naturephilosophy are caught within the infinitely reciprocating circuit of Fichtean *life*, 'wavering' on the thresholds of *physis* and *ethos*"[99]—that is, of nature's *to be* and freedom's *ought to be*. Consequently, the convergence of ontology with ethics based on the conviction that "there are never any criteria other than the tenor of existence, the intensification of life"[100] results in reciprocal presupposition having purchase on ontology and in unilateral, or one-sided, determination having purchase on ethics via the priority of freedom in regard of nature. In the present context, the purchase on ontological issues points yet again toward Deleuze and Guattari's proximity to the ecocentric and phenomenological traditions that take lived experience as the final horizon of analysis. Incidentally, this would include Westphal's version of geocriticism, based as it is on the notions of *Umwelt*, *Mitwelt*, and *Lebenswelt*.[101] The problem with this approach, as it applies to McCarthy's concept of nature, is that Westphal's geocriticism is qualified by the ontologization of embodiment. Regarding the purchase on the question of ethics via unilateral determination, the constitution of nature according to the norm of freedom amounts to "an ethical vision of the world" insofar as "actions and passions of the body accompany actions and passions of the soul"[102] and insofar as freedom is possible only as an aspect of "*a life*" but not, strictly speaking, within the domain of nature itself—otherwise Deleuze and Guattari would not have juxtaposed the "grace" of "becoming" with the "nature" of "history" in their last work.[103]

Grant's assessment of the Deleuzian and Deleuzo-Guattarian conception of nature, then, is as follows. Even though this project is the most sophisticated of the contemporary endeavors in terms of reconsidering nature as a philosophical problem, it cannot rid itself of its somatic drawbacks. Put simply, the materiality of nature in Deleuze and Guattari is unmistakably conceived of as the materiality of the body. Matter is corporeal and has as its counterpart the events it actualizes, although from the de facto point of view it would be difficult to differentiate between the two. In the present context—McCarthy's narrative answers to the philosophical question of nature's identity—I argue that the reproach of somaticism, which Grant has directed at Deleuze, can equally be directed at Westphal's geocritical principles, outspokenly Deleuzian interpretations of McCarthy's work, and readings that emphasize the "tenor of existence" in his fictions, according to ecocentric parameters.[104] What about the overtly speculative passages in McCarthy's novels? What about passages that describe landscapes, bodies, and ideas that his literary characters have, which point to a realm that is wholly indeterminate, formless, and incorporeal yet still somehow part of nature and fully material? What about the descendental poetics of McCarthy that links his work to transnational and transhistorical cultures of Romanticism?

In *The Logic of Sense*, Deleuze writes: "We seek to determine an impersonal and pre-individual transcendental field, which does not resemble the corresponding empirical fields, and which nevertheless is not confused with an undifferentiated depth."[105] Deleuze's inquiry into the virtual nature of events began in this book and permeates his entire oeuvre, including his works with Guattari. This notion of a transcendental field, which he expressly differentiates from the conception of formlessness, returns in "Immanence: A Life," in which he describes it as "a pure stream of a-subjective consciousness, a pre-reflexive impersonal consciousness, a qualitative duration of consciousness without a self."[106] While Deleuze's relationship to the phenomenological tradition is still much debated by scholars, his concept of the transcendental field is nevertheless indubitably connected to the philosophical primacy ascribed to lived experience rather than "royal" abstraction—similar to Maturana and Varela's account of self-organizing systems and Westphal's account of geocriticism. The notion of the transcendental field, with which Deleuze concerns himself from 1969 onward, substantiates the impression that his is a thoroughly vitalist philosophy, as others have noted.[107] His is a theoretical position that combines the realms of ontology, epistemology, and ethics, though always in line with the "tenor of existence, the intensification of life," however "indefinite" and "impersonal" the concept of the latter might be.[108]

In the present context, then, I argue that the Deleuzian interpretation of McCarthy's work comes closest to a thorough illumination of his concept of nature so far, as it seems to synthesize the materialist and spiritualist perspectives on McCarthy and to include the ecological accounts of his prose.

Nonetheless, the grounding correlation of the actual and the virtual on a single plane of immanence—that is, the heterogeneous and contingent process of living systems that are constantly differentiating themselves—is still not enough to adequately come to terms with how McCarthy's works can be regarded as expressions of nature itself. The issue of how McCarthy "answers" the philosophical question "What is nature?" by narrative means can be resolved only to a limited extent if one adopts a Deleuzian perspective.[109]

Grant, Brassier, and Negarestani are more helpful in this regard, because, even though their respective accounts are not entirely congruent, all three of them seek to recast what Deleuze calls "an impersonal and pre-individual transcendental field" as "an undifferentiated depth"—a nothingness that, however, is generative of differentiation. It is the hypothesis of the present study that the capability of this nothingness to give rise to different and diverse phenomena and forms of life is the most basic feature of McCarthy's conception of the natural process as well; a conception according to which *inexistence is the ground of existence insofar as the former subsists in the latter, yet also insofar as the latter depends on the former*. For McCarthy, all forms of life and phenomena depend on the formlessness out of which they emerged and of which they are a part, so this very formlessness still inheres in these phenomena. Grant writes: "What is *given* but never available is, in every case, what cannot be apperceptively reproduced because it exceeds this as its source. In this sense what is *given* is formless production."[110] Underlying this statement is Grant's conviction that it is idealism rather than materialism that is capable of accounting for nature's processes.[111] More specifically, "*only a non-eliminative idealism is capable of the philosophy of matter*,"[112] which is almost synonymous with *Naturphilosophie* in light of the "fundamentality of physicality"[113] in Grant's theoretical position. The "*non-eliminative*" character of the idealist philosophy of nature proposed by Grant is so termed because, from his point of view, nature's formless productivity can fulfill its absolute inclusion of products and processes, of ideas and bodies, and of concepts and objects in the world only if it is not restricted to any determining feature, save its dynamic and ever-changing disposition. What Grant also calls the methodological process of "regionalizing matter"[114] is conceived of as the subversion of nature's potentiality, which is why even Deleuze's far-reaching conception of the plane of immanence regionalizes the physical by defining it as the corporeal differentiation of the multiplicity of events in the world and, in turn, as the instantiation of incorporeal virtualities—that is to say, the transcendental field.

To restrict nature to any one particularity that it encompasses is to undercut the reach of its concept and, consequently, to mistake nature for just one of its many facets. This is why the condition of possibility for nature to be productive needs to be "undifferentiated" and formless; otherwise, again, it would be impossible to propose a concept of nature that is all-encompassing or—to use a word that is even more Schellingian—*absolute*. Along the same lines, I would contend that the explicit identification of nature and the environment in ecocentrism and its critical practices, as well as the conflation of nature with space in Westphal's geocentric stance and his phenomenological version of a critical practice based on that conflation, can be regarded as examples of just such a regionalization of the concept of nature. Both perspectives seem incapable of adequately capturing the extent to which McCarthy's prose can be regarded as part and parcel of the realm of nature itself—a nature that necessarily includes the "plane of life"[115] and the environments of living systems, but that is not grounded in either one of them.

While Brassier is not entirely in agreement with Grant's ontology of forces, his rationalist philosophy is equally focused on the issue of a generative nothingness and the concomitant inquiry into the question of "how *that which is not* . . . is implicated in the thought of *that which is*."[116] Both Grant and Brassier make use of the Platonic distinction between essence and appearance, which they seek to revive as an argument against the correlation of being and thinking—which, for Brassier at least, appears in Deleuze's co-constitution of the actual and the virtual.[117] Here, the question of whether this allegation is ultimately justified is less important than is the question of how the philosophical move that separates essences from appearances resonates with McCarthy's poetics and the concept of nature it suggests. Given his well-documented immersion in Plato's philosophy from early in his career, it should not come as a surprise that passages in his novels evoke a concept of a material reality that upholds a certain hierarchy between the phenomenal realm and that which exceeds all phenomenality—the absolute.[118] In *The Crossing*, for instance, Billy Parham and the blind man he meets on his travels through Mexico have a conversation, and the man tells Billy about his life, how he lost his eyesight during the Mexican War, and how that changed his thoughts about the world. At one point, the man says that in the last analysis, the world is solely composed of the elements of the earth and that "because what can be touched falls into dust there can be no mistaking these things for the real. At best they are only tracings of where the real has been. Perhaps they are not even that. Perhaps they are no more than obstacles to be negotiated in the ultimate sightlessness of the world" (*TC*, 294).

While the man sees the futility of confusing the real and the corporeal as the strongest proof of "la bendición más grande de Dios" (*TC*, 293), of God's greatest blessing, the distinction between finite appearance and infinite essence is equally congruent with the Platonism endorsed by both Brassier and Grant. Here as elsewhere, McCarthy evokes a distinctly philosophical notion of matter—namely the Platonic one, as theorized in the *Timaeus*, elaborated in Schelling's 1794 essay on it, and reconstructed in Grant's writings. As Grant puts it: "Matter is a 'difficult and dark idea' . . . since it cannot be sensibly intuited but can be thought; unlike the other ideas, however, matter cannot be thought clearly but only with difficulty."[119] This is why McCarthy's story of the blind man within the overall story of *The Crossing* is allegorical of the human position within the process of nature as a whole.[120] It is a position that, according to the logic of McCarthy's fictional worlds, is fundamentally tragic. Nevertheless, it yields a beautiful outcome, if only in the form of the tale itself—which leads us back to the ethical and aesthetic formula I mentioned at the beginning of this book: *starting from grief, arriving at grace*. Bourassa argues that *The Crossing* "does not progress from a principle of addition but of subtraction," since "the world of Billy Parham eventually and relentlessly disappears."[121] The most encompassing narrative theme, therefore, is "the relentless subtraction to which his life has been subject."[122] Yet it is precisely this latter point that suggests not so much the Deleuzian perspective that Bourassa endorses, as it does Negarestani's conception of "ontological decay."[123] This conception accounts for nature's dialectical procedure of coupling subtractive and constructive forces, by which corporeal and incorporeal beings in the worlds are not correlated according to "the tenor of existence," but according to "the vectors of the *mobilization* and *effectuation* of reason" in nature.[124] Thus, Negarestani's is another account of how nature self-analyzes, or of how—in the gnostic terminology I discussed above—nature is constantly "dividing from itself via an internal will to self-understanding."[125]

The works of Grant, Brassier, and Negarestani suggest that to gain some traction on the concept of nature expressed in McCarthy's fictions, what is needed is a geocritical practice in which "the genitive is not inverted"[126]—a form of geocriticism that neither restricts the realm of nature to spatiotemporal phenomena nor determines its analysis according to a paradigm of lived experience within a particular environment. In other words, what is required is a nonphenomenological and nonvitalist geocriticism of McCarthy's fictions that would conform to the Platonic definition of matter as foreclosed to sensible intuition. Moreover, the task is to show in what sense the Schellingian and, as I demonstrate below, the Okenian conception of *Naturphilosophie* is helpful and even indispensable for the delineation of McCarthy's narrative speculations on the question "What is nature?" In turn, it seems that it is only from the point of view of Schellingianism that McCarthy's regionalism, conceived of as a narrative strategy, can be seen as a twofold enterprise. His methodological path from the particular to the universal is not just related to the evocation of metaphysical statements per se. It is also his way of elevating the American regions of his tales as worthy environments to substantiate his position as a literary contributor to the German-American conversation about the nature of nature—a conversation that has been going on at least since Emerson commented on Kant and Fichte.

I HAVE ALREADY MENTIONED, or alluded to, many key aspects of Schelling's treatment of the question concerning nature's nature. I want to mention some of them again here, providing more detail on his and Oken's respective positions along the way. From the start of this book I have pointed to Schelling's caution about the ethical overdetermination of ontology, which is the first key aspect I want to address at this point in more detail. What Deleuze has termed the "ethical vision of the world" is possible and even necessary in Schelling's construal of nature as the untranscendable horizon of thought, yet the horizon is not fundamentally determined by the vision. According to Grant, the philosophy of nature comes first, and the possibility of an ethics (of nature) comes second. In fact, the concept of nature and its philosophical development is the single theme that permeates every one of Schelling's works, either explicitly or implicitly. Yet this positing of *Naturphilosophie* as the primary figure of thought throughout Schelling's varied oeuvre is a highly contentious stance within Schelling studies, and Grant is one of only a few scholars who have argued along these lines.[127] Incidentally, this situation is similar to literary scholars' standard categorization of McCarthy's work in successive periods, or generic phases—namely, the Tennessee period, the Western phase, detective fiction, and postapocalypse. Certainly, it is valid to divide McCarthy's fiction chronologically, spatially, and thematically, as this categorization suggests. However, such a standpoint obscures the abovementioned *narrative continuity* of the novels that remains unchanged and consequently connects each of them. This continuity is established by the centrality of the author's concern with the narrative response to the philosophical question "What is nature?"

Schelling's work, too, is routinely characterized as going through various stages of a conceptual trajectory. It starts with the Fichte-inspired works that he published between 1794 and 1797, presenting his own version of transcendentalism. Then it continues with the early treatises of *Naturphilosophie* (written up until 1800 and marking his departure from Fichte), and with the identity philosophy and the philosophy of art from 1800 to 1807. Next comes the abovementioned *Freedom* essay, in 1809. After this defining work, there is the development of a philosophical project that Schelling constantly revises between 1810 and 1828, called *The Ages of the World*. Eventually he formulates his so-called positive philosophy between 1830 and 1854.[128] I will not delve into the specifics of each of these stages, which would distract too much from the current task to clarify in what sense the Schellingian concept of nature is helpful for a reconsideration of McCarthy's vision of nature. However, it is safe to say that both the early work on the nascent philosophy of nature (*Ideas for a Philosophy of Nature* [first published in 1797], *On the World Soul* [1798], and *First Outline of a System of the Philosophy of Nature* [1799]) and the late texts (including the lecture courses *Philosophy of Mythology* and *Philosophy of Revelation* [1842–54]) are characterized by an overt spiritualism and even mystical aspects that are sometimes regarded with suspicion by scholars. In contrast, it is in the works of the middle period (*System of Transcendental Idealism* [1800] and the *Philosophical Investigations into the Essence of Human Freedom*) that Schelling develops a theory of art, human freedom, and absolute identity, and that exegetes and commentators seem to cherish the most.[129] While it can be helpful to use these stages of Schelling's thought to keep in mind the particular focus he had in his many different works of philosophy, Grant still argues that there is a *theoretical continuity* in the oeuvre. This continuity, according to Grant, has to do with Schelling's persistent concern with the question concerning nature's identity, which yields his sense of the absolute. This is the first of two reasons why I am following Grant's interpretation of Schelling's complex thought out of all of the vast literature on that German idealist, especially in the context of McCarthy's literary speculations on natural processes and their unified character. The second reason is Grant's association with speculative realism as a new option in continental theory, after the long reign of poststructuralist philosophy, which provides some critical purchase on the dissimilarity between McCarthy's poetics and those of his postmodern contemporaries in American literature.

What is at stake in the project of *Naturphilosophie* is the persistence of a kind of speculation that is set to advance beyond the bounds of the sensible but that also grounds the latter—a kind of thinking that focuses on nature's infinite dynamism, which necessarily gives rise to that thinking but which is not grounded ontologically in anything but itself. It is this persistence of speculation that characterizes not only the Schellingian philosophy of nature (including Oken's systematic account in his *Elements of Physiophilosophy* [first published in 1809–11 and, in a revised version, in 1843])[130] but also McCarthy's fiction. Conversely, it is not just in McCarthy's novelistic work that an ethical and aesthetic formula like *starting from grief, arriving at grace* can be found. Also, in Schelling's philosophy of freedom and the writings of his later period there are passages demonstrating that even "the essence of God" is to be understood "as a resplendent glimpse of life in the darkness of the depths" (that is, in "primordial nature"[131]) and that "the destiny of the world and of mankind is a tragic one by nature."[132] Although nature is sometimes said to be divine, the divine is still merely one part of natural history among others, however central. Or, as Schelling writes in *The Ages of the World*, the continuum of "the physical, far from being the last, is rather the first from which everything, even the development of the divine life, originates."[133]

Along these lines, then, I want to proceed to the second key aspect of Schelling's concept of nature that I implied in chapter 1, when I pointed out the descendentalism of McCarthy's poetics: the fact that the passages of his novels in which the narrators speculate on the essential forces that underlie the apparent, tangible, and generally sensible world are more often than not linked to contexts of destruction, putrefaction, or death. A similar approach can be found in Grant's assessment of the concept of "ungrounding"[134] in Schelling's thought. Following Wolfgang Hogrebe, Grant recasts Schelling's counterargument to Fichte's subjectivist transcendentalism, a position that is dependent on a "generative antithesis of I and not-I."[135] Grant recasts this as a "descendental philosophy" that is merely concerned neither with how the human subject can be depicted as a free rational being that cognizes the "not-I" of corporeal nature around it, nor with the uniquely rational activity that lies at the normative root of human freedom.[136] Instead, descendentalism yields a kind of thinking focused on the issue of how "nature . . . is the *prius* of all cognition."[137] Whenever there is an attempt to establish the grounds of freedom in a supposedly non-natural realm of the normative, the philosophy of nature *ungrounds* it in the sense that it exposes the falsity of both its epistemological and ontological purpose and of the postulated supervenience of the latter upon the former, which really is the metaphysical consequence of ascendentalism's "upward mobility."[138] Moreover, this notion of ungrounding brings us back to the geophilosophical and geocritical context, since it plays a role in Deleuze's *Difference and Repetition*, as Grant points out.[139] Deleuze writes of "a universal *ungrounding*," which he defines as "the freedom of the un-mediated ground, the discovery of a ground behind every other ground, the relation between the groundless and the ungrounded,"[140] a passage that is in many ways a precursor to Grant's reconstruction of Schelling's descendental concept.

Oken's Schelling-inspired *Elements of Physiophilosophy* also resonates with these descendental practices of ungrounding, already giving direction to the discussion of nature's material disposition that, consequently, relegates a certain authority to *Naturphilosophie* (or "physiophilosophy," as Alfred Tulk translates it) in contrast to the case of other thematic fields in the discipline. As Oken writes early in the text: "Physio- and Pneumato-philosophy [*Natur- und Geistesphilosophie*] range . . . parallel to each other. . . . Physio-philosophy, however, holds the first rank, Pneumato-philosophy the second: the former, therefore, is the ground and foundation of the latter, for nature is antecedent to the human spirit."[141] Furthermore, Oken's *Elements* adds yet another dimension to the present discussion—namely, that of mathematics. Oken's work sets out to develop a metaphysics of nature on mathematical grounds, claiming that "the doctrine of matter is the Philosophy of Nature [and] therefore the science also of all Singulars, like geometry and arithmetic."[142] Like Schelling, Oken has a concept that accounts for the dark origins of the world's phenomena and forms of life. While the Schelling of the *Freedom* essay calls it "the indivisible remainder"—referring to how "the understanding is born in the genuine sense from that which is without understanding" and how "without this preceding darkness creatures have no reality [since] darkness is their necessary inheritance"[143]—Oken proposes many names for this preconceptual realm in his *Elements*, one of these being "time," and another being "nothing." At one point, he writes: "All things are created in time; for time is the totality of Singulars. . . . There is no endless, still less an eternal thing; for things are only positions of time. Time itself is, however, only repetition, and thus also a suppression of these positions."[144] Finite phenomena are thus relative to time, which Oken also defines as the counting of numbers and "the act of numbering,"[145] suggesting a kind of *creatio ex nihilo* (the emergence of something out of nothing), albeit one in which nothingness is merely posited as an ideational void like the zero in arithmetic. This is congruent with his statement on the first page of the main body of the text that "Physio-philosophy has to show how, and in accordance indeed with what laws, the Material took its origin; and, therefore, how something derived its existence from nothing."[146] As Negarestani states in his commentary on Oken's philosophy of nature, "devoid of any intrinsic expression, the sign of the eternal is 0—indivisible and indifferent. . . . Oken understood the eternal as the nothing of nature or zero. 0 is the first act, yet one that has no substratum and no ground. Generation out of the eternal—or in Oken's terms position by zero—is already an expression of universal contingency."[147] The genesis of something out of nothing that is evoked here is not merely a theological plea for necessity over contingency, but the argument for there being an ungrounded contingency at the heart of all necessity in natural processes. Contingency is thus sustained in the systemic necessities of nature's structuration and constant evolution: *that which is* entails *that which is not* since, in ontological terms, being is enveloped in nonbeing, or the former presupposes the latter as its condition of possibility. "The continuance of Being is a continuous positing of the Eternal, or of nothing, a ceaseless process of becoming real in that which is not," as Oken puts it.[148] All of this affirms a *physio*centric continuum, rather than a bio- or ecocentric one, since there is no term that grounds the "ceaseless process" that is the realization of inexistence in existence, of time in temporality, or of contingency in necessity. Physiocentrism is a discourse of ungrounded materiality, rather than of living environments—even though the former does not exclude the latter but is its natural condition of possibility.

This line of reasoning connects with some of McCarthy's notes in one of the draft folders for his unpublished screenplay "Whales and Men." In one passage, for instance, he writes of a "ground of potentiality," a "foam of non-being," which "is time."[149] In the same folder he also writes something that is closely aligned with Oken's and Schelling's philosophies of nature: "All that becomes known becomes aborted (for the purpose of survival) from the numinal. It becomes a thing. The reality is not a thing but a no-thing."[150] This remark demonstrates once again the Platonic distinction between essence and appearance that McCarthy's second volume of the Border Trilogy refers to, and it also exposes the problem of "how every appearance has a kind of reality, but only insofar as it is split from within by what it does not reveal," as Brassier put it in a 2012 interview.[151] It is in this sense in which Oken's notion of an eternal time can be understood—namely, as the formless being that is not a thing but an undetermined "transcendental field" outside of human temporality, or a "no-thing."

The two generic instances of descendentalism (of a literary kind in McCarthy, and of a philosophical kind in Schelling and Oken) can be further brought in contact by making use of McCarthy's "favorite book,"[152] Herman Melville's *Moby-Dick* (1851), as an intermediary source text. Sanford Marovitz notes the similarities between Schelling's essay on freedom and *Moby-Dick* on terms of both content and form: "Schelling explains in very complex and paradoxical language the manner in which cosmic order and reason have been created from chaos and unreason; although disorder was then submerged, a residue remains below. Schelling depicts this with images of light and darkness—what would be for Melville 'love' and 'fright.'"[153] Marovitz goes on to note that "Schelling describes the 'primal longing' that eventuates in the creation of the cosmos as a longing which 'moves in anticipation like a surging, billowing sea.'"[154] The notion of a "primal longing" in Schelling's text is very much aligned with a passage from the end of McCarthy's "Whales and Men," in which one of the characters, Kelly, reads aloud a letter from John, the main protagonist of the screenplay. John concludes his speculations about a somewhat mystical oneness of the world of whales with the world of humanity by claiming that even though "the universe is cold and black and silent and our loneliness becomes us," there is still some other force that counteracts this silent indifference at the heart of the cosmos—or rather, this other force is precisely the descendental feature of ungrounding that is the only means by which the given formlessness can be met on equal terms: "I cannot believe that whales and men are alien beings. I believe we are arks of the covenant and our true nature is not rage or deceit or terror or logic or craft or even sorrow. It is longing."[155]

Both Melville and Schelling inquire into the evil ground of the good in the world, the irrational at the heart of the rational, and the raging madness at the root of scientific progress. All the same, both men are interested in, as Jason Wirth notes, "the renewal of art, philosophy, and religion" in terms of nature, "as each in their own way negotiates the madness and gravitational monstrosity at the heart of the imagination."[156] This claim arguably extends to the novelistic work of McCarthy, as Christopher Dacus implies. In his examination of *Blood Meridian* and the Border Trilogy, Dacus argues that "directly or indirectly," Schelling's diagnosis of "the correlation of freedom and evil seems to have found its way into McCarthy's thoughts," yet he misinterprets the German idealist's theory when he claims "that freedom is the source of evil."[157] According to Grant's reconstruction of *Naturphilosophie* as a consistent theme throughout Schelling's work, especially in terms of the logic of ungrounding, it would seem that while evil is a necessary possibility within the bounds of human freedom in nature, conversely (and in keeping with the doctrine of the "indivisible remainder" and the Platonic concept of matter), it is evil that is "the source of" freedom, not the other way round.[158]

The descendental practice of ungrounding, which in Melville, Schelling, Oken, and McCarthy is coterminous with the "longing" for "primordial nature,"[159] can also be evaluated in the context of Shaviro's reading of *Blood Meridian*. Like other critics, he notes that the *optical democracy* passage in McCarthy's text rejects what he calls "the prejudices of anthropocentric perceptions." But in accordance with this antianthropocentrism, which also seems to be almost a mantra among ecocritical approaches to McCarthy, Shaviro goes on to argue for the importance of the question of optics, or the notion of vision itself, in that passage:

> The eye no longer constitutes the axis of vision. We are given instead a kind of perception before or beyond the human. This is not a perspective *upon* the world, and not a vision that *intends* its objects: but an immanent perspective that already *is* the world, and a primordial visibility, a luminescence, that is indifferent to our acts of vision because it is always passively at work in whatever objects we may or may not happen to look at.[160]

These remarks lead me to the third key aspect I alluded to above: in McCarthy's fictions, as well as in Schellingianism, nature is depicted as being capable of self-analysis, which is but one feature of its self-organization, or *autopoiesis*.[161] Nature is self-sufficient in the sense that it does not need a further concept that would have to ground it. Furthermore, the orderly structuration of the natural is precisely a consequence of the formlessness that generates the phenomena and forms of life. However, this leaves us with a paradox: if nature is said to be all-encompassing, or if an existence outside of nature is ruled out in Schelling's ontology, it is thus necessary that nature be self-organizing—otherwise, there would be organization of nature that includes all of its aspects, spaces, and facets. Yet according to the descendentalism I have just outlined in Melville, Schelling, Oken, and McCarthy, the phenomena and forms of life in the world are, in fact, grounded in something—namely, the eternally productive formlessness, also called "time" by Oken and McCarthy. In turn, this formlessness is ungrounded, or not grounded in something that is not it. Nevertheless, if, according to Schelling, nature extends maximally, then both the grounded and the ungrounded portions of it would be immanent to it, or would inhere in the physiocentric continuum that is nature. It is important to note at this point that the "physio" in "physiocentric" refers to *phusis*, the Platonic conception of nature as material yet not necessarily corporeal.[162] Consequently, the issue of self-organization once again begs the question what exactly is meant by "nature," if one refers to its self-organization. What exactly is self-organizing when *autopoiesis* (literally: "self-making") occurs?

In their important work "Autopoiesis: The Organization of the Living" (1972), Maturana and Varela discuss two key notions that seem crucial to the question I just posed: they "make a distinction between 'autopoietic machines' and 'allopoietic machines,'" with the former being "simultaneously determined by, and directed towards production of, their own production," while the "productive processes" of the latter "are directed towards the production of something other than themselves."[163] Now, if "living systems" is really what they are interested in,[164] and if these systems are essentially what is self-organizing, then the question becomes what happens to those machines that do not organize themselves but instead are constitutive of machines other than themselves, and are also manufactured by machines other than themselves? Furthermore, what is the implied concept of nature here other than *existence*, as opposed to that which does not exist? As others have noted, Maturana and Varela's theory of *autopoiesis* and *allopoiesis*—meaning the self-production and reproduction of beings independent from a source that exceeds them, on the one hand, and, on the other hand, the production of individual beings from such a source—has had a strong impact on ecology, sociology, philosophy, and other fields, not least because the conception of nature in their theory is so very similar to that of ecocentrism or biocentrism. The theory has taken hold even though their rhetoric of machines is intended to obviate what they take to be the damaging thrust of "vitalism"—the "postulation of some peculiar organizational force."[165]

In fact, Maturana and Varela premise their discourse on the specifics of particular forms of life, or, rather, on the importance and irreducibility of that particularity, "the necessity of looking at the autonomous nature of living unities for the understanding of the biological phenomenology."[166]

What these passages already demonstrate, at the most basic level, is that although Maturana and Varela's essay represents "a prototype for the proliferation of theories of . . . self-organization within complex system theory over the following decades,"[167] the descendental notion of self-organization in Schelling, Oken, and McCarthy is fundamentally different on two counts. First, if the practice of *Naturphilosophie* takes place as a succession of events during which "nature is its own analyst,"[168] it is not necessarily grounded in the epistemological framework of the "biological phenomenology" of "living unities."[169] In metaphysical terms, the descendental perspective is based on physiocentrism, which is concomitant with the postulation of the incorporeality of material nature, rather than on biocentrism and its emphasis on the lived experience of single entities, or what Oken also calls "Singulars."[170] The second difference between the descendental standpoint and what Varela calls "the enactive alternative" to representationalist forms of cognitive science—which really is what he takes his and Maturana's work to be[171]—hinges on the issue of the bounds of self-organization itself. Indeed, if the objective is to inquire into the disposition of "an organization that is common to all living systems, whichever the nature of their components," and if Maturana and Varela's "subject is this organization, not the particular ways in which it may be realized,"[172] then it must be the case that what is meant by *autopoietic* and *allopoietic* machines is *that those processes exist*—as banal as that might sound.

In the context of the present discussion, however, the disposition of these machines to exist is not a banality but a crucial factor, since in Schelling, Melville, Oken, and McCarthy there is considerable interest in precisely those processes that might give rise to existing forms of organization (including the *autopoietic* machines constitutive of the processes of living systems) but that are not necessarily part of the latter. If, in Maturana and Varela, the prime example of an *autopoietic* machine would be a "living organism," an *allopoietic* machine would be an object that is not constitutive of itself, such as "a motorcar or a computer or a machine in a factory,"[173] to use the examples provided by Jeremy Dunham, Iain Grant, and Sean Watson in their discussion of enactivism. The implications of this distinction are fundamentally different in the philosophy of nature suggested by Schellingian *Naturphilosophie* and McCarthy's poetics. Neither Schelling nor McCarthy are merely interested in the biological (and partly nonbiological, or *allopoietic*) setup of self-organizing processes in the world, but also in the metaphysical basis for how that process came to pass in the first place. *Naturphilosophie* opposes the biocentric yet "non-animistic view" of the sort that Maturana and Varela promote, insofar as it does not premise its notion of self-organization and self-analysis on "living unities" or "observer[s]"[174] distinct from manufactured objects that are incapable of self-maintenance. Instead, it is based on a certain concept of the absolute reach of natural process, and the description of that absolute, in the last analysis, by itself—an idea toward which Maturana and Varela express their unmistakable contempt near the end of their study.[175]

If we transpose the concepts of *autopoiesis* and *allopoiesis* to what I have cast as the physiocentric continuum, both of them are relevant not just to the existing domains of living systems, but also to those domains of nature that are inexistent and hence are not alive—which brings us back to the logic of Schelling's and Oken's philosophies of nature, and, by the same token, their reiteration in the works of Grant, Brassier, and Negarestani. What I mean is the understanding of *the given as a formless productivity*, which gives rise to forms and phenomena in the world but which is partly independent of the latter. To use Maturana and Varela's terminology, nature consists of both *autopoietic* and *allopoietic* forms of organization, yet it is only the given dynamics of formlessness that are truly *autopoietic*, while corporeal and ideational forms and phenomena are constituted by both *autopoietic* and *allopoietic* machines. This accords with the Platonic argument that existence, or *that which is*, is preceded by and hence grounded in inexistence, or *that which is not*. In other words, disintegration is not the limit of self-organizing nature; it is the potency of the former that paradoxically gives rise to the latter. Reflecting this nonbiocentric yet animist account, McCarthy writes: "All matter is informed by spirit, and lacking this *sense* of being so, it is difficult to know where to begin with such a person and such a lack. I do not cease to be . . . in death, but only cease to explain myself."[176]

This line of reasoning leads me to the fourth key aspect in the Schellingian philosophy of nature that I want to highlight—namely, that nature cannot be locally restricted to its vital or ecological aspect (or any aspect, apart from its dynamic inclination to constantly evolve), even though it must include both aspects of life and the environment to be *what it is*.[177] Schellingianism conceptualizes matter in terms of forces rather than bodies, since for it materiality is not coterminous with corporeality. Yet neither is it constituted by some life force. At this point, Wirth's discussion of Schelling's easily misunderstood notion that nature is alive proves to be useful. Wirth clarifies:

> To say that the universe is alive is not to say that it is a living thing, the superorganism that contains all other organisms. . . . The life of nature holds

> together organically the living and dying of living things and the coming and going of nonliving things. This should not be confused with some élan vital or vitalism or life force (*Lebenskraft*). Life is not external to the living, coming into the living from afar.[178]

Therefore, according to a nonvitalist Schellingianism, the process of nature is itself contingent, yet it necessitates phenomena and forms of life that in turn enjoy a limited amount of freedom. Or, to use a phrasing that combines Schelling's theory and McCarthy's poetics, compared to the uninhibited freedom of nature's formless productivity that nevertheless adheres to irreducibly physical dynamics, the particular bodies and ideas that exist in the world are merely "shreds of matter" (*S*, 96).

Contrary to what many scholars have argued, therefore, Schelling's *Naturphilosophie* is not an organic philosophy in the sense that it is modeled on the image of biological organisms, or what Maturana and Varela call "living unities."[179] Naturephilosophy is not premised on any parallelism between life and nature as unified in terms of their respective organicity. Perhaps it is safe to say that to a certain degree the philosophy of nature *is* organic, insofar as it is enveloped in the self-organizing processes of nature; otherwise, that philosophy would not at all be *of* nature itself, which is inadmissible from a Schellingian stance. Yet according to this stance, "Nature in itself is a primordial *unconditioned* unity which divides itself into opposing forces in order to become manifest"[180] and, therefore, cannot be circumscribed by any one particular feature. Recalling Deleuze's closeness to Schellingianism here, mentioned by Grant and others, a good way of clarifying the issue of organicism hinges on what it is that should be opposed to a concept with foundational aspirations. If Deleuze (with and without Guattari) opposes the rhetoric of an all-too-rigid "Organization [in favor of] a body without organs" or the terminology of "an absolute immanent life,"[181] Schelling proposes in his early work *On the World Soul* (the German original of which had a subtitle that could be translated as *A Hypothesis of Higher Physics for the Explanation of the General Organism*) that "organization and life do not in themselves express anything enduring, but only a particular *form* of being, a commonality of many interconnected causes. The principle of life is thus merely the cause of a distinct *form* of being, not that of life itself."[182] What this suggests is that matter is not coextensive with corporeality, nor is Schelling's use of "the organic" synonymous with biological processes of organization and their environments.[183] Instead, materiality is at least partly isomorphic with an organization that, like "the understanding" in the *Freedom* essay, presupposes its "indivisible remainder" that is not it—namely, the inorganic, which is the given formlessness that is at the very root of all genesis of forms.[184] This is precisely what is argued by Grant, who stresses the importance of Schelling's theory of potencies (*Potenzenlehre*) in contrast to the transcendental logic according to which "nature is only the visible organism of our understanding," as Schelling puts it.[185] "In other words," Grant writes, "rather than a projection of organicism 'downstream' in the scale of nature, organization is a power or *Potenz* of the 'self-construction of matter.'"[186] Nature is indeed capable of organization, but the latter is merely *a potency*, rather than nature's identity.

Finally, then, I turn to the fifth key aspect I want to examine at this point: the reason why I have consistently referred to the centrality of the question of nature's *identity*, rather than its self-generating differences (which would be in accordance with poststructuralism in general and with Deleuze's ontology in particular) has to do with the fact that in the Schellingian and Okenian philosophy of nature it is identity, rather than difference, which gives rise to the genesis of forms in the world.[187] In a passage that might seem appalling for any post-1960s politically engaged cultural theory that would reject essentialism at all costs, Oken writes: "The identity of every Manifold [*Manchfaltigen*], or of all things among themselves and with the highest unity, is the *essence* [*Wesen*] of things. The limitation or definition of the Ideal is their *form*. Limitation is the Impartient of form [*das Formgebende*]."[188] It might be possible to take the word "essence" here as a cue to dismiss the Okenian theory of nature, given the term's often-cited static character in ontological but also political terms. Yet in the context of *Naturphilosophie*, and the direction this philosophy takes, as I have demonstrated in this chapter, it is precisely the opposite of stasis that characterizes Oken's as well as Schelling's accounts (one of the reasons why their theories of natural dynamics might be useful in the context of today's resurgence of metaphysical and nature-oriented investigation in the humanities, in general, not just in the circles of speculative realism or ecocriticism). In spite of Morton's objections, nature's identity qua essence is a becoming (*Wesen*), rather than some thing that is constantly reproduced. When Oken states that "there is only one essence in all things, the 0, the highest identity; but there are infinitely numerous forms,"[189] it is not some basic feature in things, objects, bodies, or ideas in the world that accounts for their identity, but precisely the opposite—namely, an irreducibility of formlessness intrinsic to all forms and phenomena. This logic, according to which all bodies and ideas in the world are in themselves devoid of any definite and unchanging identity rather than being defined by one, relays the specifics of the Schellingian account of identity, which is fundamentally different from Georg W. F. Hegel's version of it.

At this point, I want to clarify that in the present context of McCarthy's concept of nature's identity, the idea of a connection to German idealism in general, and to Schelling's thought in particular, is neither far-fetched nor unprecedented.[190] McCarthy has indeed taken note of German idealist philosophy to some extent. For instance, in his notes for "Whales and Men," he ponders the following metaphysical questions, revealing yet again the intertwined themes of the scientific and the religious in human cultural practices: "The noncommutative nature of reality is derived from our notions about time. Our skepticism regarding the reality of communal entities. . . . If the parts are other than their sum, whence this other? Hegel says the spiritual alone is the actual."[191] This fragmentary passage confirms McCarthy's interest in Hegel's *Phenomenology of Spirit* (1807), from which the latter sentence is, in fact, quoted, but it does much more than that.[192] To be sure, it seems to substantiate Steven Frye's argument that McCarthy's Border Trilogy channels Hegel's notion of "history as a record of the developing 'World-Spirit,' revealed through a 'World-Process' and 'Self-Realizing Idea.'"[193] Yet McCarthy's notion of history is arguably even more complex and discontinuous than the image Frye paints of it in evoking Hegel's philosophy: "History involves a meaningful and divinely ordained forward movement, a poetic narrative in which humankind is the hero in a sweeping process of positive movement."[194]

From the descendental point of view, Frye's reading stops short of the ways in which the divine is imbricated with the natural in McCarthy's later Western fiction. For example, when Frye concedes that the narrative of *The Crossing* never actually resolves in the manner suggested by the Hegelian vision of an all-encompassing history of the spirit, and that the "characters in the novel . . . never come to a complete and intellectually coherent understanding of the tale's purpose or meaning," he immediately adds that this does not obviate a Hegelian reading per se, since "that meaning [of the divine World-Spirit] remains a distant reality built into the assumption that there is order in the one tale and implied purpose in its forward movement."[195] That there is no final and harmonious meaning attained by *any* of McCarthy's characters in the second volume of the Border Trilogy—nor in any novel of his before *The Road*—is an indubitably correct assessment of the narrative dynamics of *The Crossing*. But the "distant reality" assumed by Frye in his subsequent inference does not necessarily have to be of a Hegelian kind. The fact that this realm is described as a real force (albeit in the background of the plot), and that it is said to be divine in the sense that it is not something that is itself sensibly intuitable, demonstrates an affinity also with the philosophies of Schelling and Oken.

Thus, even though it is not Schelling or Oken but Hegel who is mentioned in McCarthy's notes from the archive—which, as Dianne Luce and

Frye suggest, seem to have had an influence on the writing process of the Border Trilogy—I argue that in the context of the passages from McCarthy's novels as well as the archival material I have cited and discussed so far, it is in fact the Schellingian and Okenian conceptions of identity that are evoked in McCarthy's narratives. The ways in which nature is expressed in these narratives (namely, as a physical process all the way down) suggests a metaphysics that is much closer to Schelling's and Oken's account of nature's identity than it is to Hegel's. As Elaine Miller puts it: "What Hegel accomplished for the moral world, customs, social life, politics, and history . . . , Schelling first outlined for the physical world of nature. In nature, spirit should recognize itself."[196] This means that according to Schelling, it is only in nature that the spiritual should be able to examine its own existence.

But the difference between Hegel's and Schelling's respective notions of the spirit's identity—meaning the normative and the natural—goes even further than Miller would admit. As Grant suggests, Schelling's notion of identity is not merely congruent with Hegel's instantiation of the spiritual in the organic realm of the world, nor is it structurally similar to Hegel's account of the identification between two terms that are antithetical (as in the synthesis of two oppositional standpoints).[197] Clearly, Schelling's metaphysics harbors a concept of dialectics, but one that is understood as a thoroughly *physical* operation, not a merely formal or discursive one.[198] Moreover, as was already implied by the citations from Oken's *Elements*, what is meant by identity is not primarily that of single organisms or individuals, but always of nature as a whole. Thus, it necessarily remains undifferentiated and precisely *non-static*, other than in the harmonious syntheses of the Hegelian kind.

What this means is that the Schellingian notion of identity is not that of a particular subject, body, or idea in the world but that of "nature as subject" conceived of in the Spinozist terminology of "*natura naturans*" in contradistinction to the particularity of differential forms represented conceptually as the "*natura naturata*" (with the "natured" forms being the determined products of the overall process that constitutes the only givenness there is: meaning, nature's activity, its continuous production).[199] Grant puts it succinctly when he writes that "for Hegel, identity is latent in opposition, while for Schelling, 'bifurcation' is dynamic in precisely the sense that it is symmetry breaking. Identity, in consequence, is not the recovery or 'integration' . . . of differences, but causes difference to proliferate."[200] This definition, which casts identity not merely as the actuality of spirit in its capability of uniting diametrically opposed normative standpoints, but "as the contraction or retardation of the infinite in the finite, or productivity in the product," arrives at the concluding thesis concerning the activity of identity—namely, that "for Schelling, *identity differentiates rather than integrates*."[201] Identity is itself the formless production of differences. It is precisely that which cannot be intuited by the senses and, therefore, can be described as "the ultimate sightlessness of the world" (*TC*, 294), as the blind man intimates to John Grady in *The Crossing*.

Yet in addition to the work of Hegel and his idealist contemporaries Schelling and Oken, it is also important to note that the short citation from the archive sheds light on crucial areas of research within McCarthy scholarship in general, such as his conception of time, his notion of spirituality, and above all his relationship to the world of science. For instance, when he writes that "the noncommutative nature of reality is derived from our notions about time. Our skepticism regarding the reality of communal entities," he juxtaposes a mathematical notion with a humanistic concept.[202] The mathematical notion is that of "the commutative property of addition [and] multiplication," which dictates that in any equation that involves either adding or multiplying numbers, "changing the order of the numbers does not change the answer."[203] The humanistic concept is that of a community or group of people. Interestingly, McCarthy seems to compare the experiential account of time that passes in a seemingly continuous and linear fashion (with each single event following after the other—namely, insofar as time is said to be noncommutative, owing to the precise order of its events, or numbers) with "our skepticism" or distrust with respect to the idea of a community, before he adds a philosophically invested question and finally the direct reference to Hegel: "If the parts are other than their sum, whence this other? Hegel says the spiritual alone is the actual."

McCarthy's reasoning, the way he phrases this short but highly complex passage concerning the human notion of time, and his allusion to the metaphysical problem of the part and the whole—the one and the many, or the spiritual and the actual—can certainly be interpreted in many different ways. One of these interpretations, however, would emphasize the parallel between the words "noncommutative" in the first sentence, and "sum" and "other" in the question, since his open question is only inconclusively followed by the quote from Hegel's *Phenomenology*. In other words, if the parts of an equation or the individuals of a community (or, to use Oken's terminology, the singulars of material nature) are "other" than is suggested by their commutative relationship of integration and symmetrical distribution, then the question of the origin of this fundamental difference cannot be solved from a Hegelian standpoint of identity that integrates two oppositional terms or theses. Instead, it can be approached from the perspective of Schellingian and Okenian *Naturphilosophie*, in which "identity differentiates rather than integrates,"[204] and therefore provides an adequate account of the otherness between "the parts" and "their sum."

Having thus examined in detail the five key aspects of the Schellingian and Okenian versions of *Naturphilosophie*—namely, the dismissal of the supervenience of ontology upon ethics; the proposition of a descendental, rather than transcendental, stance toward the question "What is nature?"; the claim of a self-organizing and self-analyzing nature; the insistence of an unconditioned kernel, or formless disposition, within nature's processes; and the emphasis on the notion of a differentiating identity of natural process, rather than its ontological difference—I conclude this chapter by turning to the aspect of Schelling's philosophy that is indispensable in the parallelism I draw between literary and philosophical modes of nature's self-analysis. This is the role and concept of artistic practice both in Schelling and in McCarthy.

As I mentioned in chapter 1, McCarthy "believes that the novel can, in his words, 'encompass all the various disciplines and interests of humanity.'"[205] I suggested that this trust in the power of literary narrative can be seen alongside Emerson's stipulation that "all science has one aim, namely, to find a theory of nature,"[206] and that this suggests that McCarthy's understanding of literature's conceptual and methodological reach certainly includes the critical disciplines of philosophy and science. Along these lines, I argue that there is yet another connection that illuminates just how much the Schellingian (and, by extension, Okenian) concept of nature resonates with McCarthy's narrative expression of the latter. This connection is Schelling's understanding of what art actually is, and what characterizes its relationship to philosophical thought. In the last of fourteen lectures *On University Studies* (1803), he argues that "the philosophy of art is a presentation of the absolute world in the form of art."[207] Yet this is not to say that only because of philosophy can art be said to harbor "the absolute world," which is the unconditioned disposition of nature, since "forms of art are the forms of things in and for themselves," rather than forms that merely reflect or report about things and phenomena in the world.[208] Finally, this is so because, according to Schelling, these "forms of art" contain "sensuous images which have their origin in nature,"[209] a claim that seems to repeat his earlier and indubitably more famous claim that "the objective world is simply the original, as yet unconscious, poetry of the spirit; the universal organon of philosophy—and the keystone of its entire arch—*is the philosophy of art*."[210]

In what follows, I will show in more detail how McCarthy's novels can be described as narrative works of art that are not merely *about* nature but that are part and parcel *of* it, since by virtue of their being works of art, in terms of Schellingianism, they already implicate the undifferentiated and formless givenness that is the process of nature. Nevertheless, these novels are by necessity also about certain themes other than their entanglement with that givenness. Consequently, the next four chapters will have two chief objectives—namely, to explicate what is only implicated in McCarthy's fictions vis-à-vis nature's identity, and to show how that which is implicated is an explicative activity of nature itself.

[3]

"CLOACA MAXIMA": ONTOLOGICAL DECAY, OR THE DECOMPOSITION OF NATURE

Still the rain, eating at the roads, cutting gullies in the hills till they ran red and livid as open wounds. The creek came up into the fields, a river of mud questing among the honeysuckles. —Cormac McCarthy, *The Orchard Keeper*

I observe that nature is satisfied only by the greatest dominion of forms, and . . . that it delights in *arbitrariness* in the deathly management of decomposition.
—Friedrich W. J. Schelling, *On the World Soul*

OF ALL THE IMPLICATIONS in the foregoing outline of the physiocentric continuum for the inquiry into what sort of concept of nature is expressed in McCarthy's fiction, perhaps the most glaring is the discrepancy between his use of regionalism and the insistence that the realm of the absolute, the divine, and nature cannot be regionalized—that is, identified in terms of a particular feature. What this means is that the narrative strategy I discussed in chapter 1 is merely that: a strategy for storytelling, rather than an ontological claim about nature. Regionalism in literary terms is not necessarily coextensive with the philosophical move that Iain Grant has termed "regionalizing matter,"[1] the isolation of a specific feature or phenomenon of nature to count for all other phenomena. Typical variations of this isolation are vitalism, ecocentrism, and somatism, in which the question "What is nature?" is answered by referring either to life, the environment, or the body, respectively. Even though it may seem counterintuitive, McCarthy's use of literary regionalism as a means to an end turns out to be diametrically opposed to the reduction of *phusis* to merely one of its multiple facets, in terms of its metaphysical orientation. I have argued that McCarthy does not merely revere the subject matter of his fictions, as is customary in other regionalist writings, but that he also uses the time- and site-specific themes to speculate on that which is not temporally or locally bound at all or, better still, which is not determined by the temporal because "this ground of potentiality, this foam of nonbeing, is time" itself, as McCarthy notes in "Whales and Men."[2]

It could be objected at this point that as soon as one adapts a regionalist perspective, in the broadest sense of the term, there is no denying the bias of conceptual isolation on the author's part toward the question concerning nature's identity. Put simply, it is always from a certain perspective that this identity is conceived of and, consequently, delimited. In Husserlian parlance, the expression of that identity necessarily adumbrates only a demarcated part of nature, not nature as a whole. Yet what is so unique about McCarthy's style is not that his narrative speculations from the particular to the universal are irreducibly partial contemplations of the latter. Nor do his fictions suggest a concept of a nature as some thing that is whole. Instead, his refusal to engage in any overt critique of American exceptionalism by means of storytelling becomes the expression of an exceptionally American stance on metaphysical questions such as the inexistence of nature's identity as capable of differentiations. It also becomes the recoding of ethical views within a rigorously ontological register, rather than the categorization of the question "What is nature?" in line with the framework of practical reason (meaning the ethical translation and connotation of ontology).

The importance of locality, so crucial for any understanding of McCarthy's poetics, turns out to be an indispensable component of the fictional apparatus of writing nature. Yet it is only indispensable insofar as it is the starting point for the author's narrative contribution to what might be termed the culture of transnational speculation, including the juxtaposition of literature and philosophy regarding the issue of regionalization. Just how this juxtaposition is worked out by McCarthy is arguably best examined in terms of the rhetorical devices he uses in those novels that most extensively treat the issue of decay and disintegration: *The Orchard Keeper*, *Child of God*, and *Suttree*. This is because the problematic of structural overlay between literary and philosophical regionalism directly concerns the question of whether there is a metonymic relationship between a particular semantic unit of the regionalist text and the nature it refers to (in terms of isolating a specific feature of that nature), or whether there is a different kind of procedure at play that concerns both the poetic material of McCarthy's prose and its narrative structure. In other words, as soon as the investigation into the concept of nature takes account of the problem of writing nature, the question becomes how is it even possible, in line with a metaphysics that dictates the absolute yet ever-changing character of *phusis*, to differentiate between the expression *about* nature's identity and the expression *of* nature's identity, since—given that nature is identical to itself, and that each new feature of nature must be conceived of as a result of its potency—both expressions amount to one and the same thing.

It is here that I want to consider Schelling's distinction between the "*allegorical*" and what he calls, in following Samuel Taylor Coleridge, the "*taute-*

gorical" dimensions of mythography.[3] As Edward Allen Beach has stated, Schelling's later philosophy was very critical of the allegorical interpretation of Western myths—meaning "all attempts to treat mythical narratives as ciphers or signs for other things, whether for natural phenomena, for great historical events, for moral principles, for esoteric metaphysical doctrines, or whatever else"—whereas his "tautegorical" interpretation would hold that "the content of mythology is identical to its form."[4]

Schelling's distinction between these two modes of interpreting myths, but also between two ways of approaching narrative per se, is helpful in the present context because it is capable of resolving some of the problems I examined in chapter 1 (in particular those of periodization and ecocentrism). In fact, it is even more helpful than the postulation of Schelling's concept of the indivisible remainder, which, however, is linked by necessity to the notion of tautegory as *the self-presentation of nature's potencies in the form of myth*.[5] After examining the diverse and often mutually exclusive periodizations of McCarthy's oeuvre, I suggested in that chapter that McCarthy's evocation of every period of American literature from that of Ralph Waldo Emerson onward can be seen as a performance of McCarthy's concept of nature's differentiation and cross-fertilization—very close, indeed, to John Elder's theory of "culture as a process of decay."[6] Yet like so many other ecocritical perspectives on literature, this theory merely transposes the organic features of the corporeal environment onto that of literature, the obverse of which is the projection of juridical questions onto the realm of organic nature in the form of postulating the latter's "intrinsic rights" and "significance, independent of human utility."[7] Consequently, to say that the respective dispositions of natural and literary objects are isomorphic, insofar as both inhere in one and the same process that I have termed the physiocentric continuum, does not necessarily coincide with the metaphorical extension of the environment's living ground onto the development of literary creativity. Apparently, however, this is precisely what Elder proposes. While he is right in saying that "regrounding culture in the natural world involves a descent," this descent should not stop at metaphors that liken "the decay of old systems" in literature and ecology that supposedly need "fresh attention to the soil's process of regeneration."[8]

Schelling's own descendentalism offers a recontextualization of narrative art within nature's bounds that is yet more radical because it does not restrict those bounds to corporeality or to existence, but only to the genesis of forms that might or might not come into existence. In other words, Schelling's approach with respect to the relationship between the natural and the narrative is maximally extensive: to pit tautegory against allegory—that is, an understanding of narrative as a self-referring construction against a theory of mythography as referring to themes that lie outside the plot itself—is more than a critique of the allegorical interpretation of myth. It is a veritable subversion of its aspiration to serve as the key feature of mythography, while incorporating it within its own framework as merely one aspect of mythmaking among others. In the context of Elder's account of literary "culture as a process of decay," this means that the claim that literature is *just like* "the soil's process of regeneration"[9] is not to be entirely dismissed, since these kinds of rhetorical devices (metaphor, metonymy, simile, and many others) are part of the literary apparatus in the first place.[10] I suggest that especially in the work of McCarthy, the distinction between allegory and tautegory offers an insight that is simultaneously modest and bold, and that implicitly recalls many of the themes discussed in the previous chapter: while the allegorical reconsideration of literary culture and corporeal nature on the same plane is certainly valid up to a point, the tautegorical interpretation accounts for the self-sufficiency of that plane, which mythography, in particular, demonstrates. Along these lines, *allopoiesis* and *autopoiesis*—that is, the manufacture of what Oken calls singulars from a source that differs from them and the self-sufficient manufacture of these singulars themselves—are to be seen in a hierarchical fashion that entirely dismisses neither mythography's *allopoietic* (read: *allegorical*) character, nor its *autopoietic* (read: *tautegorical*) disposition; nor, indeed, does it merely restrict the self-organization of nature to that of existing forms and phenomena, meaning those within the organic realm.[11]

To an extent, then, I agree with those McCarthy scholars who find a profoundly allegorical character in his works. Owing to the spiritualist tendencies within the narratives—in the form of a recurrent biblical diction, for instance—and to the existentially dreamlike imagery propelled by his signature style of writing, McCarthy's depictions of American life seem to represent something other than the subject matter of which they speak.[12] However, more than merely conforming to the sociopolitical parameters of what Fredric Jameson calls "national allegory,"[13] McCarthy's fiction amounts to *natural* allegories that paradoxically point toward the features and consequences of an otherwise featureless givenness. Yet this is only one part of the poetic methodology underlying McCarthy's narrative speculations. The other, and arguably larger, part consists of McCarthy's idiosyncratic phrases and the frequent situations in his work that do not refer to anything else outside of the specificity of both the fictional world of the relevant novel and of McCarthy's oeuvre as a whole. Therefore, I argue that it is this tautegorical type of mythmaking in his work that both evokes nature's self-sufficiency by literary means *and* constitutes the condition of possibility for the allegorical type.

What I have termed *the givenness of formlessness* is what McCarthy hints at in those passages that have no logic or referentiality but their own. This is because that formlessness is *ungrounded*, instead of being grounded in that which is not it but to which it might refer. According to Daniel Whistler, the discrepancy between the allegorical and the tautegorical mirrors that between signification and symbolization, as "the symbol does not refer to a referent outside itself; it participates in and so shares its being with this referent. The symbol presents *itself* and does not refer to anything outside but itself" because it "is not just a copy of its referent; it is its referent."[14] The upshot of this with respect to McCarthy's fiction is that the self-referentiality of symbolism is the condition of possibility for the allegorical passages that metaphorically speak of literature's embeddedness in nature's processes—which are both organic and inorganic, continuous and discontinuous, and necessary and contingent. If one accepts the Schellingian claim of nature's all-encompassing reach, and if the literary phenomenon of referential language is therefore part and parcel of that reach, then even the allegorical interpretation of mythography (of the narrative's pointing to its outside) is based on the tautegorical interpretation insofar as every literary signification of its outside must, in the last analysis, be conceived of as an expression inside of, or inherent to, natural process. Whenever a natural allegory occurs in McCarthy's fiction, that occurrence is certainly an expression about the outside of the novel at hand. Yet in the sense that it is still within the physiocentric continuum that this outside is referred to, every one of these allegories is also an expression of nature itself. In terms of form and content, then, McCarthy's works arguably constitute a stylistic hybrid between allegory and tautegory, yet this hybrid gives tautegory the ontological priority because this approach to mythography is as ungrounded as the formlessness of "primordial nature" itself.[15]

This reasoning, then, expounds one of the ways in which McCarthy's fiction can be regarded as both narrative speculations *about* nature and expressions *of* its singular processes. This interpretation is in line with Schelling's tautegorical approach to mythology, according to which a "symbol . . . simultaneously represents a particular object or image as standing for some universal idea, while it also represents the universal idea, in turn, as being concretely active in some particular object or event."[16] Moreover, we have arrived at the point where it becomes imperative to address the dialectic of subtraction and construction, or of decomposition and composition, in McCarthy's work, simply because, according to contemporary Schellingian philosophies of nature, this process is constitutive of the emergence of phenomena. The concept of nature suggested by McCarthy's narratives harbors a notion of decay that is for the most part congruent with Elder's theory—at least in the sense in which McCarthy has recycled the modes of literary expression from transcendentalism to the present, as I argued in chapter 1. Yet in proposing the analogy between ecological and literary decay as a procedure of cross-fertilization, this theory is unable to account for the givenness of the formless. That is to say, from the perspective of *Naturphilosophie*, the dialectics of subtraction and construction that evokes ontological decay as "an infinite dissociation into ever new products"[17] must include existent forms but also inexistent properties of nature. Otherwise (and this is what Elder's account finally amounts to) what is achieved is merely a theoretical apparatus in the name of "the organicist correlation of growth and decay," as Eugene Thacker puts it.[18] The only way in which McCarthy's poetics goes beyond that correlation, and consequently achieves the inclusion of *that which is not* into his narratives about *that which is* turns out to be nothing other than the gradual development, from *The Orchard Keeper* onward, of a style that is entirely his own, by mixing the allegorical with the tautegorical in a way that narratively establishes a supervenience of the former upon the latter. *Pace* Lydia Cooper's argument that there is an "ethics of empathy"[19] in McCarthy's fiction, ethical questions about human conduct result from ontological questions about nature's identity.

In what follows, I examine first how decay is a motif in *The Orchard Keeper* in terms of the traumatic persistence of the inorganic in the organic realm of nature, second how *Child of God* treats of the dialectic of subtraction and construction in social as well as biophysical terms, and third how McCarthy combines the narrative dynamics between allegory and tautegory to recast the function of the narrator as a conductor of literary experiments that simultaneously construct and analyze the cathartic disintegration (both corporeal and incorporeal) of *Suttree*'s protagonist. Throughout, I provide evidence to support the claim that the notion of the tautegorical is especially helpful for such a reconsideration of decay in McCarthy's work.

PERHAPS THE MOST EFFECTIVE way to demonstrate in literature the continuously physical reality that goes from the inorganic—or, as Schelling writes, "anorgic"[20]—realm of nature to that of the organic, and from nonhuman to human nature, is through the narrative depiction of trauma. The reader of *The Orchard Keeper* encounters such depictions from the very first page onward: the prologue, which is set in a cemetery where three men are trying to cut through the stump of a tree, offers a depiction of the traumatic intervention of the inorganic into the realm of the organic. As one of the men laments, in the dialect of the Appalachian region where most of the novel's action takes place, the iron fence has "*growed all through the tree. . . . We cain't cut no more on it*" (TOK, 3). In chapter 1, I have argued that this prologue demonstrates both McCarthy's stance on the interaction between organic and the inorganic processes in the world and the ways in which he depicts this interaction in literature. I pointed out that the phrasing suggests that the fence (which has "*growed all through the tree*") has an agency and possibly even a minimal form of intentionality toward the tree: the object with which it is entangled. Yet this is not to say, as in Graham Harman's object-oriented approach, that the fence is an object that, like any other, is endowed with the capability of interacting with other objects in the world, in an endless regress of what Harman terms "sensual objects" of connection and mediation, and "real objects" of separation and withdrawal.[21] Nor is it enough, in ontological terms, to proclaim that this first scene in McCarthy's novel is a portrayal of "the sacrifice of a nonhuman living organism [the tree] for the benefit of dead humans,"[22] which again lets ethical questions prescribe the ontological or nature-philosophical inquiry.

The intertwinement of the iron fence and the organic tree can alternatively be interpreted as an allegory of the interpenetration of the organic and the inorganic realms of nature in general, yet not in maximally reciprocal terms (which would be akin to a Deleuzian interpretation) but in line with a minimal reciprocity that is premised upon the ontological priority of the inorganic material of the fence. What this means is that, while the materiality of the fence and that of the stump are necessarily engaged in a biochemical exchange on the molecular level, this exchange is based on the way in which the inorganic reaches into the organic realm in an experience that is fundamentally traumatic for the latter. "Trauma," Cathy Caruth writes, "does not simply serve as record of the past but precisely registers the force of an experience that is not yet fully owned."[23] Along these lines, the interaction between inorganicity and the living organism must be traumatic because the former precedes the latter as its history and because this supervenience of the organic upon the inorganic leaves the ecology of living systems (including humans and trees) almost as secondary additions to the formlessness of nonliving matter that is nevertheless capable of interaction. Yet this still begs the question of why the iron fence should be a candidate to represent the formlessness of matter, when it is actually only imaginable as a form—namely, that of a fence-like structure?

I suggest that it is imperative at this point to note the first example of the phrases I had in mind earlier when I pointed out the tautegorical counterpoint to McCarthy's clearly allegorical setting.[24] In this one-page prologue of his first novel, McCarthy has already introduced the adjective that will be one of the many tautegorical terms that define his style of writing: after the three men give up trying to saw through the stump, the older white man has a closer look at what is wrong with the "*damned old elum*" and shows the younger one: "*Here, said the man, look sideways here. See? He looked. All the way up here? he said. Yep, the man said. He took hold of the twisted wrought-iron, the mangled fragment of the fence, and shook it. It didn't shake. It's growed all through the tree, the man said*" (TOK, 3). What I am identifying here as a tautegorically qualified term (the first of several that will be identified in the course of my close reading of McCarthy's novels) is "*sideways*," a word that occurs again and again throughout McCarthy's oeuvre, and that more often than not depicts or predicts scenes of violence or despair.[25] To be sure, the word "sideways" is semantically very rich. For instance, it can denote looking in a certain direction or in a particular way, but it can also describe a baleful situation in which "things go sideways." In the case of the prologue, I argue, this only ostensibly insignificant term is the first occurrence in McCarthy's fiction of what Schelling would call a *tautegorical* form of narration: the description of a perspective on a specific object, or a character's movement in a particular scene, that is accordingly not meant to connote anything outside of the space in which it is uttered or written. It is not an allegorical term in the sense in which "the soil's process of regeneration"[26] is metaphorically charged to signify the correlation between literary tradition and organic nature. Rather, "sideways" is an example of symbolic language, the function of which is immanent to the system in which it appears (the fictional world of McCarthy *tout court*). Nonetheless, this tautegorical interpretation does not ignore the semantic content of that world—far from it. Rather, it is a different construction of meaning as it is in the allegorical mode. The chief characteristic, in fact, is the self-sufficient or ungrounded character of the term's identity vis-à-vis its semantic context. In the case of the word "sideways," this means that the term does not function according to a framework of resemblance (as in "the fertile ground of literary periods is like that of organic nature") but instead according to the notion of identity that I outlined in the previous chapter. The self-identical disposition of tautegory is conceptually separate from, yet generative of, the differentiated nature of allegory. Along the lines of Schelling's, Oken's, and McCarthy's generally Platonic ontology, the manifestation of beings in the world is necessarily a retardation of original forces, a deviation of *that which is* from *that which is not*. This process of deviation, in fact, is regarded as the obverse of the subsistence of *that which is not* in *that which is*, of inexistence (or infinite potency) in existence (or finite necessity), and this is why the seemingly nondescript word "sideways" carries so much more semantic weight than a mere depiction of a person's angle of vision on an object like a tree stump.

As will become clear during this chapter and subsequent analyses, for McCarthy, nature essentially behaves "sideways" and by necessity produces more or less deviant creatures, both human and nonhuman. Arguably, then, even in those passages that are not overtly speculative (meaning that they do not contain allegorical statements about the disposition of nature's dynamics in the way in which Elder's theory of decay likens literary cross-fertilization to that of ecology), McCarthy's narratives conceive of natural process as, first, the generation of forms through the deviation and sideways movements of bodies and ideas and, second, the condition of possibility for such deviant generation—not just an identity of process and product, but also one of process and condition. This also explains why from the start of his career, McCarthy places such importance on the locality of his novels, and how a genre like the Southern gothic is inextricably linked to McCarthy's ontological vision: Appalachian culture and the narrative expression of that culture in the form of the Southern gothic is the literary approximation of retardation and sociobiological conditioning par excellence. The generic figure of the "idiot child," or "retard," in prominent novels of that form is just one of the many features that make it seem the ideal candidate (or, rather, ideal literary environment) for a rendering of a speculative philosophy of nature by means of narrative.[27]

Cooper has noted that McCarthy's Southern "novels combine a horror-drenched and heavily allegorical style with historically rooted commentary on social ills, such as issues of race, class, urbanization, and industrialization, to bring into focus repressed social anxieties."[28] While this assessment certainly rings true, it is also possible to argue, in light of the ontologically determined conceptual pair of the allegorical and the tautegorical, that McCarthy's allegorical style is conditioned in terms of the sideways tautegory specific to Eastern Tennessee, to develop a well-nigh ontological narrative that outlines nature's decomposition as a proliferating process. Thus, in allegorical terms, it seems as if the poverty-stricken Southern anxiety provides the most fertile ground for the fictional construction of such a concept of nature. The lived experience of Appalachia—as a culture and a spatial practice, in geocritical terms—makes it the ideal framework for a concept of human and nonhuman nature as a continuously deviant production of bodies and ideas. Tautegorically speaking, however, McCarthy's regionalism generates meaning in terms of the Schellingian mythology of nature precisely because its idiosyncratic phrases and literary tableaus are expressions of the relentlessly grim Southern realities.

In accordance with McCarthy's "poetics of descent,"[29] I take it that the allegorical embeddedness of human culture in nonhuman nature, which in his works is contextualized in a tautegorical frame of narration, is routinely expressed by scenes of trauma: the convergence of organic and inorganic material (that is, the exemplification of how the formless origin of living matter is recapitulated by its contact with nonliving objects, such as the iron fence at the cemetery) is always a violently unrepresentable one. The same aesthetic pertains to the way in which geological time makes itself felt in the anxiety-ridden environs of the South. This is why a general theory of what Nick Land calls "geotraumatic tension," along the lines of the process of retardation throughout nature, seems more useful than a merely ecocritical account of "ecological holocaust."[30] That is, in terms of the philosophy of nature that McCarthy's prose evokes, "the collapse of the earth as we know it lurks [not only] in the near future, . . . spurred by our fossil-fuel-driven, hurry-up economy of fire,"[31] but is already premeditated in the past as the geotraumatic experience that can never be fully recovered, never "fully owned."[32] In other words, the psychic trauma of individuals and the ecological, as well as economical, disasters on earth appear to be premised upon a much older and more encompassing trauma that is remembered unconsciously; "a planetary trauma" that "is an ongoing process, whose tension is continually expressed—partially frozen—in biological organization."[33] In contrast to the psychosexual tension induced in the individual by what Sigmund Freud calls the "primal scene,"[34] the "geotraumatic tension" that Land outlines, and that Schellingian *Naturphilosophie* suggests as well, is related to the connection between *natura naturans* and *natura naturata* (with the latter being the "partially frozen" instances of the "ongoing process" of the former—that is, of nature's productivity itself, its formless givenness). Glossing Schelling's Platonic notion of the "world-soul," Sean McGrath writes: "The soul of the world is a drive to self-manifest which is universally distributed in nature. It presupposes a material upon which it works even if it itself is not bound to any particular matter. It is not a determinate drive, not sex drive, nor is it associated with any other qualitative determination; it is, Schelling adds, a *qualitas occulta*."[35] Nevertheless, in coupling some of the terms of Freudian psychoanalysis with Gilles Deleuze and Félix Guattari's geophilosophy, Land's theory concerns "the descent into the body of the earth" that "corresponds to a regression through geocosmic time."[36]

In the remainder of this section, I examine how the trauma of the earth and its impact on the human psyche are portrayed in the Appalachian environments of deviation in McCarthy's first novel, and how this perspective is inclusive of, yet ontologically more extensive than, the ethical approach that centers on the correlation between literary sophistication and organic complexity—a relation that is almost identical to that of the tautegorical with the respect to the allegorical. This, in fact, is why *Naturphilosophie* is capable of ungrounding ecocentrism's answer to the question of "What is nature?": it addresses that question against the backdrop of a theoretical ontology rather than one of a practical ethics.

After the prologue of *The Orchard Keeper*, the constitutive deviation inherent in any phenomenon that exists is already evident in the depiction of the landscape near the place where "the community called Red Branch" is located:

> In the relative cool of the timber stands, possum grapes and muscadine flourish with a cynical fecundity, and the floor of the forest—littered with old mossbacked logs, peopled with toadstools strange and solemn among the ferns and creepers and leaning to show their delicate livercolored gills—has about it a primordial quality, some steamy carboniferous swamp where ancient saurians lurk in feigned sleep. (*TOK*, 11)

The ornamental prose and its gothic imagery affirm the narrator's conviction of how transient the existence of these organic forms is, compared to the geological time of natural history. Rather than just showing the bond between humanity and animality, which the later novels of the Border Trilogy also depict at great length, this short but significant passage likens the quasi-posture of the "mossbacked logs" to that of fish whose "gills" are in motion to keep them alive; meaning that it is not only *intra*connections among the species of the animal world that the narrative is concerned with, but also *inter*connections across all phenomena.[37] The "primordial quality" of this scene alludes to the ancient time in which this forest in Appalachia was not yet existent—a time that is still implicitly present in the forest's "steamy carboniferous swamp." However, the inexorable link between all of these phenomena in the process of natural cross-fertilization is not restricted to the organic realm of the Tennessean flora and fauna. On the contrary, the next paragraph of the novel describes how the Red Branch community consists of

> a dozen jerrybuilt shacks . . . , squatting over their gullied purlieus like great brooding animals rigid with constipation, and yet endowed with an air transient and happenstantial as if set there by the recession of floodwaters. Even the speed with which they were constructed could not *outdistance the decay for which they held such affinity*. Gangrenous molds took to the foundations before the roofs were fairly nailed down. (*TOK*, 11, emphasis added)

Thus, in these two passages, the author manages to define the basic premises for his aesthetics of decay. In the first instance, the organic phenomena of the natural process, such as logs lying in a forest, already allude to the time and space from which they emerged—namely, a time when ancestral creatures such as "saurians" were still alive, and an imaginary space where they are still lurking. In the second passage, even manmade structures like the shacks of Red Branch are compared to animals that seem to be deformed in grotesque ways, yet whose very "demeanor" betrays their fleetingly short life expectancy, the time they have to be that which they are before the process of putrefaction returns them to the forest and the "obscene waste matter" of inorganicity (*TOK*, 39). McCarthy's anthropomorphism is particularly interesting here in his mention of the shacks' supposed "affinity" for their own downfall, effectuated by the "gangrenous mold" nested in their very foundation. Yet consider how, after the depiction of the timberland ecology and of the moldy architecture of Red Branch, McCarthy's reference to its inhabitants continues the descendental poetics in which the setting of East Tennessee seems to be both a stand-in for the whole of nature and a mythographical expression of nature's process itself: "They came and went, unencumbered as migratory birds, each succeeding family a replica of the one before and only the names on the mailboxes altered, the new ones lettered crudely in above a rack of paint smears that obliterated the former occupants back into the anonymity from which they sprang" (12). Organic life, manmade architecture, and human community—each of these domains within nature seems to be part of a larger "dynamic community,"[38] which is arguably best described along the lines of what I have termed the physiocentric continuum, in which all phenomena emerge out of the formless "anonymity" to which they return indefinitely.[39]

I mentioned in the introduction one of the buildings (the Green Fly Inn) in the surroundings of Red Branch—or rather, the destruction of that building. The local folk regularly meet and drink there, and their community is founded upon a special kind of "solidarity," as the narrator remarks, "a solidarity due largely to its precariousness" (*TOK*, 13). John Grammer notes the significance of the Green Fly Inn for the population of Red Branch, but also the metaphorical richness of McCarthy's wording at the beginning of the novel—the connotation of which is related not just to the particularity of the region but also to the universal "reality of communal entities" as such:[40] "The interdependence of 'solidarity' and 'precariousness' is an essential idea for McCarthy; for him it seems that the only sort of permanence ultimately available to us is one based upon an intense awareness of impermanence; life is possible only in a continual and more or less cordial dialogue with death."[41] Arguably, what Grammer claims here in existential terms (that is, in terms of human temporality) can be extended in terms of the descendental ontology I have delineated above. The "dynamic community"[42] of the physiocentric continuum is what is at stake in McCarthy's delineation of the drinking folk at the Green Fly Inn precisely because of the continued possibility of the state of things (like temporarily functioning communities in a tavern) to be ungrounded or subverted by revealing yet deeper, or ontologically prior, states of being. While Grammer is right in suggesting that McCarthy's narratives are always in a "more or less cordial dialogue with death," it is imperative to recognize that this dialogical relationship extends, formally, to that between ground and unground and, narratively, to that between living and nonliving entities, and to that between them and their undoing.

This relationship on the level of the physiocentric is evidenced also by the foreboding of the tavern's eventual dissolution by fire from a moldy scaffolding into the "imponderable archeological phenomenon" comprised of "a single sheet, shaped in ripples and flutings, encysted with crisp and blackened rubble, murrhined with bottlecaps" (*TOK*, 48), when one of the drinkers, Ef Hobie, joins those who have gathered outside on the wooden porch beneath which all the litter from previous nights is piled up in an accumulation of dust and empty beer bottles. As he does so, what the country folk hear is "*a long creaking sound like a nail being pulled and again the sharp detonation of strained wood giving away. There followed a dead and immobile silence during which the faces searched from one to the other uncertainly. A few began to rise and mill about, still not saying anything*" (24). After a few moments, the wooden planks give way to fall down into the pit, and the men anxiously try to get inside the inn so as not fall down into the pile of dirt and broken beer bottles: "*There ensued a single rush as of so many marionettes on one string being drawn in violent acceleration toward the door while above the noise of their retreat the joists popped like riflefire*" (ibid.). Some unlucky ones, though, do not make it inside and indeed fall down into the pile, in an image that allegorically signifies the descent of the organic to the inorganic realm of nature:

> *Now from the knot of men clawing at the door single figures began to be sucked away in attitudes of mute supplication one by one down the dangling incline of the porch, gaining momentum among leaping cans and bottles, and dropping at last with wild cries into the pit below. A few caught at the rails and dangled there with stricken looks eying their fellows rocketing past into the night.* (25)

To be sure, this scene could be interpreted as just one irregular event among many in the long history of drunken mayhem that has taken place in that particular tavern in Eastern Tennessee. Yet McCarthy's phrasing suggests otherwise, because the scene in fact is the second instance in which the author couples allegory with tautegory by introducing another one of his trademark notions that, from that point on, occur frequently throughout his oeuvre: what I mean here is the religious term "*supplication*," which denotes the gesture involved in some forms of prayer—in particular, when someone asks for a favor or mercy for him- or herself or a beloved one.[43] Typically, supplication is the act of begging for help in a desperate situation, a form of communication that is more often than not directly addressed to God. In the passage cited above, the term "*mute supplication*" arguably signifies that the tavern's drunkards represent the whole of humanity. Their poses are the way in which humans beg for mercy in the face of the nonhuman, formless abyss that awaits them and that, ultimately, is one of the causes of their emergence in the first place. In terms of the formal mixture of allegory and tautegory, I hold that the figure of the supplicant can be readily described as partaking in both of the interpretations of myth that I outlined at the beginning of this chapter. This figure (so crucial to the spiritualist side of McCarthy's poetics) is one of the most striking images of the allegorical—namely, the metonymical depositing of many people's grief or sins onto the shoulders of a single human being. Of course, the Bible's paradigmatic example of this is Jesus Christ, who begs for mercy for himself and for forgiveness in the name of humanity at the time of his crucifixion. But the gesture of the supplicant also can be seen as a tautegorical figuration: the way in which the notion of supplication, like that of being sideways, constitutes one of the many idiosyncratic poetic markers that McCarthy uses to establish a consistency or continuity that runs throughout his oeuvre. In that sense, the notion of supplication both has religious connotations and refers to itself, and the world immanent to McCarthy's fiction *tout court*.

The moral overtone of this term is not accidental, and indeed this is one of the ways McCarthy's work has consistently referred to the phenomenon of conscience within the human psyche. The fact that the terror of inevitable descent is poetically coupled with the idea of not only begging for one's own life but also for the lives of others reveals one of the ways in which the question of ethics is a result of that of ontology in McCarthy's poetics. It brings to light how McCarthy's narratives demonstrate that the issues of the normative realm within human conduct are posterior to, or an effect of, their biophysical emergence as well as their decline. I come back to the term "supplication" (and the term "supplicant"), particularly in the discussions of the Border Trilogy in chapters 4 and 5. For the moment, I want to focus on my working hypothesis that McCarthy's use of supplication, or begging for mercy or asking a superior being (God) for help, is inextricably linked to his understanding of human conscience, which does not merely refer to the ability to act according to a normative code. In the ontological terms proposed by Schelling's discussion of the human soul in *The Ages of the World* and reconstructed by Grant etymologically and vis-à-vis the German idealist's concept of nature, conscience can also be understood in the sense of a "co-science" (*Mitwissenschaft*) with the nonhuman (or rather, pre-human) past: "Drawn from the source of things and akin to it, the human soul has a [co-science (*Mitwissenschaft*)] of creation."[44] Grant's ingenious recasting of

Schelling's notion of *Mitwissenschaft* in the context of the nature of human conscience suggests that Schelling does not seem to distinguish here between the practice of scientific inquiry (particularly in the physical sciences) and the moral conduct of human beings. Both activities can be deemed to be a witnessing of creation itself. In Schelling's terminology, the capacities to think scientifically and morally have a "point of indifference" (*Indifferenzpunkt*)—that is, they have a common nature, which is their disposition to generate accounts of, or "commentaries" on, the genesis of forms.[45] As Grant puts it, even the discussion of philosophical treatises is a commentary in this sense of *Mitwissenschaft*: "Commentary, therefore, is . . . a *collaborative* ideating, a species of 'co-mentation,' not merely with regard to 'meanings,' but rather to the *objects* of thought. [It] grounds collaborative thinking in the nature of thought and its objects."[46] According to this understanding of Schellingianism, conscience partakes in the reiteration of God's creation, in parallel, not in opposition, to the making intelligible of natural objects by the empirical sciences. Furthermore, in terms of literary inquiry, the commentary on a text like *The Orchard Keeper* is to be seen as similar to the interpretation of natural objects and ethical practices by the empirical sciences and religious practice.[47] But this similarity is apparent not because, after postmodernism, all inquiry is a hermeneutical activity, but because every literary commentary and scientific experiment is as much a co-mentation with the creation of the world as is the phenomenon of human conscience. While I elaborate on these parallels below, in the present context of the relaying of geotrauma onto the human psyche, Schelling's philosophy assumes that every instance of this co-science results in a necessarily traumatic experience. The narrator's further description of the descent of the Green Fly Inn's porch in *The Orchard Keeper* certainly testifies to that aspect:

> *The porch had swung out and downward and now tottered for a moment in the strength of a single two-by-six before it too snapped and the whole affair slewed away with a great splintering sound. The figures clutching at the rails began to turn loose their holds, coming away by ones and twos like beetles shaken from a limb, and the entire wreckage descended in a slow tableau of ruin to pitch thunderously into the hollow. The atmosphere inside seethed with an inchoate violence.* (TOK, 25)

As before in the novel, human beings are likened to animals in their moments of descent: this, once again, pertains to the allegorical aspect of a passage like the disintegration of the porch and its descent into the pit of empty bottles from past nights at the tavern. Conversely, the phrase that describes the final fall of the remaining men and wooden planks—"*the entire wreckage descended in a slow tableau of ruin*"—contains an expression that not only allegorically points to the descendental metaphysics that it connotes but also tautegorically describes the whole section within the novel, which indeed is a veritable literary "tableau of ruin." That expression first denotes the referential markers of what it describes—drunkards falling down into a pit of beer bottles. Second, it connotes the gothic imagery of descent and its philosophical implications, including the Schellingian *Naturphilosophie* with which I have just connected it. Third, the expression refers to itself and the immanence of its poetic function within the novel, but also within the oeuvre of McCarthy. This last aspect, though, is not to be understood as an instance of literary self-reflexivity along the lines of postmodern fiction, but as a tautegorical instance, in the sense that the phrasing is itself a co-mentation of its creation as a literary object (a literary tableau) and, eventually, a form of poetic conscience (*Mitwissenschaft*) of natural creation as such. What I mean by this is that the tautegorical function of the phrase "tableau of ruin" is textually immanent, yet due to its self-reference—and, by the same token, its *autopoiesis*—it repeats the immanence of nature in general, and its past in particular. Insofar as there is no outside of the realm of nature, the capacity of self-analysis is equally part of that realm and occurs in just such tautegorical instances of (not only) literary expression. The trauma of the earth is thus a fundamentally "*slow*" and therefore irrecoverable process, yet it creates an "*atmosphere*" of "*inchoate violence*," just as the disintegration of the inn's porch is described by the narrator in another instance of regionalism as a narrative strategy.[48] Finally, we need to take into account the fact that McCarthy italicizes the whole passage to mark it as the memory of Kenneth Rattner. In light of the Schellingian account of the soul as being capable of the co-science or co-knowledge of nature's productivity, it is not surprising that this metaphorically charged passage in McCarthy's first novel, suggestive as it is of the philosophical conceptualization of historical thinking, is itself an example of a single individual's memory of a past incident.

As in Schelling's philosophy of nature, the following discrepancy seems to be key to McCarthy's poetics: on the one hand, there is a singular aspect to the human soul, which is the ideational co-creation of the universe through the sophistication of normative structures and forms of inquiry that are markedly different from the animal world (namely, science, philosophy, art, and religion); on the other hand, the human soul and, therefore, the people to which particular souls supposedly belong are still part of the continuous realm of *phusis*, like other biophysical organisms, precisely because the abovementioned forms of inquiry are the necessary expressions of the diverse processes within the *autopoietic* system that is nature, given its all-encompassing reach. Taking philosophy as a particular example of such an inquiry that remains embedded within the physical realm, or the cultural activity of conceptualization in general, it could be argued that, the discrepancy that has the human soul both be capable of the *Mitwissenschaft* of the world's creation and, at the same time, be a part of that creation is displayed in the existence of nature as a simultaneously preconceptual and conceptual realm. If the capacity of conceptual thinking is the result of the preconceptual realm of biophysical processes of the body, for instance, and if nature is still said to encompass the capacity and its cause, then nature exists both prior to its concept and only as that what it is insofar as it includes conceptual thinking. It does not *depend* on its partial capture in thought's representation simply because it ontologically exceeds thinking; yet according to the thesis of its wholly immanent process, it must also be the case that nature *includes* thinking as one of its self-reflexive activities, as a reiteration of its preconceptual ones.[49]

This is why, in particular sections within his novels, McCarthy's narrators frequently describe the protagonists and antagonists as though their intentions, thoughts, and even personal traits, were simultaneously both their own and foreign to them. One of these sections can be found in *The Orchard Keeper*, when Marion Sylder finds Rattner sitting in his car, after drinking at the roadhouse:

> The face stared at him with an expression bland and meaningless and Sylder groped for some, not cause or explanation, but mere association with rational experience by which he could comprehend a man sitting in his car as if conjured there simultaneously with the flick of light by the very act of opening the door. The mouth stretched across the lower face in a slow cheesy rictus, *a* voice said: You goin t'wards Knoxville?—A strained octave above normal, the pitch of supplication. (*TOK*, 33, emphasis added)

Sylder is repelled by Rattner's appearance. However, what is particularly of interest here is not the tattered and imposing figure of the man, an unwanted and almost abject passenger, but rather the way in which the narrator describes the situation. It is not the person Rattner who looks at Sylder but "the face . . . bland and meaningless," and it is not the person who speaks to the driver, but "a voice" that asks, in a typical Southern drawl, whether Sylder is "goin t'wards Knoxville" in "a strained octave," which the narrator terms "the pitch of supplication." I argue that this passage reveals just how ambivalent McCarthy's view of supplication really is, with respect to its semantic relationship to the idea of the human soul as the capacity to have a conscience. The geotraumatic tension of the nonhuman world paradoxically finds its most elaborate determination in the fact that all humans—whether a hero-like figure such as John Grady in *All the Pretty Horses* or a drunkard like Rattner—are capable of asking for help in desperate times. This is because it is not the individual human being that is responsible for the pitch in which the question is uttered, but rather the mouth, the voice, and the face. The nondescript facial expression also reflects the nonhuman origin of the tension that is eventually released in the supplicant's question, and Sylder's intuitive animosity toward the hitchhiking apparition clearly points toward, and even foreshadows, a threat that is to come: "It was not presentiment that warned Sylder to get shed of his guest but a profound and unshakable knowledge of the presence of evil" (*TOK*, 33)—an evil so primal that it transcends the filthy appearance of his new passenger and, in line with the archaic diction, almost suggests that what is at issue here is the notion of evil's using Rattner as a vessel, as if the person's face, mouth, and voice express the nonhuman trauma of the earth itself.[50]

What we need to remember about the Schellingian context of evil as a primordial and necessary force in the dynamic process of nature is that not only repulsive individuals like Rattner are objects of what may be called nature's ventriloquism, but that all bodies and ideas in the world of McCarthy implicitly acknowledge the tension that evolves from an evil ground to its eventual diversification in the form of the human soul. It is this diversification in the course of natural production that entails a constant relationship of the product to its irrecoverable genesis. It is in this sense that I interpret the frequent reminders from McCarthy's first novel onward of the natural trajectory from the inorganic (read: *evil*) to the organic (read: *good*) and back again. This is why the organic landscape is described as supposedly contaminated by inorganic materials, above all metal components such as iron fences, cars, and the "sounds" of iron objects clanking against one another. Rather than a critique of "ecological holocaust,"[51] the image of this physiocentric continuum presents a deeply conflicted, yet entirely natural, process of cross-fertilization between organic and inorganic phenomena.[52] Rather than an elevation of "human communion," nature's capability of supplication is the most advanced expression of the "dynamic community" of forces:[53] it is the very posture in, or gesture by, which nature repeatedly witnesses, through the human vessels of individual persons, its traumatic genesis of forms.

As regards the cross-fertilization of the organic and the inorganic, consider the following exemplary passages from the novel. When the narrator gives an account of how Arthur Ownby—the old recluse who is also called Uncle Ather—goes to bed one evening, we read that: "He fell asleep to the water and *metal sounds of the rain* runneling over the tin and sluicing through the gutterpipe, the rapid slash of it in a gust of wind and the fine mist spraying his face through the bellying screen. The oaks stirred restlessly, low admonitions, shhh" (*TOK*, 65, emphasis added). Besides the modernist description of the trees moving in the wind, it is remarkable that a literary image of tranquility in solitary nature, as in the manner of Henry David Thoreau, is importantly qualified by the fact that the rain transmits sounds that do not seem "natural" in the sense of the term that connotes the peaceful and hence undisturbed image of an Edenic habitat. Even in the morning, the birds that are already awake confirm what was only suggested in the evening, that the inorganic realm participates in that of organic nature: "Jays were in the blackoaks mornings and the grackles had come back, great flocks of them bending the trees, their feathers glinting dark metal colors and their calls harshly musical, *like a rusty swing*" (TOK, 65, emphasis added). Much later in the novel, there is a season of rain, so the inhabitants of Red Branch need to brace themselves in their flooded environs, which are allegorically likened to the traumatic effects of nature's dynamics: "Still the rain, eating at the roads, cutting gullies in the hills till they ran *red and livid as open wounds*. The creek came up into the fields, a river of mud questing among the honeysuckles" (173, emphasis added). Like the beginning of the narrative, with its description of the moldy shacks of the small settlement, this passage recalls the antecedent natural history of the land where the East Tennesseans now live—a plot that seems susceptible of disintegration by the metallic sounding rain, just like the porch of the Green Fly Inn was predestined to descend into the pit of waste, and the corrosive effects of the iron fence in the cemetery scene in the novel's prologue: "Great scaly gars from the river invaded the flats, fierce and primitive of aspect, long beaks full of teeth, ancient fishes survived unchanged from Mesozoic fens, their yellowed boneless skeletons graced the cracked clay-beds later in the season where the water left them to what querulous harridans, fishcrow or buzzard, might come to glean their frames, the smelly marvel of small boys" (173). This mythographical blurring of the reality of floods in the Southeastern region and the nearly imaginary survival of "ancient fishes" from a prehuman past arguably mirrors the communion between organic and inorganic products of nature that can be detected in the narrator's descriptions of rain. McCarthy here formally repeats the motif of cross-fertilization of nature's products in the unlikely, yet ingenious, juxtaposition of literary realism with a veritably Romantic mythography.

This earthly trauma is recounted yet again when Sylder drives his car into a creek: "He heard the motor building speed and then there was a sudden explosion, a doglike yelp, followed by a suspension of all sound, a momentary eclipse of animation even to the water and his own breathing" (TOK, 99). Note that besides the temporary cessation of the water's motion and Sylder's breath, the crashing of the car into and through the formerly tranquil spot in the woods evokes a kind of communicative relation between these different forms, narratively facilitated through an anthropomorphic language that, as in the earlier sections, is nevertheless grounded metaphysically in a tautegorical framework: "The trees at his left leaped, wild with light, went out again. There came an eruption of *limbs cracking, splitting, of wrenched metal screaming like slate*, a heavy and final concussion like a steel drum bursting. Silence again through which filtered a thin and diminishing rain of glass" (99, emphasis added).

Yet apart from the multiple contact zones of organic and inorganic nature, sometimes reflected on a formal level in the hybrid style that combines realism and Romanticism, there are also instances in which the impressions of human temporality are exceeded by, or point toward, a prehuman past that is somehow carried over into the present. In a passage in which Ownby remembers how he climbed down the water tank and (unknowingly) saw Rattner's corpse for the first time, we read: "Coming back he glanced down at the water again. The thing seemed to leap at him, the green face leering and coming up through the lucent rotting water with eyeless sockets and green fleshless grin, the hair dark and ebbing like seaweed" (TOK, 54). To Erik Hage, this description is "suggesting a corruption of both the natural and human worlds."[54] In contrast, I argue that it is evocative of a commonality between human and nonhuman nature, in line with the earlier passage about the dormant "saurians" (11) in the forest near Red Branch, as if this state of putrefaction is not only a ceasing but also a becoming of sorts and alludes to a pool of a strange dynamics beneath the earth's surface. It also recalls McCarthy's fondness for Melville's most famous novel by comparing the corpse's hair to "seaweed."[55]

What is more, McCarthy's aesthetics of decay is not merely determined by the natural history of biological formations and their entanglement in an immanent and material process. It also points to the mathematically grounded facet of that process. At a later point in the novel, Ownby returns to the water tank in which Rattner's remains are lying. He "stepped up on it and looked into the black square of the pit incised geometrically into the earth" (TOK, 90).[56] Believing that every word and phrase in McCarthy's fiction is chosen carefully and accorded a special function in terms of the particular narrative at hand, as well as the author's poetics in general, I take it that this applies to the adverb "geometrically" in this sentence, which can be regarded as the first connection in McCarthy's oeuvre to Oken's *Elements of Physiophilosophy*—a paradigmatic example of Schelling-inspired *Naturphilosophie* in which the process of narrative (that is, *recounting*) is set parallel to the arithmetical activity of *counting*, as well as the geometrical procedure of *delineation*. While it is in *Blood Meridian* and *The Crossing* that one can find the strongest affinity to Oken's metaphysical stance within

McCarthy's narrative speculations on nature's dynamic process, already in this short, but highly allusive, passage the writer confirms the Okenian identification of "the doctrine of matter" with "geometry and arithmetic."[57]

Lastly, before I turn to the dialectical relation between construction and subtraction in *Child of God*, I want to mention two other passages that illustrate how Land's concept of geotraumatic tension is aligned with McCarthy's descendental poetics. The first is about a group of local boys, including John Wesley, who explore the depths of a cave near Ownby's home, trying to hunt raccoons by setting up traps and kindling a fire in the cave where they live. Consider how the narrator depicts the adventurous enterprise in a downright gothic manner, almost as if McCarthy wanted to allude to H. P. Lovecraft's *At the Mountains of Madness* (1936) when writing the first of many scenes that feature cave explorations in his fiction: "They followed the strip of red clay that traced the cave floor into another and larger room, hooted at their lapping echoes, their laughter rebounding in hollow and mocking derision. Water dripped ceaselessly, small ping and spatter on stone. The two dogs hung close to them, stepping nervously" (*TOK*, 139). Even though all of them are excited about their plot to trap the raccoons, the plan to smoke the animals out does not work. The way in which the narrator depicts their escape from the smoke-filled cave once again veers between a Twainesque realism and a strange kind of mythography that feeds off the supposed imagination of the boys, but that also demonstrates McCarthy's strong interest in the mythological as well as the philosophical potential of the cave motif, as many scholars have noted:[58]

> They crawled and stumbled to the mouth of the cave—a shifting patch of murky light weaving beyond the smoke combers, came red-eyed and weeping from their crypt, their jacket fronts encrusted with slick red mud. When they had dried their eyes and could see again they were in some volcanic and infernal under-region, the whole of the quarry woods wrapped in haze and smoke boiling up out of the ground from every cleft and fissure. (141–42)

The other passage I wanted to mention before turning to McCarthy's 1973 novel is found in the last pages of *The Orchard Keeper*. After being thrown into jail as a result of his shooting four law enforcement officers who wanted to expel him and his dog from his premises near an peach orchard in the rural quiet of the Tennessean mountains, the unnerved Ownby is interviewed by a young social worker from the Welfare Bureau. The brief conversation ends with Ownby falling silent in apparent apathy and for a moment obstructing his face with his hand "as if to wipe away some image" (222). A few lines later, the narrative voice comments that "the old man felt the circle of years closing, the final increment of the curve returning him again to the inchoate, the prismatic flux of sound and color wherein he had drifted once before and now beyond the world of men" (ibid.). This sentence depicts a site and time "beyond the world of men," but not that of the transcendent and divine in terms of what Robert Tally Jr. has conceptualized as an ascendental poetics of "upward mobility."[59] Rather, this indeterminate locality is that of a preconceptual and therefore prehuman nature, one that cannot be "sensibly intuited"[60] yet can be speculated about. In this sense, the function of the narrator in McCarthy's novel can be compared to that of the "conceptual personae" in Deleuze and Guattari's sense of ideational vehicles that, on the one hand, indicate a certain key direction of a given philosophical stance (almost in an allegorical fashion), and, on the other hand, serve as the subjectivities of thought (almost tautegorically speaking), according to which the philosopher orients his or her discourse—almost as if the narrative voice had an agency of its own.[61] Yet from a Schellingian perspective, this voice, which is reflected in Rattner's "pitch of supplication" (TOK, 33) when he asks Sylder to help him get to Knoxville, can also be compared to the stance or subject position of the philosopher of nature *at the time of thinking nature*. This is because other than "the transcendental idealist," who "raises himself above the adulterated 'I' of ordinary experience through an act of abstraction, so too in a mirror image or subversion of the idealist, the *Naturphilosoph* transcends 'beneath' the limits of consciousness into the depths of nature."[62] In other words, what the narrator of *The Orchard Keeper* generates in a passage like the one foreshadowing Ownby's death via the image of that formless space "beyond the world of men" (TOK, 222) is closely related to the point of view assumed in "Schellingian abstraction" insofar as it "performs a kind of transformational enactment of the origins of natural becoming."[63]

Perhaps this "inchoate" and "prismatic flux" that constitutes the said formless space is the most condensed and, therefore, the most immediately suggestive of all images in this novel that testify to McCarthy's literary depiction of geotrauma, simply because it is the clearest example in which the outside of human temporality is grounded in the formless, incomplete, yet transcendental field. It is surely no coincidence that one of Schelling's names for "the primitive idea of an inexhaustible *primal matter*," that is, "of *aether*,"[64] has an almost homophonic resonance with Arthur Ownby's other name, "Uncle Ather" (TOK, 145). Between allegory and tautegory, between the regional pronunciation of "Arthur" and the metaphysical connotation of an "*ethereal, universally distributed fluid*,"[65] and finally between human temporality and natural history, McCarthy's first novel turns out to be clearly focused on the examination of nature's identity by narrative, not philosophical, means—even though there is undeniably a philosophical undercurrent to this kind of examination. *The Orchard Keeper* expresses the trauma of the earth as the generative occurrence in natural history, of which the human soul has a necessary, if limited, co-knowledge (*Mitwissenschaft*). This co-science (meaning both a conscience in terms of moral conduct and a consciousness in terms of intelligence) establishes the uneasy position of humanity within the perpetual composition and decomposition of organic and inorganic beings in the world.

If *The Orchard Keeper* is the novel that dramatizes the traumatic partaking of the human soul in the creation and re-creation of the world, thereby establishing the core element of McCarthy's equally religiously and scientifically oriented descendentalism, *Child of God* most explicitly reveals the complicated process of disintegration on both the corporeal and incorporeal levels of natural process. Building on the themes of decay and alienation that McCarthy's first two novels outlined, as well as the general hybrid style of allegory and tautegory, his third novel to be set in the Southeastern region alludes to the intricate relationship between nature's immanence and the transcendence of society. It addresses the issue of *allopoietic* representation starting with its title—which refers to the central figure, Lester Ballard, who is a supplicant or stand-in for the whole of humanity. Thus, the title points to an issue in McCarthy's work that guides the reader to biblical references and other religious as well as cosmological texts and contexts. Like nearly all of McCarthy's narratives, this novel is also intimately concerned with the question of how humans relate to their surroundings, to the environment of which they are a part and to which they give shape in turn. Furthermore, and this is my central thesis with regard to this novel, it is in *Child of God* that the author's notion of decay as an ontological category is most clearly evident, even though it is also important in other texts (including *The Orchard Keeper*, *Suttree*, and even *No Country for Old Men*, as I show in chapter 6). *Child of God* is McCarthy's quintessential text about decay's many forms, biological, social, and ecological. Yet while the novel seems to have been built on *The Orchard Keeper*'s characterization of the interconnections of geological and human expressions of trauma, it can be seen as the foundation for other novels that are focused on the decomposition of nature, like McCarthy's last Southern novel before *Blood Meridian* and like his first neo-Western from 2005.

Child of God tells the story of a social deviant and ex-convict from Sevier County, Tennessee. The man who will murder ruthlessly as well as indulge in necrophilic practices is called "a child of God much like yourself perhaps" (*COG*, 6) on the second page. Later in the novel, McCarthy again depicts Ballard's place among his kind by directly addressing the reader: "See him. You could say that he's sustained by his fellow men, like you. Has peopled the shore with them calling to him. A race that gives suck to the maimed and crazed, that wants their wrong blood in its history and will have it" (147). Ballard's horrific tale will be told in the course of the novel, from the first dead girl he has "intercourse" with all the way to the assembly of a whole society of corpses. He is said to be at once a product of society and its vices and to be a man who, like Ownby in *The Orchard Keeper*, has a harmonious relationship with the flora and fauna surrounding him, his nonhuman environment.[66] This relationship, however, which is to be seen in parallel to the semantic placement of organic and inorganic bodies on an equal footing in McCarthy's first novel, is rendered intelligible on a syntactic level, as in the following example from the first part of the narrative: "He sat hourlong in the windy sedge with the sun on his back. As if he'd store the warmth of it against the coming winter. *He* watched a *cornpicker* go snarling through the fields and in the evening *he* and the doves went husbanding among the chewed and broken stalks" (39, emphasis added). What is so striking in these sentences is that because the personal pronoun "he" is used so many times, there is an increasing ambiguity as to whom or what it refers to, meaning either Ballard or the machine. The passage thereby demonstrates yet another dimension of McCarthy's use of tautegory—namely, the temporary disentangling or problematization of referential nouns or common names by representative functional words, like pronouns, that are used to denote their identity in their stead. By creating such kinds of syntactic ambiguities, the narrator here proposes the imaginative scenario in which the human being goes "husbanding among the chewed and broken stalks" or the "cornpicker." By accumulating instances of the same pronominal reference, the semantic connection becomes blurred. This ambiguity generates a performative variation on, or adumbration of, the metaphysical undercurrent of the novel's plot, thus pointing to the progressively fragile identity of its central figure.[67] This is one of the ways in which tautegory, which I have identified as the narratological twin of *autopoiesis*, is ontologically prior to allegory, which is the twin of *allopoiesis*.

This syntactic conceit, which McCarthy employs in several of his novels (most recently in *The Road*), also reflects one side of the dialectical process of disintegration narrated by this text, the act of subtraction, while the corresponding act would be construction. The purely functional subtraction of a pronoun from its reference point thus mirrors, on the level of content, the ways in which social impoverishment finds its outlet in violent excess and in a tainted form of the pastoral that Georg Guillemin also discusses in his examination of McCarthy's third novel.[68] McCarthy's narrative not only connects Ballard, the psychopathic "child of God," and his flawed character to the whole of society but also makes clear that even Ballard's most terrible mistreatments of his victims are continuous with both the normative principles on which that society rests and the laws of community among the plants and animals he encounters in the forests and mountains of Sevier County. As Willard Greenwood notes, "the narrative chronicles the rapid *descent* of . . . Ballard from social outcast to deranged serial killer and necrophiliac," "a true anti-hero."[69] However, despite (or maybe because of) all of his evil conduct, the narrative still depicts him as a "child of God much like yourself perhaps" (COG, 6).

If the novel is indeed rooted in the Romantic tradition of literary and philosophical thought, as Hillary Gamblin has argued,[70] I want to suggest that McCarthy's poetics shares major features with both Schelling's and Oken's philosophies of nature, and the work of their contemporary heirs in speculative realist circles. Above all, there is a similar understanding of humankind's relationship to, and its conditioning by, the nature within and without it. In terms of the dichotomy that is largely dismissed nowadays in cultural studies, environmental thought, and continental philosophy, for McCarthy, the German idealists, and the relevant speculative realists whose work resumes the project of *Naturphilosophie*, human culture continually emerges in the environment of a nonhuman nature, even though the former conceives of the latter in a particular manner and thereby shapes it in turn. This epistemologically reciprocal relationship is based on an ontologically hierarchical relationship that is premised on the conviction that nonconceptual reality is the basis for conceptual reality, whereas the difference between the two is itself conceptual. In Deleuze and Guattari's terms, the distinction is a de jure reality, while their mixture is a de facto dimension. As many scholars have convincingly argued, Deleuze and Guattari are among the few philosophers of the past few decades to have not only taken the concept of nature seriously but to have also continuously strived to account for the ways in which the separation and mixture of these realities (conceptual and nonconceptual, corporeal and incorporeal, actual and virtual) can be thought of on one and the same plane, that of immanence.[71]

However, although for Deleuze and Guattari it would be a mistake to accord priority to either the conceptual or the nonconceptual reality on de facto terms and, by the same token, on ontological terms (since the nonobjective concept evolves with its nonconceptual object and vice versa), the idealist philosophy of nature that resonates with McCarthy's poetics actually does accord a certain priority to the nonconceptual realm. Furthermore, it does so on markedly ontological grounds that border on a downright spiritual as well as a scientific understanding of indeterminate being that remains indeterminate while being productive of determinate forms and phenomena: a formlessness that is given because it attests to the existence of diversification and differentiation in the first place. "For it is not because there is thinking that there is being, but rather because there is being that there is thinking," as Schelling writes.[72] The resulting determination of "humanity's place within the cosmos," according to Dianne Luce a central tenet of McCarthy's "bedrock philosophical concerns,"[73] results in a threefold metaphysical schema that aligns the author's narrative treatment of these concerns with the German idealists and speculative realists whom I have mentioned. According to this schema there is, first, an *ontological priority* ascribed to a formless being that is ontologically prior to thought and that is entirely natural; second, there is an *epistemological reciprocity* of influence between conception and the nonconceptual and, to a certain extent, between the human and the nonhuman; and third, there is nevertheless an *epistemological particularity* in the human soul, which is capable of the co-science of nature's productivity—or rather, which serves as a vessel for nature's self-analysis. These three conceptions are arguably indispensable for an understanding of McCarthy's concept of nature and the ways he delineates that concept through an idiosyncratic type of narrative speculation.

The notion of decay is central to this concept precisely because it touches in a decisive manner on questions of ontology, epistemology, hierarchy, and reciprocity raised in the schema: the diversification of nature, Schellingian and post-Schellingian philosophy of nature suggests, is articulated by "the progressive decomposition of nature," a "serial decomposition that is never finished" because physical dynamics are not a thing but a process.[74] Decay, in McCarthy's *Child of God*, is a notion capable of encompassing the social dimension of its central character ("a child of God like yourself perhaps") with respect to the community from which he becomes increasingly alienated—and from which he thus normatively subtracts himself, "a man much to himself" (*COG*, 39)—and the community through which he becomes once again a self-constructed social being. However, the latter is a community that itself progressively decays since it is composed of his dead victims. Ballard, the supplicant for humanity and for himself, is thus also an allegory of nature's continual and indifferent process of arbitrary or indifferent subtraction and construction: a dialectics of decay. As Schelling writes in *On the World Soul*, "nature is satisfied only by the greatest dominion of forms, and . . . it delights in *arbitrariness* in the deathly management of decomposition."[75] McCarthy's third novel, in contrast with his first, demonstrates not only the general inter- and intraconnections between organic and inorganic nature but also the reciprocating forces of disintegrating processes within these two realms (which are really two realms only in terms of a de jure stance but are one immanent realm in terms of a de facto standpoint, to use the terminology of Deleuze and Guattari again). As Grant reconstructs the *World Soul*'s dialectics of positive and negative forces, "ideally separable, . . . they nevertheless lack *real* conditions of dissociability."[76]

Finally, and this is the most important advantage of the physiocentric interpretation of decay as a grounding principle with respect to *Child of God*, its conceptually inclusive disposition compared to other interpretations of the text renders such an approach viable: while logocentrism, ethicocentrism, ecocentrism, biocentrism, or even phenomenologically inflected geocentrism all offer potentially important perspectives on this novel, the abject sexuality and ecological awareness of which is certainly worthy of examination, the present interpretation affirms these perspectives on the text and contradicts every one of them at the same time—which is very similar to the situation related to the periodization of McCarthy's work as a whole, which I discussed in chapter 1. Physiocentrism renders each of these perspectives as vital adumbrations of, or perspectives on, the narrative, yet it demonstrates that these points of view are merely regional perspectives whose partial view sometimes means that they miss categories that are larger than their conceptual framework would allow. I have shown above that this is precisely what happens with ecocentric and biocentric accounts, which tend to equate the concepts of the environment or life with that of nature. In like fashion, readings of McCarthy's work in terms of the linguistic bounds of literature *tout court* at best entail a similar conflation on the level of ontology (namely, the reciprocal determination of the terms "literature" and "nature," which results in the identification of the literature of nature with the nature of literature) and at worst exclude the question of nature's identity altogether. The physiocentric perspective, by contrast, examines the imbrication of literature and nature, and, more importantly, *the natural genesis of literature as part of nature's self-analysis*.

This examination is not dependent, however, on any substantialist essentialism in terms of a definition of literature once and for all, but on the conviction that if nature is immanent and therefore has no outside, then literature is not merely *about* nature but necessarily *of* it. If the theory of a veritable literature of nature (*Naturliteratur*), in the context of McCarthy's fiction, gives the impression of being a general theory about literary practice, this is in part accidental and in part a necessary result of the theme of this book. It is McCarthy's fiction (the author's narrative exploration of such an idea of literature as part and parcel of nature) that gives rise to the present conception of literature as such. Put differently, the caution inherent in McCarthy's style of writing—namely, that literature cannot exist in a reciprocal relationship with the entirety of natural process, since the latter is the condition of possibility of literature and is in itself a merely heuristic or idealized concept due to the infinite capacity of that process—may be applicable to a general theory of literature or narrativity, but that is beyond the scope of the present book. Instead, what is at issue here is the way in which McCarthy is able to construct narrative speculations on the identity of nature, not literature, even though the fact that the interpretation of these speculations inevitably has consequences for an account of literature attests to the far-reaching conceptual implications of McCarthy's narratives. In any case, I hold that of all thematic focuses that seem crucial to his literary "answer" to the question "What is nature?," the inquiry into nature's decompositions appears to be a quintessential point of reference, above all in *Child of God.*

The richness of the notion of decay, then, read vis-à-vis the *Naturphilosophie* of Schelling and his contemporary followers and modern heirs, makes possible the most fruitful account of those deeply metaphysical problems at the heart of the novel's tragic as well as poetic rendering of the outcast Ballard and his world: What is the development of an individual's personality when measured against, or compared to, the particular territory in which it evolves? How is social deviance not only a matter of becoming less and less connected with one's community, but also a matter of remaining and, therefore, resisting as a natural being, regardless of one's normatively unacceptable behavior, given the supervenience of the social upon the natural? In other words, how is it possible for the reader to conceive of the almost religious, but certainly ethical, problem of showing tolerance in the face of Ballard's transgressive activity throughout the narrative, as a fundamentally natural problem? Given the immanence of nature suggested by McCarthy's style of writing, is it possible to argue for a *natural* interpretation of Ballard's repulsive deeds, after having accepted the description of him as "a child of God much like yourself perhaps" (*COG*, 6)?

Certainly less controversial than this last question is my claim that McCarthy's third novel displays the fundamental notion of a natural dialectic in which processes of subtraction or diminution co-determine those of construction or organization. Although *Child of God* has been connected to literary Romanticism before, I argue that it is not so much the *memento mori*, understood as humanity's condition of finitude, that determines the Romantic decadence of McCarthy's narrative but instead what Reza Negarestani aptly terms the "Memento Tabere"[77] or instance of disentanglement, putrefaction, corrosion, or becoming fluid that eventually occurs in worldly corporeal and incorporeal matters of all kind, from rocks to vegetable life-forms, and from nonhuman carnivores to the human brain. While both instances or mementos have a common origin—the Romantic tradition of thought, generally—the latter focuses less on notions of melancholia and nostalgia, on which the former feeds.[78] Or rather, it deals with these notions in a different way, not by remaining in a state of mourning for a lost object, but by investigating and reiterating the infinite process or development of materiality. The *memento tabere*, or acknowledgement of decay as something productive, is indeed a recurring motif in McCarthy's novel, which illustrates both bodily and incorporeal transitions of living beings, objects, or ideas to formlessness and the inorganic. Thus, in *Child of God*, Ballard's alienation from society goes hand in hand with the organization of a new society of rotting corpses in a cave he discovers in the Appalachian Mountains after his house has burned down. Social decay (meaning both voluntary and involuntary alienation) becomes the "infinite dis*sociation* into ever new products."[79] It becomes a particular narrative about an ex-convict in the Southeastern United States who tries to come to grips with his new situation in the old environs, and it thus also becomes a general treatise on the dynamics of composition and decomposition in nature.

I suggest that McCarthy's third novel, in which Ballard progressively divests himself of his fellows through murder and self-isolation in a manner that resonates with Negarestani's idea of "ontological decay," thereby entails or rather presumes a theory of "being qua being" expressed by means of fiction rather than philosophy.[80] Instead of "nature writing" and environmental awareness, or what Lawrence Buell terms "writing for an endangered world,"[81] the "writing of nature" itself is at stake here, the literary dramatization of how both "*that which is*" and "*that which is not*"[82] co-determine one another in the dynamic ways of natural processes. The writing of nature, then, is understood as a conceptual as well as an artistic grasping of the fermentation of the old in the new by way of "the chemical potency of putrefaction (*tabes*)."[83] It is understood as the unintentional expression of the dead in the living and vice versa, and the continuity (or maximal extensity) of the concept of nature in literary production.

For Negarestani, ontology must account for the difficulties that the chemical and biological processes of living and dead bodies represent for the philosophical and fictional depiction of nature.[84] If the question of being is coupled with that of becoming, as Platonic physics suggests with its emphasis on the transience of corporeality and the dynamics of materiality, this question is equally connected with the issue of *what remains* in the process of that unceasing becoming, the persisting (if nonintentional) striving for change. For Negarestani, "being qua being is a genus of being which persists and remains under any condition or environment synthesized by other beings whatsoever. In other words, being qua being is that which continues to remain after all belongings are shed, removed and taken away."[85] Ballard's trajectory, during which he loses his home, his human acquaintances (both living and dead), and one of his arms after being shot at (COG, 165–66), may thus be read allegorically as the narration of the decomposition of nature's products, giving rise to ever new products and forms. *Child of God* dramatizes the simultaneity of subtraction and production in nature, by which "the continuity of remaining . . . is only attainable, and must be conducted, through diminution and decay."[86] McCarthy's narrative thereby speculates on the metaphysical problem of decay in two senses: it examines the "problem of the *infinitesimal persistence* of the decaying object" and how the subject takes part in a state of "becoming infinitely close to zero but never effectively becoming zero."[87] This is a process in which the complete subtraction of personal traits from the individual human subject can only be approximated but never achieved, and in which this approximation makes for the becoming, or construction, of this particular "child of God" called Lester Ballard (COG, 6). In psychological terms, this dramatization can be traced back to Carl Jung's elaboration of the alchemical notion of *nigredo*, a confrontational practice of facing one's personality's "*Shadow*" that is linked to the mystical idea of the "*Anima*" in his last major study, *Mysterium Coniunctionis* (1955–57).[88] As other scholars have made clear, Jungian psychology is useful not only with regard to *Child of God*'s narratological setup, but also with respect to other novels by McCarthy.[89] Yet as will become apparent, it is above all those passages in *Child of God* that depict Ballard's descent into cave-like structures that reveal the narrative treatment of both *nigredo* and the closely linked *katabatic* activity.[90] What is more, the deviant sexuality of the novel's antihero is equally linked to this notion of subterranean exploration, simply because his necrophilic "sexual intercourse is [also] a sort of physiological *katábasis*."[91]

At this point in my argument, I want to consider those passages in which the context of abominable scenery gives rise to the narrator's metaphysical speculations that are so characteristic of how McCarthy's fictions narratively respond to a question that is usually resolved by philosophical means—namely, "What is nature?" Consequently, the following sections give examples of how, in the overall narrative, Ballard's social decay and intensified depravity (which flourishes with acts of depredation, mutilation, and necrophilia) are bound to the practice of cosmological speculation on the part of the narrative voice that registers the actions in a well-nigh "detached" mode of storytelling, to use Dana Phillips's terminology yet again.[92] Consider the following passage, arguably one of the most revolting parts of the book, in which Ballard for the first time indulges in necrophilia after he has discovered a young couple of lovers who accidentally suffocated to death inside their car:

> The dead man was watching him from the floor of the car. Ballard kicked his feet out of the way and picked the girl's panties up from the floor and sniffed

> at them and put them in his pocket. He looked out the rear window and he listened. Kneeling there between the girl's legs he undid his buckle and lowered his trousers. A crazed gymnast laboring over a cold corpse. He poured into that waxen ear everything he'd ever thought of saying to a woman. Who could say she did not hear him? (*COG*, 84)

It is this detached mode of narration, as well as the questioning at the end of the section, which projects the situation of a local deviant having intercourse with a female corpse onto a veritably ontological problematic. At which point does the capacity to perceive sounds, or words in this case, cease in the human body that has died? Where does sentience go after sapience has vanished? Does the ability to perceive vanish in the organism or does it remain in the form of an infinitely small and subtle activity that has become imperceptible to other organisms? In short, does a dead man continue to watch what is in front of him as long as his eyes are still open? According to Negarestani, "the persistence in remaining or the act of remaining (to remain)—as the continual result of the subtractive operation—can only invest itself in *remaining less* and as ontological decay. The continuity of remaining . . . is only attainable, and must be conducted, through diminution and decay: $R > r' > r''$ . . . ."[93] Negarestani's theory is not only adequate for a rigorous analysis of Ballard's alienation from society, or his deviation from the latter's normative structures that very much reflect this "persistence in remaining." It is also shedding light on the function of the corpses that Ballard brings to his cabin and later groups together in his caves.

A little later in the novel, Ballard has managed to carry the female body to his cabin and has started to make her "feel at home," however grotesque that might sound. Placing her before his fireplace and getting the fire going, in this way he even increases the speed of putrefaction, accelerating the subtractive operation, and thereby summoning the abovementioned *memento tabere*:

> He came in with an armload of firewood and got a fire going in the hearth and sat before it and rested. Then he turned to the girl. He took off all her clothes and looked at her, inspecting her body carefully, as if he would *see how she were made*. He went outside and looked in through the window at her lying naked before the fire. When he came back in he unbuckled his trousers and stepped out of them and laid next to her. He pulled the blanket over them. (*COG*, 87, emphasis added)

Note how McCarthy's phrasing here already prefigures the passage from *The Road* that I cited at the beginning of the introduction to this study, starting with a sentence that is strikingly similar to the italicized words in the above quote: "Perhaps in the world's destruction it would be possible at last to *see how it was made*. Oceans, mountains. The ponderous counter-spectacle of things ceasing to be. The sweeping waste, hydroptic and coldly secular" (*TR*, 274, emphasis added). I have argued above that these sentences do not allude to a transcendent realm that is somehow outside the world, or to a supernatural dimension of what might be called an ascendental imaginary. Rather, they allude to the descendental realm of the formless givenness that I have described above. This is the same transcendental field of indeterminacy that the passage from *Child of God* refers to, because the narrator uses nearly the same phrase to allude to it—which is again testament to the narrative continuity within McCarthy's entire oeuvre.

Shortly afterward, Ballard's home burns down, and with it the female corpse for which he felt affection. In a scene reminiscent of the destruction of the Green Fly Inn that I discussed in the last chapter, Ballard witnesses the disintegration of his home, "[standing] there in the snow with his jaw hanging" (*COG*, 100). Note how the narrative voice renders the melting of the cabin's structure, once again emphasizing the interconnectedness of the organic and the inorganic, the animal world and biochemical phenomena: "The flames ran down the batboards and up again like burning squirrels. . . . The few panes of glass crackled and fell from their sash in a myriad rupture and the roof dropped with a whooshing noise down into the house. . . . Long before morning the house that had kept Ballard from the elements was only a blackened chimney with a pile of smoldering boards at its feet" (ibid.). If we concede that the notion of decomposition or decay extends to the disintegration of architectural structures, such as Ballard's home, then Negarestani's concept is useful: even the loss of Ballard's cabin is productive, as it further amplifies the protagonist's psychological *katabasis*. "Decay builds without creation . . . [and] introduces power to the misadventures of matter. But it is 'entities as beings' which *narrate* the adventures of decay as a cosmic odyssey between themselves," Negarestani states.[94] Ballard's new home in the cave he finds in the mountains at a later stage of his alienation from human society will gradually be filled with the corpses he finds and the Tennesseans he murders. The literal dissection of Ballard's identity as a human being, on both a social and a physical level, gives way to the multiplication of relationships between him and the bodies he assembles, and with whose scalps and clothing he dresses himself. In ontological terms, Ballard's social and physical body displays the "misadventures of matter" as explorations into the process of decay in acts of construction or building without intention—that is, shorn of the creative aspect of anything that develops into an increasingly complex, if fragile, structure. It is, therefore, imperative to examine the depictions of the caves the necrophiliac inhabits after burning down his own house. The following passage thus again speculates on "some strange underground force" (COG, 126) that, in a complicated narratological conceit on the part of McCarthy, paradoxically serves as an allegorical image for that part of nature that is the total opposite of allegorical or *allopoietic* logic: the tautegorical or self-analytic capacity of nature. What I mean is that the "underground force," an allegory of nature's dynamic and ever-changing processes, is linked to the principal rendition of *autopoiesis*—namely, the image of "the stream" in the grotto, "rushing off into the darkness . . . , descending from pool to pool in stone cups of its own devising." This, then, is how the narrator depicts Ballard's *nigredo*-like survey of his first cavernous home:

> From the floor of the room an underground stream rose. It welled up blackly in a calcite basin and flowed down a narrow aqueduct where the room tailed off through a black hole. Ballard's light glanced from the surface of the pool unaltered, as if bent back by *some strange underground force.* Everywhere water dripped and spattered and the wet cave walls looked waxed or lacquered in the beam of light. He crossed the room and followed the stream out and down the narrow gorge through which it flowed, the water rushing off into the darkness before him, *descending* from pool to pool in stone cups *of its own devising.* (126, emphasis added)

Picking up where the narrative of *The Orchard Keeper* left off, regarding the description of underground systems "[below] the world of men" (TOK, 222), this passage is also steeped in the gothic tradition of American literature and possibly in that of the Lovecraftian weird. The narrator's rendering of Ballard's descent into the corporeal depths of the earth and his psychological *katabasis* has a strange, hybrid quality to it, equally scientific and mythological: "Here the walls with their softlooking convulsions, slavered over as they were with wet and blood-red mud, had an organic look to them, *like the innards of some great beast.* Here in *the bowels* of the mountain Ballard turned his light on ledges or pallets of stone where dead people lay like saints" (COG, 126–27, emphasis added). Here is yet another connection to McCarthy's 2006 novel *The Road*, which is established by the dream of the father at the beginning of that novel: "In the dream from which he'd wakened he had wandered in a cave where the child led him by the hand. Their light playing over the wet flowstone walls. Like pilgrims in a fable swallowed up and lost among *the inward parts of some granitic beast*" (TR, 3).[95] Dream or waking state, myth or laboratory—McCarthy's narrative speculations clearly incorporate both fantastic and forensic practices that are fundamentally human forms of the co-science of morphogenesis.

Once again I want to return to a section I have examined above. In light of the concept of nature's decomposition and other aspects that I have already elaborated on, this passage can now be seen from a newly informed perspective: "In the spring or warmer weather when the snow thaws in the woods the tracks of winter reappear on slender pedestals and the snow reveals in palimpsest old buried wanderings, struggles, scenes of death. Tales of winter brought to light again like time turned back upon itself. Ballard went through the woods kicking down his old trails where they veered over the hill toward his onetime homeplace" (*COG*, 130). These "tales of winter," one of which includes the burning down of the antihero's cabin, are the narrative ground of the ensuing madness of Ballard, a madness that increasingly allows for moments of contemplation in tandem with a decline of social adaptability. The "palimpsest" mentioned here is really the constantly evolving dynamics of reciprocal determination on the minimal level of decompositional and compositional influence between the individual and his new home, a subterranean corridor. Yet it is also ontologically posterior to the formless givenness that functions as the predisposition to—or, better still, the unground of—the reciprocating processes across nature's corporeal and incorporeal phenomena.

One of the contemplative moments to which I just referred is captured in a paragraph about Ballard lying in his cave at night, this time speculating on the cosmos and himself, rather than on the flesh of a victim. It is a section that is still set in spring, a season that is a most fertile ground for the cross-fertilization of the "misadventures of matter,"[96] as McCarthy's poetics suggests. Note how the narrator employs the syntactic ambiguity of the pronoun "they" in the last sentence of the following passage, almost as though this were a recapitulation of the earlier pronominal ungrounding of the references to Ballard's and the cornpicker's identities (which as a result become blurred and nearly interchangeable). The fact that here the pronoun "they" most likely refers to the stars on the night sky, yet may also function refer to the bats and is moreover connected semantically with Ballard in the last clause of this complicated sentence, again confirms the claim that McCarthy's conception of the natural realm encompasses more than the flora and fauna of the environment and certainly is the antecedent of its own depiction in literary practice:

> False spring came again with a warm wind. The snow melted off into little patches of gray ice among the wet leaves. With the advent of this weather bats began to stir from somewhere deep in the cave. Ballard lying on his pallet by the fire one evening saw them come from the dark of the tunnel and ascend through the hole overhead fluttering wildly in the ash and smoke like souls rising from hades. When *they* were gone he watched the *hordes of cold stars*

> sprawled across the smokehole and wondered *what stuff they were made of, or himself*. (*COG*, 133, emphasis added)

Before turning to *Suttree* at last, I want to point out how the ending of *Child of God* subverts or parodies (in other words, *ungrounds*) the ascendental stance that Edgar Allan Poe, one of McCarthy's precursors in the gothic tradition, equally despised for its false notion of a God-given mobility.[97] As is clearly indicated in the title of McCarthy's 1973 novel, the only motion that is given is that of the return to the formlessness or indeterminacy of the transcendental field. This is the Romantic idea of a downward mobility, or what Negarestani calls "the compulsion to return toward pure contingencies of cosmic time,"[98] which is facilitated by the dialectical process of decomposition and composition on a corporeal and incorporeal level, an allegorical and tautegorical level, and, finally, in the purely linguistic domain of semantics and syntax as well as its *memento tabere*, to use Negarestani's terminology again.

In 1965, the year Ballard dies, a farmer "named Arthur Ogle was plowing an upland field one evening when the plow was snatched from his hands" (*COG*, 185). Suddenly the whole apparatus, including the mules and the plow, falls down into the opening of Ballard's last cavernous home where he stored his victims' moldy corpses, camouflaged as they are by "scallops of light fungus [that] grew along them as they do on logs rotting in the forest" (186). This is indubitably a reference to the "old mossbacked logs, peopled with toadstools strange and solemn" (*TOK*, 11) at the beginning of McCarthy's first novel. Now, what I mean by the subversion of the ascendental standpoint and, by the same token, the ethicist antithesis to any possibility of a nature-philosophical account of *Child of God* is the subsequent description of the police dragging the first body out of the cave with a rope, a description that proceeds in a grotesque fashion:

> The sheriff and the deputy made a noose from a rope and they slipped it around the upper body of the first corpse and drew it tight. They pulled her from the slab and dragged her across the stone floor of the vault and down a corridor to where daylight fell against the wall of the sink. . . . The rope grew taut and first of the dead sat up on the cave floor, the hands that hauled the rope above sorting the shadows like puppeteers. Gray soapy clots of matter fell from the cadaver's chin. She ascended dangling. She sloughed in the weem of the noose. A gray rheum dripped. (*COG*, 186)

The horrific imagery presented here certainly does not connote a preestablished harmony sought after by the preservationist tenets within ecocriticism. If anything is preestablished or premeditated by McCarthy's vision of nature's dynamics in his third novel, it is a "pre-established universal chemistry"[99] that merely points to a dynamically katabatic procedure whereby the blackening of the body and the descent of the soul (*nigredo*) each participate in the interdependence of individual *being*, *becoming*, and *remaining*. What is so remarkable in the passage just cited from the ending of *Child of God* is not just the almost satirical counterimage to the ideal of ascension in religious terms, but the fact that the very instrument of such an upward mobility, the rope, is itself the cause for another cavernous structure that inevitably forms itself onto the dead flesh of the first corpse—namely, "the weem of the noose." This term arguably suggests that any ascendental rhetoric or ideal is grounded on, or unthinkable without, a descendental practice. This is precisely because, metaphysically speaking, the cord (or, in this case, the rope) by which souls and bodies are said to ascend toward the sky leaves behind a cut, which eventually will develop into a cavernous structure or traumatic scar on the corporeal or incorporeal entity—until, that is, part of the entity falls off into the ground (in this case, "a gray rheum") to provide the soil with new and fertile components for it to thrive.

This is one of the ways, finally, that the ecocentric and ethicist question concerning the "child of God," Lester Ballard, is reframed in terms of a physiocentric approach: the difficulty of accepting the humanity behind the gruesome acts of the novel's antihero pales in comparison with the narrator's subversion of the apparatus of traction that is put to use in the ascendental activity at the ending of the novel. Thus, as readers and fellow human beings, it is on nature-philosophical grounds that not only must we accept that the revolting crimes committed by Ballard are a testament to his humanity, but we must also concede that those speculative moments of his soul (his sincere and yet sincerely flawed "co-knowing [*Mitwissenschaft*] of creation,"[100] when he contemplates "what stuff [he is] made of" [COG, 133]) are mirrored in the complicity with which we accept the development of the narrative by reading on after having witnessed the first of many heinous acts of violence and scenes of depravity.

An ascendental ethics of reading *Child of God* is therefore always grounded in its descendental condition of possibility, just as the co-science of the genesis of forms is structurally similar to complicity in a criminal act. As I discuss in later chapters, the etymological relationship between *Mitwissenschaft* (co-science) and *Mitwisserschaft* (complicity) is reflected in the semantic relation between the respective functions of the supplicant and the witness: the former is able to feel morally conscious of him- or herself, as well as of others, while the latter stands apart from the activities and events in the world and who bears witness instead of bearing the cross of a bad conscience.[101]

The question of how the ethical dimension of *Child of God* is ultimately tied to the notion of a "pre-established universal chemistry"[102] rather than to the harmonious relationship of the individual to the environment is even more appropriate in the context of McCarthy's forth novel. This is because in *Suttree* the imagery of caves, the moldy wastes of homeless people's corpses, and above all the flux of materiality—the Tennessee River, which the narrator calls "Cloaca Maxima" (*S*, 13)—not only reveals the continuation of the poetics of disintegrating objects begun in *The Orchard Keeper* but also constitutes the aesthetic as well as conceptual scaffolding for the ethical and phenomenological dimensions of the novel, which is centered on Cornelius Suttree.[103] I suggest, moreover, that this literary character is the one in McCarthy's fiction who most clearly fits the description of what Deleuze and Guattari call a "conceptual persona,"[104] due, in part, to the well-documented parallels between Suttree's life and McCarthy's own time in Knoxville. One of the most captivating aspects of this narrative is its treatment of the genre of autobiography vis-à-vis the mythographical intersection of allegory and tautegory. On the one hand, *Suttree* may be the one of McCarthy novels that relies the most on the literary portraiture of "lived experience," to use the terminology of Bertrand Westphal's geocritical practice of reading.[105] On the other hand, this phenomenological accounting of events by the novel's protagonist is ontologically dependent on the same realm of the given formlessness that is evoked in McCarthy's earlier tales set in Appalachia. In other words, Suttree's narrative of existential anxiety, familial disconnection, and sexual and alcoholic excess ultimately constitutes the literary search for or investigation of this realm, expressed in the regional vernacular of 1950s Knoxville and its downtrodden inhabitants like Harrogate or Red Callahan.

As I reemphasize the consonance of Schelling's *System of Transcendental Idealism* with McCarthy's work, including the philosopher's thesis of nature's all-encompassing reach[106] and his description of "the objective world [as] simply the original, as yet unconscious, poetry of the spirit,"[107] it is important to note that although most of the narrative speculations in McCarthy point to a realm of the ineffable that is generative of its own analysis, we must also acknowledge the diversity of these speculations. If some of these metaphysically informed passages amid the realist descriptions of particularly American lives (like those of Harrogate or J-Bone) outline a natural history of which these lives are part yet which cannot be recounted by them, other passages in *Suttree* are *poetic leaps* that somehow allow us to imagine that exact history in delirious and, by the same token, aesthetic states of mind. This is why, in one of McCarthy's nods toward the Romantic notion of an aesthetically inscribed yet nonetheless enlightened madness, or what could also be called *an understanding evoked by psychological excess*, a passage describing Suttree's typhoid fever dreams is presented as conveying some metaphysical insight "into a cold dimension without time without space and where all was motion" (*S*, 452).[108]

How should one characterize this search for a realm "where all [is] motion"? I claim that *Suttree* amounts to a literary experiment in the sense of experimental science rather than in terms of formal experiments in literature (even if the regionalism employed in McCarthy's novels in general can be regarded in connection to the history of experiments in constraint writing, as I suggested above). What I mean by this notion of literature as a scientific experiment in a laboratory situation, say, is that the narrative perspective taken up in *Suttree*, from its prologue until its last page, shares Émile Zola's proviso that "the novelist is equally an observer and an experimentalist. The observer in him gives the facts as he has observed them, . . . [t]hen the experimentalist appears and introduces an experiment, that is to say, sets his characters going in a certain story so as to show that the succession of facts will be such as the requirements of the determinism of the phenomena under examination call for."[109] Among the many possible candidate natural sciences, which would be the most apt allegorical reference point in terms of the narrative stance taken by McCarthy in his fourth Southern novel, the longest one of his career? In other words, if one assumes that the narrative voice of *Suttree*, conceived of as a near-naturalist novel, has both an observing and an experimenting component, would it not be possible to identify a certain scientific discipline that would be both formally and aesthetically related to the scenes, landscapes, and plotlines of that novel?

In light of the themes discussed above with respect to *The Orchard Keeper* and *Child of God*, and the way in which these texts outline a particular ontological conception that gives rise to (yet is partially independent of) any ethical, ecocritical, or biocentric perspective on them, I suggest that it is the experimental practices of chemistry and especially of its protoscientific antecedent, alchemy, that serve as the model for the poetic rendering of decay in *Suttree*. If this novel is shot through with speculative passages that suggest a certain understanding of the disposition or nature of materiality, then it does so by means of imaginative episodes that allude to the idea of chemistry and its origin in the alchemical practices of the premodern world. This is not to say that McCarthy's fourth novel is much different, in this respect, from *The Orchard Keeper* or *Child of God*. Yet it is here that the dimension of katabatic explorations in cave structures and the psyche of an individual character, such as the protagonist, is directly related to chemical processes of intoxication and alchemical ritual. Put differently, it is in *Suttree* that the well-nigh chemical aspects of the cross-fertilization of the organic and the inorganic and the dialectical relationship between subtraction and construction are spelled out. In this context, then, and especially with respect to the ethical problem I raised in regard to the reader's partial acceptance of Ballard's crimes, as he or she keeps on reading after having witnessed the first shedding of blood, consider the following passage from McCarthy's notes for his screenplay "Whales and Men." The passage clearly indicates the author's ontological interest in the issue of complicity: "Truth? Forgiveness? Are they the same thing? If pain is excruciating enough will it not at last ferret out God himself? Ultimately it's not the confession of crimes or the whereabouts of companions that the torturer hopes to elicit. It's the whereabouts of the spirit. *What we are talking about is a form of alchemy*." McCarthy continues: "With these howls we hope to provoke the silence of the universe into its own betrayal. [For what we require is a witness.] [S]omething to say that we are here and . . . are justified to be so. What else could this man possibly be seeking with his thumbscrews . . . ? This man who goes home at night to supper with his family. This man whose hands are so bloody. This man who is me." And McCarthy ponders, "What can he be seeking except evidence for the reality of the world? That is why we cannot stop. . . . Because deep in our hearts we fear that we do not exist."[110]

It must be conceded that this note does not directly refer to any of McCarthy's Southern novels. Even so (or maybe especially because of this unspecified reference), it is possible to interpret the statement in terms of McCarthy's fiction in general and in particular of his function as an author who to a certain extent becomes "the torturer" of the fictional characters and animal creatures he creates. Or rather, the author becomes the one who orders his respective narrators to inflict pain and grief on these bodies and their souls for them to arrive at a state of grace, at least on a poetic level.[111] The statement therefore sheds light on the role of the narrative voice and the perspective from which specific characters and their hardships are to be read—namely, in terms of Zola's proviso, as necessary ingredients of a literary experiment on the reactions of the character at hand after "a series of trials, placing him amid certain surroundings in order to exhibit how the complicated machinery of his passions works."[112] Thus, while in *Child of God* the perpetrator of crimes is doubled in the forms of the antihero Ballard and the narrator who constructs the narrative of Ballard's decline from his return to Sevierville from jail until his death, the circumstances of *Suttree* are dictated by a narrative voice that lets the protagonist go through a number of ordeals (corporeal and incorporeal) in the environs of Knoxville in the early 1950s. This narrative voice arguably defines the conditions of possibility of these ordeals by addressing the reader directly in the novel's first paragraph, thereby instigating both the narrative and the reader's complicity in bringing about the trying events and resulting burdens on the central character: "*Dear friend now in the dusty clockless hours of the town when the streets lie black and steaming in the wake of the watertrucks . . . , now in these sootblacked brick or cobbled corridors where lightwire shadows make a gothic harp of cellar doors no soul shall walk save you*" (*S*, 3). If, as McCarthy's notes from "Whales and Men" suggest, the narrative voice is itself in the position of torturing its literary figures, and if, as the novel's prologue suggests, it is principally the witness-as-reader of these figures' ordeals who "shall walk" through the underground passages of the tale, then the characters' psychological torment and speculative statements can be regarded as "evidence for the reality of the world," given that this is what the narrator intends to produce as a result of the literary experiment that is fiction. Fiction thus becomes both the narrative *about* nature (allegory), the expression *of* nature (tautegory), and the search for proof *that* nature exists (literary alchemy).

How does McCarthy fuse the scientific history of chemistry and the protoscientific legacy of alchemy with the poetic setup of his largely autobiographical fiction from 1979? What, for that matter, is the connection between chemical and alchemical practice? First of all, the descriptions of the Knoxville environment and its low-life characters, who are the protagonist's fellow ex-convicts or drinking buddies, and the depictions of the cavernous systems beneath the city and the Appalachian forest ecologies (depicted in the course of Suttree's mountain sojourn during his temporary escape from the events he had previously endured) have one thing in common, which is a conceptual link between the cleansing dissociation from externally normative structures (like that of the protagonist's father who, in "his last letter [to his son had] said that the world is run by those willing to take responsibility for the running of it" [*S*, 13]) and the excessive use of intoxicating substances, particularly alcohol. Suttree has his hands full with figuring out what is best for him as an individual and how he can help those who are in real need, like Harrogate or his African American friend Abnego Jones (who at the end of the narrative is beaten to death by the local police for behaving inappropriately to them [*S*, 447]). Furthermore, there are Suttree's repeatedly troubled affairs with women, only two of which result in passionate, though short-lived, relationships: first with a very young girl named Wanda, the daughter of Reese (his business partner in fishing for mussels in the Tennessee River), and second with Joyce, a prostitute with whom he tries to share an apartment in the city—a situation that does not work for long.[113] The episodes that recount the developments in these relationships often reflect the narrator's stance toward nature, often from the perspective of Suttree. Thus, scenes of violence seem to be on par with those of love and sexuality, as is the case with McCarthy's speculative passages and those of violent disintegration or death. This is not at all surprising, since the indifference of death and decay seems best counterbalanced in this novel by the frequent introspective remarks of Suttree as a narrator who is in love, as well as those of the narrative voice that accounts for scenes and events in the novel beyond the phenomenological reach of its protagonist's psyche.

"McCarthy's recreated Knoxville [is] set for the most part in subterranean structures, tunnels, and caverns populated by the sinking human detritus of the rising Sun Belt South," as Joseph Millichap remarks.[114] The novel's aesthetics of decay is certainly apparent beginning with the untitled prologue, a section that introduces the reader to an environment of dirt and dust, simultaneously mythologized and naturalized: "*A world beyond all fantasy, malevolent and tactile and dissociate*" (*S*, 4), composed of "*interstitial wastes . . . afreight with the past, dreams dispersed in the water someday, nothing ever lost*" (4). The narrator goes on to tell us: "*The night is quiet. Like a camp before battle. The city beset by a thing unknown and will it come from forest or sea?*" (4). All of these seemingly gothic qualifications of Knoxville's surroundings—its malevolence and dissociation, the way in which the dirt of the streets and that of the gaping sewage systems beneath those streets finds its mirror image in the intricate thoughts of both the wakeful and dreamlike mental states of Suttree, as well as those of the many other inhabitants of the city—can be connected meaningfully to the history of alchemical and chemical practice precisely because, as Grant notes (following the work of Bernadette Bensaude-Vincent and Isabelle Stengers), "chemistry has always been the science and art of the imperceptible, of what escapes the imprisonment of sensibility . . . to go directly to the earth, or to earths, to be dispersed and molecularised in the black. Even etymology serves to remind us of this: '*chemistry* derives from the Egyptian word for 'black,' which is itself named for the black earth of Egypt.'"[115] While this etymological origin clearly resonates with McCarthy's aesthetics of the "black earth" (*S*, 80) and of the katabatic tendencies so prevalent in his Southern novels (and elsewhere), the second etymological inference that Bensaude-Vincent and Stengers provide is even more striking with regard to *Suttree*—namely, "that the same word may derive from the Greek word *cheo*, which means to pour a liquid or cast a metal. Greek or Egyptian etymology? The question cannot be settled, because it sends us back to the great Hellenistic city of Alexandria, where it was already the subject not only of legends but also of speculations and discussions."[116] This adds another dimension to the link between McCarthy's literary experimentation and the history of protochemical practice, meaning not only the mythographical aspect that is evidenced by one possible origin of the term, "the black earth of Egypt," but also the inventory or constructive aspect of this science, which can be traced back the Greek origin that indexes liquefying processes of all sorts. Surely having Deleuze and Guattari in mind here, Grant writes, "chemistry [thus] gives us a geophilosophy based on manufacture or metallurgy."[117] Consequently, it is much more than just a matter of understanding nature's processes. In other words, much like Zola's ideal novelist with a literary naturalist bent, or what I have conceptualized in the context of *Suttree* as a narrative persona, the stance of the chemist is almost isomorphic with that of the mythographer: "analysis is one part of the equation, but one understands nothing until synthesis has taken place. . . . That synthetic ambition is unique to chemistry—it's about production as well as analysis."[118]

These aspects are worth considering in the context of a reinterpretation of McCarthy's concept of nature in *Suttree* simply because the alchemical roots of chemistry provide a fitting model for the kind of literary experiment that this novel constitutes. For instance, the prologue is clearly rooted in Greco-Egyptian mythology, as other scholars have noted. For example, Knoxville's environs are characterized by the following: "*Old stone walls unplumbed by weathers, lodged in their striae fossil bones, limestone scarabs rucked in the floor of this once inland sea. . . . Curious marble architecture, stele and obelisk and cross and little rainworn stones where names grow dim with years. Earth packed with samples of the casketmaker's trade, the dusty bones and rotted silk, the deathwear stained with carrion*" (*S*, 3). These peculiarly ancestral surroundings clearly allude to the mythical past of Egyptian origin, as Rick Wallach argues with reference to this particular section: "The recurrent Egyptian references—scarabs, stelae, obelisks—. . . suggest an evolution from prehistoric to ancient to contemporary, not just in architectural terms but in spiritual terms as well."[119] Like *The Orchard Keeper*, *Suttree* combines the mythical past and natural history in a poetic rendering of the interrelatedness of physical and narrative construction, in line with the alchemical (and chemical) standpoint "that both synthesizes and self-analyses"[120] and with the narrator's perspective as both observer and experimenter, prescribed in the tradition of literary naturalism.

Returning once more to Bensaude-Vincent and Stengers's fascinating account of the discipline's Western beginnings in Egypt's capital, we see another parallel between the "'chemical paradigm' for thinking"[121] and the poetics of McCarthy. The two historians write: "Alexandria, center of the mingling and re-creation of Greek traditions—Pythagorean, Platonic, Stoic, Egyptian or Asian, Gnostic—and heir to a past that she revered, is the origin of the specific character of *alchemy*. . . . Today we associate alchemy with magic, but originally it encompassed *both mysticism and practical techniques for manipulating matter*."[122] While this latter phrase is certainly important, again pointing to the experimental or constructive disposition of chemistry at all stages in its long history (meaning, the minute tracings of material reactions induced by the experimenter) it is the authors' mention of "the Hellenistic alchemists [who] believed knowledge led to salvation, in the gnostic way,"[123] that once and for all substantiates the complex relationship implied in McCarthy's text. What I am referring to here is the complex of alchemy's originary and intertwined promises of "*recreating* nature,"[124] catharsis, and eventually salvation. Alchemy and its modern successor, chemistry, thus provide the reader of McCarthy's intricately layered narrative with a particular formal vision or scientific outlook that both describes and creates its object of investigation, a paradoxical activity in which manipulation and examination go hand in hand—again, very much like Zola's proposed dual stance of the naturalist writer as observer and experimenter at the same time.

There is yet another feature of the etymological derivation of Greek or Hellenistic origin that homes in on the metallurgical term "*cheo*, which means to pour a liquid or cast a metal,"[125] as Bensaude-Vincent and Stengers explain in the passage cited above. I have already mentioned in passing McCarthy's obsession with metal or iron substances in *The Orchard Keeper*. *Child of God* even has a passage in which Ballard dumbly watches a blacksmith at work, without being able to comprehend the metallurgical procedure of reforging Ballard's axe in the fire (COG, 67–71). In *Suttree*, however, there is yet another interpretation of what it means "to pour a liquid." In effect, the protagonist's alcoholism is more than just the remembrance of McCarthy's own adolescent experiences as one heavy drinker among others in the city he grew up in. The process of nature's disintegration in his fourth novel is likened to the habits of intoxication, the decomposition of nature that includes many forms—most of which are based on chemical grounds. The depictions of excessive drinking and, more often than not, the sexual encounters that this activity leads to, are arguably allegorical of the practice of alchemy as a mode of protoscientific experimentation and, simultaneously, tautegorical insofar as the alteration of states of consciousness (*Mitwissenschaft*) is precisely coextensive with the manipulation of *phusis*, which is the precondition of alchemical practice to start off with. It is this tradition (equally scientific and aesthetic) that is at the heart of *Suttree*'s speculations about nature's identity that consequently become speculations of nature, regardless of whether the passage at hand refers to the caves of the sewer; the dirtiness and "light surmise of putrefaction and decay" (*S*, 66) on Market Street, where Suttree sells the fish he catches in the Tennessee River; or his "final corridors of the brain, small watchmen to see that all is quiet for the advent of eternal night" (29).

The protagonist's hilariously rendered states of delirium and elaborate episodes of drunkenness can thus be seen in a new context, as both Romantically conceived cathartic moments and, in consequence, as chemically effectuated manipulations of one's own psychological geography. In other words, a scene like the one in which the narrator describes Suttree wandering through Knoxville at night after having drunk too much serves as an opportunity to explicate the novel's embeddedness in a poetics of alchemy: the protagonist's drunken visions of fragmentary recollections of his twin brother ("a dead child in a glass bier") and his dreamlike personifications of death as such ("mansized at times and how so?") are certainly not unrelated to the fact that after these moments and a night spent in the midst of "iron-colored nettles and sedge in the reeking fields like mock weeds made from wire", the ground on which he has been sleeping is described as a "packed *black earth* . . . with its bedded cinders and bits of crockery" (*S*, 80, emphasis added). To be sure, the description of the central character's moments of drunkenness on its own does not immediately bring to mind any particular facets of the scientific history I have just mentioned; or rather, it might not seem necessary to connect a description of landscape as "black earth" to that history. I nevertheless argue that the narrative treatments of Suttree's intoxication are as much instances of the abovementioned practice of *nigredo* as the narrative explorations of the caves beneath Knoxville is the *katabasis* necessary for the alchemical effectuation of "salvation, in the gnostic way."[126]

This argument is warranted because McCarthy's narrative about Knoxville's surroundings contains many passages that poetically evoke that very context. The frequency of these passages is too great to be coincidental. Except for Harrogate's and Suttree's wanderings in the underground systems of the sewer, which I examine below, the context I am referring to is even nominally defined: while the narrator describes the Tennessee River on various occasions throughout the text, its appearance is not only that of a "Cloaca Maxima" (*S*, 13), "a rippled sludge" (210) whose animalistic body is "like a giant trematode curling down out of the city, welling heavy and septic past these fine homes on the north shore" (119), but it is presented as the ontological basis for both the existence of the world around it and as the decisive element that determines Suttree's psyche and even his mood. Thus, in the latter part of the novel, "in the spring of his third year on the river" (306), the following passage intimates how this rainy season amplifies Suttree's contemplative tendencies, while living on his houseboat that drifts in the thick current among trash cans, animal cadavers, and even "a dead baby" (ibid.) floating in the mud:

> Oaring his way lightly through the rain among these curiosa he felt little more than yet another artifact leached out of the earth and washed along, drain-

> ing down out of the city. . . . Suttree among the leavings like a mote in the floor of a beaker, come summer a bit of matter stunned and drying in the curing mud, *the terra damnata of the city's dead alchemy*. The fish he raised up from the flood in this season themselves looked stunned. (ibid., emphasis added)[127]

What is slightly different, then, from the earlier Southern novels I have examined in this chapter is the emphasis on the phenomenological aspects of McCarthy's descendentalism, on the central character's lived experience and his psychological processing of events, as "he felt little more than yet another artifact leached out of the earth." Writing about this descendental variation in McCarthy's great book about Knoxville and the troubled mind of its author's alter ego, Thomas Young Jr. notes that Suttree's "attempt to live simply on the river, to penetrate into ever more primitive realms of being, is the same as his other great quest in the novel: the attempt to understand his own past."[128] The latter "quest" of Suttree's, related to the way in which his past continues to shape his troubled mental life, is inextricably linked to "the stillbirth of his twin brother," an event of which he has only heard "because of a drunken lapse of his Uncle John, and presumably he holds this concealment against his family as well." In a sense, this crucial relationship between Suttree and his stillborn twin brother, which leads the former's "ruminations [to] come to center around more fundamental questions of being,"[129] can be seen not only as referring to the long list of twin motifs and doppelgängers in American literature, but also as allegorical of the constancy of what in Romantic philosophies of nature has been called by various names, such as the unground, the abyss, and pure productivity. In other words, the two brothers' relationship refers to the persistence of *that which is not* in *that which is*. Concerning this relationship between "Suttree and Antisuttree" (*S*, 28), Young further argues that "the existence of this spectral other . . . is the constant reminder of [his] own putative nonexistence," a perpetual presence of the well-nigh metaphysical outlook that "*Life* [simply amounts to] *an improbable deviation from the eternally uniform, comfortable stasis of inorganicism*."[130] While the relationship of individual lives to the realm of the inorganic is nicely captured in Young's sentence, it is nevertheless a formulation with which I can agree only in part, since in the novel both the organic and inorganic realms of nature are said to be perpetually moving. Toward the end of the narrative, when the protagonist lies in bed with typhus, a Catholic priest comes to talk to him about his life—in case he does not survive his severe illness. The priest remarks, "God must have been watching over you. You very nearly died." Suttree replies: "You would not believe what watches." As the priest is obviously surprised at that answer, Suttree clarifies that God "is not a thing. *Nothing ever stops moving*" (*S*, 461, emphasis added).

In a much earlier passage that recalls Ballard looking up at the night sky from one of his corpse-filled caves, the narrator of McCarthy's 1979 novel depicts Suttree lying in the yard of a church outside of Stanton, Tennessee, on his way back from a very dramatic episode in which he has attended his son's funeral from a distance, due to the ties he had cut not only to his parents and other relatives but also to his own family, which he had abandoned for a solitary life on his houseboat. On his way back, he is unable to hitchhike at night, so he lies down on the grass in the churchyard, holding a bottle of whiskey in his hands. After drinking and crying himself to sleep, he wakes in the night and—as Ballard would have done—contemplates the nature without and his own nature within. The narrator evokes alchemically significant substances like iron and salt in the same sentences in which Suttree broods over the connection between his own mental state and that of the black nothingness apparent in the distant regions of outer space (the "ether," or what Schelling called the "inexhaustible *primal matter*"):[131] "He must have slept. When he woke he was lying in the grass looking up at the heavens. A cloudless night strewn with stars. Salt taste of sorrow in his throat. He saw a star spill across the sky, a light trail of fire and then nothing. Hot spalls of matter rifling through the icy ether. Misshapen globs of iron slag" (*S*, 159).[132] Where can the expressions of nature as ugly "globs of iron slag" be found, apart from the cosmic environs of the ethereal night sky?

As before in *The Orchard Keeper* and *Child of God*, in this novel McCarthy's most idiosyncratic depiction of what Suttree also calls "blind slime" (*S*, 23) (in one of his many drunken gatherings with his friends J-Bone, Bobbyjohn, and others, "this fellowship of the doomed" [23]) refers to the cave or sewage systems through which Harrogate will crawl—followed a little later by Suttree who is searching for the helpless adolescent ex-convict for whom he cares, almost like a supplicant would care for his or her neighbor.[133] And as in the earlier Southern novels, in *Suttree* the depiction of caves features scenes reminiscent of Plato's cave, in which the shadows on the wall are only representations, or symptoms, of the real forces behind these appearances.[134] Consider how the narrator of McCarthy's fourth novel recapitulates the diction of the earlier novels that pointed toward the dark materiality in the very depths of the earth: "In the summer of his second year in the city Harrogate began to tunnel toward the vaults underground where the city's wealth was kept" (*S*, 259). Suttree's companion thus explores "the dark of dripping caverns, stone bowels whereon was founded the city itself, holding his lantern before him, a bloodcolored troglodyte stooped and muttering down foul corridors, assaying vectors by a stolen scout compass that spun inanely in this nether region so gravid with seam and lode" (ibid.). And a little later, after Harrogate has told Suttree about his adventures underground and his plan to return to the caves beneath the city, in "foul corridors" where the organic and inorganic realms of nature bleed into one, the narrator continues to depict Harrogate's katabatic movements that yet again reveal the both allegorical and tautegorical method at the heart of McCarthy's own exploration of the formlessness of generative materiality—simultaneously a practice of *nigredo* (facing one's own shadow) on multiple levels of narration, and a literary experiment that both describes and manipulates its own course of events:[135]

> In the damp and alveolar deeps beneath the city he probed with a torch he'd stolen, sighting courses from stone to stone to reckon by and charting with his crazed compass a fix of compounded errors. Down old caverns where carbon-colored water leaked from overhead or treacly sipes of sewage. Through a region of ruptured ducting and old clay drains and into a dark stone gullet skewered by a jointed cesspipe. Everywhere a liquid dripping, something gone awry in the earth's organs to which this measured bleeding clocked a constantly eluded doom. . . . Gray sewage percolating down through faults and bedding planes. Dark leachings from the city's undersides and speleothems accresced out of some grim slime quietly oozing in the dark. (*S*, 261–62)

After Harrogate's repeated explorations of these depths, described in the narrator's typically archaic or mythographic diction,[136] once again reminiscent of earlier representative works of descendentalist fictions of the American gothic, "the city mouse" (*S*, 260) (as he is sometimes called in the novel) eventually finds a casing of dynamite, which he then intends to detonate—perhaps to impress his mentor, Suttree. Harrogate's plan actually succeeds, so that in the humorous beginning of a paragraph that has Suttree starting to search for his friend, we read: "When Suttree saw the piece in the paper that said: *Earthquake?* he read and knew. He folded the paper and rose and went out the door" (270). When Suttree finds Harrogate at last, after four days of inspecting the various corridors of the sewer and the adjacent tunnels within the earth, "down the carious undersides of the city, through the black and slaverous cavities where foul liquors seeped" (276), the narrator describes the two friends' "faces [as] blackened like miners or minstrels and the city mouse wore only shreds of clothing and he was covered with dried sewage." At the sight of this, but also at their underground surroundings, Suttree says almost with a touch of black humor: "True news of man here below" (ibid.), which indicates once more the allegorical and tautegorical dimensions of McCarthy's text. I am referring here to the novel's regional disposition, particularly in this passage, that functions as a stand-in for the "true news" that is tales about the ancient times of mankind's origin. But I am also referring to the self-referentiality of which this sentence fragment is capable, since it functions not only at the level of content but also at the level of material form: the narrator (and, in all likelihood, the author) suggests here that it is in the book itself—in *Suttree*—that this type of ancient news may be discovered.

Finally, before turning to McCarthy's 1985 novel *Blood Meridian* in the next chapter, I want to mention yet another strand in the narrative of *Suttree*: the series of encounters between the novel's protagonist and Mother She, an old African American woman living on the outskirts of Knoxville, who Ab Jones calls an "old nigger witch" (*S*, 278). Suttree once watches her "hobbling through the gloom with [a] knobbly cane . . . in the last hours of night to gather herbs from the bluff on the river's south shore" (ibid.). When he visits her with Jones to have her read the old man's palm, she tells Suttree that he "should of come alone" (282). Much later in the novel (after his affair with the prostitute, Joyce, and his return to his houseboat after he had lived with her in an apartment in the city—all the while shunning his friends, one of whom remarks when he returns to the circle of drunkards and hobos, "Ah he's back, God spare his blackened soul, another hero home from the whores" [412]) Suttree returns to Mother She's shack. At that meeting, with just the two of them present, she seems determined to examine the young man's soul and, perhaps, cleanse it. She prepares a tincture that is highly reminiscent, again, of the alchemical roots of the science that according to Grant, both synthesizes its object and analyzes it at the same time. McCarthy writes: "she had taken out an old bottle handblown that held an oily unguent and seemed gone on to philters now, spooning some grim powder from the tin into the pot where the oil began to smoke and sputter with a stench like frying dung." When it is ready, Suttree is asked to drink it: "A tasteless slime impacted with a harsh grit. He swallowed." The tincture soon produces its effect, so that "pieces of a dream unreeled down the back of his brain" (424). What I am interested in here is not merely the description of Suttree's visions, which mostly recall scenes from his childhood. I am also interested in the short yet philosophically significant dialogue between the old woman and Suttree, before he drinks the "tasteless slime." After she advertises her skills by referring to a patient who could walk again after having been treated by her, Suttree clarifies that he is actually in good health, thereby indicating that his problem is of a psychological nature:

> I can walk, said Suttree.
> You can walk, she said. But you caint see where you goin.
> Can you?
> To know what will come is the same as to make it so. (*S*, 423)

This, then, is the clearest explanation of the novel's evocation of alchemy's signature method: the simultaneity of understanding materiality and constructing it as part of that material's own activity. In other words, and almost referring to a reciprocal epistemology, humanity's co-knowing of creation is also a *co-creating*, because according what Grant calls the "'chemical paradigm' for thinking,"[137] to know is to make. What is new, however (as already implied in the passage just quoted), is yet another facet of McCarthy's work, the relationship between freedom (or agency) and determinism (or resignation), and how that relationship is aligned with the dichotomies of allegory and tautegory, and analysis and synthesis, as determined by German *Naturphilosophie* of the kind endorsed in the present study. The next chapter will demonstrate how these motifs are used in McCarthy's first Western *Blood Meridian*, and the stylistically and metaphysically related narrative of *The Crossing*.

[4]

"ANOTHER KIND OF CLAY": PHYSIOPHILOSOPHY AND WAR

The passing of armies and the passing of sands in the desert are one. There is no favoring, you see. How could there be? At whose behest?
—Cormac McCarthy, *The Crossing*

The word has become world. Worldly things have no more reality for God, than our words or our language for us. We carry a world within us while we think; we posit or create a world without us while we speak. —Lorenz Oken, *Elements of Physiophilosophy*

IF THE THEMATIC COMPLEX of decay and decomposition, or of the relationship between the organic and the inorganic, figures prominently in novels like *The Orchard Keeper*, *Child of God*, and *Suttree*, similar claims could be made regarding the fiction of McCarthy's middle period—in particular, *Blood Meridian* and *The Crossing*, both of which will be analyzed in this chapter. However, the focus shifts slightly, and the context here is neither the caves, mountains, and forests of Tennessee nor the human psyche and its moral degradation (even though nearly every one of McCarthy's works deals with the latter in one way or other). Instead, I discuss the function of warfare in the later novels, and a possible theory of language in the light of the idea that nature is all-encompassing—an idea that is part of McCarthy's literary vision of nature and the philosophical stance described in the two preceding chapters. If *Suttree* is the novel in which the author draws parallels between alchemical and literary experimentation, as I argued in the last chapter, the works of McCarthy's middle period echo the philosophical developments of nineteenth-century forms of Schellingianism in ways closely related to the scientific unfolding of modern biology and mathematics.

This chapter thus further explores McCarthy's interest in the natural sciences and the possibility of retaining a certain image of God at the same time that one accepts the immanence of material nature. My reading of *Blood Meridian* in particular builds on chapter 3, and I demonstrate the relationship of the novel to the work of Lorenz Oken, who was inspired by Schelling. But my discussion of *The Crossing*'s three interpolated tales (of the priest, the blind man, and the gypsy) also refers to Oken's philosophy of nature (in addition to the overall Schellingian framework), since it is in these tales that the reader finds the clearest exposition of a conception of language in any novel by McCarthy. The second volume of the Border Trilogy, therefore, adds new facets not only to the author's narrative delineation of "the void" (*TC*, 173)—conceived of as the source or locus of nature's generative energy—but also to his understanding of narrative in the first place. Drawing on the following close reading of *Blood Meridian* in terms of Oken's philosophy and theology of nature, my interpretation of *The Crossing* will combine the Okenian image of God with the Melvillean image of the "weaver-god,"[1] both of which illuminate McCarthy's complicated idea of purposiveness—central to his concept of nature—that implicitly subverts the postmodern dismissal of all things teleological.

BLOOD MERIDIAN, OR *the Evening Redness in the West*, a novel that depicts the journey of a group of scalp hunters through the borderlands of the United States and Mexico in the mid-nineteenth century, contains a passage that deserves more critical attention. This passage considers the notions of fate and agency from the point of view of one of the two leaders of the group, John Joel Glanton. Late in the novel—after many of Glanton's fellow mercenaries have died, together with their Native American scouts ("the Delawares all slain" [*BM*, 243])—the narrative voice describes Glanton's mind-set as a peculiar mixture of resignation and affirmation:

> He'd long forsworn all weighing of consequence and allowing as he did that men's destinies are given yet he usurped to contain within him all that he would ever be in the world and all that the world would be to him and be his charter written in the urstone itself he claimed agency and said so and he'd drive the remorseless sun on to its final endarkenment as if he'd ordered it all ages since, before there were paths anywhere, before there were men or suns to go upon them. (ibid.)

As Kirk Essary has shown, this passage recalls Captain Ahab's view of nature in general and the sun in particular in Herman Melville's *Moby-Dick*, a novel that McCarthy calls his "favorite book,"[2] as I noted in chapter 2. The *Blood Meridian* passage depicts Glanton as he meets his seeming fate with a perspective that combines indifference and absolute control. While he concedes the givenness of everyone's fate, he paradoxically strives to master his own by trying to literally make it his own, "as if he'd ordered it all ages since," as if he had authored or decided it himself: his own fate and the cosmic fate of extinction pertaining to the sun. As Steven Shaviro puts it, "Glanton affirms his own agency through an identification with the whole of fate, so that it is as if he has willed even the event that destroys him."[3] It is, above all, McCarthy's phrasing that is of interest here, especially his representation of a sense of inevitability or unavoidable determination. Glanton's claim to be an agent in ordering the world is described as an attempt to "to contain within him all that he would ever be in the world and all that the world would be to him" (*BM*, 243), even if this containment of agency would be prefigured in those schemes and their ostensible teleology. To communicate this notion of prefiguration, McCarthy writes that Glanton's "charter [is] written in the *urstone* itself" (ibid., emphasis added). What exactly is this urstone, and what is this neologism's importance with respect to the rest of the novel?

While the word might seem to be one of McCarthy's archaic-sounding neologisms, its lexical source and meaning for the narrative are complex matters. There are two possibilities for the source of and reason behind the author's use of the word. First, the mythologies of some Native American tribes, such as the Seneca, the Ponca, and the Omaha, include the notion of a large stone that is somehow fruitful and from which smaller forms of life may emerge. In *Landscapes of the Sacred* (1988), Belden Lane writes: "The Seneca Iroquois traveled often to a large hill at the head of Canandaigua Lake in Western New York. Unremarkable in any outward way, they nevertheless saw it to be the great *Ur-Stone* of their people, the primitive place of emergence where life began."[4] Along similar lines, in a paper on the grammar of Ponca and Omaha, "two . . . highly endangered languages of the Missouri River Valley," Bryan Gordon interprets a section from James Dorsey's collection of nineteenth-century Omaha stories (published in 1890 as *The Cegiha Language*) which reads, in Gordon's explication: "They say *the stone* cracked all over and was ground very finely by the fall. They say that from there *that one round stone* was ground and scattered far, and became all *the scattered stones* of all the lands everywhere." In Gordon's reading, the phrase "*that one round stone*" refers to what he calls "the *Ur*stone, so large it blocked the sun."[5]

All of this sounds like material that McCarthy might have been engrossed in when doing research before publishing his first Western. Yet however compelling these etymological references and inferences might be, the notes he made at the time shed a slightly different light on the hitherto unresolved issue of the "urstone" and thereby suggest another source for McCarthy's phrasing, one that demonstrates the transatlantic cultures of literary and philosophical speculation in whose tradition the author's work as a whole should be regarded. The source for this word, which in *Blood Meridian* simultaneously refers to a space in which the individual fates of human beings are inscribed and to the very protean thing that Glanton strives to contain by sheer force of will, could very well be a concept found in the nature-philosophical writings of Oken. In the notes that McCarthy used to draft *Blood Meridian*, he writes: "URSTONE (URSCHLEIN [*sic*]) OUT."[6] This is a misspelled but clear reference to a word used by Oken that Alfred Tulk's 1847 translation renders as "protoplasma." Oken's neologism, is "*Ur-Schleim*," which denotes the concept of a biologically primordial and formless sludge from which all forms of life and phenomena issue forth.[7] This idea partially continues the metaphysics of the "Cloaca Maxima" (*S*, 13) from McCarthy's previous novel in a different setting—namely, the Mexican-American borderlands of the mid-nineteenth century.

Certainly, McCarthy may also have known of the Native American notion of the "Ur-Stone." Yet it is striking that the notions of "Ur-Stone" and "*Ur-Schleim*" are in some ways conceptually coincident and even have similar pronunciations: "Ur-stone" is "Ur-Stein" in German, which is remarkably close to Oken's "*Ur-Schleim*." McCarthy's notes suggest that he might have been aware of this resonance and that he used the word "urstone" to refer to Oken's concept, playfully concealing his source. In any event, the *Ur-Schleim* in Oken's *Elements of Physiophilosophy*[8] represents, ontologically speaking, the inexistent grounding for the world's phenomena and is alternatively called the "Nature-Nothing [*Natur-Nichts*]"[9] as well as likened to the zero in mathematics and the conception of time that is not correlated to human temporality, as I mentioned in chapter 2. In the present chapter I argue that this obscure reference in McCarthy's manuscripts to a similarly obscure figure in the history of the philosophy of nature opens up a new way of reading *Blood Meridian*—namely, by determining the concept of nature underlying it. My claim is that Oken's "physiophilosophy," which is Tulk's translation of the idiosyncratic German term *Naturphilosophie*, can be traced in the narrative voice, the narrative dynamics, and the philosophical monologues of the scalp hunters' second leader, Judge Holden. In other words, the seemingly antinomic propositions in Oken's *Elements*—a strange hybrid of post-Kantian transcendental thought and the natural sciences of his day—are mirrored not only in the novel's most violent if "childlike" (*BM*, 79) figure but also in descriptions, statements, and metaphysical speculations of the narrative voice itself. As the reference to the "urstone" and its Okenian influence suggests, the question of fate versus agency—which is also that of determination versus freedom, or (nonhuman) nature versus (human) reason—is central to any understanding of the novel. What distinguishes my reading from the major interpretive frameworks in McCarthy scholarship, however, is the way in which the novel's question of fate versus agency—crystallized in the notion of the urstone—is raised, in contrast to critical accounts that identify a biocentric or ecopastoral standpoint in *Blood Meridian*. By the same token, my reading is equally critical of postmodern accounts in the scholarship that detect a literary subversion of Western rationality in the novel.

The question at hand mirrors what Jay Ellis has called the "central problem"[10] of *Blood Meridian*—namely, the discrepancy between man's intentions and nature's indifference, or in the terms of my analysis, between reason's containment of the order of the world and the urstone that precedes it. This chapter, therefore, develops Ellis's articulation of what may be called the "clay issue" in McCarthy's first Western novel. According to Ellis, a by now often-cited passage in the book formulates the "central problem" as it depicts the novel's setting, the American Southwest. The passage occurs shortly after the kid has been introduced: "not again in all the world's turning will there be terrains so wild and barbarous to try whether the stuff of creation may be shaped to man's will or whether his own heart is not another kind of clay" (*BM*, 4–5). Much later, the judge gives an answer in another often-cited passage: "If war is not holy man is nothing but antic clay" (307). The question and its ostensibly authoritative answer in many ways frame the plot, especially because of their respective positions in the course of the narrative and because of what they convey. While the question is established by asking "whether . . . or not" something is the case, its answer rhetorically suggests the divine nature of war, whose negation would affirm that the heart of man is "another kind of clay." This seems like an either-or logic at work that echoes familiar debates in the philosophy of nature and, by extension, in environmental criticism about the ontological priority between humans and nature—that is, product and productivity, or object and process. Yet in a sense McCarthy's negotiation and expression of the "clay issue" rejects both options and affirms them at the same time. There is no decision made between a nature subordinated by humans via "a caricatured Enlightenment"[11] and the antiscientific stance based on humanity's lack of agency in an irrational world, inherited from Theodor Adorno and Max Horkheimer's *Dialectic of Enlightenment* (1944). The biocentrism of deep ecology and the subversive matrices of deconstruction are both evident in the novel, but they are insufficient to serve as critical frameworks, as I have discussed above.[12] In effect, the novel seems to proclaim the divine nature of war *and* the nature of the human heart as immanent in the "earthen causeways" (*BM*, 5) of the American West.

It must be said that this reading of the novel is to be distinguished from ethically motivated accounts of the book that detect the literary vision of a reconciliation between humankind and its environment, such as Georg Guillemin's and Andrew Keller Estes's studies of McCarthy.[13] As I showed in chapter 1, these two scholars proclaim that a biocentric perspective (as opposed to an anthropocentric or logocentric one) is essential for understanding *Blood Meridian*. For Guillemin, "the desert scenes" in the novel signify "the resistance of wilderness to the logocentric encoding of nature as a cultural artifact."[14] And, to reiterate Estes's argument, passages in McCarthy's book such as the section about the often-cited notion of "*optical democracy*" that represents "a strange equality" between "all phenomena" (BM, 247, emphasis added) should be read as "biocentric maps" whose message is that "the natural world possesses intrinsic rights and does not exist purely for the benefit of man."[15] Conversely, the affirmations that war is holy and that man is substantially made of clay (of a conglomerate of dust and liquids, in other words) necessitate an account of McCarthy's novel that captures its dramatization of the indifference of natural processes to humankind and, in turn, the indifference of the human characters to the order of nature. As Judge Holden claims when he and the kid reencounter each other after a long time, referring to the ignorance of the men who spend their time in the tavern: "They do not have to have a reason [to be here]. But order is not set aside because of their indifference" (BM, 328).

Far from devaluing the specific ecology of the American Southwest as an important part within the narrative, I demonstrate in this chapter that a mainly biocentric reading intended as a rebuttal of an anthropocentric or language-based perspective on the clay issue disregards the entanglement of both positions in the narrative. In McCarthy's rendering of living nature and its partial encapsulation within language, it is not so much the "intrinsic rights"[16] of the former that devaluate the adequacy of the latter; nor is the linguistic description of its outside all there is to the understanding of a novel—in which, after all, the importance of an argument concerning linguistics pales when compared to the brutal reality of a scalp hunter's everyday life. Rather, as the notion of the "urstone" suggests, nature *exceeds* the bounds of living organisms while simultaneously *including* the workings of language. In *Blood Meridian*, therefore, *bios* and *logos*—the immanence of living nature and the transcendence of human reason—are entwined in a way that is grounded in what I have called a physiocentric, rather than biocentric, stance with respect to nature's identity.[17] Based on McCarthy's reference to Oken's neologism and, as I will show below, the novelist's accordance with the philosopher's major ideas about the concept of nature, I will substantiate the claim that *Blood Meridian* resonates with a philosophy that ascribes to nature a generally dynamic and material character, encompassing both creatures and concepts—that is, both living organisms (*bios*) and their registration in linguistic inferences (*logos*). As in *The Orchard Keeper*, *Child of God*, and *Suttree*, in this novel nature is grounded in, or defined as, a primordial formlessness (*phusis*) that is indifferent to the bodies and ideas it generates. Other than its historical setting, what sets McCarthy's 1985 novel apart, though, is its emphasis on the disposition of war, and the way in which that topic relates to the decomposition of objects and ideas in the world.

This conceptual entwinement of *bios* and *logos* resembles many tendencies in nineteenth-century philosophical thought about nature and its processes, and Oken's *Elements of Physiophilosophy* provides a fitting synthesis for *Blood Meridian*'s "central problem" even beyond the reference to the concept of the *Ur-Schleim*: while man's ideality remains bounded by nature's potencies, in the practice of war the event of the world's creation may be repeated. Or as Oken puts it: "By the process of destruction [*Tödtungsproceß*], the finite being seeks to become the universe itself [because] man is a complex of all that surrounds him, namely of element, mineral, plant and animal."[18] To develop a new framework for the problem of natural determination regarding the novel's individual beings and their grim surroundings, the issue of the determining "urstone" and the "charter[s] written" therein (BM, 243), I argue that Oken's philosophy of nature offers valuable clues to the *narrative continuity* that extends from the judge's monologues to the narrator's descriptions of the barren landscape traversed by Glanton's warring gang of scalp hunters and, eventually, to other novels of McCarthy, chief among them the second volume of the Border Trilogy. Along the lines of recent scholarly work that identifies the author's strong relationship with science and its history,[19] then, this interpretation runs counter to both predominantly biocentric or ecopastoral readings and, above all, to accounts of *Blood Meridian* that detect an outspokenly critical or even subversive tendency with respect to the evils of nineteenth-century imperialism and ideology in America.[20] Better still, the question of whether or not McCarthy's "new mythic vision presented in *Blood Meridian* offers a postmodern challenge to notions of essentialized ethnic and national identities and borders"[21] seems less pressing compared to the issues of contemporary philosophical and scientific inquiry. This is because, according to the physiocentric basis of McCarthy's poetics, it is ethics that results from ontology, not the other way around, and thus any ostensibly subversive inclination in McCarthy's fiction is the product of his generally descendental poetics, his use of images and scenes of disintegration for allegorical and tautegorical effect.

I will show in two main steps how *Blood Meridian* expresses an Okenian philosophy of nature by narrative means. First, after having introduced Oken in chapters 2 and 3, I will now examine his theories in detail, showing the parallels between his *Elements* and McCarthy's *Blood Meridian*—chief among them the similarities between the "protoplasma"[22] and the "primal mud" (BM, 146) and between the generative zero in mathematics and the quantification of life in acts of war. Second, I will discuss another link between Oken and McCarthy besides the "urstone" reference—namely, the influence that Oken had on Melville, the author of McCarthy's favorite novel, *Moby-Dick*. This discussion includes an examination of the ways in which the sea imagery in that novel resembles *Blood Meridian*'s Okenian physiophilosophy on an aesthetic level.

McCarthy's novel begins with three epigraphs that portend what is to come in this extraordinarily violent narrative about issues ranging from scalp hunting to cosmology. One of these is a quote from Jacob Boehme, the gnostic thinker who would become important for nineteenth-century idealists such as Schelling and Oken.[23] As Shane Schimpf explains, Boehme had a "concept of the Ungrund or the Abyss . . . an undifferentiated entity that was defined as the absence of everything. Creation, according to Boehme, arises from the Ungrund dividing from itself via an internal will to self-understanding."[24] Schimpf further notes that *Blood Meridian*'s subtitle ("*Or the Evening Redness in the West*") can be interpreted as "a clever reference" to Boehme's first work *Aurora* (1612), the full title of which is: "*Aurora. That is, the Day Spring. Or Dawning of the Day in the Orient or Morning Redness in the Rising of the Sun. That is the Root or Mother of Philosophie, Astrologie, and Theologie from the true Ground. Or A Description of Nature.*"[25]

Without trying to merely reiterate an interpretation of McCarthy's novel and its central figures as motivated by Boehmian gnosticism,[26] I want to emphasize *Blood Meridian*'s status as a comprehensive or fundamental "*Description of Nature*" by means of narrative, and this, it seems to me, is very much in accordance with Oken's ontological (that is to say, *mathetic*) conception of an abyssal or void-like grounding of terrestrial forms of life. In the preface to the third edition of his *Elements of Physiophilosophy*, Oken, "the speculative scientist," as René Wellek once described him, states "that all organic beings originate from and consist of [an] infusorial mass, or the protoplasma (*Ur-Schleim*) from whence all larger organisms fashion themselves or are evolved."[27] Similar to Schelling's "primal ground [*Urgrund*] of existence" or the "indivisible remainder" from his *Freedom* essay, the philosophical concept of this protoplasma is a prime example of what Peirce Mullen has characterized as "Romantic science," the idea of an originary structure or archetype from which all forms of life would evolve.[28] Oken goes on to state that "the Organism is none other than a combination of all the Universe's activities within a single individual body," a proposition that is rephrased later as "the finite thing seeks to become the universe itself."[29]

Already, we are reminded of Glanton's wish to "to contain within him all that he would ever be in the world" (*BM*, 243) and his desire to "drive the remorseless sun on to its final endarkenment" (ibid.)—that is, his twin intentions of containment and destruction, which are so emblematic of Oken's thought. The reader of *Blood Meridian* might also be reminded of Judge Holden's remark that "every man is tabernacled in every other and he in exchange and so on in an endless complexity of being and witness to the uttermost edge of the world" (141), a remark that reiterates Suttree's statements that "a man is all men" and that "all souls are one" (*S*, 422 and 459). The "combination[s]"[30] of nature's actions in Holden's remark—focusing on humankind while also accounting for other life-forms and phenomena, as I discuss below—are somehow immanent in each and every body as well as the overall entanglement. Furthermore, the "complexity of being and witness" (*BM*, 141) gives rise to a concept of nature that extends indefinitely and a part of which is self-aware. The interdependency of finite beings in the world according to both Oken and the judge denotes something different from any semiotic or linguistic theory according to which meaning is to be generated by the co-constitution of differences. Oken's definition of "Organism" is related to an ontological thesis that anticipates his paradoxical statement that finite beings are the results of an originary nothing or contingency that is both slimy and inexistent—*a given formlessness*. The judge reflects this statement in his twisted anthropology, which both debases man and elevates him (or some elements of the human species) as nature's pinnacle: "For whoever makes a shelter of reeds and hides has joined his spirit to the common destiny of creatures and he will subside back into the primal mud with scarcely a cry. But who builds in stone seeks to alter the structure of the universe" (146). The reader of Oken's *Elements* will find similar depictions of the "primal mud" out of which the as yet unaltered "structure of the universe" emerges. It is this "primal mud" from which each finite thing originates, as Oken reasons in his philosophy of nature—a theoretical practice that he also terms "mathematics endowed with substance."[31]

But why is mathematics so important for Oken's *Naturphilosophie*? And how can the void be coterminous with the protoplasma? Protoplasma is the Platonic template of which actual phenomena are only temporary products, or "retardations," and enjoy a merely "fallacious existence [*Trugexistenz*]."[32] These phenomena, therefore, exist in contrast with yet are immanent to what Oken calls "the Eternal [or] the *nothing* of Nature," which is functionally coterminous with the template.[33] Parallel to the judge's preoccupation with the taxonomy of natural and cultural forms, as seen in his quantification of their properties and sketching of their shapes (*BM*, 140), Oken's notion of a *creatio ex nihilo* has as its foundation the christening of mathematics understood along the lines of what Deleuze and Guattari term the "royal science"[34] upon whose structure supposedly any philosophical and scientific inference is built.[35] Oken conceptualizes the continuous generation of the necessary out of the contingent—or, in Platonic terms, the persistence of *that which is not* in *that which is*—in this way:

> The principle of nature, or of the universe, must be of one and the same kind with the principle of mathematics. For there cannot be two kinds of monades, nor of eternities, nor of certainties. The highest unity of the universe is thus the Eternal. The Eternal is one and the same with the zero of mathematics. The Eternal and zero are only denominations differing in accordance with their respective sciences, but which are essentially one. . . . The Eternal is the *nothing* of Nature. As the whole of mathematics emerges out of zero, so must everything which is a Singular have emerged from the Eternal or the *Nature-Nothing* [*Natur-Nichts*].[36]

The zero of mathematics, on a formal level, is the absence of the phenomena on which that discipline operates, and which is thereby present in each and every instance of a number and every act of numbering. As is also the case in Cantorian set theory, developed at the beginning of the twentieth century, the zero subsists in every group of numbers or magnitudes. Every act of counting tacitly re-counts the zero as the condition of possibility for the numbers generated. As Grant explains: "Oken's account of zero's generative potential can be rendered in the form of the generation of natural numbers from the empty set."[37] Before the count, "the empty set Ø, on its own, contains nothing; wrap a set around it, however {Ø}, and this second set allows the empty set to 'emerge out of itself as number,' since the set containing the empty set contains thereby one member {Ø} = 1. An infinite number of sets can be added in like fashion."[38] In a similar way, the genesis of a given plant or animal species is recapitulated in the individual development of a given member of that species. Put differently, in Oken's physiophilosophy there is a consistent parallelism between the formal or abstract, on the one hand, and the real or concrete, on the other hand. The importance of the mathematical zero for ontology is constitutive of the necessity of natural nothingness—the "Nature-Nothing"—for biology, and vice versa. The recapitulation of the zero in each number, or (in the language of axiomatic set theory) of the empty set in each set of numbers, in this sense correlates with the repetition in each human being of the slimy ascendancy of the entire species.[39]

Oken sees the incipient discipline of modern biology as premised on the principles of a mathematized ontology, in which the concept of the zero, or the "*nothing* of Nature," somehow lives on (or, in literary terms, *is cited*) in every occurrence of a phenomenon or form of life.[40] In biological terms, "*ontogeny recapitulates phylogeny*."[41] Although this phrase was coined by Ernst Haeckel in the second half of the nineteenth century, the concept has a long history that was shaped in large part by the work of Oken and his fellow *Naturphilosophen*. Put differently, the "'biogenetic' or 'Meckel-Serres law,'" as it is also called, is the result of a general understanding in the circles that practiced Romantic science, starting at least as early as 1793.[42]

It should be noted that the early account of recapitulation in the *Elements* has at least two directions, due to its structurally reciprocating polarities of "mathematics" and "substance," in the words of Oken. The parallelism exists between these polarities and their individual developments—that is, both diachronic and synchronic—and between the developments of single organisms with respect to the evolution of their phyla (animals) and divisions (plants). In addition to this, however, is the principle dictated by "the highest unity of the universe"—namely, that all phenomena are related in the sense that they are finite expressions of an infinite process. They are the ornamental retardations, the transient beings, of the formless yet generative zero, the "Nature-Nothing." In other words, Okenian recapitulation works both vertically and horizontally, on both a formal and a real level, and it must allow for diagonal (that is to say, transitional) relationships across the unceasing continuum of nature.[43] As Robert Richards informs us, already in *Die Zeugung* (1805), Oken had argued that "the organic could not arise out of the inorganic."[44] Yet this meant only that there is no supernatural moment in which, suddenly, life emerges from the stasis of inorganicity. Rather than *creatio ex nihilo* in the sense in which the respective creations, or products, of nature simply exist (that is, by way of a divine transformation of the inorganic into the organic realm), the forces of the "Organism" are constituted only insofar as they are themselves appearances of the inorganic, similar to the way in which every number is merely a positing of zero.

Regarding *Blood Meridian*'s clay issue—whether or not humankind is subordinated to nature, and whether or not humankind is part of nature to begin with—Oken is quick to affirm that "nature is antecedent to the human spirit."[45] Yet while nature is ontologically prior to mankind, the latter is nevertheless part and parcel of the former, as can be concluded from the identity of the respective "principle[s] of nature, or of the universe" and those of mathematics.[46] "On Oken's evidence, then," Grant writes, "number is inseparable from animal precisely because *animals are the numbers of nature*."[47] In turn, numbers are the formalizations or abstractions of singular beings, including animals but also the plants, rocks, and dust that are part of the empirical, or corporeal, world. Furthermore, it is possible to deduce nature's ontological priority from Oken's thesis about the combination of universal elements in every singular being, the striving of each singularity "to become the universe itself."[48] According to Oken, this act of attempting to incorporate that which exists without (that is, the whole universe) into that which lies within (that is, a singular) is performed by all individual beings in the world but is best done by humankind, or what he calls "man." This is because "Man is the summit, the crown of nature's development, and must comprehend everything that has preceded him, even as the fruit includes within itself all the earlier developed parts of the plant. In a word, Man must represent the whole world in miniature."[49] While mankind appears to be the summit of the natural domain, it is grounded upon that which has preceded it and is itself the ground for future generations of forms of life that will supersede it. This is because "the field of the eternal or nature is continuous [in] an unbroken field of transition," given that "evolution is nothing but a concatenation of zeros," as Reza Negarestani paraphrases Oken's account.[50]

All of this establishes one of Oken's antinomic propositions: that man is nature's pinnacle—the creature that "builds in stone to alter the structure of the universe" [BM, 146]—*and* simultaneously is nothing other than a manifestation or positing of "the primal mud," the zero, or the nothing of nature. In McCarthy's words, man is indeed "another kind of clay." To repeat Judge Holden's solution to the clay issue: "If war is not holy man is nothing but antic clay" (307). In terms of the larger narrative of *Blood Meridian*, as well as Oken's account of the partial inclusion of mankind in (and its exclusion from) the material universe that surrounds it, war is holy—and the substance of man is coincident with that of other materials. McCarthy's novel depicts again and again how the group of scalp hunters is both embedded in the darkness of the surrounding desertscapes and alien to it. Further, what Grant has called the "antecedence criterion"[51] is elaborated narratively in passages that depict the monotonous yet bloody journey of Glanton's gang. As I mentioned above, according to this criterion, the fact "that ground may not be substantial does not mean that it cedes priority with respect to the grounded, which is [also not] the totality of the actual."[52] In effect, this understanding of the dynamics of the antecedent and that which succeeds it is conveyed in Oken's ontological prioritization of the nonhuman grounding of nature vis-à-vis the groundedness of the human spirit.

Consider, for instance, *Blood Meridian*'s elaboration of such a standpoint: "They rode on. They rode like men invested with a purpose whose origins were antecedent to them, like blood legatees of an order both imperative and remote" (BM, 152). However, this is not a teleological purpose of the kind that has been rejected time and again by cultural critics inspired by postmodern philosophies and those philosophies' opposition to the grand narratives of the modern. Rather, the distinct purpose of the scalp hunters is the partial fulfillment or recapitulation of the long line of warring individuals that preceded them. They act according to an "order both imperative and remote" (that is, both unconditional and nonrecoverable), because they cannot fully grasp what it is that gives rise to their existence. They cannot do so because if they did, the generation of finite bodies and ideas on the basis of the antecedent *phusis* would cease to be ontologically prior with regard to its products. The eternal and the Nature-Nothing would consequently switch places with the ephemeral and the singular within nature. Conversely, if war is "the ultimate trade," as the judge proclaims, the tradition of its art is what "its ultimate practitioner" (248) must honor. As a band of "ultimate practitioner[s]," of which he and Glanton are the leaders, the men "moved like migrants under a drifting star and their track across the land reflected in its faint arcature the movements of the earth itself" (153). These movements of dust and rain, and of blood and dirt, are repeated in the motions and deadly activities of the scalp hunters who are consequently one with the "primal mud," the clay of which they are built.

This warring group of murderers is just that: an assembly intended to kill, thereby fulfilling the noblest act performed by the summit of nature, which is man, according to Oken, Judge Holden, and the narrative voice (even though the latter is not to be understood as identical to the author's). If, as Christopher Dacus reasons, there is an "obvious penchant for number symbolism" in McCarthy that "can be interpreted as something like Plato's definition of time as the moving image of eternity,"[53] this can be seen particularly in the sections of the novel that deal with warlike scenes and the descriptions of related settings. For instance, when the kid joins the army of filibusters under the command of Captain White, we read that their "camp was upriver at the edge of the town. A tent patched up from old wagon canvas, a few wikiups made of brush and beyond them a corral in the form of a figure eight likewise made from brush where a few small painted ponies stood sulking in the sun" (*BM*, 36). The passage foreshadows the impending and inevitable doom of the filibusters by alluding to the infinite, the divine nature of war. After all, if you turn the number eight on its side it is the symbol for infinity, or the eternal (∞).

The divine nature of war reveals the implications of understanding the positing of numbers out of and within the primary zero in the formal realm of mathematics and understanding the manifestation of forms, or morphogenesis, out of and within the eternally contingent in the realm of physiophilosophy. The formal and real actualization of forms juxtaposes the realm of the infinite zero, which ideally exists, with the realm of finitude, which actually exists. In tandem with the act of positing, then, another act comes to pass—that of negating either the single being or other finite singularities, be they humans, animals, or plants. While it is the numbering act of scientific discourse that quantifies the world and exposes the indifference of antecedent nature toward humankind, it is the killing act of war, "the process of destruction [*Tödtungsproceß*]"[54] that rationalizes or equalizes a life as "another kind of clay"—"the human mind itself being but a fact among others" (*BM*, 245) as the judge states later in *Blood Meridian*.

Finally, a dual process that Oken variously calls "individualizing" and "universalizing," "positing and negating," or "presentation" and "retrogression"[55] makes intelligible the sacred character of the triumvirate of mathematics, philosophy, and war, which is echoed not only in the judge's claims that "War is god," and its art "the truest form of divination," which comprises "all other trades" of human conduct (*BM*, 249), but also on the last page of the *Elements of Physiophilosophy*. For Oken, "the art of War is the highest, most exalted art; the art of freedom and of right."[56] It combines the characteristics of "all sciences and all arts"[57] because it repeats the primal act of numbering, the emergent realization of the Nature-Nothing in the struggle of will against will, with each individual will retrogressing toward zero. Ontology in Oken's sense, then, is the self-consciousness of the act of positing and negating by philosophical means, whereas the calculus of war is the nearest approximation of the contingency within which forms of life emerge. Or, as Grant puts it: "Philosophy is the *formal* repetition of cosmogony, while war is its *essential* repetition."[58]

I turn now to Oken's definition of God and the divine. Curiously, this definition is almost exactly reiterated in one of Judge Holden's metaphysical speeches. In one of the many instances in which he examines the landscape surrounding the band of scalp hunters after they have set up a camp, a remarkable dialogue takes place that is not only emblematic of the judge's philosophy of nature but arguably of the whole novel's underlying presumptions about the identity and extensity of natural processes. After the judge has been "breaking ore samples with a hammer," thereby adding to the taxonomy of material forms and phenomena in his ledger book—refining "his ordering up of eons out of the ancient chaos" (*BM*, 116)—his audience of murderers, adventurers, and half-wits confronts him by objecting to his reasoning by citing passages from the Bible. Holden remains unaffected and depreciative as usual:

> The judge smiled.
> Books lie, he said.
> God dont lie.
> No, he does not. And these are his words.
> He held up a chunk of rock.
> He speaks in stones and trees, the bones of things. (*BM*, 116)

His reaction resonates uncannily with Oken's *Naturphilosophie*.[59] After having added his numbers and schemata into his register of plants, animals, and other objects, the judge debates with a man in the audience about a given book's veracity, and the content of his argument seems to be a paraphrasing of Oken's conception of God and his divine language. When the judge affirms the word-like character of "stones and trees, the bones of things" (*BM*, 116), he means God's words, utterances whose most approximating practice is the art of war. In turn, Oken defines God as the "self-consciousness [and] ceaseless presentation" of the zero, the "self-manifestation of the primary act"[60] in which and through which the zero is counted and the slime is molded. The following passage may very well have been the blueprint for Holden's speech in front of his fellow scalp hunters:

> The presentations are, however, manifested or attain only reality through *expression*. The world is therefore the language of God; the creation of the world the speaking of God. . . . This is the created, realized system of thought. The thought is only the idea of the world, but speech is the idea actualized. . . . As thought differs from speaking, so does God from the world. Our world consists in our apparent thoughts, namely, the words. The universe is the *language* of God.[61]

Apart from giving philosophical context to the judge's argument, this paragraph (which combines a theodicy, an account of creation, and a theory of language in just a few sentences) also evokes the notion of "presentation" having a genuinely expressive character. Presentation can be understood as both the actualization of the eternally formless into mortal forms and phenomena and as the construction of phenomena from the perspective of singulars, such as human beings. Put differently, while "words are things," and while "their authority transcends his ignorance of their meaning" (*BM*, 85)—referring to whoever is unable to decipher them—it is still the experiential horizon of every human being that defines his or her world—otherwise, again, the ontological priority between product and process would be inverted. In line with the antecedence criterion, which posits a perpetually unequal relationship between the ground and the grounded, and between the eternal and the singular, the judge argues that "the order in creation which you see is that which you have put there, like a string in a maze, so that you shall not lose your way. For existence has its own order and that no man's mind can compass, that mind itself being but a fact among others" (245).

Oken's theory of language as well as the greater nature-philosophical framework of Romantic science can thus be found in a novel published in 1985. *Blood Meridian* is thereby at odds with the general cultural tendencies of literary postmodernism that tried to unmask scientific and religious master narratives. Instead of criticizing the destructive character of scientific progress and religious regress, *Blood Meridian* suggests a post-Kantian mind-set that is built on the notion of a fundamental gap, or contingency—a conception of a dark ground whose creator, Boehme, became one of the major sources of McCarthy's work.[62] Rather than postulating the relative and arbitrary character of language and its fictional denotation of physical objects such as stones or trees, *Blood Meridian*'s most violent character proclaims the coincidence of spoken words and these objects in a recapitulation of what Oken terms the "primary act"[63] by which singular and finite forms of life come into being.

In addition to postmodernism's preoccupation with linguistic and textual matters, broadly conceived, *Blood Meridian* is also at odds with the straightforwardly biocentric orientation that has been ascribed to it. The question at the heart of the clay issue in the novel—whether war is holy and concomitant with a commitment to rational and scientific inquiry, or whether man is wholly embedded in the irrational fabric of nature like any other animal, rational or not—is treated in a way that affirms either both options or none, rather than indicating a choice between the two. Furthermore, and against all appearances, Grant argues,

> Biocentrism does not . . . define nature against languagephilosophy, as we might think, but rather defines the moment beyond which the phenomenological envelope will not extend, precisely because life is thought not in itself, but *for consciousness*. 'Biocentrism' marks the point, that is, where a *phenomenology* of nature . . . turns back from nature itself, through 'life,' and towards the consciousness that life vehiculates.[64]

Unlike *Suttree*, the work that preceded McCarthy's 1985 novel, or *The Road*, *Blood Meridian* contains no evidence of a phenomenological introspection provided by means of narrative. Since "biocentrism and logocentrism . . . both hinge around an essentially phenomenological approach to nature,"[65] either both must be affirmed with regard to an analysis of the novel or neither used. The logic behind any subversion of the rational in the name of a nonanthropocentric nature as imagined in the vitalist strands of literary ecology runs counter to McCarthy's narrative about the indifference of the deserts and plains to its nomadic marauders, and the indifference of the judge's practice of a scientific naturalism with regard to the natural and cultural objects he scrutinizes and subsequently destroys. Neither bio- nor logocentrism seem to be able to escape the conceptual horizon of phenomenal consciousness, the perspective of lived experience. Neither a discourse based on life nor one based on discourse itself enters the realm of indifference that *Blood Meridian* evokes. In actual fact, the novel depicts a double indifference, which juxtaposes the immanence of living nature and the transcendence of practical reason with the transcendence of death-in-nature and the immanence of theoretical reason. To unpack this doubling we could say, in Cormackian diction, that it is precisely because "men are made of the dust of the earth" (BM, 297) and there is "a strange equality" between "spider," "stone," and "blade of grass" (247) that the judge's conception of science as indifferent to its objects of inquiry equals the indifference of nature with respect to mankind. Okenian physiophilosophy is a framework that succinctly explicates this double indifference, mirrored in the entanglement of man and dust, of practical human reason in discursive form and living nature in the forms of singular organisms. Recalling Oken's statement that the zero and the eternal are one, and that the empty set and the Nature-Nothing are functionally equivalent, given the identity of the respective "principle[s] of nature, or of the universe" and those "of mathematics,"[66] then Ø equals ∞. In the same way, the spoken word is on a par with the physical object (or better, coincides with it), according to the philosophy of nature underlying *Blood Meridian.*

The line of reasoning concerning the embeddedness of humanity in its physical environment appears for the last time in the epilogue. In these last sentences of the novel's postscript we read of "*a man progressing over the plain by means of holes which he is making in the ground*" (BM, 337), with two groups of wanderers behind him—one of which collects the bones lying on the ground, while the other might consist of cartographers or "surveyors," as Ellis calls them.[67] The petrified remains probably belong to the dead buffalo that are mentioned toward the end of the novel,[68] but they may belong to the men, women, and children who have died in the course of the many massacres that have taken place in the book and in the brutal history of the American West. *Pace* Ellis, it is arguably both groups of nameless wanderers who "*cross in their progress one by one that track of holes that runs to the rim of the visible ground and which seems less the pursuit of some continuance than the verification of a principle, a validation of sequence and causality as if each round and perfect hole owed its existence to the one before it there on that prairie*" (BM, 337). The italicization of this epilogue, its placement in the novel as a coda, and its almost transhistorical and mystical tone suggest that the passage refers to more than simply the cruelties of westward expansion and the political consequences of the very idea of progress. Arguably, the "*progress*" described as "*a validation of sequence and causality*" also aptly delineates what is so central to the logic of Oken's philosophy of nature: the deductive method of constructing speculative inferences, in which each proposition is built on the one that preceded it, point by point, "*hole by hole*" (337)—very much like the generation in the natural realm of forms, including animal species and plants, all the way to the protoplasma from which each of these phyla and divisions emerged in the first place.[69] Cartography (the measuring of the world) and the collecting of bones (which presupposes the dynamics of what Oken termed the *Tödtungsproceß*) go hand in hand, at least in *Blood Meridian*'s epilogue. As Manuel DeLanda writes in *A Thousand Years of Nonlinear History* (1997), a book that may be seen in the tradition of works like Oken's *Elements* inasmuch as it mixes historical with philosophical, physical, biological, economic, and linguistic perspectives on world history: "While bone allowed the complexification of the animal phylum to which we, as vertebrates, belong, it never forgot its mineral origins: it is the living material that most easily petrifies, that most readily crosses the threshold back into the world of rocks. For that reason, much of the geological record is written with fossil bone."[70]

There are indeed many organic materials in the novel that are in the transition "back into the world of rocks," or the world of raw matter, due to the all-pervasive practice of war. This transitional space (part solid, part slimy) is the realm of clay between the organic and the inorganic, and in the tradition of depicting this space in literature another link between Oken and McCarthy may be established. This connection is *Moby-Dick*, McCarthy's "favorite book."[71] Jill Barnum shows the connections between the Romantic scientist and his *Ur-Schleim* and the creator of the literary leviathan. What is more, she cites historical evidence that while Melville, like his contemporaries Ralph Waldo Emerson and Henry David Thoreau, "owed a debt to German Romantic thought in general," it was "Oken in particular" that he was interested in.[72] Barnum writes that Melville "was reading Oken's *Elements of Physiophilosophy* while composing *Moby-Dick*. In 1854 he presented a copy of *The Whale* to John C. Hoadley inscribed with these lines from Oken's *Elements*: 'All life is from the sea; none from the continent. Man also is a child of the warm and shallow parts of the sea in the neighborhood of the land.'"[73] As Barnum further shows, apart from the mention of generative protoplasma as "sea," *Moby-Dick* even contains a reference to the early version of the biogenetic law—namely, that ontogeny recapitulates the development of the entire species. According to her, "the phenomenon that most securely binds Oken to Melville centers on a discovery claimed by Oken . . . that the cranial bones in the skull were mirror-images of an animal's spinal vertebrae. This discovery thrilled Oken because he had long been searching for a primordial unity in nature that could at the same time account for particularities of individual organisms."[74] In chapter 80 of Melville's novel, when Ishmael is "referring to the image of a strung skull necklace, [the narrative voice] declares flat out: 'It is a German conceit, that the vertebræ are absolutely undeveloped skulls' [382], an incontestable endorsement of Oken."[75] Here again, and via Melville, we see the resonance between McCarthy and Oken's foundational, if rudimentary, version of the recapitulation thesis. Perhaps Bathcat's "necklace of human ears," which the narrator compares to "a string of dried black figs" (*BM*, 87), points specifically to this resonance and is not merely an allusion to the brutal practices of American imperialism in general and during the Vietnam War in particular.[76]

In connection with the "German conceit," as the author of *Moby-Dick* called Oken's discovery of the unifying image of natural forms via the morphological similarities between the skull and the vertebral column, another recent find in the McCarthy archive indicates McCarthy's knowledge of the nineteenth-century theory of recapitulation. McCarthy's unpublished screenplay "Whales and Men" demonstrates that he does not just know about Oken (as evidenced by his reference to the *Ur-Schleim* in the early manuscripts of *Blood Meridian*) but that he is well versed in the main aspects of the biogenetic law, of which Oken was an early theorist. That understanding can be seen in a dialogue between the screenplay's two main characters, John and Guy. John asks if Guy has ever seen a whale fetus, and Guy answers that he has seen photos of them. "Yes," John responds. "You know the theory that ontology recapitulates phylogeny." Guy calls this a "pseudo-theory," but John affirms it, noting that early in the process of development a human fetus has what appear to be "vestigial gills." He adds that a whale fetus "looks alarmingly like a human fetus," with hind feet, fingers, nostrils, and ears. At the Oceanographic Institute, John looked at one in a vial and "had an uncanny sense that we were somehow included in the whale's history. That we were what the whale might have been. And that he was what we would never be."[77]

What is peculiar here is not just that the example McCarthy chooses to use in discussing the recapitulation thesis is the relationship between whales and men, in yet another echo of Melville's reading of Oken, but also that he writes "ontology" when it should have been "ontogeny." While there are undoubtedly many different ways to interpret McCarthy's (intentional or unintentional) misspelling, the phrase "ontology recapitulates phylogeny" is a rather ingenious juxtaposition of the linguistic realm and that of organic matter. This is because the theory of recapitulation was not only influential in the life sciences of the nineteenth century but also resulted in the phrase "ontology recapitulates philology"—a motto credited to James Grier Miller by the twentieth-century American philosopher of language Willard V. O. Quine.[78] In light of this analysis, moreover, McCarthy's combination of both traditions that have used the notion of recapitulation as a motif to imagine a generative dynamic between the whole and the part, and between systems and their individuals, displays what I described above as the entanglement of *bios* and *logos* in the novel.

Thus, while it is not clear whether McCarthy was aware of Melville's indebtedness to Oken when he was writing *Blood Meridian*, it is nevertheless striking how McCarthy's work is a literary example of the biological idea of recapitulation in particular, and how *Blood Meridian*'s philosophy of nature appears to be a literary expression of Oken's Romantic science.[79] Given the strong link between Melville's and McCarthy's works, it should not surprise the reader to find passages that refer back to the Melvillean "sea" and its monsters, even when McCarthy is describing the deserts, forests, or Mexican towns through which the scalp hunters roam. Indeed, on a number of occasions Melville's literary transformation of Oken's *Ur-Schleim* (which the latter regarded as identical to what he called "sea-mucus [*Meerschleim*]"[80]) seems to be the "unconscious" of McCarthy's text, looming in the background, repeated while being transformed itself whenever the word "sea" is used.

For example, when the Glanton gang rides past a cathedral early in their blood-soaked journey, McCarthy describes the building as being decorated with "the dried scalps of slaughtered indians strung on cords, the long dull hair swinging like the filaments of *certain seaforms* and the dry hides clapping against the stones" (*BM*, 72, emphasis added). And a few pages later, there is a "church where old Spanish bells *seagreen with age* hung from a pole between low mud dolmens" (97, emphasis added). When a bear mutilates one of the Delaware Indians who for a time accompany the scalp hunters, "the bear swung with the indian dangling from its mouth like a doll and passed over him in a *sea* of honey-colored hair smeared with blood and a reek of carrion and the rooty smell of the creature itself" (137, emphasis added). Another scene in the desert provides a more focused analogy: "They were riding in pure sand and the horses labored so hugely that the men were obliged to dismount and lead them, toiling up steep eskers where the wind blew the white pumice from the crests *like the spume from sea swells* and the sand was scalloped and fraily shaped and nothing else was there save *random polished bones*" (175, emphasis added), while "adamantine ranges" are "rising *out of nothing like the backs of seabeasts* in a devonian dawn" (187, emphasis added) when the band of murderers is "[passing] through a highland meadow" (187). A more lengthy passage, which also grotesquely combines the sea and bone imagery as well as the motif of "the mathematical certainty of death" (*S*, 295), is also set in the desert. It describes a still life in a typically Cormackian style:

> The riders looked off to the north. They rode on. Beyond a shallow rise in cold ash lay the blackened wreckage of a pair of wagons and the nude torsos of the party. The wind had shifted the ashes and *the iron axletrees marked the shapes of the wagons as keelsons do the bones of ships on the sea's floors.* The

> bodies had been partly eaten and rooks flew up as the riders approached and a pair of buzzards began to trot off across the sand with their wings outheld like soiled chorines, their boiled-looking heads jerking obscenely. (*BM*, 220, emphasis added)

This still life projects the Nature-Nothing that is so central to *Blood Meridian* (and, to a certain extent, *Moby-Dick*) onto the plain of dust that is the desert, the most indifferent ecology imaginable. It is not just the body parts of those who once traveled in the wagons that are now broken, but also the vehicles themselves. Given to the decay of that life-threatening ecology, their remains are likened to the "bones of ships on the sea's floors." It is as if not just supposedly living nature is susceptible to the petrifaction of which DeLanda writes, the transit "back into the world of rocks,"[81] but actually all that is corporeal in the world eventually strives toward its point of manufacture—even if this goal must remain unattainable, the process of disintegration notwithstanding.

The last and arguably most powerful image that serves to demonstrate the strong link between Melville's version of the *Ur-Schleim* and McCarthy's narrative explication of it is found in the closing paragraph of chapter 21 of *Blood Meridian*. At this point, the kid and the ex-priest have been rescued by Native Americans of the Digueño tribe from certain death in the Californian desert and have reached the western shore, at the edge of San Diego. In the evening, while Tobin has "turned off to find them a doctor" (*BM*, 303), the kid wanders toward the beach and watches a horse and its colt there, as "the sun dipped hissing in the swells" (304). Like the dialogue between John and Guy from "Whales and Men," the following passage captures the simultaneous kinship and alterity of humankind and the animal kingdom:

> He rose and turned toward the lights of the town. The tide-pools bright as smelterpots among the dark rocks where the phosphorescent seacrabs clambered back. Passing through the salt grass he looked back. The horse had not moved. A ship's light winked in the swells. The colt stood against the horse with its head down and the horse was watching, out there past men's knowing, where the stars are drowning and whales ferry their vast souls through the black and seamless sea. (ibid.)

If we consider the references to "the primal mud" (*BM*, 146) and the simultaneously progressive and destructive character of Judge Holden's scientific theory and practice; the latter's as well as Oken's characterization of war as the "highest, most exalted art" of humankind;[82] and, finally, the possibility of an implicit channeling of Okenian Romanticism through the subtle but explicit references to McCarthy's "favorite book" in *Blood Me-*

ridian's narrative, it is possible to conclude that *Blood Meridian* indeed reveals an Okenian philosophy of nature. With regard to the book's "central problem,"[83] therefore, McCarthy's narrative rendering of Okenian thought affirms man's substance as "another kind of clay" (*BM*, 5) and reiterates the idea that this species recapitulates the natural history of plant and animal life that preceded it. *Blood Meridian* evokes Oken's idea that the sacred nature of mathematics, philosophy, and (above all) war depicts the approximation of *that which is not* in the addition and subtraction of finite beings in the world.

However, this does not mean that the link between Oken's ideas and McCarthy's poetics is a somehow definitive reading that disproves other predominantly philosophical interpretations of *Blood Meridian*, even if it shows that physiophilosophy is a helpful framework for any analysis of the novel's underlying philosophy of nature.[84] Nor does the established connection between the views on the nature of war of Oken, the judge, and the narrative voice in any way entail a straightforward endorsement of their politics. Instead, this connection raises questions about the assumption that McCarthy's novel is a simple denunciation of the practices of war, American imperialism, and bloodshed in general, and it challenges the standpoint according to which the novel's characterization of humanity as "another kind of clay" is a postmodern rebuttal of the *logos* of rationality. Oken's concept of the Nature-Nothing—of the acknowledgment of a generative negativity, or primordial formlessness, at work in both human and nonhuman phenomena and forms of life—provides a new perspective on the concept of nature construed in the worlds of McCarthy's 1985 novel and others. Not only a "historical romance," then, "in which characters move in intertextual regions between fiction and myth," as John Sepich has noted,[85] *Blood Meridian* can also be understood as the novelistic expression of a speculative kind of Romanticism that navigates between science and philosophy.

It is this space between science and philosophy that *The Crossing* delves into as well, even though this novel was not the first one that McCarthy published after *Blood Meridian*. However, there is a certain sequential order between them if one looks at the historical settings of the 1985 novel (the mid-nineteenth century) and the adventurous tale about Billy Parham and his brother Boyd from 1994 (set roughly in the period between the First and the Second World Wars). Although the later novel's style of writing, tone, and atmosphere are, at times, very different from those of *Blood Meridian*, the philosophical themes echo the ones in McCarthy's first Western.[86] *The Crossing* can be viewed as both a variation on and a supplement to the physiophilosophical underpinnings of the earlier novel. This is because the author returns to the notion of the generative zero (repeatedly using the term "the void"[87]) and thereby revisits the theme of the corporeal world and its human inhabitants understood as "dust" in direct comparison to this originary nothingness—Oken's Nature-Nothing—or what is also called "the true and ageless world" (*TC*, 283) by the blind man in the second of three interpolated stories within the novel.

Here, as elsewhere, McCarthy's "narrative textures mirror the mysteries of the natural world. The three interwoven stories . . . suggest a metaphysical source and an underlying order in nature, which he renders in detailed description."[88] Many scholars have emphasized the importance of these tales within *The Crossing*, as well as the notion of "tale" or "story." According to Dianne Luce, for instance, "*The Crossing* suggests that rather than any physical sense, the human capability for narrative—not for language, which is another kind of artifact, but for formulating the tale that carries our past, gives meaning to our present, and right intention to our future—is one primary means of accessing and perhaps communicating the thing itself: *the world which is a tale*."[89] Even though I agree with Luce's assessment that McCarthy's conception of storytelling goes beyond the bounds of particular languages, I would modify this interpretation by arguing that it is precisely because it is a physical activity—in the sense in which, according to Schellingian and Okenian *Naturphilosophie*, even ideas are expressions of physical nature, or what I have termed the physiocentric continuum—that "the human capability for narrative" has its origin in the world itself and not merely in the exceptionally human capacity to forge sentences in distinct idioms. Similar to the Okenian theory of language that I have outlined in my reading of *Blood Meridian*, McCarthy's notion of *the void*, as it is depicted in the second volume of the Border Trilogy, is recounted in that volume by means of literature. Narrative is understood here as an allegorical means of implicating something other than itself (extratextual reference—a technique for understanding that "one thing can be another thing" [*KP*, 26]) and a tautegorical means of self-reference pertaining to text and world (intra- and intertextual reference). I am specifically concerned with how the narrator delineates that "unknowable void" (*TC*, 73) in *The Crossing* and the fact that the delineation is not merely a tale *about* that void but a narrative *of* it—structurally isomorphic, to be sure, with McCarthy's earlier narratives that veer stylistically between allegory and tautegory.

I want to focus here on the ontological importance of the three tales of the priest, the blind man, and the gypsy within the overarching story of Billy's adventures with and without his brother Boyd, north and south of the border between New Mexico and Mexico. Beside these interpolated stories, there are passages in the novel where the narrator refers to *the void* in terms that are consonant with Oken's notion of the Nature-Nothing

(*Natur-Nichts*), or what I have conceptualized as the formless givenness of nature.

Arguably, the first of these passages alluding to a domain of nature that is somehow other than that of lived experience, yet still recapitulated in and generative of its processes, can be found on the second page of the novel in a paragraph that describes Billy's reverence for the packs of wolves that roam near his home in the plains of New Mexico. The special relationship that is established in the first part of the narrative is set in place here: as a young boy, not even fourteen years old, he sneaks out of his home "on a winter's night" (*TC*, 3), in search of the wolves, after having heard them howl. Following the tracks they have left in the snow, he eventually sees them and watches them excitedly: "They were running on the plain harrying the antelope and the antelope moved like phantoms in the snow and circled and wheeled and the dry powder blew about them in the cold moonlight and their breath smoked palely in the cold as if they burned with some inner fire and the wolves twisted and turned and leapt in a silence such that they seemed of another world entire" (4). What the narrative bears out in this passage is arguably not an affirmative stance of vitalist origin that would underscore the "inner fire" of life's unbound powers, represented not just by those animals that Jack London also revered in his novels a little less than a hundred years before the publication of *The Crossing*, but by their eventual prey. Contrary to what Edwin Arnold claims,[90] the image of the circling wolves is not grounded in a biocentric ontology, because the wolves' movements give them the posture of a type of species that seems otherworldly or downright mythological. Moreover, we should recall that the eyes of the she-wolf whom Billy brings back to Mexico in the first part of the novel evoke a realm that the narrator described as an unlivable space that cannot be accessed by means of one's senses but that seems to constitute the ontological and epistemological basis of human sensibility. When Billy and the wolf are camping in the Mexican desert, he cannot sleep properly because of the coldness during the night. So he must see that unlivable realm: "He'd rise and mend back the fire and [the wolf] was always watching him. When the flames came up her eyes burned out there like gatelamps to another world. A world burning on the shore of an unknowable void. A world construed out of blood" (*TC*, 73).

This passage is worth reconsidering in light of the philosophies of nature examined in previous chapters, as well as in the discussion of the metaphysics underlying *Blood Meridian*—a metaphysics based, in part, on the scientific histories of biology and mathematics in the nineteenth and twentieth centuries. This scene takes place on the night before Billy crosses the border to Mexico for the first time, taking his she-wolf back to where she came from. The narrator describes how "the darkness that passed over them came in a sudden breath of cold and stillness and passed on. As if the darkness had a soul itself that was the sun's assassin hurrying to the west as once men did believe, as they may believe again" (*TC*, 72–73). In this nearly gnostic depiction of landscape, the narrator suggests that the darkness that envelops both Billy and his wolf has a pneumatic quality.[91] The expression "as if" in this sentence arguably signals its allegorical capacity to connote more than the immediate, or immanent, context in which it is narratively enveloped (the novel, the author's oeuvre, and the mode of literary narration), which would conversely be the tautegorical dimension that is still arguably its stylistic base. The expression thus points to the metaphysical outlook expressed by the entire novel—namely, a stance in which *the void*, like the darkness of the night passing over Billy, the she-wolf, and his horse, has "a soul itself." The succeeding section, then, is the point in the novel when the narrative voice depicts the she-wolf's eyes as mediating entities between existence and "another world." This paragraph also determines what is actually meant in the section of the novel's first few pages, when Billy watches the wolves on the wintry plains of New Mexico. The paragraph could, on a first superficial reading or if isolated from the rest of the novel, be seen in the context of a reverent vitalism that worships the animality of wolves for itself, as life's affirmation:

> He'd rise and mend back the fire and [the wolf] was always watching him. When the flames came up her eyes burned out there like gatelamps to another world. A world burning on the shore of an unknowable void. A world construed out of blood and blood's alcahest and blood in its core and in its integument because it was that nothing save blood had power to resonate against that void which threatened hourly to devour it. He wrapped himself in the blanket and watched her. When those eyes and the nation to which they stood witness were gone at last with their dignity back into their origins there would perhaps be other fires and other witnesses and other worlds otherwise beheld. But they would not be this one. (73–74)

These speculations on the part of the narrator, I suggest, are more than reflections on a supposed realm of transcendence that is closed off from the existing world. Certainly, the "world burning on the shore of an unknowable void" is different from the existing one, or "this one," in which Billy intends to return the wolf to Mexican soil. Yet the complex phrasing here suggests that *the void* mentioned here may be viewed not only as the futural space in which the contemporary world has ceased, but also the predispositional realm that renders possible the realm of existing forms and phenomena.

The second part of the passage—like the mention of the antelopes' "inner fire" and their hunters' predatory appearance that "seemed of another world entire" in the earlier passage from the novel (*TC*, 4)—again makes two ways of reading McCarthy possible: he can be seen either as an ecocentric writer or as a physiocentric one.[92] Arnold opts for the former interpretation, while I endorse the latter. Surprisingly perhaps, the philosophical and religious contexts in which both readings are positioned are nearly identical, while the estimation of the ontological priority of specific terms yields different, sometimes even contradicting, conclusions. In other words, my reading takes some of Arnold's premises as a starting point yet combines these in terms of *Naturphilosophie* rather than in terms of an approach that above all champions the ethical dimension of McCarthy's text. For instance, Arnold writes that "in ecological terms" the novel "asks that we reconsider our position in the natural world," and that "in religious terms, it asks that we recognize how limited our perception of the spiritual realm remains."[93] He thereby both affirms the general tendency in ecocriticism to conflate the notion of the ecological with that of nature and advocates for the literary stance that supports religious humility—all the while arguing for the narrative's "biocentric view of nature."[94] While I agree with him that the poetics of *The Crossing* are closely related to the philosophical mysticism of Boehme (who is the source of one of *Blood Meridian*'s epigraphs), and that "we might rightly, in fact, identify McCarthy as a spiritual writer himself, a spiritual author . . . who believes in a source of being and order deeper than that manifested in outward show and pretense of human individuality," and, finally, that "the [novel's] title alone encourages a kind of religious exegesis,"[95] I disagree with Arnold's estimation that this necessarily supports the view that the narrative contains an ecological, biocentric, or ethically based conception of *the void*.

To return to the second part of the lengthy paragraph that has the Mexican wolf watching Billy with eyes "like gatelamps to another world" (*TC*, 73), I would argue that the motifs recalled in the last two sentences recapitulate issues that were also key motifs in earlier fiction by McCarthy—namely, the concept of nationality and of witnessing: "When those eyes and the nation to which they stood witness were gone at last with their dignity back into their origins there would perhaps be other fires and other witnesses and other worlds otherwise beheld. But they would not be this one" (74). Is it Billy's nationality that is at stake here—the American nation, which is so integral a theme throughout McCarthy's Western fiction, as many scholars have noted—or are we dealing with an expanded concept of "the nation" (meaning that of wolves, or animals generally, who are gradually becoming extinct in New Mexico because humans set traps for them)? Are the wolf's eyes witnessing the deeds of Americans (and of humanity as a whole), or are they the witnesses of an animal species, looking toward future times and future "worlds" about which one can only speculate? Furthermore, we need to ask in what way the witness of specific worlds must have the capacity to think in a certain way to qualify as a witness, or, to give substance to those worlds (which "perhaps" would no longer exist if the act of witnessing ceased altogether). Is it only "man [who] is tabernacled in every other and he in exchange and so on in an endless complexity of being and witness to the uttermost edge of the world" (*BM*, 141), as Judge Holden claims in *Blood Meridian*, or does this also hold for other animals apart from the human animal?

To be sure, these questions are related to the issue of what kind of thought is required to be able to count as witnessing, according to the logic proposed in McCarthy's fictional world of *The Crossing*. The narrator of that world seems to have a well-nigh *panpsychist* standpoint regarding the requirement of either witnessing or thinking as such, given that even "the darkness" that surrounds the tale's main figure appears to have "a soul itself . . . as once men did believe, as they may believe again" (*TC*, 72–73). When I discuss the interpolated story of the blind man, I will come back to McCarthy's allusions to this tradition of thought—a tradition that posits the existence of a level of thought (or better, a psychical capacity) throughout nature.[96] For the moment, it will be enough to state that the second volume of the Border Trilogy, as well as other novels by McCarthy, suggest an understanding of the term "psyche" that is in many ways consonant with Schelling's in his exegesis of Plato's *Timaeus*. This is because, like McCarthy's narrator, Schelling suggests that the Platonic conception of "*psyche* means nothing but: *original principle of motion*, *arche kineseos*"; it does not merely denote the capacity to contemplate.[97] Thus, McCarthy's narrative will eventually identify the notion of *the void* as the predisposition of this "*original principle of motion*," and thus link it to the condition of possibility that I have examined as the posture, or figure, of supplication in McCarthy's early fiction.

In line with this contextualization of *The Crossing* against the backdrop of the metaphysical tradition of panpsychism (or, rather, a certain version of the latter), the novel's title should indeed be interpreted in religious terms, as Arnold proposes,[98] yet this does not mean that those terms should extend beyond their materiality, since they must still count as terms *within* nature's conceptual process, given the latter's immanence evoked throughout McCarthy's novelistic work. What I mean by this is that although "the crossing" of *The Crossing* refers to the complicated distinction between the realm of secular phenomena and that of their ideal grounding in the divine, I claim that this distinction should be reframed as that between corporeal and incorporeal materiality, or what could also be called the resonance between the physics of the body and "the physics of the idea."[99] One reason for this is the Platonic understanding of the "soul" as the engine of orderly motion, while the "ataxia of forces"[100] refers to the material consolidation of becoming, which is also identical with and recapitulates the primal matter from which order arises.[101] In other words, "Platonic physics concerns the emergence of order from disorderly and unceasing motion,"[102] recasting the capacity of thought, first, as the condition of possibility both for consciousness and for conscience, and, second, as part of an entirely material dynamics. As will become apparent, this reframing of the question of which kinds of realms or worlds the narrative of *The Crossing* refers to is supported by the centrality of the concept of *the void* and its generative potential for thinking (namely, as "unceasing motion") and by the enlargement of the notion of the witness by including nonhuman forms of thought that are directly related to that potential—forms that McCarthy also calls "*the sentience of rocks*" in his notes for "Whales and Men."[103]

In any event, the figure of the wolf seems to have a relationship to the questions of who or what kind of entity qualifies as witness and how that "world construed out of blood and blood's alcahest" (*TC*, 73) might be accessed by means of narratively speculating on the resonance between the two kinds of physics I have just mentioned—those of concepts and creatures.[104] This assessment is confirmed by several passages in the first part of the novel. For instance, when Billy visits him in search of advice on how to capture the she-wolf, Don Arnulfo, who is regarded as a blasphemous "brujo [sorcerer]" by his people (48), says: "Each hunter must have his own formula. He said that things were rightly named its attributes which could in no way be counted back into its substance" (45). This is a claim that is surely resonant with the "antecedence criterion" inspired by Schelling and Oken,[105] which dictates the ontological priority of natural process with regard to its products that can in no way be returned to their nascent state of nonbeing, due to their dynamic evolvement ad infinitum. It is a proposition that holds for both concepts and objects, since the material potentiality of their existence exceeds their ontological status as natural product, a status that has to be regarded as posterior to that potentiality as ground. The brujo goes on to contend, almost as if to outline the desperate and tragic path that Billy will traverse throughout the narrative,

> that no man knew what the wolf knew. . . . El lobo es una cosa incognoscible, he said. Le que se tiene en la trampa no es mas que dientes y forro. El lobo propio no se puede conocer. Lobo o lo que sabe el lobo. Tan como preguntar lo que saben las piedras. Los arboles. El mundo [The wolf is an unknowable

> thing, that which one has in the trap is more than teeth and fur. One cannot know the true wolf. Wolf or what the wolf knows. It's like asking what the stones know. The trees. The world.] (*TC*, 45)[106]

I read this passage not as an admonition to once again affirm the virtue of humility in the face of the perils and joys of a God-given world but, in fact, as the direct opposite of such an admonition: Billy's tale is an allegorical narrative that is concerned with *the void* in "the crossing" not only between Mexico and New Mexico, or between the divine and the secular, but also between human and nonhuman knowledge, and between the things humans can know and the "ideas" of wolves, stones, trees, and eventually *nature itself* ("el mundo"). The conversation between Billy and Don Arnulfo continues: "The old man went on to say that the hunter was a different thing than men supposed. He said that men believe the blood of the slain to be of no consequence but that the wolf knows better. He said that the wolf is a being of great order and that it knows what men do not: that *there is no order in the world save that which death has put there*" (*TC*, 45, emphasis added). This claim clearly forebodes the plotline of the she-wolf's death; some aspects of Billy's later conversations with the priest, the blind man, and the gypsy; and the tragic events in the narrative such as the murder of Billy's parents and the equally untimely death of his brother, Boyd. More than that, the order generated by death—the "ataxia of forces"[107]—will later be identified with the order of *the void*, which is precisely what is meant by the generative potential of the latter.

The brujo goes on to tell Billy that it will be hard to capture the she-wolf he is looking for, simply because of its particular disposition as a wolf, which substantiates the claim that perhaps the wolf, as well as human beings, can fulfill the role of witness:

> You catch [it] but when you look in your hand you dont have it no more. . . . If you want to see it you have to see it on its own ground. If you catch it you lose it. And where it goes there is no coming back from. Not even God can bring it back. . . . The wolf is made the way the world is made. You cannot touch the world. You cannot hold it in your hand for it is made of breath only. (*TC*, 46)

The concluding remark in particular once again recapitulates the idea of the pneuma of darkness mentioned above, for which the animal nature of the she-wolf generally (and her eyes particularly) figures as a medium. Finally, after the old man mythologically describes the she-wolf's peculiar character, he advises the sixteen-year-old boy to "find that place where acts of God and those of man are of a piece. Where they cannot be distinguished" (*TC*, 47). When Billy asks where those places are to be found, Don Arnulfo claims "that it was not a question of finding such a place but rather of knowing it when it presented itself. He said that it was at such places that God sits and conspires in the destruction of that which he has been at such pains to create" (ibid.). In other words, the places where the activity of humankind and those of the divine coincide are not places one can trace in the existing world but those where the genesis and the dissolution of the world's forms and phenomena become identical. Furthermore, the notion that darkness itself is capable of a certain pneumatic activity—as the narrator of *The Crossing* had suggested earlier in the text (72)—entails the notion that the "place where acts of God and those of man are of a piece" (47) is precisely not an ascendentally inscribed locality but the undetectable space that defines the hegemonically determined imbalance between nature's antecedent productivity and the consequent products it spawns. The identity (both ontologically prior and posterior to the realm of existing forms, yet nevertheless entangled with it) is established in what Oken calls the Nature-Nothing (*Natur-Nichts*), or the generative void out of which and into which phenomena move ceaselessly, all the while emerging and ceasing to be and not be, according to the dialectic of presentation and negation (or, as I called it in chapter 3, of construction and subtraction) out of and back into the protoplasma (*Ur-Schleim*) of natural processes.

Before turning to the three interpolated tales, each of which present variations on the Okenian theories of language and narrative "presentation"[108] from *Blood Meridian*, I want to comment on two additional passages that are important in the context of the generative void depicted in *The Crossing*. The first of these depicts the moment when the she-wolf has died from the wounds inflicted by Mexican dogs and from the coup de grâce from Billy's rifle, when he finds the animal (which had been taken away from him by Mexicans) nearly dead in a barn in which dog fights are held. In a compassionate act of caring for the wolf, Billy (who is her supplicant) shoots her. Subsequently, he rides out of the little town where he had attempted to rescue the she-wolf and ultimately grieves for her, which the narrative voice depicts in a fashion that is typical of the other instances in McCarthy's oeuvre when the painful sadness of the content is compensated for by the poetic beauty of the writing:

> He took up her stiff head out of the leaves and held it or he reached to hold what cannot be held, what already ran among the mountains at once terrible and of a great beauty, like flowers that feed on flesh. What blood and bone are made of but can themselves not make on any altar nor by any wound of war. What we may well believe has power to cut and shape and hollow out the dark form of the world surely if wind can, if rain can. But which cannot be

> held never be held and is no flower but is swift and a huntress and the wind itself is in terror of it and the world cannot lose it. (*TC*, 127)

After Billy has buried the wolf and has started back north toward New Mexico, the narrator describes how one night Billy lies half-awake on the plains—a passage that recalls both the *optical democracy* scene from *Blood Meridian* (*BM*, 247) and the speculations in *The Road* concerning the revelation of the genesis of forms "in the world's destruction" (*TR*, 272). The passage is also linked to McCarthy's penchant for the history of mathematics, demonstrated in many other novels including *The Orchard Keeper*, *Outer Dark*, *Suttree*, and, of course, the author's first Western from 1985:

> In that wild high country he'd lie in the cold and the dark and listen to the wind and watch the last few embers of his fire at their dying and the red crazings in the wood coals where they broke along their *unguessed gridlines*. As if in the trying of the wood were elicited *hidden geometries* and their orders which *could only stand fully revealed*, such is the way of the world, *in darkness and ashes*. (*TC*, 130, emphasis added)

These sentences recall the alchemical connotations of the Southern novels and the notion of the "mathematical certainty of death" (*S*, 295) to the same degree that they constitute a variation of the "inner fire" (*TC*, 4) of the antelope from the beginning of *The Crossing*. Moreover, they are part of the long list of campfire descriptions in the Border Trilogy and most other tales by McCarthy, and they arguably resonate with Oken's definition of fire as the most divine and thus most powerful element of all, due to its simultaneous connotation of emergence and destruction. As Oken writes, in a passage that clearly echoes Schelling's treatise *On the World Soul*: "Fire is the totality of *æther*, is *God manifested in his totality*. God, previous to his determination to create a world, was darkness; in the first act of creation, however, he appeared as fire. There is no higher, more perfect symbol of divinity than fire. God's whole consciousness, apart from individual thoughts, is fire."[109] In what follows, then, I show how this cosmology, concomitant as it is with McCarthy's curious poetics of a yet to be determined form of panpsychism—according to which, as the protagonist of *Suttree* put it, "nothing ever stops moving" (*S*, 461)—is also reflected by the three interpolated tales of the priest, the blind veteran, and the gypsy.

The first of these three tales in *The Crossing* begins when Billy meets a priest in front of the church of a deserted town called Huisiachepic on his way home from the tragic and adventurous events with the she-wolf. The priest tells him that the reason why he had moved to that town was that he "was seeking evidence for the hand of God in the world. I had come to believe that hand a wrathful one and I thought that men had not inquired sufficiently into miracles of destruction. Into disasters of a certain magnitude" (*TC*, 142). In light of the previous analyses, it is difficult not to categorize this statement as a tautegorical one—that is, as a self-referential instance that points to the immanent and thus autogenerative process of McCarthy's fiction and the way his narratives are construed in tandem with speculations on the identity of nature. In other words, the self-reflexivity of the priest's tale (the fact that the narrative in which the priest figures is one of many "miracles of destruction" and "disasters of a certain magnitude") is not merely a claim about the textual realm of literary processes, but, since McCarthy's fictions are also *about* nature's all-encompassing reach, this kind of *autopoiesis* is part and parcel *of* nature. Billy asks the priest if he suspects that "the people that lived here had done something bad," to which the priest replies, "I thought it possible, yes" (ibid.). Eventually, he declares that the reason for his being in that town is because of the tale about a certain man—a tale, it becomes clear, that really is about the nature of tales or *the tale as such*:

> What was here to be found was not a thing. Things separate from their stories have no meaning. They are only shapes. Of a certain size and color. A certain weight. When their meaning has become lost to us they no longer have even a name. The story on the other hand can never be lost from its place in the world for it is that place. And that is what was to be found here. The corrido. The tale. And like all corridos it ultimately told one story only, for there is only one to tell. (142–43)

The sentiment expressed by those words connotes, once again, Boehme's gnostic cosmology, which prefigures the theory of ungrounding that is so integral to Schelling's and Oken's philosophies of nature: "In *Forty Questions on the Soul*, Boehme describes the Deity's mystical essence as the 'Ungrund' (the 'unground'), implying both nothingness and all, that which in being everything is equally an incomprehensible 'No thing.'"[110] Boehme's is a metaphysical source text that necessarily brings to mind McCarthy's notes about the "foam of nonbeing," which "is time,"[111] or, in the language of *Blood Meridian*, *the urstone itself*. Unsurprisingly perhaps, at this point, the priest's understanding of a given tale's disposition is inclined to be tragic, like his own story about the heretic who rejects God's existence after having experienced the traumatic event of having outlived his own son, due to the natural catastrophe of an earthquake—incidentally, perhaps the most pertinent example of what I have been describing, via Nick Land's geophilosophy, as McCarthy's investment in the literary rendition of "geotraumatic tension."[112] The priest's understanding also always concerns the same structure of the tale—a process that I suggest is related to the conception of self-similarity, or fractality, that is integral to the type of complexity studies practiced at the Santa Fe Institute, where McCarthy has been a fellow for decades. The priest continues his theory of what a tale is by contending that two different places in the existing world (for example, two cities) can be conceived of as two "different worlds" (*TC*, 143), as in two distinct lived spaces, with different inhabitants, life stories, and customs:

> Yet even so there is but one world and everything that is imaginable is necessary to it. For this world also which seems to us a thing of stone and flower and blood is not a thing at all but is a tale. And all in it is a tale and each tale the sum of all lesser tales and yet these also are the selfsame tale and contain as well all else within them. . . . I say again all tales are one. Rightly heard all tales are one. (143)

As I have indicated, the priest's tale is that of a loving father from Huisiachepic, the town in which the priest tells Billy this story. This man loses his son due to an earthquake in a different place. Stricken by grief, he eventually meets the priest in the small deserted town, supposedly having renounced God, and as "a heretic" (*TC*, 47), having adopted a worldview that can also be described as a practice of cultivating an utter indifference toward the world. It is a view according to which "the world . . . can have no cause to favor certain enterprises over others. The passing of armies and the passing of sands in the desert are one. There is no favoring, you see" (148), the priest explains to Billy. However, at that point in his life, the heretic's view of the world does not entail the complete dismissal of the idea of God: in fact, "there was God and there was the world. He knew that the world would forget him but that God could not. And yet that was the very thing he wished for" (ibid.). Feeling more and more contempt for that God who, in his view, had ungrounded his life, the heretic starts dreaming about the divine:

> In his dreams God was much occupied. Spoken to He did not answer. Called to did not hear. The man could see him bent at His work. . . . Seated solely in the light of his own presence. Weaving the world. In his hands it flowed out of nothing and in his hands it vanished into nothing once again. Endlessly. Endlessly. So. Here was a God to study. A God who seemed a slave to his own selfordinated duties. A God with a fathomless capacity to bend all to an inscrutable purpose. Not chaos itself lay outside of that matrix. And somewhere in that tapestry that was the world in its making and in its unmaking was a thread that was he and he woke weeping. (149)

Recalling, yet again, the relation between observation and construction in the last part of this depiction of Billy's dream, the paragraph as a whole refers back to the notion of the "weaver-god . . . drawn from *Moby-Dick*," although, as Steven Frye rightly states, "McCarthy is less ambiguous than Melville, since he posits an underlying unity in his characters' lives. In *The Crossing* the notion of individual stories unified in the 'matrix' of the one story lends singularity to a multiplicity of perspectives."[113] What, then, is Melville's image of the weaving divinity? Frye notes that it can be found in a scene in chapter 102 of Melville's famous novel, in which Ishmael gives an account of his whereabouts on one of the Solomon Islands, Tranque. "For Ishmael, the earth is 'a weaver's loom,' the vegetation the 'warp and woof' [Melville, *Moby-Dick*, 489], and the sunlight 'a flying shuttle' [ibid., 490] operated by a silent, invisible, and ceaselessly working divinity that transcends the visible world. Yet this god paradoxically shares humanity's dilemma in this vast world-factory,"[114] since this supposedly transcendent being is still part of that which it constructs by means of its constant weaving: "The weaver-god, he weaves; and by that weaving is he deafened, that he hears no mortal voice; and by that *humming*, we, too, who look on the loom are deafened; and *only when we escape it shall we hear the thousand voices that speak through it*."[115] Of the many aspects that could be noted regarding this passage and its influence, perhaps one of the less obvious yet particularly pertinent aspect is the word "humming," which McCarthy uses again and again in his fiction.[116]

To return to the passage at hand, which is evidently a riff on Melville's tale of the weaver-god, Frye writes that it is this "humming" frequency that "unites all the 'voices' of humankind in a single inarticulate sound."[117] Thus, like human beings, the divine being in the weaver's workshop signifying the world in the dream "is both inside and outside" the world, "a conception that appears similar to the 'panentheist' view" according to "which the divine exists both within and outside his creation."[118] While Melville's source might suggest a conception that is both theological and philosophical, McCarthy's text arguably exceeds this framework due to his conception of nature as all-encompassing productivity. God exists as part of the primordial materiality that is nature, or better, the "*nothing* of Nature"[119] that is the very space "out of" which the world gets woven and "into" which it disappears "once again. Endlessly. Endlessly" (TC, 149). Yet even though the weaving God appears to be "a slave to his own selfordinated duties" (like the "thread . . . in that tapestry that was the world in its making and in its unmaking" that turns out to be the dreaming man himself, who, above all, loathes the thought of a divine being that let his child die for no reason) this conception does not necessitate the panentheist view, according to which God alone is the grounding for the construction of the world. Rather, in an even more expansive viewpoint, the conception champions the "nothing" out of which the threads "in his hands" emerge and into which they return indefinitely. I suggest that it is, therefore, a "weak" form of panpsychism (as opposed to the stronger thesis of a universal mindedness) that characterizes the weaving divinity in *The Crossing*, not only because this position is consistent with McCarthy's frequent allusions to the sentience of nonhuman entities in the world, but also because it aligns well with Oken's understanding of God's identity as the "self-consciousness [and] ceaseless presentation" of natural nothingness.[120] What is so remarkably consistent in this literary, as well as metaphysical, lineage from Oken to Melville to McCarthy vis-à-vis the notion of the weaver-god is the equating of *language* (narrative expression) and *construction* (material practice). Yet even more striking in McCarthy's narrative evocation of that lineage is its minimally panpsychist framework, given that it is concerned above all with the unceasing motion in the becoming of the material world. While God is weaving the world and thus figures as the ostensibly transcendent *ground* of the world's products, the void from which and into which the divinity fabricates those bodies and ideas *ungrounds* the latter, and with them the ontological priority of the respective vessel of construction at hand—be it God, a human being, or any body whatsoever.

Trying to make sense of his dreams and the unfortunate events that have determined his life since the earthquake, the heretic goes to a town called Caborca, where he eventually argues about the nature of God with the same priest who is telling Billy this tale. After those debates with the priest, the heretic comes to the conclusion that the events of the world are substantiated by their witnesses, and not the other way around; that the tragic occurrences of his life, for example, exist only insofar as they are witnessed by him as their observer, the person who generates meaning out of them, by the very means of their impact as events. But what may at first seem a worldview that is a type of constructivism akin to postmodern views on history is in fact thoroughly rooted in the Romantic science that is Okenian physiophilosophy: "[The man] saw the world pass into nothing in the very multiplicity of its instancing. Only the witness stood firm. And the witness to that witness" (*TC*, 154)—a stance that once more echoes Judge Holden's remark that "every man is tabernacled in every other and he in exchange and so on in an endless complexity of being and witness to the uttermost edge of the world" (*BM*, 141). Consider how the priest continues to present the heretic's point of view, which roughly delineates a dismissal of God despite the dream he had of that uncontrollably weaving divinity:

> If the world was a tale who but the witness could give it life? Where else could it have its being? . . . And he began to see in God a terrible tragedy. That the existence of the Deity lay imperiled for want of this simple thing. That for

> God there could be no witness. Nothing against which He terminated. Nothing by way of which His being could be announced to Him. . . . He could create everything save that which would say him no. (*TC*, 154)

About this final stance of the heretic, the priest tells Billy that "we may speak of madness" (*TC*, 154). Yet consistent with the conception of natural dynamics in *The Crossing* as a whole, as well as other novels by McCarthy, this stance is much more complex than that: if existence is dependent on its being witnessed by some observer or listener, and if there cannot be a witness for God's existence (given God's function as the constructive vessel, or narrative persona, of the world as tale) then the only witness for God cannot be a thing or a body but is "nothing by way of which His being could be announced to him." Now, this conclusion does not entail that there is no God at all, but that God merely *inexists* insofar as the space of witnessing is not a thing but its opposite, "an incomprehensible 'No thing'"[121] that is fundamentally inchoate. Furthermore, if God cannot be witnessed, he is by the same token unknowable, since, as McCarthy writes elsewhere, "all that becomes known becomes . . . a thing. The reality is not a thing but a no-thing,"[122] in keeping with the Platonic distinction between unified appearance and formless essence, of which the former (that is, appearance) is necessarily part of existence, while the latter (that is, essence) is not. The old man thus arrives at the theological viewpoint that God does not exist—or, rather, *inexists*—because otherwise there would be a witness to give an adequate account of Him, and there would be a narrative that would entirely enclose its own being as narrative at the same time that it is told. When the heretic eventually lies on his deathbed, he sends for the priest to tell him "what he had learned" (*TC*, 156) in their debates and otherwise. He states that in the last analysis,

> no man can see his life until his life is done and where then to make a mending? It is God's grace alone that we are bound by this thread of life. . . . This flesh is but a memento, yet it tells the true. Ultimately, every man's path is every other's. There are no separate journeys for there are no separate men to make them. All men are one and there is no other tale to tell. (156–57)

These last words, then, confirm the being of God as an inexistent entity whose "witness" is precisely the void, or—to use Oken's terminology—the eternal Nature-Nothing that is the material out of which and into which God's constructions are woven and spoken as beings in the world. The fact that it is not a thing but a formless materiality that constitutes the past and the future place for the weaver-god's creations attests to another fact: that in this first, and possibly most central, of the three interpolated narratives, theological and philosophical speculation is ultimately grounded in the physiological process that is nature.[123]

Concerning the notion of *the void* in *The Crossing*, note how the narrator describes the scene when Boyd gets shot by the Mexicans who have tracked down the two brothers for stealing back their horses: after the bullet has hit Boyd it "slow[s] down from having passed through his brother's body but still moving faster than sound and passing his left ear with the suck of the air like a whisper from *the void* and the small jar of the shockwave" (*TC*, 270, emphasis added). This description once again reminds the reader that "*the void*" is not merely the conceptual conceit used to finally account for the divine construction of the world (that is, God's inexistence) but that it also coincides with death and the trauma of disintegration. In the context of McCarthy's earlier work, which I examined in the previous chapter, the space of witnessing the divine and "ceaseless presentation"[124] of natural nothingness is reflected in the *memento tabere*—that is to say, the disentanglement or *ungrounding* not just of bodies and ideas, but also, on a different level, of *that which can be known*.

After Billy has sent his wounded brother away with a group of Mexican workers who have offered their help, he wanders around the Mexican plains, praying for Boyd, and eventually comes to the place where a blind man lives with his wife. This is the point in the novel that introduces the second interpolated narrative, which is about how this blind man lost his eyesight in 1913, during the Mexican Revolution, and subsequently tried to cope with his new condition. As Frye perceptively remarks, this story is predominantly told by the man's wife: "It is a horrific tale of revolution and violence in which the blind man's eyes are sucked from their sockets by a sadistic commander,"[125] serving under General Huerta, as the future blind man is taken prisoner by the federal army. What interests me here is the way the wife retrospectively describes her husband's then-new world of darkness to Billy and how he supposedly tries to deal with his new situation as a blinded human being. According to Frye, "McCarthy violates a basic principle in storytelling by allowing a second-hand account to render events in vivid clarity, but this violation is entirely consistent with his theme" of the material nature of narrative as such: "Just as the husband's experience is the woman's as well, so it will become Billy's. Her retelling moves beyond the sensory and her sense of its gravity and meaning allows her to delve beneath mere chronicle."[126] This is an assessment of the woman's mode of narration that also fits McCarthy's own mode of "speculative fiction," which does indeed point to a realm "beyond the sensory"—to the conceptual space of Platonic matter, which is approximated on an allegorical level by the deprivation of eyesight in the blind man's tale.[127] His new and pitiful condition yields a world that is depicted in terms that parallel those of the "world construed out of blood and blood's alcahest" (*TC*, 73) in the eyes of the she-wolf from the passage I cited above. The blind man's wife recounts that "he was surprised at the authority which his blindness conferred upon him. He seemed to want for nothing" (278). I take it that, like some of the phrasings in the first interpolated tale of the priest, this formulation is semantically ambiguous, in the sense that it both connotes a paradoxical state of completeness (meaning that the man had everything he needed) and a desire for "nothing," for *that which is not*. While the first reading might seem more plausible initially, the second reading is supported by the way in which she describes this realm of nothingness to which the man seems to have come closer, due to his having lost his power of vision—clearly an evocation by McCarthy of the figure of *the blind seer*, so central to Western mythology.

Again, what complicates this situation is that it is the wife who reports the blind man's past feelings, precisely like a witness who can only speculate about those feelings but can never even try to represent them as the practice of witnessing is often understood. Yet due to the narrator's conceit from the first interpolated story (that even within the tale that is recounted by her, "all tales are one" [*TC*, 143]) the construction of narrative is determined not by its representative value or mimetic power but by the fact of its world-constructing nature. The woman also tells Billy about how once, as the blind man was struggling with the burden of adjusting to the loss of his sight, he met a man on the road who tried to uplift him morally. His response to that man's verbal support culminates in a short monologue, which arguably resonates with both the physiophilosophy underlying McCarthy's earlier Western and the weak form of panpsychism according to which, up to a point, thinking extends beyond the realm of concepts insofar as the notion of the *psyche* indexes material and dynamic forms of motion on an ontological level before it can function as the epistemological carrier of semantic constructions:[128]

> He spoke of the broad dryland barrial and the river and the road and the mountains beyond and the blue sky over them as entertainments to keep the world at bay, the true and ageless world. He said that *the light of the world was in men's eyes only for the world itself moved in eternal darkness and darkness was its true nature and true condition* and that in this darkness it turned with perfect cohesion in all its parts but that there was naught there to see. He said that *the world was sentient to its core and secret and black beyond men's imagining and that its nature did not reside in what could be seen or not seen.* He said that he could stare down the sun and what use was that? (*TC*, 283, emphasis added)

One of the things that the blinded man realizes is "that the world hid more than it revealed" (*TC*, 289), and that therefore the difference between that which appears and that which exists, similar to the fundamental chasm between that which is and that which is not, is integral for any understanding—however speculative—of "the ultimate sightlessness of the world" (294), *the void* in *The Crossing*. The crushing monologue, after which the stranger leaves him, thus substantiates once more the generative capacity of *the void*, which is said to harbor a certain kind of mentality that is compatible with Schelling's recasting of Plato's "world soul."

Late in the novel, after Billy has retrieved the remains of his dead brother, one night he dreams that "Boyd came to him and squatted by the deep embers of the fire as he'd done times by the hundreds and smiled his soft smile that was *not quite cynical* and he took off his hat and held it before him and looked down into it" (*TC*, 400, emphasis added). What is interesting here is that the narrator's description of Boyd's smile as "*not quite cynical*" could also apply to the way in which the narrator's perspective is characterized throughout the novel with respect to the almost continual tragic events. It is a stance, or an angle, on these events that happen to the protagonists Billy and Boyd that is "not quite cynical," so Boyd's smile replicates the whole novel's narrative perspective. In other words, I suggest that this is an instance in which McCarthy makes two poetic moves, one having to do with the history of science, the other with the mythology of nature (both of which I discussed above). To say that the smile of Billy's brother is "not quite cynical" is to assume that it is on the verge of both bitterness and brotherly care (also thereby echoing Glanton's stance, in the urstone passage in *Blood Meridian*, between resignation and affirmation), which arguably reflects the point of view of the book's narrator as well, in this respect clearly revealing the Romantic naturalism that others have noted in McCarthy's work.[129] What I find much more intriguing than the periodization of *The Crossing*, in this case, is how the narrator's stance that is here imitated in the facial expression of a character is thereby replicated in a narrative reiteration of the biogenetic law, or recapitulation thesis, on the level of form. This really is the scientific backbone of the novel. The mythographical side to this is arguably that the narrator's insertion of a specific phrase into the description of Billy's dream, which also describes the narrative stance of the entire novel, can be deemed tautegorical in the sense that self-reflexivity here is not merely textual but a function of nature itself. Nature's *autopoiesis*, in McCarthy's case, is "not quite cynical." In its existence between bitterness and care, and between resignation and affirmation, the self-making of nature also refers to Oken's *Natur-Nichts*, which allopoietically gives rise to the possibility of the protagonist's dream in the first place:

> In his dream he knew that Boyd was dead and that the subject of his being so must be approached with a certain caution for that which was circumspect in life must be doubly so in death and he'd no way to know what word or gesture might subtract him *back again into that nothingness out of which he'd come.* When finally he did ask him what it was like to be dead Boyd only smiled and looked away and would not answer. (400, emphasis added)

Finally, we have come to the third narrative interpolation, the tale of the gypsy who is part of a group of ox drovers who, strangely enough, carry the dismantled remains of an airplane "on old truckaxles" (*TC*, 401). When Billy wants to know where that plane comes from, the gipsy says: "Con respecto al aeroplano . . . hay tres historias. Cuál quiere oír? [With respect to the airplane, there are three histories. Which do you want to hear?]" (403), and Billy responds that he wants "to hear the true history" (404).[130] This already mirrors the situation in the first of the interpolated narratives within the general narrative of *The Crossing*, when the priest claims that it makes no difference which particular tale is told because, in the end, "there is only one to tell" (143)—namely, that of the continuous, tragic, and "dynamic evolution"[131] of nature. Nonetheless, the gypsy recounts parts of the individual history of this nonfunctioning plane, which, to a certain degree, is constituted by that very narrative:

> He said that men assume the truth of a thing to reside in that thing without regard to the opinions of those beholding it while that which is fraudulent is held to be so no matter how closely it might duplicate the required appearance. If the airplane which their client has paid to be freighted out of the wilderness and brought to the border were in fact not the machine in which the son has died then its close resemblance to that machine is hardly a thing in its favor but is rather one more twist in the warp of the world for the deceiving of men. Where then is the truth of this? The reverence attached to the artifacts of history is a thing men feel. One could even say that what endows any thing with significance is solely the history in which it has participated. Yet wherein does that history lie? (*TC*, 405)

Along the lines of Oken's physiophilosophy, as used in the present chapter, the history of any particular entity, such as the gypsies' airplane, would indeed inhere in a larger history, which remains foreclosed to any individual perspective since it would not just include the past and the present, but the future as well: "For God will not permit that we shall know what is to come. He is bound to no one that the world unfold just so upon its course and those who by some sorcery or by some dream might come to pierce the veil that lies so darkly over all that is before them may serve by just that vision to cause that God should wrench the world from its heading and set it upon another course altogether and then where stands the sorcerer?" (*TC*, 407). In fact, is it a sorcerer at all?

The gypsy concludes his long monologue by recalling how he and his father used to travel together and "would come upon old photographs and tintypes" (*TC*, 412). He says that "these likenesses had value only to the living who had known them and with the passage of years of such there were none" (ibid.), but that his father, who was a gypsy himself, was fond of these photographic portraits of the dead. Indeed, the father collected these photos on the journey with his son to accompany them and, as the gypsy tells Billy, "he came to see that . . . in truth every journey was so accompanied. . . . In those faces that shall now be forever nameless among their outworn chattels there is writ a message that can never be spoken because time would always slay the messenger before he could ever arrive" (413)—a poetic image that once again resonates with Oken's theory of time as that which presents and negates, and by this dual process antecedes human temporality as that which "slays the messenger" who would try to reverse the ontological process of the temporal hierarchy between geocosmic and anthropic time. Yet there is still another twist to the gypsy's narrative, which he himself christens as the "historia de las historias [the narrative of all narratives]"—namely, that the truth has no specific place but is evoked in its telling itself, "the history that each man makes alone out of what is left to him. Bits of wreckage" (411) (or as McCarthy phrased it 1979 in *Suttree*, "shreds of matter" [*S*, 96]). Along these lines, then, the final twist in the gypsy's narrative is revealed when he says:

> Pensamos . . . que somos las víctimas del tiempo. En realidad la vía del mundo no es fijada en ningún lugar. Cómo sería posible? Nosotros mismos somos nuestra propia jornada. Y por eso somos el tiempo también. Somos lo mismo. Fugitivo. Inescrutable. Desapíadado. [We think that we are the victims of time. In reality the way of the world is not fixed in any place. How could this be possible? We ourselves are our own journey. And for this we are time as well. We are the same. Fugitive. Inscrutable. Unpitied.] (*TC* 413–14)

These claims raise questions about the construction of the self and nature's determination. For the moment, however, they must remain unanswered, while the next chapter outlines in detail the relationship between the notions of identity and indifference and the concept of life in McCarthy's early work *Outer Dark*, as well as the two novels that preceded and followed *The Crossing*, *All the Pretty Horses* and *Cities of the Plain*. In any event, the tautegorical upshot of the gypsy's tale in terms of the novel's underlying question about the nature of storytelling itself (that is, of the diegetic act) is that nature's immanent productivity is identical to the activity of narrative: nature is what it is as long as it self-analyzes, as it tells the tale *of* its self *to* itself.

[5]

"MALIGNANT LIFE": INDIFFERENCE, IDENTITY, AND NARRATIVE EXTAINMENT

There aint but one truth . . . . The truth is what happened. It aint what come out of somebody's mouth. —Cormac McCarthy, *All the Pretty Horses*

Reality has an essence that fiction cannot subsume.
—Bertrand Westphal, *Geocriticism*

IN THE PREVIOUS TWO chapters I have discerned an ontologically based form of literary experimentation in McCarthy's fiction from his Tennessee period and a theory of narrative construction that can be traced back to nineteenth- and twentieth-century biology and mathematics, as well as the theological strands of German idealism. At this point of the argument I want to caution against any possible misinterpretation of this largely narratological account of McCarthy's fiction as a warrant to confuse the identification of "world" and "tale" with the postmodern equation of "world" and "text." McCarthy's conception of narrative *does not* conform to the view that "there is nothing outside the text, and a text is a text is a text," as Bertrand Westphal puts it somewhat flippantly in his account of postmodern literary theory.[1] Yet, as Judge Holden's Okenian definition of God and the deeply philosophical speculations in the interpolated tales of *The Crossing* suggest, McCarthy does regard the realms of narrative and natural production as isomorphic spaces that are determined by coextensive processes. How is this apparent contradiction to be resolved? What kind of narrative is meant here, if not a purely textual one that would be the lens of human culture through which nature's processes must be viewed and judged, precisely as "as a retro-effect of culture"?[2] Conversely, how are nature and narrative to be articulated in a common, yet noncorrelational, space? Given that McCarthy's fiction cannot be reduced to any literary style of writing from the period of transcendentalism to the present, and that it is therefore not susceptible to any representational or antirepresentational approach to the question of how fiction may either give an adequate account of the referential world or forge a visionary counterhistory to it, what particular notion of space is necessary that would both be aligned with the twofold framework of allegory and tautegory and be capable of coming to terms with the conceptual interplay between nature's identity and its indifference?

If nature is the antecedent ground of narrative yet is only that which it is on the condition that narrative structures depict it *as such*, then narrative is both part of nature and necessarily incapable of adequately representing it because it is merely one of many "fictional additions" to it.[3] In turn, these "additions" change nature in ways that are incorporeal yet material, given the immanently physical disposition of nature. The problem at hand really is whether or not one assumes a certain hierarchy between being and thinking: whereas a correlational attitude would posit a fundamental reciprocity between the two terms (since, after all, the one cannot be without the other, while, by the same token, the other cannot be thought without the one) the attitude of *Naturphilosophie* places an emphasis on nature's antecedence and thought's consequence, "for it is not because there is thinking that there is being, but rather because there is being that there is thinking," as Schelling writes.[4] Nevertheless, he wonders how it is possible for nature to be the object of thought? As he states in his treatise *On the History of Modern Philosophy*,[5] "The whole world lies, so to speak, in the nets of the understanding or of reason, but the question is *how* exactly it got into those nets, since there is obviously something other and something *more* than mere reason in the world, indeed there is something which strives beyond these barriers."[6] What is at stake here, then, is the question of how human reason (including all possible forms of *Mitwissenschaft* that have nature as their content) is capable of having an object like nature (or "the whole world") as its content, while this object—more than any other notion that could be thought—necessarily escapes its conceptual framework, since "there is something which strives beyond these barriers" of conception. In other words, any attempt to answer the question "What is nature?" has to regard itself as an almost quixotic enterprise since it seeks to capture what is essentially bound to escape any scientific, theological, philosophical, and (most important in the present context) narrative form of understanding, if it is the case that nature is always more than what is said about it, and if, therefore, "reality has an essence that fiction cannot subsume."[7]

As a result, it is imperative to show both the fictional iterations and reiterations of the indifference inherent in antecedent nature in the form of McCarthy's narratives about nature's identity and the way in which these narratives are capable of demonstrating just that portion of nature that escapes its "nets"—that exists, in other words, "beyond" its role or function as the content of literary practice. I have already suggested that McCarthy's novels are both narratives *about* nature and products *of* it. Yet it also must be said that with respect to the literary determination of what is "more than" their content these novels constitute a singular narrative space with regard to their object. This is a space that is neither strictly representational (that is, mimetic) nor antirepresentational in the postmodern sense, but one that is comparable to what Iain Grant, following Gilles Châtelet and Louis Kauffmann, has conceptualized as the space of "extainment," rather than that of the partial "containment" of the objects of thought.[8] As Grant proposes in his explanation of this space, there has to be a difference between conception and containment in the thought about nature because otherwise the object of this form of thinking would eventually be exhausted:

> It is only if thinking about nature always involves more nature than can be thought that nature is in fact being thought. This is why something's being conceived is not identical to its containment. That something is conceived *does* entail that something is contained in the conceiving; but this does not mean that what is antecedent to the conceiving is . . . contained in the conceiving.[9]

What this means is that the conception of nature's identity is capable of speculating on that which lies outside of its actual content because of its origination in the same nature to which its object of thought (that is, nature) is identical. That which is extained is merely the larger space involved in the operation of thinking nature, compared to that which is contained (meaning simply the content of thought). "Thought is [thus] set within an interiority constituted by its extainment of what is not thought," and "from nature to thought the passage is irreversible such that thought cannot think the nature prior to it"[10]—or rather, it cannot contain it by conception but nevertheless is able to extain it by speculation (and in particular, I would add, narrative forms of the latter). This reasoning is supported by Grant's definition of the effect of "extainment," namely, that it "integrates the concept into its environment at the point of the concept's emergence."[11] Extainment (and especially its narrative form) situates the concept within the material nature of which it is an expression rather than a mere representation.

Along these lines, I hold that a slightly altered form of geocritical practice (or rather, a mode of geocriticism that is properly wedded to the Schellingian and Okenian understanding of human reason) is possible, if that practice is defined as an "additional rearticulation of a reality that, far from being distant from it, is what is active in it."[12] The concept of nature can never exhaust its object of thought, yet it expands that object's existential reach, given the impossibility of escaping nature's immanence. According to Westphal, "representation *reproduces the real* or, better, an experience of the real. . . . *Any work*, no matter how far from sensed reality, as paradoxical as it seems, is part of the real—and, perhaps, *participates in forming the real*."[13] While the present book is not concerned with judging whether the formation of reality is an activity that applies to any work of art (literary, cinematic, or otherwise), regardless of the themes that are negotiated in or by it, I want to use Westphal's consideration of literature's impact on natural processes in my analysis of McCarthy's writings, since this is precisely what his fiction attempts to determine: "the warp of the world" (*TC*, 405) and "the sentience of rocks."[14] Moreover, I want to underscore the ontological, rather than epistemological, import of Westphal's claim because this claim is consonant with Grant's reading of Schelling's inquiry in *On the History of Modern Philosophy*: "If the whole world does indeed come to lie in the nets of reason, but if it is not of another nature than the reason that arises in the world, it is importantly *not false* that the whole world is indeed contained in reason, as a multiplication or 'potentiation' of the world as that world in which reason arises."[15] For Grant, the antecedent world can never be whole because the "fictional additions"[16]—the expansion of nature by humanity's "co-knowing" (*Mitwissenschaft*)—give rise to "a multiplication or 'potentiation'" of that world, insofar as "the wholeness of the world is an artefact of the reason that contains it,"[17] due to the ever-changing dynamics of natural processes that consequently subvert this logic of completeness at every turn.[18] In other words, what is additional and therefore consequent *is* multiplication, whereas what is subtractive and therefore antecedent is what could be called "indivision"—that is, it can be described, adumbrated, and exceeded, but it cannot be violated, diminished, or recovered.

This is, finally, what I suggest vis-à-vis McCarthy's determination of that portion of nature that necessarily escapes its literary content: if narrative is an "additional rearticulation" of nature, yet also still part of nature, since the latter's "reality" is constantly "active in it,"[19] then what escapes the content of McCarthy's speculations on nature's identity is what is extained, rather than contained, by it. However, it is due to the metaphysical undercurrent of McCarthy's works that this logically excluded element is itself brought into focus in them.

This narratological problem brings us back to the distinction between allegory and tautegory: if the former mode of narrative would point out more than what it merely denotes (in terms of a literary *allopoiesis*), the latter would, in turn, point toward itself *tout court* (literary *autopoiesis*). If we keep the question of nature's narrative containment in mind, the issue of the ontological priority of the tautegorical mode becomes qualified in a new sense, because the self-organizing part of nature can never be semantically contained (strictly speaking), as containment implies a certain form that needs to be captured "in the nets of the understanding."[20] Conversely, the opposite of nature's semantic approximation must account for what is intentionally excluded from any distinctive signification—namely, what is extained rather than contained by the content of narrative. Nonetheless, one of the prime characteristics of the disposition of antecedence or identity is that it is neither formed nor diverse, but the condition of possibility for diversification or formation. If there were an actually determining facet of antecedence, it would be *indifference*, because that is what defines nature's stance toward its constant reiterations and recountings by means of narrative practice (among other forms of *Mitwissenschaft*).

Therefore, I seek to examine McCarthy's reiteration of nature's identity in the following readings of those novels that depict the issue of indifference in its most intricate yet simultaneously devastating ways: *Outer Dark*, *All the Pretty Horses*, and *Cities of the Plain*. In line with some of the arguments from chapter 4 about the reiteration of the genesis of forms in the practice of war, an integral part of this examination is the testing of a hypothesis in light of McCarthy's second novel and the first and third volumes of the Border Trilogy. I investigate in what way the narrative depiction of the world's indifference toward human life and the indifference of human life toward itself and other forms of life are related to what Schelling writes in his *Ideas for a Philosophy of Nature* about the identity of nature and thought: "For what we want is not that Nature should coincide with the laws of our mind *by chance* (as if through some third intermediary) but that *she herself*, necessarily and originally, should not only express, but even *realize*, the laws of our mind, and that she is, and is called, Nature only insofar as she does so."[21] The hypothesis of this chapter, therefore, is that McCarthy's depiction of indifference in *Outer Dark*, *All the Pretty Horses*, and *Cities of the Plain* can be described as *the narrative extainment of nature's identity* and, consequently, as an exemplary realization of "the laws of our mind" in nature.

ABOVE I INTRODUCED MCCARTHY'S 1968 novel as a tale that narrates the tragic search of an incestuous couple (Rinthy and Culla Holme) for their nameless child, after it has been abandoned by Culla in the woods nearby the little cabin in which the child was born. The birth was very traumatic and conveyed in a naturalist style of writing, as I showed in chapter 1. Katie Owens-Murphy and others have already noted that *Outer Dark* "invites symbolic readings," in the sense that it has many connotations to religious and metaphysical texts and contexts, while at the same time it "depicts the physical body with gruesome accuracy."[22] Furthermore, what James Giles has called the "multilayered determinism" of the novel highlights the fact that the grim reality that results, for instance, from the siblings' sexual intercourse (which occurs before the narrative starts) is not to be viewed within the framework of a "largely uncomplicated biological determinism" or that of an "economic determinism,"[23] but (as is also the case of McCarthy's other

Southern novels) within one that yields a dialectics of subtraction and construction, of decomposition and composition that I examined in previous chapters. What I am primarily interested in here, however, is neither the relationship between the siblings nor the way in which their social decay determines their journey in a mostly unspecified Tennessean countryside. Rather, I am interested in how the narrator develops the motif of indifference-in-nature, as it reaches into the lives of the novel's characters—above all in the form of the "*grim triune*" (*OD*, 133) who by the ending of the book have slaughtered the nameless child in the presence of its indifferent father. In the course of my reading, I argue against the ethicist interpretation of *Outer Dark* as a novel that "throws us into epistemological uncertainty at every turn" and simultaneously emphasizes "the mysteries of faith,"[24] and that also "reflects the breakdown of the grand narratives of the past, of progress, rationality and of God, and instead presents a view of a world provisional, contingent, deeply suspect."[25] This is because in light of the narrative's depiction of nature's identity and indifference (and McCarthy's treatment of the latter throughout his oeuvre), the dichotomies of uncertainty and rationality, teleology and contingency, and belief and alienation do not hold: in *Outer Dark*, it is not "epistemological uncertainty"[26] but ontological fragility that is at the heart of the narrator's concern with the world of Rinthy and Culla. McCarthy's notion of the divine is not premised on a naïve understanding of teleological processes in the world but informed by an ontological notion of a form of contingency that is fundamental for, and generative of, the ideas and bodies that populate the world of the novel. Consequently, the narrative extainment of this type of divine contingency is evoked in the passages that depict indifference on multiple levels, chief among them both the passages in which the characters commit atrocious acts without showing any affective response to their deeds and those sections that melancholically depict the victims of the tale as content with their fate. However, before discussing these instances in the novel—with particular emphasis on the three murderers who haunt its surreal environs—I first briefly discuss the title of McCarthy's second novel and connect it to a passage from McCarthy's first Western, *Blood Meridian*, since it already determines the primary stylistic conceit of the novel's poetics: the narrative extainment of nature's identity.

Following William Schafer, Edwin Arnold notes that the title, *Outer Dark*, is taken from the Bible, specifically "from the eighth chapter of Matthew, in which Jesus comments on" various levels of being committed to one's "faith," which, in turn, result in "two possibilities: the kingdom of heaven as well as the 'outer darkness' of hell."[27] Yet as with the urstone (discussed in the previous chapter), there is an alternative source here. *Outer Dark* does not refer only to the biblical dichotomy between "the kingdom of heaven" and "the 'outer darkness' of hell" but is also a reference to the disciplinary trajectory of mathematics. Certainly, the biblical reference is the most striking of the title's allusions, and it makes a lot of sense to use the Bible as an intertextual reference here, given the context of the sin of incest between Rinthy and Culla and the subsequent abandonment of their child in the woods. Yet the expression "outer dark" can also be found in the fragmentary notes for the first drafts of *Blood Meridian*, in which McCarthy writes: "outer dark—black lemniscate? (OK)."[28] In *Blood Meridian*, the unusual term "black lemniscate" appears in Chapter 16, in the description of an incident in which Glanton's horse bites into the ear of an Apache's horse: "Blood flew. The horse screamed and reared and the Apache struggled to keep his seat and drew his sword and found himself staring into the black lemniscate that was the paired bores of Glanton's doublerifle" (BM, 228–9). McCarthy here uses the mathematical notion of "the *lemniscate*, a curve shaped like a figure-eight . . . that gets its name from the Greek word *lemniskos*, a ribbon used for fastening a garland on one's head," and "that turns into the infinity symbol ∞"[29] to describe the shape of the end of Glanton's double-barreled rifle, which metaphorically connotes the infinitude of death and the act of killing.

Thus, on a first reading, the mathematical sign of the eternal seems to reverse the gnostic logic—according to which the corporeal world is the realm of finitude and the spiritual (or pneumatic) world is the realm of infinitude—by viewing the eternity of violence and disintegration as opposed to, or constitutive of, the transience of the forms of life.[30] On closer inspection, however, the reversal of gnosis is not exactly warranted, given that the seeming iconology of divine warfare, which I examined in chapter 4, signifies the infinitude of the inorganic by emphasizing the finitude of corporeality. Thus, it is the simultaneous emphasizing of war as a metaphysical category and the claim that the bodies and ideas of the world are results of the spiritual realm that points in the direction of gnosticism, yet all of this still functions according to a nature-philosophical logic. The equation of "the 'outer darkness' of hell" with the mathematical sign of infinity, therefore, once again connects McCarthy's writings with the work of both Schelling and Oken, emphasizing also the Boehmian influence on the writer and the two philosophers.[31] In particular, Schelling's abovementioned notion of the "indivisible remainder" from his *Freedom* essay comes to mind.[32] In the passage where he outlines his concept, he writes that this "remainder" is irresolvable, that it cannot be apprehended "in understanding" or rational practice but rather "remains eternally in the ground." It is crucial to consider the two subsequent sentences, which I quoted above: "The understanding is born in the genuine sense from that which is without understanding. Without this preceding darkness creatures have no reality; darkness is their necessary inheritance."[33] I suggest that the corresponding notion of this "indivisible remainder" has many names in McCarthy's oeuvre, which he uses synonymously. In fact, two of them may be the "black lemniscate" and the "outer dark." This interpretation is reasonable in light of the baleful "inheritance" of virtually all of the characters in McCarthy's Southern fiction, and especially of Rinthy, Culla, and their child, set in Appalachia "under a black sun" (*OD*, 5) at the beginning of the twentieth century. I am not solely relying on the fortuitous, yet nevertheless illuminating, find at the McCarthy archive at Texas State University. Rather, my interpretation integrates the materialist-scientific and the spiritualist-religious aspects of his work—which are equally important, considering the frequency of references to God throughout his work and his decades-long affiliation with the Santa Fe Institute in New Mexico.

In light of the present argument concerning McCarthy's second novel, this short, yet substantial, digression back to *Blood Meridian*, mathematical etymology, and Schelling's notion of the "indivisible remainder" tests the hypothesis that the depiction of nature's indifference in *Outer Dark* is coextensive with the narrative extainment of nature's identity. Going back even further to the issue of nature's decomposition, it is really the descendental poetics that opposes McCarthy's fiction to the image of a "kingdom of heaven"—or, rather, "the 'outer darkness' of hell"[34] is not merely a reminder of humans' sinful ways, and on a more fundamental level, the "black lemniscate" can be figured in terms of what (following Reza Negarestani) I have conceptualized as the *memento tabere*, and which (to recapitulate chapters 3 and 4) might be called nature's ribbon of decomposition. The function, then, of these contexts in terms of the dialectical relationship between identity and indifference in McCarthy's work, and the way the latter depicts that dialectics, is perhaps best represented by the notion of the indivisible remainder in natural processes: the irrecoverable discrepancy between production and product that is the "substance" of extainment (even though, it would almost be false to call it that, since that which is extained is precisely without substance, it is indiscrete, formless, and unfixed). It is precisely "this preceding darkness" of which Schelling writes,[35] the evil ground of beings in the world that makes possible their freedom—the identity of which, however, can only be conceived of in part. Whatever is not contained and whatever cannot be divided into distinct forms and phenomena, therefore, can be extained only by the various forms of witnessing, with human reason and narrative imagination chief among them. The given formlessness (being indivisible) cannot be contained by narrative as content, but it is always already recapitulated as that which remains, in the process of narrative itself, as the outside of the text. This is what I mean by narrative extainment.

In many ways indebted to the Romantic idea of "aesthetic intuition,"[36] the concept of narrative extainment accounts for the way McCarthy's narrative voices render explicit what is essentially given and therefore cannot be fully rendered, but only partially contained. The indivisible remainder is precisely what literature extains in the narrative expression of indifferent acts of human beings toward another, and responses to violence that are almost without affect whatsoever.

This line of reasoning is supported by the process of revision McCarthy used to produce the published version of the novel. In an early draft of *Outer Dark*, for instance, the scene in which Culla places his unwanted child in the woods contains a short passage that McCarthy omitted in the published version. In its sincere and almost confessionalist attitude, this inner monologue is exceptionally rare in McCarthy's novels from his Tennessee period and perhaps in his work as a whole. The absence of this passage from the published version may demonstrate McCarthy's probable intention of emphasizing the indifference the father develops toward his own child, rather than his more humane care for his own flesh and blood. Allegorically speaking, the father's cruelty in abandoning the son out of guilt and later indifferently witnessing the child's slaughter by the triune signifies, among other things, the indifference of nature toward its creatures. Tautegorically speaking, the father's cruelty *is* an expression of nature's indifferent attitudes and acts because intrafamilial violence remains intranatural violence, given the immanence of natural process.[37]

In the typescript passage, after Culla has put his son down on the moss, this is what he apparently says both to himself and to his son: "It aint your fault, he said. We'd be some kind of double kin. . . . His lip began to jerk and then he said: Goddamn me, rose, spinning and walking fast, his arms again at his sides, staggering with a kind of desperate aimlessness through the brush like something blind."[38] Although this passage does not appear in the final version of the novel, it informs us that McCarthy originally conceived of Culla's fear as intense and saw him as feeling guilt at having fathered a child on his sister. He tries to convince himself that "it aint your fault" and convince the child that it has no part in how it is treated by him, thus trying to deal with the worst of what might happen (the child's death) via denial and subsequent repression, in Freudian terms. In fact, Culla is aware of committing a crime in betraying his sister and another having an incestuous relationship with her—an act almost universally prohibited as described by anthropological accounts and psychoanalytical theories from the early twentieth century onward.[39]

It is because Culla feels guilty that his quick walk turns into a run the more he distances himself from his child. In a very gothic prose style worthy of Nathaniel Hawthorne, McCarthy's narrator in the published version describes how as soon as he abandons his son and turns back in the direction of the cabin in which he lives with his sister, "night fell long and cool through the woods about him and a spectral quietude set in. As if something were about that croquets and nightbirds held in dread. He went on faster" (*OD*, 17). In the earlier version, the narrator's description of Culla rushing through the woods is even more ornamental: "He . . . turned to his right and took a new course, moving faster, the wild and sleepless and stricken look of him now rescinded by a single face of fear, an aura of it in which he moved with impeded progress as if loaded beyond all bearing with the soul's warfare. As if darkness itself were a weight."[40] Soon he is accelerating more and more, and "with full dark" he rushes back to the cabin, "the trees beginning to close him in, malign and baleful shapes that reared like enormous androids provoked by the alien insubstantiality of this flesh colliding among them. Long and long after he should have reached the river he was careering through the woods with his hands outstretched before him against whatever the dark might hold" (*OD*, 17).

I take it that this whole scene of Culla's guilt-ridden escape from the spot in the forest where he has left his newborn son resonates on various levels with the philosophies of nature provided by Schelling and Oken, more so than with Freudian psychoanalytic theory. One of these resonances concerns Culla's outstretched hands, which he uses to fight both any wooden branches that he might run into *and* the sin that so plagues him, but against which he cannot do anything but return. What I want to stress at this point, in recalling the themes touched on in the last chapter, is that this double reference to corporeal and ideational materiality is apparently expressed as an empty space (a void, or nothingness) that is material because it has "a weight," as we read in the typescript. Culla's intention is to ward off "whatever the dark might hold," meaning the darkness itself is not merely a danger, but the very condition of possibility for the perils that necessarily come to pass in the world of the novel. Yet they come from both without and within. Otherwise humanity would not be implicated in the generative process of what Oken calls the "Nature-Nothing"[41] and what the narrator of *Outer Dark* describes as "a hall forever empty" (*OD*, 219), which is synonymous with "the outer dark" (218) through which both Rinthy and Culla must wander. McCarthy's second novel appears from its beginning to be a parable about the indifference of time and its infinitely generative nothingness that mostly lies dormant, like the "saurians" (*TOK*, 11) in the Appalachian forest of *The Orchard Keeper*, but that sometimes makes itself felt in baleful ways.

In the context of narrative extainment, Culla's guilt is more than the result of fearing the consequences of his incestuous relationship with Rinthy.

To be sure, the expression of guilt is not an indifferent behavior but one that functions on an affective level. Yet the result of Culla's affect and his repressive tendencies is not only an inhumane gesture toward his own child, but it also allegorically recapitulates the way in which nature is indifferent to the lives of its creatures. This is aligned not only with Schelling's view in his essay on freedom that the dark and evil ground of the organism is also the predisposition of nature's capacity of free action, but also his reasoning that even though "indifference arises only out of difference,"[42] it is nevertheless the case that the prime reason for the existence of difference is its function as "a *striving toward indifference*, a striving which is conditioned by the difference itself, and by which it, on the other hand, is conditioned."[43] Similar to *Suttree*'s narrative voice, in *Outer Dark*, the narrator's depiction of Culla's behavior in the face of personal decline and the eventually coextensive development of a new self (or *selves*) that can accept the existence of the nameless child suggests that the allegorical content of the novel as a tale about the indifference of both human and inhuman nature with regard to the beings in the world that embody it is grounded on what is extained by the tautegorical aspect of the novel. What this means is that Culla's bad conscience in the beginning of the novel, his subsequent "denial"[44] that he knew the three murderers, and his indifference with regard to what they do with his child at the end of the novel all render visible the darkness that both precedes him as a literary character and succeeds him as an individual. This rendition of the inchoate that haunts Culla, yet which from the narrator's perspective must be realized in form, is expressed most clearly by the depiction of the triune of murderers, which Dianne Luce describes as "a manifestation of Culla's *psyche*, a status that is hinted early in the novel when the tinker," who eventually picks up the crying newborn in the woods, "finds Culla's tracks converging from separate directions, 'as if their maker had met in this forest *some dark other self in chemistry* with whom he had been *fused traceless* from the earth' [*OD* 20]."[45] What I want to stress here is not only the consistency with which the narrators of McCarthy's Southern novels mention literary quasi-chemical, or alchemical, experimentation but also how McCarthy's weak form of panpsychism blurs the boundary between corporeal and incorporeal materiality. That is, since the narrator to a certain degree leaves it up to the reader to decide what to make of the peculiar relationship between Culla and the three strangers who not only kill his child in the end but also assassinate some of the rather hostile people he meets on his journey (like the squire Salter, for instance),[46] the uncertainty about whether the triune is "a manifestation of Culla's psyche" or a band of bloodthirsty psychopaths distinct from Rinthy's brother raises the question of what is meant by the notion of *psyche* in the first place.

Regarding this production of an alternative personality (or three personalities), scholars do not seem to agree whether or not these three killers are merely figments of Culla's imagination. Similar to Luce, Tim Parrish writes: "The marauders of *Outer Dark* surely prefigure the killer gangs of *Blood Meridian*; moreover, the former novel implicates Culla Holme as belonging to their universe."[47] Taking the opposite stance, John Grammer holds that the "grim triune" is not a figment of Culla's imagination, or a projection of his guilt. Instead, "these menacing riders, armed with farming tools, are of course figures of *time*, reapers who move through the novel, leaving a trail of violent death behind them; the farm tools they carry will indeed become weapons as their spree commences."[48] While Grammer is right in interpreting the triune as in some way "figures of *time*," his reading is problematic for several reasons. First, he equates the notion of time in *Outer Dark* with that of history, when he says that the three murderers "embody the deadly threat which history poses to the pastoral realm. And yet they are themselves pastoral figures, or at least parodic versions of such figures, bearing spades and brush hooks through a barnyard, frightening the stock."[49] This equation of time with history, in Grammer's reading, hinges on the assumption that in McCarthy's second novel, the predominant temporality is that of modern historicity disturbing pastoral mythology. Yet as with so many of McCarthy's narratives, it is arguably instead geological time that is disturbing the realm of human temporality. However, this former time of nature's temporal stratification really cannot be contained by human reason, including narrative; it is that which is extained as the manifestation of nature's indifference by means of the triune's acts. Second, Grammer writes: "Whatever threat they represent, that is, emerges in some sense *from* the pastoral realm they scourge; they are that community's nightmare, the seed of destruction which lurks within the pastoral realm."[50] Although it is not entirely obvious in the published novel, as I mentioned above, the triune does not represent the underside of the pastoral idyll at all, but as Parrish, Luce, and others have claimed, they are indeed figurations of Culla's guilt and, consequently, figments of his imagination.[51] This origin of the triune in Culla's psyche can be seen in the following section (omitted in the published novel) from a dialogue between the group's leader and Culla, at a late point in the narrative:

> [Culla] said: You aim to kill me?
>
> No, the man said. You ought to know that. Except you dont know do ye? No. You dont care, that's all. . . . Don't talk to me about killin. I dont talk about that. Besides if it wasn't for you where would we be?[52]

This is not the only instance in the novel's various drafts that supports the claim that the triune is part of Culla's psyche. In an earlier version of *Outer*

Dark than the one containing the dialogue quoted above, there is a sentence that evidently expresses Culla's thoughts concerning the triune: "He speaks to me of the Trinity of the Godhead but how am I to be astonished who find in myself the selfsame triune, the three persons neither sacred nor profane but simply warring."[53] Once again underscoring the relationship in McCarthy's fiction between war, narrative, and mathematics, what is conceived yet not contained in *Outer Dark* is what involves narrative extainment: the speculation on nature's irrecoverable identity in the most indifferent scenes and expressions that narrative is able to evoke. It is this irrecoverable indifference that I have characterized as the inchoate givenness of natural process.

Yet the narrative blurring of inside and outside in terms of the extension of Culla's personality also reframes the question of McCarthy's arguably Platonic, as well as Schellingian, definition of the psyche—namely, not just in commonly *psycho*logical terms as the locus of individual thoughts, but also in *onto*logical terms as the "*original principle of motion*, *arche kineseos*."[54] In the end, it seems, it is not really important whether the grim triune is part of Culla's imagination or whether it is a phenomenon external to his body, because the extended concept of the psyche as the idea of movement as such affirms both options. Consider, in this respect, the narrator's description of the triune and its defining aspect of movement, wedded to the indifferent account of how they assault the squire who is on his way to track down Culla—who is himself on the run after having stolen the squire's boots:

> *They came across the field attended by a constant circus of grasshoppers catapulting from the sedge and entered the wood deployed in the same ragged phalanx while before them passed solitary over no visible road a horse and a wagon surmounted by a harriedlooking man in a white hat. They altered their course and came upon a log road down which the wagon receded in two thin tracks and upon a burst lizard who dragged his small blue bowels through the dirt, breaking into a trot, a run, the first of them reaching the horse and seizing the reins and turning up to the driver a mindless smile, clutching the horse's withers and clinging there like some small and vicious anthroparian and the driver rising in remonstration from the wagon box so that when the next one came up behind him sideways in a sort of dance and swung the brush-hook it missed his neck and took him in the small of the back severing his spine and when he fell he unhinged sideways and without a cry.* (OD, 53)

In this passage (which I quoted at length here to demonstrate its effect on the reader), the narrative voice emphasizes the importance of types of movement in two long sentences and repeatedly makes use of what I have conceptualized in chapter 3 as one of McCarthy's tautegorical notions ("*sideways*"), which signify the view of the world as essentially tragic and *ungrounded* in the Boehmian, Schellingian, and Okenian sense. Another integral aspect of the passage is the possibility that since it is in italics (which often denotes a memory of one of McCarthy's characters, as in the descent of the Green Fly Inn of *The Orchard Keeper*, or a perspective outside that of the main narrative, as in the prologue of *Suttree*), the description of the triune's movement and assassination of Salter could very well be from the perspective of Culla while at the same time being an action outside his corporeal reach, as if the psyche were somehow part of a person yet, in the last analysis, unbounded by that person's body.[55] What is more, if the darkness of the world (or what Schelling calls the "ataxia of forces"[56]) is the origin of the psyche, then the depiction of the triune is the narrator's speculative attempt at extaining, rather than containing, this originary emergence of ordered movement out of chaotic motion by contextualizing it in a scene that depicts the cold and indifferent murder of Culla's pursuer. Furthermore, the detached rendering of this scene suggests Culla's narrative perspective, since it is directly mirrored in the much later section that describes the death of his and Rinthy's child—a death that somehow figures as a monstrously conclusive event that connotes the psycho-physiological fusion of the triune and Culla, their apparent creator (or conspirator).

By the time of this second and last meeting between the three murderers and Culla at the campsite of the triune, who look "like revenants that reoccur in lands laid waste with fever," "spectral, palpable as stone" (*OD*, 239), the child has already been tortured (Culla "saw one eyeless and angry red socket like a stokehole to a brain in flames" [240]) and its father is compelled to turn his eyes away from it. This reaction is, in fact, one of the most typical gestures of a given crime's "co-knowing (*Mitwissenschaft*)": looking away, trying to act as if nothing has happened at all.[57] This holds both for the sins or crimes of the past (Culla's incestuous relationship) and those that are to come—namely, the killing of the "chap" (244) by one of the three strangers and the subsequent cannibalization of it by another: "The man took hold of the child and lifted it up. It was watching the fire. Holme saw the blade wink in the light like a long cat's eye slant and malevolent and a dark smile erupted on the child's throat and went all broken down the front of it. The child made no sound" (ibid.). The brutality conveyed above all in the narrator's detached style is poetically consistent with the account of Salter's murder in the longer passage quoted above. This appalling image of the triune's leader slitting the child's throat is surpassed only by the following subversion of any sincere motives ostensibly inherent in the figure of the supplicant, whose arms are usually outstretched in the act of begging for mercy in the name of himself or his fellow human beings. In the cannibalization of the child by Culla or the triune, this moral side of supplication (which, as I argued in chapter 3, is presented as the "[co-science (*Mitwissenschaft*)] of creation"[58] throughout McCarthy's oeuvre) finds its underside in the posture of the second stranger who drinks the blood of Culla's son: "[The child] hung there with its one eye glazing over like a wet stone and the black blood pumping down its naked belly. The mute one knelt forward. He was drooling and making little whimpering noises in his throat. He knelt with his hands outstretched and his nostrils rimpled delicately. The man handed him the child and he seized it up, looked once at Holme with witless eyes, and buried his moaning face in its throat" (OD, 244–45).[59]

Now that we have considered these revolting acts of murder and indifference, what about Rinthy, the other half of the incestuous relationship that is the condition of possibility for the narrative? Lydia Cooper is right in cautioning that "*Outer Dark* cannot be read as presenting an argument for total human corruption without risking a gross oversimplification of the novel's nuances. Rinthy's quest, for instance, is not immoral at all, and readers who overlook her purity and love are guilty of a blindness that even the minor characters in the novel overcome."[60] In fact, she cares deeply for her lost child. Her journey is a quest to rescue from certain death an offspring she has accepted as her own, as she makes clear in a conversation with a doctor she visits because of her leaking breasts. When the doctor asks her where she currently lives, she answers with conviction as well as resignation: "I don't live nowheres no more. . . . I never did much. I just go around huntin my chap. That's about all I do any more" (OD, 162). Nonetheless, the largely positive or uncorrupted stance of the mother in pain does not manage to survive the ending of the tale, as she comes too late to save her only child.[61] Indeed, what I have conceptualized as McCarthy's trademark ethical and aesthetic formula—*starting from grief, arriving at grace*—finds yet another unforgettable expression that, by the same token, reflects Schelling's logic of the unilateral movement from nature's progressive movement that has identity revealed as a nonaffective form,[62] so that on a poetic level, nature's identity (that is, *grief*) becomes identical with its indifference (that is, *grace*). The only redemption that is granted—if we can call it that—as Rinthy's journey comes to an end is impossible on the level of content (that is, a narrative containment of natural dynamics) yet has become a matter of poetic necessity on the level of form (meaning the narrative extainment of the "before" and the "after" of the tale, the *outside of the text* embedded, or extained within it).

This is how the narrative voice describes Rinthy's almost otherworldly response to the sight where her "chap" has been murdered, pointing at itself as a tautegorical form of nature's graceful process of indifferent motion and rest: "Late in the afternoon she entered the glade, . . . slender and trembling and pale with wandlike hands to speak the boneless shapes attending her. And stepping softly with her air of blooded ruin about the glade in a frail agony of grace she trailed her rags through dust and ashes, circling the dead fire, the charred billets and chalk bones, the little calcined ribcage" (*OD*, 246). Inspecting the site of slaughter, however, Rinthy does not burst into tears: "She did not know what to make of it. She waited, but no one returned" (ibid.). Instead of grief, Rinthy is a graceful figure, indifferent to the site of bestial slaughter—the one thing that usually would evoke the worst kind of trauma one could imagine. However, as Ann Fisher-Wirth convincingly argues, the narrator's description of her reaction is "a comment not on her ignorance" or on the melancholy of a shattered life, "but on the preposterousness of the scene, the sense that it profoundly fails to make her."[63] This is how the narrator accounts for the childless mother's reaction to the profane surroundings of the campfire's remains: "She waited all through the blue twilight and into the dark. Bats came and went. Wind stirred the ashes and . . . [s]hadows grew cold across the wood and night rang down upon these lonely figures and after a while little sister was sleeping" (246–47).

The tranquility that is conveyed through these simple yet carefully crafted sentences alludes to another form of indifference than the merciless behavior toward life expressed by Culla (or the triune) and other fundamentally violent characters in McCarthy's fiction. This form is the graceful indifference that is involved in accepting one's fate by remaining unbroken in the face of even the greatest difficulties, thereby removing oneself from the sadness and clamor of the world and, almost in a state of epiphany, avoiding all of the perilous forces of natural process, both within and without. This indifference of grace is the closest McCarthy's early fiction gets to a genuine ethics that is not, however, premised on the ecocentric projection of human values onto the environment but remains an entirely human problematic, which is nonetheless inexorably linked to the embeddedness of the human in nonhuman nature: "There we leave her, 'little sister' [*OD* 247], in the clearing, where time continues, natural process continues, birds and wind and seasons clean the relics of the dead, and death mingles with life in terrible beauty."[64]

Two kinds of literary expressions of indifference in nature, then, can be registered in McCarthy's second novel; two kinds of narrative extainment that, in line with the Romanticist ideal of evoking the infinite in a finite work of art, are narrating the "black lemniscate" in a regionalist work of fiction.[65] Affirming once again McCarthy's thematic consistency, I will now show how the dialectics between these two types of extainment are treated in the two novels that depict the life of that particular protagonist in the author's oeuvre who resembles Rinthy most strikingly, yet also in the most unexpected ways—namely, John Grady Cole.

Both *All the Pretty Horses* and *Cities of the Plain*—the first and the third novels of the Border Trilogy—have a different tone and style of writing than McCarthy's earlier work. They do not have the fiercely bleak atmosphere of a tale like *Outer Dark*, and the hope of redemption is not as strongly shattered in the course of their respective narratives. It has to be said, however, that in the end, the central figure of these two novels dies from the wounds inflicted on him in a knife fight that, he seems to have known from the start, he could not win. I am referring to John Grady Cole, who shares some of the traits of Rinthy in McCarthy's second novel. Even if Rinthy cannot foresee the death of her child, the love she sincerely feels for the nameless chap and her motherly concern for him link her to the central figure of *All the Pretty Horses* and *Cities of the Plain*, simply because (more than Cornelius Suttree in McCarthy's 1979 novel, Billy Parham in *The Crossing*, and arguably even the son in *The Road*) among McCarthy's diverse cast of characters, John Grady best embodies the heroism inherent in McCarthy's later work.

The first reason why I am analyzing these two novels in tandem here is that John Grady is arguably the main protagonist in both narratives, even though Billy certainly plays a significant role in the latter work.[66] Second, as I mentioned above, the tale of *Cities of the Plain* closely follows that of *All the Pretty Horses*, historically speaking: while the first volume in the Border Trilogy is set in 1949, the narrative of the third volume resumes the story of John Grady's life almost seamlessly in 1952 on a ranch in southern New Mexico, near the Mexican border. Third, and perhaps unexpectedly, it is imperative to discuss John Grady's tale in the context of what I have theorized as narrative extainment because this character functions as the antithesis to a figure like Culla, who can be described as the incarnation of nature's indifference, with the travesty of the supplicant's posture being counterbalanced by John Grady's heroic sincerity. It is perhaps helpful to recapitulate the plot of the first novel and then outline that of *Cities of the Plain*, for the reader to immediately understand why it might at first seem peculiar to choose John Grady's narrative, as it is told in McCarthy's 1992 and 1998 novels, to demonstrate the author's narrative extainment of nature's identity, or his literary depiction of indifference in its various forms. In the context of the revolting scenes of *Outer Dark*, it is indeed a peculiar (albeit entirely warranted) choice, not least because the one character trait that makes John Grady's life supposedly unsusceptible to any consideration of nature's indifference is his capacity to fall in love—behavior that is usually regarded as the opposite of indifference on an emotional level.

John Grady—a sixteen-year-old whose family's ranch is for sale and whose uncaring parents ignore, and thus alienate, him—dreams of being a cowboy south of the border, making a living by breaking horses. On horseback, he crosses the Rio Grande with Lacey Rawlins, his cousin, in search of a ranch that will give them work. On their way they meet a strange-looking boy who calls himself Jimmy Blevins, and whose actions will eventually lead to their doom—as he will entangle them in the theft of horses and other crimes (including murder) that he commits in the Mexican state of Coahuila. Before they are put in jail in the third part of the book, however, they find a ranch owner named Don Héctor, who hires them. At the ranch, John Grady falls in love with Alejandra, Don Héctor's daughter. However, after a few months, both John Grady and Rawlins are put in prison where they must fight for their lives on a daily basis, and Jimmy is killed by the Mexican police for murder and for horse theft. After the cousins' eventual escape from prison and a series of violent encounters with the Mexicans who got them incarcerated, the two return separately to their home in San Angelo, Texas.

The plot of *Cities of the Plain* is even more straightforward, as it presents John Grady's life shortly after the events of *All the Pretty Horses*. He is working on a ranch in Alamogordo, New Mexico, with an older character, Billy, as well as a few other cowboys. This ranch is close to El Paso and Ciudad Juárez, and at the beginning of the narrative, John Grady, Billy, and the others visit a whorehouse in the Mexican border town. This is where John Grady sees Magdalena for the first time, a young Mexican prostitute whom he falls in love with. This is another romance that is doomed to fail, since although Magdalena is an epileptic, she is the favorite prostitute of the pimp Eduardo, who owns the whorehouse. After John Grady has secretly visited Magdalena a few times and after they have confessed their sincere love for each other, they plan for her to get across the border so they can be married in New Mexico and to live near the ranch. Yet, as usual in McCarthy's fictional worlds, this plan "goes sideways": Eduardo sends Tiburcio, his right-hand man, to intercept Magdalena, and he cuts her throat. Having waited for her for hours, John Grady finally discovers her mutilated body at a local hospital in Juárez and, with revenge on his mind, challenges Eduardo in a knife fight that none of the two adversaries survive. Eduardo dies first, and John Grady dies a little later, in the arms of Billy—who arrives after a local boy who has hidden the dying John Grady tells Billy where he is.[67]

The central protagonist of these two narratives is a very different character than McCarthy's average killer, who is bloodthirsty and unaffected by his experiences, a literary figure whose face and demeanor remain essentially "without expression" (BM, 84). John Grady's heroism does not seem to fit the descendentalism of the earlier novels and the seemingly negative concept of the world's "co-science" (*Mitwissenschaft*) in terms of being complicit in a crime. It is not exactly obvious to liken the indifference that characterizes Culla to John Grady's affective and respectful relationship to his environment and, more important, his fellow human beings.[68] Yet in contrast to any biocentrism that might be evoked by the frequent comparisons of the lives of men to those of horses (who in John Grady's view are related as no other species are, repeating the Melville-inspired relationship between whales and human beings), the narrator describes the protagonist on the very first page in terms of *supplication*—the practice that McCarthy's earlier work depicted in the gothic contexts of descent and nature's decomposition. The night before his grandfather's funeral, John Grady steps outside his family's ranch: "Dark and cold and no wind and a thin gray reef along the eastern rim of the world. He walked out on the prairie and stood holding his hat *like some supplicant to the darkness over them all* and he stood there for a long time" (*PH*, 3, emphasis added). This formulation attests to the fact that there is a certain narrative continuity regarding the motif of supplication from *The Orchard Keeper* to *All the Pretty Horses* and, consequently, also to the last volume of the Border Trilogy. Even though in McCarthy's first novel it was the repulsive apparition of Kenneth Rattner and "the pitch of supplication" (*TOK*, 33) in his voice, rather than the youthful and almost naïve determination of the young cowboy (who as death approaches in *Cities of the Plain* prays to God in the most candid manner [*CP*, 257]), the ontological vision of McCarthy remains the same in all three of these texts.[69] That is, due to the religious aspect of the author's poetics, it does not really matter who takes on the function of the person who begs for him- or herself or for others, insofar as the attitude of supplication remains essentially the same, regardless of its temporary subject. If in the context of geotraumatic tension in *The Orchard Keeper*, I have described nature's capacity of supplication as the most sophisticated expression of the "dynamic community"[70] of forces, rather than merely an appraisal of "human communion,"[71] to a certain extent this also holds for the representation of the supplicant in the case of John Grady. However, in both *All the Pretty Horses* and *Cities of the Plain*, it is less the traumatic genesis of forms that is witnessed than the way in which nature's identity can be revealed only by the stoic endurance of hardship, of the seemingly unbearable turn of events in one's life.

This is precisely what I mean by the supervenience of ethics upon ontology in McCarthy's border fiction: the narrator's depiction of John Grady assuming the function of the supplicant from his first appearance in *All the Pretty Horses* to his last breath in *Cities of the Plain* can be described as the narrative extainment of nature's identity insofar as the unwavering determination of individual will in the face of certain defeat is to meet nature's indifference with a behavior that is in turn indifferent to it. If one stipulates (like McCarthy and the early Schelling of the 1799 introduction to the *First Outline of a System of the Philosophy of Nature*) that identity is not the property of things in the world but a formless process of differentiation, then there are two aspects of this stance in terms of identity's narrative extainment in *All the Pretty Horses* and *Cities of the Plain*—one philosophical, the other literary. The philosophical aspect is in line with the Platonic idea of love (*philea*) as the characteristic with which humanity is endowed that is conceived of as "unconditioned by authorial directives, tradition, [or] prejudice"[72] and that is similar to the indifference of grace that I referred to above in the discussion of Rinthy's perspective in *Outer Dark*: love is a singular form of *Mitwissenschaft* insofar as it is not "mute supplication" (*TOK*, 25) but unconditioned affection for a person (in the case of John Grady, for Alejandra and, in the later narrative, Magdalena). This type of affection is unconditioned insofar as it is indifferent to its circumstance. For John Grady, love cannot be returned to its origin because, like the unground and time, it is not a thing but a "no-thing"—hence, as Grant has remarked, the linguistic ambiguity of love's unconditioned character in German, as the "unthinged [*das Unbedingte*]."[73]

The literary aspect has to do with the genre within which narrative extainment is articulated as graceful indifference: in other words, it is necessarily the coming-of-age narrative that expresses unconditional love in opposition to indifferent violence toward beings in the world (as in the fictional construct of Culla or the triune) because, as Schelling states: "Identity produced from difference *is* indifference."[74] That is, identity is reached on a formal or poetic level if—and only if—the character has experienced the world's circumstances (the differentiation of things in the world) and can gracefully envision identity qua indifference. In this sense, John Grady's reverence for animal life and Native American mythologies, his willingness to be responsible for his cousin and Jimmy, and his relationships with Alejandra and Magdalena can be viewed in a more encompassing light than any biocentric or ecocentric perspective would allow. Furthermore, the form of narrative extainment that is fundamentally sustained by John Grady's capacity to be affected—in spite of the indifference of fate or nature's contingencies—is consistent, or consonant, with the poetics of antecedence that I discussed in terms of John Joel Glanton's simultaneous resignation and affirmation at the beginning of the previous chapter.

In the evening after his grandfather's funeral, John Grady goes for a ride and imagines how the Native Americans, "the painted ponies and the riders of that lost nation," once went through that desert territory, "nation and ghost of a nation passing in a soft chorale across that mineral waste to darkness bearing lost to all history and all remembrance like a grail the sum of their secular and transitory and violent lives" (*PH*, 5). After he has dismounted and walked through the evening dusk, there is a short paragraph that may allude to Melville's reference to Oken's theories about the vertebral column in *Moby-Dick*, the "German conceit"[75] I discussed in the previous chapter: "There was an old horseskull in the brush and he squatted and picked it up and turned it in his hands. Frail and brittle. Bleached paper white. He squatted in the long light holding it, the comicbook teeth loose in their sockets. The joints in the cranium like a ragged welding of the bone plates. The muted run of sand in the brainbox when he turned it" (*PH*, 6). The appropriateness of interpreting this passage along the lines of the Okenian physiophilosophy I made use of in my interpretations of *Blood Meridian* and *The Crossing* is further confirmed by the paragraph that follows directly after the one I just quoted, which affirms the natural immanence of living bodies in the world, the oneness of human and nonhuman animality: "What [John Grady] loved in horses was what he loved in men, the blood and the heat of the blood that ran them. All the reverence and all his fondness and all the leanings of his life were for the ardenthearted and they would always be so and never be otherwise" (ibid.). Certainly, it would be possible to assert a vitalist standpoint in these sentences, a "reverence" for "the heat of the blood," the supposed life-force that animates creatures like horses and humans.[76] Yet this standpoint is not enough to account for the ontological reach of the concept of nature that is consistently evoked throughout McCarthy's Westerns alone: the interrelated mythologies of blood and animality are neither wholly affirmative nor entirely negative, since both point to the nonhuman origin of humanity and—in line with Oken's paradoxical logic in the *Elements*—to the recapitulation of life's originary emergence in the practice of war.

When John Grady and Rawlins are starting out to break horses for Don Héctor, they ride into the nearby mountains to look for wild mares, together with a few young Mexican cowboys and an old cook whose name is Luis. Like other literary figures of McCarthy's who present aphorisms or short tales to the respective protagonists (above all in *Blood Meridian* and *The Crossing*), the cook falls into a contemplative mood and tells John Grady and Rawlins that he is convinced "that the souls of horses mirror the souls of men more closely than men suppose and that horses also love war. Men say they only learn this but he said that no creature can learn that which his heart has no shape to hold" (*PH*, 111). Further problematizing any straightforwardly vitalist reading of *All the Pretty Horses* that would emphasize what Arnold has called the "affirmation of life and of humanity,"[77] Luis adds that "he had seen the souls of horses and that it was a terrible thing to see. He said that it could be seen under certain circumstances attending the death of a horse because the horse shares a common soul and its separate life only forms it out of all horses and makes it mortal. He said that if a person understood the soul of the horse then he would understand all horses that ever were" (ibid.). When Rawlins asks him how this commonality among horses compares to humankind, Luis replies after some hesitation "that among men there was no such communion as among horses and the notion that men can be understood at all was probably an illusion" (ibid.).[78]

Luis's reasoning does not conform to Cooper's ethical standard of "human communion,"[79] nor does it purport a "vital materialism" of the sort that Jane Bennett suggests, since his speculations on animal and human souls do not expound the virtues of any "thing-power" or "human power" that would exist in an ecologically grounded correlation.[80] Rather, the cook is concerned with the locus of emergence of these powers, the space that by necessity has to be extained by living bodies and actual ideas, since it consists of the formless inexistence that precedes and succeeds these creatures and concepts, judged according to the unconditioned and thus unknowable "no-thing" of nature.[81] What I am claiming here is not that Cooper's spiritual interpretation of McCarthy or Bennett's ecocentric materialism is fundamentally at odds with the animist metaphysics of Luis and other characters or narrators in McCarthy's fiction. Rather, I am claiming that these perspectives are insufficient to account for the all-encompassing reach of natural process in McCarthy's narrative answer to the question "What is nature?" For McCarthy, the realm of nature is not defined by, yet nevertheless includes, the human capacity to feel empathy, as well as the sensible features of objects in the world. Conversely, the realm of nature includes all that exists as well as inexistence, the identity of which can never be contained in human reason (or "communion," for that matter), but it can be extained by violent or graceful expressions of indifference. Supplication (or the conscience of the world) is thus expressed either in the practice of war as the recapitulation of the zero or in the practice of affirmation as the persistence of love.

After John Grady has talked to Alejandra for the first time and apparently fallen in love with her, he returns to the mountains with Rawlins and the *vaqueros*, or Mexican cowboys. At the campfire he talks about Alejandra with Rawlins, and after the cousins have bid each other good night, the narrator describes John Grady contemplating the night sky as the other cowboys sleep:

> He lay looking up at the stars in their places and the hot belt of matter that ran the chord of the dark vault overhead and he put his hands on the ground at ei-

> ther side of him and pressed them against the earth and in that coldly burning canopy of black he slowly turned dead center to the world, all of it taut and trembling and moving enormous and alive under his hands.
>
> What's her name? said Rawlins in the darkness.
>
> Alejandra. Her name is Alejandra. (*PH*, 119)

I take it that any supposed vitalism of this passage is not an ontological one that conditions the way in which John Grady views the world. On the contrary, his impression that "the world" is "taut and trembling and moving enormous and alive under his hands" is possible only because of his unconditional love for Alejandra, which is further emphasized by McCarthy by the fact that her name is the very last word in this scene in the mountains.

The romantic image of the cowboy's special relationship to the world of horses is linked to the affair with Alejandra when we read the following description: "she rode all seeming unaware down through the low hills while the first spits of rain blew on the wind and onto the upper pasturelands and past the pale and reedy lakes riding erect and stately until the rain caught her up and shrouded her figure away in that wild summer landscape: real horse, real rider, real land and sky and yet a dream withal" (*PH*, 131–32). The narrator follows this remarkable depiction almost immediately with the first conversation between John Grady and the Dueña Alfonsa (Alejandra's godmother), when the latter states: "They have a long life, dreams. . . . They have an odd durability for something not quite real" (134). It is this space of the "not quite real" (the space that cannot be contained but only extained) that is equated in this case with the realm of dreams that occupies a prominent place in the Border Trilogy. In other words, it is a space where the unconscious processes in individual minds like those of the Dueña Alfonsa, John Grady, Rawlins, and Billy Parham coincide with, or take part in, "the community of forces"[82] in nature. This space—arguably synonymous with what Schelling calls "the world soul"—is also evoked in one of John Grady's dreams after he and Rawlins are captured by Mexican authorities for being complicit in Blevins's horse theft earlier in the novel. John Grady once again dreams of horses in the first night of their incarceration, at the small town of Encantada, and in this dream the "resonance" of the world's soul is even more apparent:

> In the dream he was among the horses running and in the dream he himself could run with the horses and they coursed the young mares and fillies over the plain where their rich bay and their rich chestnut colors shone in the sun and the young colts ran with their dams . . . and they ran he and the horses out along the high mesas where the ground resounded under their running hooves and they flowed and changed and ran their manes and tails blew off of them

> like spume and there was nothing else at all in that high world and they moved all of them in a resonance that was like a music among them and they were none of them afraid horse nor colt nor mare and they ran in that resonance which is the world itself and which cannot be spoken but only praised. (*PH*, 161–62)

In line with the strongly Platonic imagery of John Grady's dream,[83] his answer to the fabrications of the Mexican captain who tries to implicate him in Blevins' crimes (which include murder as well as theft) is related to the metaphysics of nature that I have traced throughout McCarthy's works. The captain threatens John Grady by saying he would do better to confess the truth in the local prison in Encantada than in the more dangerous one in Saltillo, where Rawlins and he are eventually headed: "Then the truth will be in other hands. You see. We can make the truth here. Or we can lose it. But when you leave here it will be too late" (*PH*, 168). John Grady replies: "There aint but one truth. . . . The truth is what happened. It aint what come out of somebody's mouth" (ibid.). This statement does not discredit the truth of narrative, which the interpolated tales of *The Crossing* will extol, but it renders insufficient the ontological aspiration of veracity provided by the conditions of lived experience. In other words, the truth of the world's events does not lie in the way they are narrated or witnessed, but in the fact that they are told and witnessed: in the last analysis, the truth of narration consists of the process of narration itself, unconditioned by time or place.

John Grady's unbroken idealism is further demonstrated when he and his cousin are transferred to the prison in Saltillo (Blevins has been executed during the journey there from Encantada). The narrator describes the new environs of two young Americans thus: "A sense of some *brooding and malignant life* slumbering in the darkened cages they passed" (*PH*, 181, emphasis added)—to be sure, an allegorical rendering of nature's indifference toward the two cowboys' well-being. Yet this "malignant life" awaiting them also points to a perverted vision of the nascent egalitarianism suggested by that indifference: curiously, the narrator depicts daily life in the prison in terms that are not altogether negative. Recalling the diction of *optical democracy* from *Blood Meridian*, yet this time referring to the individual status of every prisoner in terms of his fighting skills, the narrator almost praises the social structure of the community of which John Grady and Rawlins have involuntarily become a part:

> The prison was no more than a small walled village and within it occurred a constant seethe of barter and exchange in everything from radios and blankets down to matches and buttons and shoenails and within this bartering ran a constant struggle for status and position. Underpinning all of it like the

> fiscal standard in commercial societies lay a bedrock of depravity and violence where in an egalitarian absolute every man was judged by a single standard and that was his readiness to kill. (182)

McCarthy's notion of the world as tale, and of the world soul as that which is extained in the act of narration, which I described in the previous chapter with regard to the concept of the void, is foreshadowed in the following scene when John Grady first gets out of his hospital bed after the death of the *cuchillero*, the assassin who was hired to kill him: "He pushed back the sheets and rolled onto his side and stepped down to the floor. He walked up and back. His feet left cold wet tracks on the polished stones that sucked up and vanished like the tale of the world itself" (*PH*, 206). The latter half of the last sentence recalls a passage from *Child of God*, which I cited above—a passage that referred to the "palimpsest" (*COG*, 130) generated by tracks in the Appalachian snow.[84] I argue that the thematic closeness of these sections once again testifies to the narrative continuity of McCarthy's literary vision of nature's identity in both the early Tennessee works and the Southwestern novels.

When John Grady returns to Don Héctor's ranch for the last time he has a long conversation with the Dueña Alfonsa, and she tells him about her childhood and her relationship to two men, Francisco and Gustavo, who fought in the Mexican Revolution. As other scholars have noted, this conversation is one of the passages in McCarthy's work that have a strong metaphysical import and an allegorical aspect, in the sense that the woman's tale is placed within the overall narrative of a novel (in this case, *All the Pretty Horses*) to communicate a certain message or statement that transcends the narrative in which it is embedded. From the perspective of the present argument, this narrative technique is in line with McCarthy's narrative strategy of regionalism: it seems as if it is only in the context of individual histories—"the deaths of great men in violence and madness" (*PH*, 231), as recounted by the elderly Mexican woman—that the speculative narrative of McCarthy's narrator can take the shape it has. The Dueña Alfonsa thus recounts to John Grady that Gustavo once told her "that those who have suffered great pain of injury or loss are joined to one another with bonds of a special authority and so it has proved to be. The closest bonds we will ever know are bonds of grief. The deepest community one of sorrow" (238). This may be a metafictional admonition on the part of the narrator, referring to the ethical and aesthetic formula that is at the root of McCarthy's entire novelistic oeuvre: *starting from grief, arriving at grace*. However, in addition to the Schellingian and Okenian resonances of the novel, this type of metafiction is based not on its own textual disposition but on its embeddedness in natural dynamics insofar as it functions as a narrative "extainment" that tautegorically "integrates the concept into its environment at the point of the concept's emergence."[85]

To return briefly to the way in which the narrative voice of *All the Pretty Horses* renders intelligible the unthinged nature of John Grady's affection for Alejandra, and how this nature is inexorably connected to the above-mentioned ethical and aesthetic formula, consider the scene in which the two lovers see each other for the last time. The appearance of his beloved seems almost otherworldly to John Grady: "As she walked toward him her beauty seemed to him a thing altogether improbable. A presence unaccountable in this place or in any place at all. . . . You are so thin, she said. He looked into those blue eyes like a man seeking some vision of the increate future of the universe" (*PH*, 248). Here John Grady's love almost directly reveals the connection to the "co-knowing of creation"[86] of which Schelling writes in *The Ages of the World*. Even more significant, however, is the manner in which John Grady's love for Alejandra's beauty is equaled by the great pain he experiences after saying goodbye to her, and how his thoughts are depicted yet again as parallel to the dying stars in the night sky:

> He listened to the wind in the emptiness and watched stars trace the arc of the hemisphere and die in the darkness at the edge of the world and as he lay there the agony in his heart was like a stake. He imagined the pain of the world to be like some formless parasitic being seeking out the warmth of human souls wherein to incubate and he thought he knew what made one liable to its visitations. What he had not known was that it was mindless and so had no way to know the limits of those souls and what he feared was that there might be no limits. (*PH*, 256–57)

Almost in confirmation of the fundamental link between McCarthy's concept of antecedent nature, the latter's indifference to its creatures, and the narrator's description of love as the unconditioned expression of graceful indifference, a few pages later the narrator clearly equates Alejandra's beauty and John Grady's grief at his loss: "He thought that in the beauty of the world were hid a secret. He thought the world's heart beat at some terrible cost and that the world's pain and its beauty moved in a relationship of diverging equity and that in this deficit the blood of multitudes might ultimately be exacted for the vision of a single flower" (*PH*, 282).

The penultimate page of the novel reprises what Megan Riley McGilchrist has termed nature's "beauty, horror and utter indifference to humanity"[87] in her account of McCarthy's Western fiction. Coinciding with John Grady's return to San Angelo is the funeral of an old Mexican woman who had been working as a housekeeper (and serving as a sort of grandmother) at his family's ranch for "fifty years" (*PH*, 301). In the following passage he is standing at her grave in despair, after the other mourners have gone:

> He stood holding his hat and he called her his abuela and he said goodbye to her in spanish and then turned and put on his hat and turned his wet face to the wind and for a moment he held out his hands as if to steady himself or as if to bless the ground there or as if to slow the world that was rushing away and seemed to care nothing for the old or the young or rich or poor or dark or pale or he or she. Nothing for their struggles, nothing for the living or the dead. (ibid.)

This paragraph is one of the clearest examples of how McCarthy's prose narrates the numbing effect of nature's indifference on those people who are affected by it and struggle to respond indifferently themselves. Yet even though John Grady cries in despair over the loss of "his abuela," as well as the loss of his Alejandra, he does not succumb for long to melancholy. Rather, after having experienced how nature "care[s] nothing for the old or the young or rich or poor or dark or pale or he or she," he emerges an unbroken and even stronger person at the start of the Border Trilogy's third volume, *Cities of the Plain*.

Just as the title of *Outer Dark* referred to the Bible, many scholars have noted that the title of *Cities of the Plain* refers to "the iniquitous cities of Sodom and Gomorrah,"[88] places of sin and moral depravity. Despite Billy's undeniable role in the narrative, I hold that the driving force of the novel is the love between John Grady and Magdalena, the young prostitute whom he eventually intends to rescue from the Mexican pimp, Eduardo. I read John Grady's approach to the world of prostitution in Ciudad Juárez, and the way he works closely with the horses at the ranch, in terms of the graceful indifference of love that is wholly alien to the materialistic aspects of the world related to money or social hierarchy. As in *All the Pretty Horses*, in *Cities of the Plain* John Grady is the one cowboy on the ranch where he works who almost intuitively knows how to communicate with these animals, and Troy, one of his coworkers on the ranch, wonders whether he is "some kind of specialist in spoiled horses" (*CP*, 14). In a conversation with Oren, another one of the ranch hands employed by McGovern, John Grady even claims that "a good horse has justice in his heart. I've seen it" (53).

Furthermore, he reveres the plains of New Mexico—a feeling that he shares with Billy. For instance, he once rides to a place called Cedar Springs (near Alamogordo, where McGovern's ranch is situated), where he takes in the scenery: "He ate his lunch in an outcropping of lava rock with a view across the floodplain to the north and to the west. There were ancient pictographs among the rocks, engravings of animals and moons and men and lost hieroglyphics whose meaning no man would ever know. The rocks were warm in the sun and he sat sheltered from the wind and watched the silent empty land. Nothing moved" (*CP*, 49). I take it that the narrator's statement that "no man would ever know" the meaning of the "ancient pictographs" is an allusion both to the strongly descendental motif of caves in many of McCarthy's works and to the epistemological importance of reverence. While the next chapter will elaborate on the latter point at length, it should be noted here that the passage I just quoted can be regarded as a prime example of what I have conceptualized as regionalism employed as a narrative strategy by McCarthy. The philosophical statement about the unknowability of these "pictographs" and "engravings" is possible only in the context of the "floodplain" scenery, and the narrative movement yet again is from the particular to the universal, from regionalist narrative to transnational speculation.

John Grady's situation in *Cities of the Plain* is very much like that in *All the Pretty Horses*, insofar as he falls in love with a girl whom he cannot have—in this case, due to the very jealous pimp, Eduardo. When John Grady returns from one of his visits to Magdalena to the ranch where he works with Billy and others, the narrator once again takes up the theme of the inseparability of grace and grief, which is also central to the two preceding novels of the Border Trilogy. Grace and grief (or, as in this particular passage, "beauty and loss") are intimately linked and, in the last analysis, can be separated only temporarily, if at all. They are two extremes that to a certain extent correspond to the two forms of extainment of nature's identity in terms of indifference that I discussed above in this chapter:

> In the cold dawn the lights were still burning out there under the dark cape of the mountains with that precious insularity common to cities of the desert. A man was coming down the road driving a donkey piled high with firewood. In the distance the churchbells had begun. The man smiled at him a sly smile. As if they knew a secret between them, these two. Something of age and youth and their claims and the justice of those claims. And of the claims upon them. The world past, the world to come. Their common transiencies. Above all a knowing deep in the bone that beauty and loss are one. (*CP*, 71)

The mystery or "secret" that the narrative voice mentions here is perhaps best seen in light of John Grady's idealist attitude toward his life and the obstacles it has had in store for him, in the course of both the first and third volumes of the trilogy. He is indifferent neither to "beauty" nor to "loss," yet his assuming responsibility for his loves, his friends, and even the horses around him is nevertheless a courageous attempt to live up to the standard of a certain kind of graceful indifference, an ethics of the unconditioned or unthinged as it appears in the world: a love that is boundless, regardless of circumstance. This ethics is also involved in a passage late in the novel, in which the blind maestro—a Mexican whom John Grady befriends and whom he asks to be the "padrino" (*CP*, 190) of Magdalena—tells the young man, "the world does have a conscience, however men dispute it. And while that conscience may be thought of as the sum of consciences of men there is another view, which is that it may stand alone and each man's share be but some small imperfect part of it" (193). These statements, significantly made by a blind man who immediately recalls the blind veteran in *The Crossing*, define John Grady's view of the world. It is almost as if the whole trilogy has been building up to this moment, which not only reflects the concept of nature's unconditioned identity but also refers to the notion of the world as the source of the phenomenon of conscience, instead of humankind alone. In other words, if the conscience of the world is always more than, or ontologically prior to, the various forms of "co-science (*Mitwissenschaft*)"[89] practiced by human beings, it is not exclusively the human mind that is the condition of possibility for moral standards, but instead the natural environment has to be integrated into the emergence of the concept of normativity.[90]

In line with these speculations on the part of the maestro, I conclude this chapter by referring to a passage in which Billy is trying one last time to convince John Grady not to go through with his plan to steal Magdalena away from Eduardo's whorehouse. The passage is striking, not least because it resonates with the narrative delineation of the world's indifference at the ending of *All the Pretty Horses*, when John Grady attends the funeral of his *abuela*. However, in this case the tragedy is yet to come and is somehow foreshadowed by the conversation between the two friends. After Billy has tried in vain to persuade John Grady not carry out his plan, the younger cowboy says:

> Well, . . . I'm willing to risk it. I've damn sure tried it the other way.
>
> Yeah.
>
> You cant tell anybody anything, bud. Hell, it's really just a way of telling yourself. Any you cant even do that. You just try and use your best judgment and that's about it.
>
> Yeah. Well. The world dont know nothin about your judgment.
>
> I know it. It's worse than that, even. It dont care. (*CP*, 219)

While the world's carelessness is what I have been discussing when I referred to indifference as the primal expression of nature's identity, along the lines of Schelling's early philosophy of nature, what is arguably most significant here, and what I discuss in the next and final chapter, is the question of time in the literary portraiture of indifference. What I mean is that the declarative statement *about* the world and its indifference toward humanity is one thing, and the narrative treatment of a course of events that, allegorically speaking, *goes sideways* is another and depends on whether the tragedy is depicted after its events have taken place, or whether the these events are somehow foreshadowed by narrative means. Even though this chapter has discussed the use of nonmimetic depictions of nature's identity in *Outer Dark*, *All the Pretty Horses*, and *Cities of the Plain*, by developing a theory of narrative extainment rather than containment, and even though the chapter has connected this theory to the earlier narratological pair of allegorical and tautegorical forms of mythography that I introduced in chapter 3, I still have to specify which kinds of concrete mythologies McCarthy is indebted to and negotiates in his fiction.

As I argue in what follows, in novels like *No Country for Old Men* and *The Road*, for instance, determining which myth or mythological figure a narrative at hand alludes to always comes down to the question of temporal perspective. This is because not only is McCarthy's work *formally* mythological (that is, in terms of allegory or tautegory) but also because his novels can be regarded as contemporary attempts at mythmaking—but from an exclusively American perspective, not a Greek or Roman one.

[6]

"THE ASHES OF ITS RUIN": WRITING NATURE BETWEEN ORPHISM AND PROMETHEANISM

Things happen to you they happen. They dont require your permission.
—Cormac McCarthy, *No Country for Old Men*

What we speak of as nature is a poem lying pent in a mysterious and wonderful script. Yet the riddle could reveal itself, were we to recognize in it the odyssey of the spirit, which marvelously deluded, seeks itself, and in seeking flies from itself.
—Friedrich W. J. Schelling, *System of Transcendental Idealism*

ABOVE I HAVE OUTLINED the literary and philosophical contours of McCarthy's concept of nature; explored the notion of ontological decay, as it unfolds narratively in *The Orchard Keeper*, *Child of God*, and *Suttree*; examined the physiophilosophy reflected in *Blood Meridian* and *The Crossing*; and described McCarthy's practice of narrative extainment in *Outer Dark*, *All the Pretty Horses*, and *Cities of the Plain*. This final chapter adds to these previous discussions and reframes them in terms of two distinct mythographical traditions. It contextualizes McCarthy's unique approach to literary practice no longer in exclusively formal terms of philosophy and narratology—that is, with respect to consequence and antecedence, allegory and tautegory, counting and recounting, and containment and extainment—but also with respect to myths that are recapitulated in McCarthy's fiction.

As the preceding chapters have shown, the question of how to relate humankind to its natural environment has a long history in Western literature and philosophy, from gnosticism all the way to geocriticism. The human perspectives on this relationship between the human and nonhuman realms of the world seem innumerable, but in this chapter I focus on two major traditions of dealing with the question concerning nature's identity that seem to be diametrically opposed to each other.[1] Both have their origins in Greek mythology and its successors, and both are alive and well to this day. One, which respects nature and honors it often in poetic form, can be traced back to the figure of Orpheus. The other, which sees nature as merely useful to humankind and subordinate to manmade technologies, can be traced back to the figure of Prometheus. Both figures have a long history of reception in

Western literature and culture at large, with various narratives about them imagined by authors and artists from Pindar to Richard Powers, and from Aeschylus to Ridley Scott.[2] As others have noted, the two figures are of great importance to McCarthy's later work but are alluded to at least from *Blood Meridian* onward.[3] The poetically inclined Orphic attitude and the scientifically oriented Promethean attitude toward the question of humanity's relationship to and position within its natural surroundings each give rise to narrative tensions within novels like *No Country for Old Men*, *The Road*, and *The Sunset Limited*. Furthermore, the two mythological figures and their characteristics in many ways summarize the style of writing nature that McCarthy espouses particularly in the latter half of his career, but also in part from its beginning. Certainly, the explorations of the cave systems, the katabatic discoveries of John Wesley in *The Orchard Keeper*, and the characters of Lester Ballard in *Child of God* and Gene Harrogate in *Suttree* confirm the Orphic sentiment of McCarthy in his early works—which again attests to his narrative continuity.

I take the distinction between the Orphic and Promethean attitudes with respect to the question in how humanity should understand its relationship to and existence within nature from Pierre Hadot's *The Veil of Isis: An Essay on the History of the Idea of Nature* (2004). The book succinctly traces various responses to and interpretations of one of Heraclitus's most famous aphorisms from "around 500 BCE": "'Nature loves to hide.'"[4] There is a rich history of responses in Western culture to this seemingly simple statement. Although I will not delve into the plethora of these interpretations and retranslations, what seems important in most of them is the issue of agency—recalling once again the notion of panpsychism, which I discussed above in connection to *The Crossing* and *Outer Dark*. That is, if "nature loves to hide," is it hiding from human perception? Is referring to nature's habit of or preference for remaining hidden just a way of saying that human perception is limited and can register only a tiny percentage of nature's being? Is human perception quintessentially human by virtue of its being limited? If so, and in line with McCarthy's predominantly tragic narrative arcs, is human action quintessentially human by virtue of its being condemned to failure, whether or not its motivation or aspiration is reasonable?

In any case, according to Hadot, there are two major perspectives on how to confront the situation evoked by this aphorism—one that is conceived of in terms of human experience, which, regarding our problem, remains unchanged in principle from ancient Greece until today. The two major perspectives that have been developed over the centuries are modeled on mythical figures that have their own distinct features, partly entangled within Heraclitus's "enigmatic saying"[5] and partly generative of the self-consciousness of humankind as a whole in distinction to its natural birthplace and subsequent habitat. Prometheanism, Hadot states, "extends from the beginnings of Greek mechanics to the mechanistic revolution of the seventeenth century and opened the way for the technological and industrialized world in which we live."[6] It corresponds to the belief in humanity's right to colonize nature, to transform wild portions of the planet into manmade landscapes. According to the mythological narrative, Prometheus is a Titan who survived the war between the gods and their enemies. He tricks Zeus into eating the unpalatable portions of an ox, and as a result Zeus withdraws fire from humans. In turn, the unruly Titan steals fire from Olympus, carries it down to earth, and gives it to humanity. To punish him, Zeus chains Prometheus to a rock. Every day an eagle comes and eats from his liver, which renews itself at night to be destroyed once again the next day. Thus, the Titan steals fire from the gods and provides humankind with the basic element from which technology is born.[7] Prometheus, whose name means "forethought,"[8] embodies the human determination to shape life according to one's needs, "to orient oneself towards the future," as Ray Brassier puts it.[9]

To be sure, the mythological figure who steals fire from the gods so that humanity may feel warm irrespective of the time of day or season also represents the project of emancipation from the laws of nature that exist indifferently with regard to its human inhabitants. For providing the human race with the means of orienting itself toward a future not dictated by the divine laws of nature, therefore, Prometheus has to be punished, in the same way in which the acquisition of more knowledge or a more sophisticated technique of reflection is punished by the pains of self-doubt and -deception. It is not by accident that the Titan who brings the fruits of knowledge (the means of self-emancipation) to humanity by reversing the hierarchical relationship between humans and nature is also the primordial "trickster," the first and greatest deceiver.[10] In addition to the concepts of emancipation and deception, there is also the will to transformation and self-transformation, however, and this third aspect is crucial in the context of McCarthy's late novels (and, I would argue, his oeuvre as a whole). As Brassier notes, "Prometheanism is simply the claim that there is no reason to assume a predetermined limit to what we can achieve or to the ways in which we can transform ourselves and our world."[11] The figure of Prometheus can be said to represent the aspiration to change one's situation, the condition within which life occurs. This change may occur in the acquisition and exchange of knowledge or the fine-tuning of the techniques of deception, both of which contribute to what is sometimes called progress or civilization. This idea of deception coupled to the accumulation of knowledge and technological know-how is a notion we find in literature including Johann Wolfgang von Goethe's poem "Prometheus" (1789) and Mary Shelley's novel *Frankenstein, or The Modern Prometheus* (1818). Like the Titan who molds the first humans "from mud or clay"[12] and subsequently brings technology and progress to humanity, thereby subverting the hierarchies between man and nature and between the created and the creating, the scientist Victor Frankenstein is punished for achieving what is supposed to be made possible only by the use of the divine powers, an activity restricted to the gods. His generative science defies the laws of nature by forging a hideous creation—namely, Frankenstein's monster.

The mythic figure of Prometheus is also depicted in film, for instance in Scott's 2012 movie *Prometheus*, in which a crew of scientists are on a mission to discover the origins of the human species, almost risking the extinction of humanity as the result of tragic events that take place on their spaceship—including contact with a superhuman race. Tellingly, the spaceship is called *Prometheus*. As Scott observes, "When you talk about the myth on which the title is based, you're dealing with humankind's relationship with the gods—the beings who created us—and what happens when we defy them."[13] Arguably McCarthy's later work also addresses this fundamentally ethical question: what if humanity disregards ontological priority in the relationship between process and product? Or rather, how much weight should this question have in comparison with the larger question about the identity of nature? Finally, which of these two questions takes precedence in McCarthy's fiction?[14]

The other approach to the enigma that is Heraclitus's phrase—"Nature loves to hide"—is in many ways at the other end of the spectrum of possible human attitudes toward their natural origins. Orpheus is not the bringer of light but the poetic incarnation of a dark past. As Schelling writes in his *Philosophy of Revelation*, Orpheus is a veritable "representative of the past, in contradistinction to the new time" of the future.[15] The Orphic perspective is oriented toward this past, or rather positioned in it to establish a view toward the present, while Prometheanism has finished with the present condition and strives to change it, often by any means necessary. One of the narratives about Orpheus tells us about his descent into Hades (that is, the underworld) to bring his wife, Eurydice, back—a plan that almost succeeds, except that he cannot help looking over his shoulder at her before both of them can manage to escape from the deeps.[16] In accordance with this narrative, Orphism describes the human ability to mourn and be touched or affected by the senses that are given by nature, entailing the capability to create music and art and thus to mimic this givenness. If "the sin of Prometheanism . . . consists in destroying the equilibrium between the made and the given," if its "trespass resides in *making the given*,"[17] in

Brassier's words, the Orphic attitude dictates a general worship of all that gives rise to affectivity in general, be it the joy of being with your loved ones or the grief after they have died: "Whereas the Promethean attitude is inspired by audacity, boundless curiosity, the will to power, and the search for utility, the Orphic attitude, by contrast, is inspired by respect in the face of mystery and disinterestedness."[18] To use one of McCarthy's phrases in *The Road*, "carrying the fire" (*TR*, 83) in the Promethean sense denotes humans' emancipation from their god-given condition, and the element of fire in Orphism points toward the repetition of the wonders of nature in poetic form. Reverence and resignation in the perspective inherited from the mythic figure of Orpheus stand in direct opposition to the emancipatory stance of the future-oriented Titan, the rebellious Enlightenment approach to the riddle about nature hiding in plain sight, recalling once again Schelling's notion of "the indivisible remainder, that which with the greatest exertion cannot be resolved in understanding but rather remains eternally in the ground."[19] In other words, the products of nature, such as human beings and some types of animals, can examine their production only up to a certain point, due to the ontological priority of production over product, and of the unconditioned over the conditioned, as well as to their aspect of being finite by nature—of having a limited amount of years to live and a limited capacity for introspection. It is this fact that engenders two different responses in the mythological traditions I have mentioned, to try to remodel life by scientific means or to value it as something god-given.

However, in line with Hadot, I want to suggest that as much as Prometheanism and Orphism seem to be completely different responses to the question concerning human identity in the larger picture of natural processes, it might be a mistake to simply view them as the negative image of each other. In other words, "the Orphic attitude and the Promethean attitude may very well succeed each other or coexist or even combine. They nevertheless remain radically and fundamentally opposed,"[20] not least because of their mutually exclusive perspectives with regard to the question of temporality. Thus, the figures of Orpheus and Prometheus, as well as the mythological narratives attached to them, can be combined in various artistic forms of expression—which is precisely what McCarthy has done in his late prose.[21]

The remainder of this chapter contains three parts, in which I point out instances in *Blood Meridian*; *No Country for Old Men*; *All the Pretty Horses*; and McCarthy's two novels from 2006, *The Road* and *The Sunset Limited*, in which he alludes to the two mythological figures. Rather than merely analyzing the novels in terms of their Orphic and Promethean poetics, however, the chapter demonstrates how McCarthy's recontextualization of myth adds to the literary dramatization of his concept of nature, emphasizing the centrality of fire as a richly symbolic element throughout.

CRITICS HAVE NOTED THAT allusions to the figure of Prometheus appear not only in *No Country for Old Men* and *The Road* but also in the middle period of McCarthy's career. For example, Scott Yarbrough notes that "the possession and creation of fire is a recurring motif in *Blood Meridian*; Judge Holden captures fire, in a sense, when he creates gunpowder at the lip of a volcano."[22] As I showed in chapter 4, the judge is an expert in all kinds of human practices and disciplines, from scalp hunting to cosmology. He is a scientist and a "great deceiver," often lecturing his companions and murderers of Indians on topics like geology or moral philosophy, while at the same time playing tricks on them. For instance, when the group of scalp hunters have set up a camp, "the judge like a great ponderous djinn step[s] through the fire and the flames [deliver] him up as if he [is] in some sense native to their element" (*BM*, 96). Along with its technological connotation, "the idea of fire refers to the basic physical needs for warmth and light," according to Andy Dumont.[23] What is more, the creation of fire (or, in the words of Jack London, the ability "to build a fire"[24]) draws a line between the given and the made, between the drives that are common to a whole range of animal species and the distinctly human features of existence: "Symbolically, fire thus becomes a means of guiding us past the baser instincts that would leave us wallowing in our animal nature."[25]

Furthermore, Prometheanism is directly evoked in one of the judge's speeches when he claims that man's task is to decide about his own destiny instead of living under "mystery and fear," which he sees as the hallmarks of "superstition" (*BM*, 199). Even if "nature loves to hide," as Heraclitus has it—and it is worth noting here that the Greek philosopher was one of McCarthy's sources for developing Judge Holden's views on the importance of war for the understanding of humanity, as others have noted[26]—and is concealed from human perception and understanding, this does not mean that the concealment is a permanent state of affairs. Instead, it is a condition that is in constant transformation. Furthermore, if nature is conceived of as immanent and thus all-encompassing, as both McCarthy's poetics and Schelling's *Naturphilosophie* suggest, then, to a certain extent, nature must hide from itself insofar as the ontological priority of process over product, and of antecedence over consequence, is merely the condition of possibility for that constant transformation of natural dynamics.[27] Because he is opposed to any kind of superstition that really is an acceptance of the given, the judge is oriented toward a future in which he is determined "to dictate the terms of his own fate" (*BM*, 199) and unwilling to accept the path he has been put on by divine powers or nature. When he mentions "the task of singling out the thread of order from the tapestry" (ibid.), he is expressing the Promethean impulse of imposing the order of the fabricated and artificial onto the chaos of the ostensibly given and natural.

I write "ostensibly given" because McCarthy's evocation of Prometheanism here reflects that his concept of nature's identity is not premised on a strict distinction between the given and the made in terms of nature and artifice (that is, between being and thinking), but on the belief that nature exists only to the extent that it analyzes itself. The given is not a natural *form* but the given formlessness that both is the predisposition of artifice and is perpetually expanded by the fictional, artistic, scientific, religious, and philosophical "rearticulation[s] of [this] reality that, far from being distant from it, [are] what is active in it."[28] In other words, the Promethean figure of the human, which is part of nature's processes, can be regarded as "another kind of clay" (*BM*, 5) that constantly remodels itself and acts as one of the most sophisticated agents of or within nature to effectuate the latter's self-construction.

Along these lines, it is important to remember that the judge is not only a light bringer, deceiver, scientist, and Enlightenment figure (as has been argued repeatedly by scholars of McCarthy's work), but he is also a great musician and advocate of the Orphic thesis that human discourse in many ways repeats the processes of nature (that is, the language of God). For Holden, "words are things. The words he is in possession of he cannot be deprived of. Their authority transcends his ignorance of their meaning" (*BM*, 85). As I discussed in chapter 4, Holden says at one point during the scalp hunters' journey, while he is holding a "chunk of rock" in his hands, that "stones and trees, the bones of things" are the words of God (116). His claim that the languages and literatures of humankind are prior to the one person using them to his or her advantage illustrates the view that the divinity of physical nature is recapitulated in the psychological scope of the discourses that constitute human culture. This is precisely why language is an expression of *Mitwissenschaft*: like physical objects that are the quasi-linguistic units of a sacred form of speech that can never be fully recovered by merely human utterances, these utterances have effects that freely repeat those of their functional predecessors. As Jason Wirth puts it succinctly, "the thought of freedom is a kind of accessory knowing, a knowing with or *Mitwissenschaft*. It is the real becoming conscious of or aware of its ideality."[29] Like his fiddle and his dance at the end of the novel, Judge Holden's speeches are part of a natural (that is, physiocentric) continuum, the products of which are always grounded in a dark past. And this past necessarily precedes the human future that tries to separate itself from its origin and simultaneously repeats that which came before it.

Paradoxically, it is *Blood Meridian*'s rendering of war that brings together both attitudes concerning human identity within a natural cosmos, Orphism and Prometheanism, even though according to the myth, "the influence of Orpheus always tended to oppose bloodshed," and despite the fact that the Orphic religious cults were "completely opposed to the spirit of war."[30] To recapitulate the argument from chapter 4, for Holden, as well as for the narrator of *Blood Meridian*, "war is god" (*BM*, 249). Like nonhuman nature, "it makes no difference what men think of war, said the judge. War endures. As well ask men what they think of stone. War was always here. Before man was, war waited for him. The ultimate trade awaiting its ultimate practitioner" (248). War is depicted in this passage as the final expression of human culture in its recapitulation of nature's indifference to the moral codes of human societies. It is significant that in the context of war and the kinds of attitudes human beings may have toward it, the judge compares war to stone, which he previously defined as the product of God's speech. It is also significant that if the antecedence of war is equated to that of nature, human beings as the "ultimate practitioner[s]" of the former are also those of the latter—they are the summit of nature's self-analysis. On the one hand, then, war is the practice in which the most sophisticated technology decides who wins and who loses. Like the impersonal aspect of the natural sciences in contrast to the poetological discourses of the humanities, war is the ultimate quantification of human life, its most effective instrumentalization and means of annihilation. On the other hand, war repeats the relentless struggle of one force against another in the schemes of natural process, of the brutal antagonisms that give rise to the hierarchical structures of animal species, predatory or not.

If we recall what Oken said about the essence of warfare in his *Elements of Physiophilosophy* (that it "is the highest, most exalted art"), we need to add that it also has a scientific character, as it contains "all sciences and all arts." Yet if we take into account the whole passage in which Oken makes this statement, what comes to the fore is the dialectical relationship between the recapitulation of nature's conflicted forces by means of warfare and the narrative and musical recounting of the agony that awaits those who mourn for the fallen soldiers on a battlefield and, more importantly, all the victims who are to be found elsewhere: "As in the art of poetry all arts have been blended, so in the art of war have all sciences and all arts. The art of War is the highest, most exalted art; the art of freedom and of right, of the blessed condition of Man and of humanity—the Principle of Peace."[31] Okenian physiophilosophy, the judge's metaphysics, and *Blood Meridian*'s narrator all seem to participate in this tension between Orphism and Prometheanism. It might seem contradictory to claim that "the Principle of Peace" is warfare, but only if Oken's physiophilosophy is not fully taken account of, since the latter derives nature's God-given creatures from the Nature-Nothing, the zero of contingency, rather than from a principle inherent in the existent world. Thus, according to the metaphysics underlying McCarthy's first Western, it is *necessarily* the case that warfare is the ground of tranquility, just as any ethical norm would result from its ontological disposition, and just as *that which is not* eternally inheres in *that which is*—existence.

In *No Country for Old Men*, we encounter a villain who, like Judge Holden, is emotionless, cold-blooded, and fond of philosophical speeches. As Yarbrough writes, "Anton Chigurh . . . in many ways recalls Holden. He too is implacable, inscrutable, a seemingly unstoppable force of nature. One can't imagine Chigurh dancing and fiddling on a stage in any context, but on the other hand, in *Blood Meridian* Holden does coin tricks with one of the children he seems to be eyeing as a potential victim."[32] Like the judge, "Chigurh . . . fancies himself a powerful agent of destiny."[33] If for Holden the human activity of war is the most advanced of all "games of chance," since in war "that which is wagered swallows up game, player, all," so that the "stake [of warfare] is at once the game and the authority and the justification" (*BM*, 249), it is the flipping of a coin that Chigurh uses to determine whether or not someone he encounters will die. He makes most of his future victims "call it" (*NC*, 56), as he says, so they can partially decide their own future. Arguably, this procedure can be read as a dramatization of the laws of probability that often determine the results of experiments in the natural sciences, always leaving aside a last uncertainty due to both chance and the inevitable imprecision of human technologies.[34] Consider the first instance in which Chigurh, after having escaped from police custody, urges a potential victim (in this case, the owner of a gas station) to call heads or tails:

> Call it, he said.
> Call it?
> Yes.
> For what?
> Just call it. Well I need to know what it is we're callin here.
> How would that change anything? . . . You need to call it, Chigurh said. I cant call it for you. It wouldnt be fair. It wouldnt even be right. (*NC*, 55–56)

When the man is lucky enough to call the side of the coin that saves his life, Chigurh cautions him to take the coin and carry it with him at all times. To explain why the man should do so, Chigurh states: "Anything can be an instrument. . . . Small things. Things you wouldnt even notice. They pass from hand to hand. People dont pay attention" (*NC*, 57). He implies that this inattention is a fatal mistake because at some point in their lives, "there's an accounting. And after that nothing is the same. Well, you say. It's just a coin. For instance. Nothing special there. What could that be an instrument of? You see the problem. *To separate the act from the thing*. As if the parts of some moment in history might be *interchangeable* with the parts of some other moment. How could that be? Well, it's just a coin. Yes. That's true. Is it?" (ibid., emphasis added). Two passages in some of the abovementioned texts and novels are arguably referred to in Chigurh's statements about the intersection of lived experience and the nature of chance: one is part of what the Dueña Alfonsa says to John Grady during their conversation in *All the Pretty Horses*, and the other is the passage from the notes for "Whales and Men," in which McCarthy fuses the mathematical notion of commutativity and the humanist notion of community, as I discussed in chapter 2. Ultimately, both of these passages, like Chigurh's, are metaphysical speculations on the notion of time and chance, as well as on the relationship between the qualitative determination of bodies in the world and the quantitative processes of construction on which these objects depend and as part of what they emerge from.

In *All the Pretty Horses*, for instance, the dueña comments with an air of resignation: "In the end we all come to be cured of our sentiments. Those whom life does not cure death will. The world is quite ruthless in selecting between the dream and the reality, even where we will not. *Between the wish and the thing the world lies waiting*" (*PH*, 238, emphasis added). This last proposition resonates with Chigurh's problematization of the notion of chance as that process in the world that multiplies the use of objects with regard to the activity in which they partake. This is because even though the dueña recognizes the discrepancy between an individual's desire for an object or a state of affairs to be in a certain way and the actual way in which the object or state exists, nonetheless there is a strong correspondence, however troubled, between "the wish" and "the thing." That is, for both Chigurh and the dueña, things are static beings that depend on the processes in which they are caught, while "the world" is identical with its process—even though the psychopathic killer of *No Country for Old Men* speaks from the perspective of the perpetrator, whereas the old Mexican lady of the first volume in the Border Trilogy speaks from the perspective of someone whose life has brought more pain than happiness.[35] The dueña goes on to recall one of her childhood memories, which ends up being a cautionary tale whose self-referential nature reveals the tautegorical (rather than the allegorical) disposition of the metaphysics evoked by McCarthy's text, since not only does this paragraph refer to the overarching theme of loss in the Border Trilogy (thus being a statement about the nature of the trilogy), but it also refers to McCarthy's literary strategy of constructing narrative voices that are both observing and experimenting. This is similar to what I conceptualized in chapter 3 as the author's literary alchemy, which the dueña casts in biological terms:

> When I was in school I studied biology. I learned that in making their experiments scientists will take some group—bacteria, mice, people—and subject that group to certain conditions. They compare the results with a second group which has not been disturbed. This second group is called the control group. It is the control group which enables the scientist to gauge the effect of his experiment. To judge the significance of what has occurred. *In history there are no control groups. There is no one to tell us what might have been. We weep over the might have been, but there is no might have been. There never was. It is supposed to be true that those who do not know history are condemned to repeat it. I dont believe knowing can save us.* (*PH*, 239, emphasis added)

What I am particularly interested in here is how these sentences seem to prefigure Chigurh's speculations vis-à-vis the irreversible nature of time as well as his contempt for the Orphic leaning toward the past. What his speculations imply, ultimately, are the projection of the experimental situation of the laboratory into that of lived experience insofar as he "subject[s]" his "group [of potential victims] to certain conditions." This leads us back to McCarthy's remark that "the noncommutative nature of reality is derived from our notions about time. Our skepticism regarding the reality of communal entities."[36] In the context of the Promethean figure of Chigurh and his view of the world, the act of killing necessitates a decision about the state of affairs that depends on a conglomerate of factors—the potential victim's choice, the weight, the spinning frequency of the coin, and so on—all of which are premised on McCarthy's problematization of reality's "noncommutative nature." In other words, if his "problem" ("to separate the act from the thing" [*NC*, 57]) is recontextualized in regard to McCarthy's note on the possibility of commutative time and its relationship to the idea of community, then Chigurh's psychopathic disposition (read as a thought experiment, first and foremost, on McCarthy's part) can be presented in Promethean terms: it is because he questions the "noncommutative nature of reality" that he is incapable of feeling or having any sense of community.[37]

Consider two other memorable passages that demonstrate the indifference of this villain toward his victims and how it reflects the novel's detached style of writing. The first is the execution of an anonymous hitman. After a shoot-out, Chigurh kills one of the men he has shot in the back but who has not yet died. The way in which the narrator describes the scene best displays the cold and cruel precision of Chigurh, who embodies all that is wrong with the world—at least from the point of view of Sheriff Ed Tom Bell, whose jeremiad-like reflections on the rising tide of violence and criminality in 1980s Texas let him represent the Orphic position in the novel (*NC*, 38–39).[38] This is how the narrator depicts the death of the hitman, which demonstrates once again the detached or forensic style of the narrative voice from the Promethean perspective: "He looked at Chigurh. He looked at the new day paling all about. Chigurh shot him through the forehead and then stood watching. Watching the capillaries break up in his eyes. The light receding. Watching his own image degrade in that squandered world" (*NC*, 122). The second passage occurs late in the novel, when Chigurh kills Carla Jean, the wife of the novel's main protagonist, Llewelyn Moss. Before Chigurh kills her, he says: "I got here the same way the coin did. . . . For things at a common destination there is a common path. Not always easy to see. But there" (*NC*, 258–59). When she responds that "everything I ever thought has turned out different," that "there aint the least part of my life I could of guessed," Chigurh says: "I had no say in the matter. Every moment in your life is a turning and every one a choosing. Somewhere you made a choice. All followed to this. The *accounting* is scrupulous. The shape is drawn. No line can be erased. I had no belief in your ability to move a coin in your bidding. How could you? A person's path through the world seldom changes and even more seldom will it change abruptly. And the shape of your path was visible from the beginning" (259, emphasis added).

These sentences also contain implicit references to McCarthy's earlier work, especially to the notion of "the urstone" (*BM*, 243) in *Blood Meridian*. Yet what is even more striking is the phrase that "the *accounting* is scrupulous," which confirms once again that the killer's logic is premised on the Promethean ideal of quantification in a ruthless manner, which is also in line with the worldview that is expressed in literary naturalism: human beings are at the mercy of the chance events of nature that happen regardless of how these characters think about them or perceive them. As Moss tells a hitchhiker he has picked up while being on the run with the drug money he stole: "Three weeks ago I was a law abiding citizen. Workin a nine to five job. Eight to four, anyways. Things happen to you they happen. They dont require your permission" (*NC*, 220).

Yet even though chance events force the novel's characters into the particular situations, the possibility of agency within those situations is always the last resort that is left to them. This tension between chance and choice is reminiscent not only of Judge Holden's lectures about war as the "ultimate game" (*BM*, 249), but also of John Joel Glanton's wish to "drive the remorseless sun on to its final endarkenment as if he'd ordered it all ages since" (243). In the context of McCarthy's converging narratives of Orphic and Promethean descent, this tension also recalls the classical dichotomy between freedom and nature—which (from both the Cormackian and the Schellingian perspectives) is not a conceptual duality that signifies oppositional terms but one that denotes the supervenience of freedom upon nature. Along the lines of the philosophy of nature endorsed throughout the present inquiry into McCarthy's concept of nature, notions of freedom are always figured as the most ingenious aspect of the production of forces *within* the natural realm, as "the real becoming conscious of or aware of its ideality."[39] Instead of positing "an insuperable gulf between nature and freedom,"[40] what Schelling's practice of *Naturphilosophie* and McCarthy's practice of writing nature in *No Country for Old Men* seem to be concerned with is to "think nature in its freedom as it develops along all possible trajectories."[41] In this way, to acknowledge the freedom of human beings in their reaction to the events shaping their lives is just as crucial for the philosophical and narrative speculation on nature as it is to concede the neutrality and the aimless and sometimes entirely contingent character of these events. In other words, the choices made by Moss are entangled with the chance events he is confronted with—just like the choices made by Chigurh's victims. Although there is an ontological priority of antecedence with regard to consequence, their relationship still allows a minimal kind of reciprocity, insofar as the additionally determining agency of making choices is itself a force within nature that feeds back into antecedence. Even though there is an ontological priority that pertains to chance, to the "urstone" in whose substance is written not only Glanton's charter but also Moss's, the decisions made by both characters are substantial forces within the narratives of which they are a part—which is exactly why they are the consequent factors of their enveloping, or antecedent, narratives.[42]

"Moss is a welder," Erika Spoden observes in her reading of McCarthy's novel. "It is his job to meld metal with fire, making him into a Promethean figure responsible for joining disconnected and separate planes: past and present, home front and war, Texas and Vietnam."[43] I would add, however, that the motif of Vietnam that haunts the American cultural unconscious via literature and film to this day is the reminder of a past that is mourned and not easily forgotten. The long-lasting effect that any war leaves on its participants can certainly be witnessed in the figure of Sheriff Bell, who is equally haunted by his experiences in the Second World War. His first-person narrative passages, which dominate the structure of the novel, show how the intensity and ferocity of crime has changed from past generations of Texan life to the 1980s, the time when the novel is set.

On many counts, Bell is a broken character whose notion of truth is reminiscent of some of the passages from *Blood Meridian* I mentioned above. Arguably, his definition is consistent with the concept of nature's indifference to the opinions human beings may have of it. Along similar lines, there is a more Orphic angle to the ruthlessness of chance, insofar as Orphism can be also identified with the givenness of natural process and the acceptance thereof. Consider the following section from the beginning of chapter 5 of *No Country for Old Men*:

> *The stories gets passed on and the truth gets passed over. As the sayin goes. Which I reckon some would take as meaning that the truth cant compete. But I dont believe that. I think that when the lies are all told and forgot the truth will be there yet. It dont move about from place to place and it dont change from time to time. You cant corrupt it any more than you can salt salt. You cant corrupt it because that's what it is. It's the thing you're talking about. I've heard it compared to the rock—maybe in the bible—and I wouldnt disagree with that. But it'll be here even when the rock is gone.* (NC, 123)

Bell does not share the Promethean view, according to which the limits of human achievement are set and overcome by the dynamics of human aspiration. He takes truth to be not something that people (strive to) reach an agreement about—in other words, an intersubjectively malleable standard of agreement within human discourse—but a fact that precedes the people who speak about it, as well as the flora and fauna that perceive it or appear as a part of it. For him, truth will outlive those forms of existence—humans, animals, plants, and rocks—to which it is given. Indeed, truth is not made (to revisit Brassier's distinction) but is *given* in a divine act and should be respected as such. Nature is not something that can be "corrupted" or deceived. Only humanity can be deceived, and is able or condemned (depending on how you look at it) to deceive itself by believing in the remanufacture or alienation of what is allegedly natural and not artificial. Even Prometheus's rock, to which he is bound in the mythological narrative about his punishment for "carrying the fire" (TR, 83) from the gods down to earth as a present for the human race, cannot endure the givenness that is also evidenced by the "indivisible remainder,"[44] the difference between the finitude of the product and the infinitude of production.[45]

As Spoden and other critics have remarked, the last few pages of *No Country for Old Men* have Bell relate a dream in which his father on horseback rides past him with a horn that contains fire—"*the way people used to*" (NC, 309), as Bell says. This phrase, which denotes a past that is long gone and shrouded from memory, recalls the longing for the American West in McCarthy's Border Trilogy. There is a certain mourning for a past that cannot be recovered but has to be reiterated in poetic form. The novel ends with Bell knowing that his father "*was going on ahead and that he was fixin to make a fire somewhere out there in all that dark and all that cold and I knew that whenever I got there he would be there. And then I woke up*" (ibid.). This ending points to the tension that any combination of Orphic and Promethean attitudes establishes in regard to the question of humanity's relationship to nature. The fire that the father carries in the dream clearly alludes to Prometheus's descent from Olympus. Yet it is also carried in a manner that is almost forgotten and lost to present generations. Torn between the two traditions of looking at nature, Bell finds both comfort and discomfort in his dream at the same time.

With *The Road* and *The Sunset Limited*, McCarthy's narrative treatment of Orphism and Prometheanism continues to address the question of how to conceive of a nature that can be disclosed only in part, yet that seems to be the agent of its own disclosure. Put differently, McCarthy's rendition and recontextualization of the mythological narratives that respond to Heraclitus's aphorism ("nature loves to hide") have to be understood as part of the way in which McCarthy aims to answer in literature the philosophical question, "What is nature?" The identity of nature, as *No Country for Old Men* and especially his last two novels suggest, might be determined not only by saying what it is, but also by delineating the major kinds of human responses to one of the most general, yet also most persistent, speculations about what nature does. Nature's hiding itself means that the possibility of recovering the given—either by forging new technologies for calculating and predicting that which is contingent in nature, or by envisioning new poetic or musical forms of expression to give the given its due—is eternally deferred like the promise of redemption, in religious terms. Bell's belief that "*whenever I got there he would be there*" (NC, 309) may be understood allegorically as the hope that nature will disclose what it hides from itself. However, as McCarthy's concept of nature seems to entail, it is precisely in this hiding that the ongoing reiteration and repetition of natural forms (the recapitulation of the zero) is assured.

The conceptions of nature's indifference, its antecedence, and its contingent character were all in *Blood Meridian* and *No Country for Old Men*, and they appear again in *The Road*. The latter novel won McCarthy the Pulitzer Prize, and it seems to manage a thematic synthesis of all of his previous books. Furthermore, *The Road* is part of the literary genre of post-apocalyptic fiction, yet its sources include the coming-of-age novel and the quest narrative, both of which also contributed to the plots of some of McCarthy's earlier works, such as *Suttree*, *All the Pretty Horses*, and *The Crossing*.[46] In fact, it could be argued that the Southern works and McCarthy's later Westerns already foreshadow the dark and sometimes nihilistic tone that dictates the atmosphere in his two latest novels,[47] one set in the wasteland of a desert landscape after a supposedly nuclear event, and the other set in a New York apartment in the midst of a dialogue that considers not the meaning but the supposed value of human life.

In *The Road* "the effects of fire are omnipresent," according to Paul Patton,[48] and indeed the phrase "carrying the fire" (*TR*, 83) is taken from this book, which presents a typically sober depiction of the few remaining human beings and their actions in the postapocalyptical scenario of "the late world" (11), as McCarthy terms it. A father and his son roam the ashen and devastated country, homeless on a road generally headed toward the southeastern coast of the United States, which they reach shortly before the father dies. In this novel, like other coming-of-age narratives (including those of the Border Trilogy), questions are raised about how to face an increasingly life-threatening environment and to accept one's own finality as a human being, a living body in a universe that cares nothing about its temporary inhabitants. "Despite his pessimism about human nature," in this novel "McCarthy embraces the belief that literature has a crucial social function that expands the education of a culture and an individual beyond the traditional venues of school and church and family."[49] As was also the case in *All the Pretty Horses* and *Cities of the Plain*, here the narrative extainment of nature's identity is approximated by the working through of difference, the consequence of which is indifference: the father and his son survive by meeting their hostile environment with love, or what I have called the indifference of grace. As other scholars have noted, "carrying the fire" (*TR*, 129) is a formula that recalls Sheriff Bell's Promethean dream, in which his father carries fire in a horn. According to Daniel Luttrull, "for the man, it seems, the divine fire that he carries is, or is at least especially present in, the boy."[50] The gift of a child for a future time and place that contradicts the gray landscapes of the postapocalyptic present can be read as a testament to the unwillingness of the man to give in to his dreary circumstances, which is why the father describes his boy as a "golden chalice, good to house a god" (*TR*, 75). Fire, in this case, symbolizes the hope of an alternative in spite of a reality that does not hint at any alternatives. Hope and forethought as a general repudiation of the given establish a consistent contradiction with what is manifestly and corporeally there in the environment through which father and son have to stagger. Along these lines, one of the unpublished early versions of *The Road* includes the following passage on the father's relationship to fire that sheds light on these mythological resonances: "The most common things are become drained of every feature. To light a fire had long seemed atavistic to him. *The hearth was within. A million years so.*

All sucked back into its origins. A fire now meant only warmth. Nothing more and nothing less."[51] Yet there is also the more sober description of fire and its construction, which is at the same time a naturalistic representation and an implicit evocation of the mythic tradition of Prometheanism: "They collected some old boxes and built a fire in the floor and [the father] found some tools and emptied out the cart and sat working on the wheel. He pulled the bolt and bored out the collet with a hand drill and resleeved it with a section of pipe he'd cut to length with a hacksaw. The he bolted it all back together and stood the cart upright and wheeled it around the floor. It ran fairly true. The boy sat watching everything" (*TR*, 16–17).

Perhaps controversially, *The Sunset Limited* can be seen as a "novel" that is complementary to *The Road* (irrespective of the former's structure as a screenplay, indicated by its subtitle *A Novel in Dramatic Form*), providing the psychological supplement to the material explication of *nigredo*—the process of the soul's "blackening," or confrontation with the realm of shadows—in the postapocalyptic wasteland through which the father and his son are wandering. This dual rendering of the alchemical narration of McCarthy's early work—in particular, *The Orchard Keeper*, *Child of God*, and above all *Suttree*—is thereby recapitulated in a manner that, parallel to the reference to the laboratory situation and its "control groups" (*PH*, 239), expands alchemy's ashen workshop of construction and discovery onto the dead floor "of the late world. . . . Everything uncoupled from its shoring. Unsupported in the ashen air. Sustained by a breath, trembling and brief" (*TR*, 11).

The way in which both *The Road* and *The Sunset Limited* negotiate the tension between the Orphic and Promethean standpoints is framed by the problem of suicide, or life's value. Early in *The Road*, the father recalls that the conditions of the postapocalyptic wasteland have compelled his wife (the mother of the young boy) to commit suicide, and the reader witnesses retrospectively the last heated discussion between the two adults before the wife leaves her family to kill herself in solitude. We learn of "the hundred nights they'd sat up debating the pros and cons of self destruction with the earnestness of philosophers chained to a madhouse wall" (*TR*, 58). In an even earlier version of the novel than the one I quoted from above, one still provisionally titled *The Grail*, McCarthy writes this passage in the first person, in contrast to the third person in the published version of *The Road*. Directly after the sentence that likens the philosophical debates between mother and father to that of the two protagonists of *The Sunset Limited*, McCarthy adds the following two sentences from the father's viewpoint: "Until I could not do it anymore and just watched her drift away. In bitter envy."[52]

As I noted above, this discussion between the father and the mother in *The Road* is, in many respects, very similar to the dialogue that makes up almost the whole text of *The Sunset Limited*, apart from minimal stage directions.[53] This dialogic novel takes place in an apartment within "a tenement building in a black ghetto in New York City," immediately after the African American resident of the apartment, Black, has saved the life of a suicidal white university professor, White, who sits in Black's room (*TSL*, 3).[54] Throughout the novel the two of them debate philosophical questions about knowledge versus faith; the pros and cons of continuing to live despite experiencing hardship and misery; and the ways in which the joy of living and the beauty that lies in the diversity of life's phenomena presuppose a painful time and traumatic space, grounded in indifference. To quote an already familiar passage from *The Road*: "All things of grace and beauty such that one holds them to one's heart have a common provenance in pain. Their birth in grief and ashes" (*TR*, 54).

Brassier's work proves very useful with respect to the discussion of "grace and beauty" having a "common provenance in pain," a discussion that is most thoroughly evoked in McCarthy's two 2006 novels. Brassier's advocacy of a forensic and seemingly disinterested notion of rationality rooted in the philosophical tradition of scientific realism echoes White's endorsement of "a gradual loss of make-believe," a "gradual enlightenment as to the nature of reality" (*TSL*, 120). Yet instead of viewing suicide as the only alternative, and deploring the reproduction of the human species, as White does toward the end of the novel, Brassier speaks in favor of the Promethean attitude mentioned above: the view that nature's forms and phenomena should be molded to serve the ideal if unattainable transformation of the human species to a state of "perfection."[55] This supposed motivation to strive to reach perfection must be viewed with caution, however. The eventual transformation, and thus utter unrecognizability of that species as a practical consequence of the theoretical sophistication and technological advancement envisioned by the Enlightenment is not ruled out, in Brassier's view. For him, one of the effects of the conceptual refinement propelled by human reason in the long run will be the wholesale transformation also of the question concerning humanity as a special case among natural species.[56] Nonetheless, this stance continues to place the human at the mercy of nature's indifference, with the caveat that humanity's technological and conceptual self-transformation is equally indifferent to nature. This juxtaposition is similar to the double indifference I described with respect to *Blood Meridian* in chapter 4—namely, the resulting juxtaposition of the immanence of "nature alive"[57] and the transcendence of practical reason, on the one hand, and of the transcendence of death-in-nature and the immanence of theoretical reason, on the other hand. Along these lines, perfectibility does not (or at least *should not*) denote the illusory objective of a supposed harmony in which each human being would live happily ever after. Rather, it describes the view that the proliferation of knowledge is a desirable objective that would make possible new experiments about the conflicted relationship "between reason and imagination"; in fact, "Prometheanism promises an overcoming of the opposition between reason and imagination: reason is fuelled by imagination, but it can also remake the limits of the imagination."[58] Thus, the question raised here is whether the ethical framework of anthropocentrism can be made moot by the ontological validation of nonhuman life, or, conversely, whether human exceptionalism should be dismissed on ontological grounds while being affirmed epistemologically. The differentiation of the anthropocentric stance in terms of ontology and epistemology rebuts ecocentrism's projection of normative questions onto the environment, while granting that human life is at the mercy of natural forces. However, the emphasis on the epistemological in this type of contemporary Prometheanism may be viewed as a recapitulation of nature's transformative powers—a conceptual dynamic that recalls Schelling's dialectic of "freedom and evil,"[59] of human reason and its unground, and finally of human reason as ungrounding.

Quoting J. G. Ballard, Brassier writes that "'all progress is savage and violent.' And indeed, the psychic and cognitive transformations undergone by Ballard's protagonists are nothing if not savage and violent. But the fact that progress is savage and violent does not necessarily disqualify as progress. There is indeed *a savagery recapitulated in rationality.*"[60] Incidentally, this is precisely the reasoning that links Brassier's writings to Oken's conceptualization of a nothingness antecedent to living organisms that is recapitulated in the *logos* of the rational, as I explained in chapter 4 in my reading of *Blood Meridian* and *The Crossing* from an Okenian perspective. According to Oken, human language is part of the same physical continuum that includes the domain of living or organic nature as well as inorganic nature. Cultural practices, therefore, with their normatively inscribed structures and rituals, recapitulate their origins in the generative zero, or what Oken calls the Nature-Nothing. By the same token, these practices affirm their continuous embeddedness within that continuum, even though they should not be conflated with the laws and principles of the natural sciences that work empirically. The specificity of each practice should be carefully considered, as Brassier also argues. Like the judge in *Blood Meridian*, Brassier sees man as what Oken calls "the summit, the crown of nature's development, and [he] must comprehend everything that has preceded him, even as the fruit includes within itself all the earlier developed parts of the plant. In a word, Man must represent the whole world in miniature."[61] Yet—again like Oken—he concedes that in the schemes of material nature, this summit will be surpassed, as other perceptive "engines" or organisms in the animal world have been surpassed in the course of evolution. With regard to the relationship between the forces of a purely corporeal matter and the forms of culturally informed materiality, both of which are immanent in nature, Brassier states that "natural history harbours temporal strata whose magnitude dwarfs that of the nature 'whose appearing to us is conditioned by our belonging to it'—for it proceeds regardless of whether anyone belongs to it or not. Even if it remains irreducible to it, cultural history is mediated by natural history, which includes both time and space, biology and geology."[62]

On a different level, Brassier's reasoning vis-à-vis recapitulation ties in neatly with McCarthy's stylistic fermentations of prior literary styles and periods from transcendentalism to the present into his distinctive mode of writing. Even if in general the notion of progress is not particularly appropriate, or even out of place, in any discussion of literary history, the characterization of McCarthy's style in terms of this notion in the Okenian and Brassierian sense is a complex matter, so that the question of a supposed "progress" in literary history vis-à-vis McCarthy becomes ambiguous. As I argued above, McCarthy's aesthetization of violence, his philosophical consideration of decay, and his notion of a geologically determined trauma that shapes human life all play roles in his mode of literary expression. Moreover, he employs these themes in the service of the narrative delineation of nature's identity—or better, to practice *Naturphilosophie* by narrative means. In this way, the cross-fertilization of literary periods in his own works structurally mirrors Brassier's claim about the often gruesome paths and detours toward cognitive achievement via the recapitulation of savagery. Moreover, the claim that it is not possible to have harmony between humankind and nature or among human beings echoes Brassier's standpoint, according to which science can neither answer any question once and for all nor avoid the spilling of blood in the name of the reconfiguration of what it means to think (whether in literary, scientific, or philosophical terms). As McCarthy famously stated in his 1992 interview with Richard Woodward: "There's no such thing as life without bloodshed. . . . I think the notion that the species can be improved in some way, that everyone could live in harmony, is a really dangerous idea. Those who are afflicted with this notion are the first ones to give up their souls, their freedom. Your desire that it be that way will enslave you and make your life vacuous."[63]

More specifically, Brassier's philosophical stance resonates with *The Road*'s bleak vision concerning a humanity that is "lost to the same indifferent sun" (*TR*, 219) and whose annihilation, together with "the accelerating expansion of the universe," will have engendered an all-encompassing apocalypse "terminating the possibility of embodiment."[64] Instead of merely being an example of ecocentric storytelling, *The Road* can thus be read as an exacting analysis of the place humanity inhabits and will inhabit within nature as a whole. This interpretation is in line with my generally critical attitude toward the majority of attempts by scholars to place McCarthy's work in the literary category of nature writing. Neither solely logocentric nor exclusively biocentric, McCarthy is arguably best understood as a writer whose novels combine certain features of the Promethean and Orphic attitudes to recount the physical continuum that is nature. Between scientific indifference and poetic reverence (or, mythologically speaking, between Prometheus and Orpheus), McCarthy creates a writing of nature, not nature writing.

The notion of a painful past that has been transformed into something beautiful gives rise to the whole tradition in which the fire of Prometheus, the spark of the intellect, becomes one with the poetic impulse that binds a human community in the Orphic sense: *starting from grief, arriving at grace*. In terms of the thematic distribution of both attitudes, we can say that, on the one hand, the father and his son in *The Road* are primarily future-oriented as they must adapt constantly to the life-threatening circumstances of postapocalyptic America. In addition, the end of the novel promises to transform the daily life of hardship by the founding of a new community when, after the man dies, the boy finds a new family that takes him in as a foster child. This is the kind of hope the narrative provides with its Promethean standpoint. On the other hand, however, it is the past that haunts the father and his son the most. Early in the narrative, the man speculates: "What had they done? He thought that in the history of the world it might even be that there was more punishment than crime but he took small comfort from it" (*TR*, 33). As Prometheanism proposes, it simply has to be the case that there is more punishment than crime, because in accordance with the myth, any human technology (beginning with the creation of fire) separates the human sphere from that of the given world. Thus, punishment without the corresponding crime in secular terms is to be seen as a reminder of the sin of Prometheus, which Brassier calls "*making the given*."[65]

While the Promethean attitude seems more visible in *The Road*, the Orphic attitude is equally present in the novel. The next quote most clearly identifies the delicate mixture of the two mythological traditions that indicates McCarthy's view of nature's identity (meaning its ultimate indivisibility or incalculability in terms of human forms of understanding and perception) and its principal activity (its self-induced concealment and disclosure, or its hiding and unveiling). Orpheus represents the dark past, Prometheus signifies "the age to come," and both traditions contribute to McCarthy's powerful image of a single human being's musical expression in a world that has no use for the recapitulations of the wonders of givenness and that does not yet have a notion of what its music, poetry, and art will be like:

> In the morning they came up out of the ravine and took to the road again. He'd carved the boy a flute from a piece of roadside cane and he took it from his coat and gave it to him. The boy took it wordlessly. After a while he fell back and after a while the man could hear him playing. A formless music for the age to come. Or perhaps the last music on earth called up from out of the ashes of its ruin. (*TR*, 77)

Finally, I want to examine the last paragraph of the novel, since it is one of the most central passages in McCarthy's work for those scholars who claim that biocentrism is the root of that work. The passage comes immediately after the boy has found a new family that has promised to protect him from the perils of "the late world" (*TR*, 11). As many scholars have remarked, this ending is very unusual for McCarthy, who typically concludes his narratives on a bleak, rather than a hopeful, note (even though in effect he leaves open the possibility of hope, rather than confirming it). Arguing against the claim that the last pages apparently keep the promise of redemption alive, since the new family of survivors represent a safe haven for the boy, Shelly Rambo writes: "It is not a triumph over death that one faces in *The Road* but, instead, a testament to the ways in which life and death can no longer be distinguished."[66] Furthermore, she states that the novel does not, in fact, end on a life-affirming note but entails a reconceptualization of "life as a *living on*. As readers, we are handed over the perilous question: 'What does it mean to witness to what remains?' The question is not who will save the world but, instead, who will witness its shattering?"[67] This is a provocative and insightful reasoning that connects the topic of *The Road* to the dialectic of subtraction and construction, which is so central to McCarthy's earlier novels. Conversely, the interpretation of the novel's ending as a redemptive narrative of life's affirmation, as in the case of Andrew Estes's critical navigation of "biocentric maps,"[68] is ostensibly justified only by the very last paragraph of *The Road*:

> Once there were brook trout in the streams in the mountains. You could see them standing in the amber current where the white edges of their fins wimpled softly in the flow. They smelled of *moss* in your hand. Polished and muscular and torsional. On their backs were vermiculate patterns that were maps of the world in its becoming. Maps and mazes. Of a thing which could not be put back. Not be made right again. In the deep glens where they lived all things were older than man and they *hummed* of mystery. (*TR*, 286–7, emphasis added)

It is easy to see how this beautifully rendered image of a functioning (that is, homeostatic) ecosystem of fish in the mountain creeks of unidentified origin figures as the prime example of what Estes depicts as a biocentric map. Yet, as always, it is important to examine McCarthy's phrasing. First, the fish "smelled of *moss* in your hand," a feature that is certainly reminiscent of nature's decomposition and its dialectics of becoming and remaining, as exemplified at the beginning of *The Orchard Keeper* by the "old mossbacked logs" in the "carboniferous swamp where ancient saurians lurk" (*TOK*, 11). Second, there is an allusion to the weaver-god that was referred to in *The Crossing*. Writing about "the deep glens where [the brook trout] lived," the narrative voice adds that in that space "all things were older than man and they *hummed* of mystery" (*TR*, 287, emphasis added). Recalling the image of Herman Melville's creator of the world, we should remember that the practice of creation (or "weaving") has a deafening effect, not only a constructive one: "The weaver-god, he weaves; and by that weaving is he deafened, that he hears no mortal voice; and by that *humming*, we, too, who look on the loom are deafened; and only when we escape it shall we hear the thousand voices that speak through it."[69] This deafening characteristic of living bodies, like McCarthy's brook trout, is not merely testament to the narrative's biocentric reverence toward, or well-nigh affirmation of, life. Rather, it identifies the activity of nature as that which, by creating itself, escapes its own cognition. As Schelling writes, in one of the well-nigh Orphic passages of his *System of Transcendental Idealism*: "What we speak of as nature is a poem lying pent in a mysterious and wonderful script. Yet the riddle could reveal itself, were we to recognize in it the odyssey of the spirit, which marvelously deluded, seeks itself, and in seeking flies from itself."[70] It is along these lines, then, that the ending of *The Road* should be interpreted, since it is the humming of creation that simultaneously makes possible the existence of forms of life and effectuates the irrecoverable identity of a nature that hides indefinitely.

CONCLUSION: *NATURPHILOSOPHIE* AND THE LITERATURE OF NATURE

The ultimate nature of a thing is its nascent unbeingness and it is this nothingness that is the declension to unity, singularity, which I must learn to love.
—Cormac McCarthy, "Whales and Men"

Hardly had the first steps of reuniting philosophy and nature taken place, when one had to acknowledge the great antiquity of the physical, and how the physical, far from being the last, is rather the first from which everything, even the development of the divine life, originates. —Friedrich W. J. Schelling, *The Ages of the World*

I STARTED THIS BOOK with a hypothesis—namely, that the deeply metaphysical question "What is nature?" most adequately captures what is unique about McCarthy's fiction. Perhaps I could be reproached for my frequent references to the priority of ontological over ethical themes in the author's narrative "answer" to the question concerning nature's identity by means of the following argument: In asking how adequate a question is, one may imply that some ways of examining an object (like the oeuvre of McCarthy) are better than others, and in determining which is the most adequate, adequacy may become a question of right and wrong, and thus of normativity. In other words, an adequate question about an object must necessarily be *the right one* and must invalidate other perspectives—at least to a certain extent. Therefore, it seems to me that the hypothesis with which I started this book actually did what it tried to circumvent, which is to evaluate McCarthy's works from an essentially ethical point of view—a point of view, moreover, that may not originate in the work itself.

Yet it should be remembered that my attempt to determine the most adequate question in regard to McCarthy's view of nature's identity merely sought to suspend the authority of the major ways of reading his work: in terms of spiritualism or materialism; in terms of approaches that would categorize the work as belonging to a particular period of American literary history; in terms of the ethical disposition of ecocentrism that would ultimately regard *Blood Meridian*, *The Crossing*, and *The Road* as literary products of a close ally; and in terms of the phenomenological and vitalist views of what has been called geocritical practice. It is imperative to note here, however, that I have written "suspend," rather than "reject," when referring to the highly influential analyses of McCarthy's works. This means that vis-à-vis the question "What is nature?" none of these analyses contains any serious examination of McCarthy's intricate narrative answers to that question. All of them are important readings of certain facets of McCarthy's poetics, yet they do not interpret what for him is arguably an all-encompassing process that has no outside except for what I have conceptualized as *the formless givenness of natural production* that results in the genesis of forms and phenomena in the world.

Thus, starting in the first two chapters of this book, I scrutinized this concept of nature in McCarthy—first by questioning the viability of the dominant critical approach of ecocentrism to his work, and second by providing an alternative theory of natural process that combined geocriticism, speculative realism, and, above all, the philosophies of nature forged by Schelling and Oken. Regardless of their theoretical character, these chapters contained crucial analyses of McCarthy's work that resonated with these philosophical strands. Chapter 3 introduced the important narratological dichotomy of allegory and tautegory and used it to examine *The Orchard Keeper*, *Child of God*, and *Suttree*, while chapter 4 clarified the complex relationship between the human practices of warfare and storytelling in *Blood Meridian* and *The Crossing*. Chapter 5 investigated McCarthy's various treatments of his crucial notion of supplication and his fictional rendering of a weak panpsychism in *Outer Dark* and the first and last volumes of the Border Trilogy, and chapter 6 examined his allusions to the mythographical traditions of Orphism and Prometheanism.

Given the emphatically theoretical nature of the present book, one might suspect that I have been guilty of misappropriating the primary material (that is, the novels) for the sake of a specific philosophical approach—namely, Schellingian *Naturphilosophie*. Yet has the argument really been tainted by a supposed projection of Schellingianism onto McCarthy's oeuvre? Has it turned out to be a mere application of theory to practice of the sort that necessarily and regrettably results in the simplified caricature of the given primary material, rather than the identification of its complexity?

In relation to this issue, Vereen Bell writes about the humbling experience of interpreting McCarthy's fiction: "Writing about McCarthy is an oddly embarrassing project because one is always saying either more or less than needs to be said, and always, in any case, in a version of the language that by comparison with McCarthy's seems poignantly inept."[1] While especially the second part of this statement is certainly true of the present book, I would argue that it is nevertheless important to note that Bell continues:

"One strength of McCarthy's novels is that they resist the imposition of theses from the outside, especially conventional ones, and that they seem finally to call all theses into question."[2] While Bell undoubtedly has a point regarding the scholar's difficulty of coming to terms with McCarthy's novels and their theoretical underpinnings (or with the impenetrability of the fiction with regard to the terms singled out during its scholarly exegesis) I hold that it is precisely this difficulty that confirms the approach I endorsed throughout the present book: it is because, according to McCarthy's poetics, there is no difference in kind between narrative and natural objects that his fictions resist theoretical determination, which is quite close to Heraclitus's statement that nature "loves to hide."[3] What I mean is that, even though Bell is right in his assessment that McCarthy's works cannot be appropriated or misrecognized by critical and cultural theory as easily (or unproblematically) as the writings of some of his postmodern contemporaries, my nature-philosophical interpretation is capable of accounting for this as it places McCarthy's works *within* nature, thereby rejecting any types of "theses from [and of] the outside."[4] And this contextualization is due to the fact that, as I have been arguing, McCarthy's novels are not just narratives *about* nature but direct expressions *of* it. Thus, to read McCarthy's literature of nature (*Naturliteratur*) from a Schellingian perspective is perfectly adequate, since there is no difference in kind or degree between the two, in spite of the disciplinary gap between literary and philosophical modes of expression.

Against this backdrop, then, and returning one last time to the question about the place of ethics within an approach to McCarthy's work in terms of Schellingian and Okenian *Naturphilosophie*, consider the following note in McCarthy's sketches for "Whales and Men": "The ultimate nature of a thing is its nascent unbeingness and it is this nothingness that is the declension to unity, singularity, which I must learn to love."[5] Arguably, this is both the closest one can get to an ethical maxim in McCarthy's writings *and* the furthest from what I have called the ethicist grounding of McCarthy scholarship. That "which I must learn to love" is not the beauty of existing life-forms but a given object's "nascent unbeingness." This is the upshot of my interpretation in ethical terms: it yields the broadest possible approach to McCarthy's understanding of natural dynamics, since that understanding includes not only *that which exists* but also that which does not: *inexistence*, or the nothing of nature. Perhaps, then, McCarthy's ethics of nature can best be defined as the acceptance of the functional identity between the disintegration and the emergence of forms of life in the realm of nature, or the world.

NOTES

Introduction: Cormac McCarthy's Concept of Nature

1. In contrast to most McCarthy scholars, I regard *The Sunset Limited*, which was initially published in the same year as *The Road*, as a novel and not as a play. Despite the prehistory of its publication as a play before the author added the subtitle *A Novel in Dramatic Form* without making any further modifications, I follow McCarthy's own final classification of the text, which emphasizes its thematic closeness to *The Road*—not the least important aspect of which is the rendering of death and the diverse forms it takes as one of the key issues in both novels. For different assessments, see Ciarán Dowd, "'A Novel in Dramatic Form': Metaphysical Tension in *The Sunset Limited*," in *Intertextual and Interdisciplinary Approaches to Cormac McCarthy: Borders and Crossings*, ed. Nicholas Monk (New York: Routledge, 2012), 116; Peter Josyph, *Cormac McCarthy's House: Reading McCarthy without Walls* (Austin: University of Texas Press, 2013), 24 and 262. For a concise history of this text's reception, see Markus Wierschem, "'It's More True but It Aint as Good': Searching for Truth in the Death-Deferring Dialogue of McCarthy's *The Sunset Limited*," in *Imaginary Dialogues in America*, ed. Till Kinzel and Jarmila Mildorf (Heidelberg: Winter, 2014), 327–28.

2. Dana Phillips, "History and the Ugly Facts of Cormac McCarthy's *Blood Meridian*," *American Literature* 68, no. 2 (1996): 450.

3. In part, here I am following Dowd's outline of two approaches to the philosophical standpoint implied by McCarthy's fictions, which Dowd describes as "naturalism (or close variants thereof) on the one hand, and supernaturalism, or mysticism, on the other" ("Dramatic," 117). Yet while I agree with Dowd's estimation that "both of these assessments of McCarthy's metaphysics are simultaneously valid" (ibid.), I do not concur with his concluding remark that "the opposite poles" are those of an "unresolved metaphysical tension" (ibid., 119). In fact, the theoretical framework of this book is designed to demonstrate how McCarthy's prose evokes particular philosophies of nature that cannot be ascribed to either of the two polarities proposed by Dowd, but that are capable of combining both of his frameworks.

4. Edwin T. Arnold, "McCarthy and the Sacred: A Reading of *The Crossing*," in *Cormac McCarthy: New Directions*, ed. James D. Lilley (2002; Albuquerque: University of New Mexico Press, 2014), 231.

5. Raymond Williams, *Marxism and Literature* (1977; Oxford: Oxford University Press, 2009), 132. While Williams conceives of his concept as a way to account for affective relations in the social dynamics of a given period in cultural history, I use the phrase to describe McCarthy's signature style of writing fiction.

6. Phillips, "Ugly Facts," 450.

7. See, for instance, David Mazel, *American Literary Environmentalism* (Athens: University of Georgia Press, 2000), 26.

8. Throughout this book, I capitalize the first letter of "Romanticism," "Romanticist," and "the Romantic" whenever the artistic and philosophical movement is at issue, and not the denotation of a sentiment between human beings in a love relationship. This capitalization, therefore, is not intended to discredit other literary epochs, such as modernism or postmodernism.

9. I am referring to two seminal works of twentieth-century criticism here: F. O. Matthiessen, *American Renaissance: Art and Expression in the Age of Emerson and Whitman* (1941; Whitefish, MT: Kessinger, 2007); Hugh Kenner, *The Pound Era* (Berkeley: University of California Press, 1971).

10. Friedrich W. J. Schelling, *SW* VII, 356, and *Philosophical Investigations into the Essence of Human Freedom*, trans. Jeff Love and Johannes Schmidt (Albany: State University of New York Press, 2006), 26. All of the citations to Schelling's work will give first the page number of the German original (either in the standard edition—*SW* I–XIV—or as otherwise noted) and then the page number of the English translation (if one is available), as shown here. In those cases in which I provide only the page number of the German original, the translation is mine.

11. Iain Hamilton Grant, *Philosophies of Nature after Schelling* (2006; London: Continuum, 2008), 32.

12. See Willard P. Greenwood, *Reading Cormac McCarthy* (Santa Barbara, CA: ABC-Clio, 2009), 90. Greenwood further elaborates, "McCarthy's combination of formal prose with debased subject matter confirms his status as a decadent novelist. In this decadent 'art for art's sake' mode, McCarthy is not heavily invested in advocating for social causes in his novels" (Ibid. 18). Compare this statement with Robert Jarrett's reading, according to which McCarthy is also less concerned with issues of race in the South than was William Faulkner, one of his literary forebears (*Cormac McCarthy* [New York: Twayne, 1997], 24–25)—a point with which Greenwood (*Reading Cormac McCarthy*, 132) concurs.

13. Olaf Breidbach, "Schelling und die Erfahrungswissenschaft," *Sudhoffs Archiv* 88, no. 2 (2004): 156.

14. Nick Land, *Fanged Noumena: Collected Writings 1987–2007* (Falmouth, UK: Urbanomic, 2012), 322. This British philosopher had an important influence on a whole array of thinkers whose writings are used in this book, including Iain Grant, Ray Brassier, and Reza Negarestani. Land's works prefigure much of the innovations in terms of the concepts of nature to be found in these philosophers, which is why I will return to him on occasion. On a different note, I want to add that in spite of my usage of Land's early material, I do not condone his recent turn to the highly questionable neoreactionary movement on the global political scene. While this turn is lamentable and has to be condemned, I deem it false to ignore the fruitful connections and resonances between Land's early philosophy and McCarthy's oeuvre (otherwise, any Heideggerian reading of McCarthy's works ought to be off the table, too). Furthermore, Land has evidently read parts of McCarthy's novels. See Nick Land, "Philosophy in a War-Zone," *Dissolution*, accessed May 1, 2018, www.larsholdhus.com/Dissolution.pdf.

15. Ralph Waldo Emerson, *Emerson's Prose and Poetry: Authoritative Texts, Contexts, Criticism*, selected and edited by Joel Porte and Saundra Morris (New York: W. W. Norton and Company, 2001), 29.

16. Bertrand Westphal, *Geocriticism: Real and Fictional Spaces*, trans. Robert T. Tally Jr. (2007; Basingstoke: Palgrave Macmillan, 2011), 86 and 87.

17. For the "Lacanian" Schelling, see Slavoj Žižek, *The Indivisible Remainder: On Schelling and Related Matters* (1996; London: Verso, 2007), 76–79. For an examination of the existentialist version of Schellingianism, see I. Grant, *Philosophies of Nature after Schelling*, 14–16 and 205. In the context of McCarthy's fictions, see also Christopher Dacus's Schellingian reading of some of the author's Western novels, which formulates an ultimately existentialist and human-centered stance with regard to Schelling's theory of freedom ("The West as Symbol of the Eschaton in Cormac McCarthy," *Cormac McCarthy Journal* 7, no. 1(2009): 13).

18. Ursula K. Heise, "The Hitchhiker's Guide to Ecocriticism," *PMLA* 121, no. 2 (2006): 505.

19. Bernd Herzogenrath, "Nature | Geophilosophy | Machinics | Ecosophy," in *Deleuze | Guattari & Ecology*, ed. Bernd Herzogenrath (New York: Palgrave Macmillan, 2009), 1.

20. Ibid.

21. Jacques Derrida, *Of Grammatology*, trans. Gayatri Chakravorty Spivak (1967; Baltimore: Johns Hopkins University Press, 1997), 163. It might seem that I use the terms "postmodern" and "poststructuralist" interchangeably. However, whereas the former term denotes the artistic, aesthetic, and critical expression of American and Western cultures since at least the early 1970s, the latter term denotes a specific period of French philosophy that has been intertwined with postmodernism on an academic level since Derrida's lectures in the United States.

22. Schelling, *SW* III, 571, and *System of Transcendental Idealism*, trans. Peter Heath (Charlottesville: University Press of Virginia, 1978), 186. This is not to say that I interpret Derrida's famous saying as literally meaning that there is no reality outside of the realm of signification. As will become clear, I am taking my cue from Westphal's notion of geocriticism to emphasize the nontextual realm that is so prominent in McCarthy's narratives.

23. Iain Hamilton Grant, "'Philosophy Become Genetic': The Physics of the World Soul," in *The New Schelling*, ed. Judith Norman and Alistair Welchman (London: Continuum, 2004), 133.

24. Peter Gratton, *Speculative Realism: Problems and Prospects* (London: Bloomsbury, 2014), 113.

25. Dustin McWerther, "Absolute Naturalism. Review of Iain Hamilton Grant's *Philosophies of Nature after Schelling*," *Radical Philosophy* 144 (2007): 50. See also I. Grant, *Philosophies of Nature after Schelling*, 61.

26. Julia Kristeva, *Powers of Horror: An Essay on Abjection*, trans. Leon S. Roudiez (1980; New York: Columbia University Press, 1982), 2.

27. For one of the more important Kristevan readings of McCarthy's work, see J. Douglas Canfield, "The Dawning of the Age of Aquarius: Abjection, Identity, and the Carnivalesque in Cormac McCarthy's *Suttree*," *Contemporary Literature* 44, no. 4 (2003): 665. For further references to Kristeva or the abject in McCarthy scholarship, see Ann Fisher-Wirth, "Abjection and 'the Feminine' in *Outer Dark*," in *Cormac McCarthy: New Directions*, ed. James D. Lilley (2002; Albuquerque: University of New Mexico Press, 2014), 127; Rachel Furey, "Sentence Fragments, Sound, and Setting in *Suttree* and *The Road*," *Cormac McCarthy Journal* 9, no. 1 (2011): 52; Christopher J. Walsh, *In the Wake of the Sun: Navigating the Southern Works of Cormac McCarthy* (Knoxville, TN: Newfound Press, 2009), 233.

28. Schelling, *SW* III, 258, and *First Outline of a System of the Philosophy of Nature*, trans. Keith Peterson (Albany: State University of New York Press, 2004), 184.

29. Reza Negarestani, "The Corpse Bride: Thinking with *Nigredo*," *Collapse* 4 (2008): 142.

30. On this point, see Dianne C. Luce, *Reading the World: Cormac McCarthy's Tennessee Period* (2009; Columbia: University of South Carolina Press, 2010), 194.

31. On McCarthy and Joyce, see John Cant, *Cormac McCarthy and the Myth of American Exceptionalism* (New York: Routledge, 2008), 104; Georg Guillemin, *The Pastoral Vision of Cormac McCarthy* (College Station: Texas A&M University Press, 2004), 6; Walsh, *In the Wake of the Sun*, 215.

32. See Luce, *Reading the World*, 194; Terri Witek, "Reeds and Hides: Cormac McCarthy's Domestic Spaces," in *Cormac McCarthy* , ed. Harold Bloom (New York: Infobase Publishing, 2009), 26.

33. John Elder, *Imagining the Earth: Poetry and the Vision of Nature* (1985; Athens: University of Georgia Press, 1996), 30.

34. Ibid.

35. Reza Negarestani, *Cyclonopedia: Complicity with Anonymous Materials* (Melbourne: re.press, 2008), 184, emphasis added.

36. The term "dialectic" does not refer

to any kind of Hegelian formalism in this context but to the way in which Schellingian philosophy of nature uses the term as the self-limitation of negative and positive forces in and of nature with respect to each other (Schelling, *SW* II, 396–397, and "On the World Soul," trans. Iain Hamilton Grant *Collapse* 6 [2012]): 93–95). Consider Breidbach's following statement, ridiculing the Hegelian master-slave dialectic in an article on Schelling's view on the empirical sciences: "Nicht Herr und Knecht, sondern Kathode und Anode konstituierten das Grundgefüge des Dialektischen" (Breidbach, "Schelling und die Erfahrungswissenschaft," 172).

37. See, above all, Steven Frye's insightful "*Blood Meridian* and the Poetics of Violence," in *The Cambridge Companion to Cormac McCarthy*, ed. Steven Frye (2013; New York: Cambridge University Press, 2014), 107.

38. Greenwood, *Reading Cormac McCarthy*, 130, emphasis added.

39. The word "correlation" is used here in the sense of Quentin Meillassoux's critical examination of this notion's philosophical import in his first book (*After Finitude: An Essay on the Necessity of Contingency*, trans. Ray Brassier [2006; London: Continuum, 2009]).

40. Vereen M. Bell, *The Achievement of Cormac McCarthy* (Baton Rouge: Louisiana State University Press, 1988), 124.

41. William Faulkner, *Wild Palms* (1939; London: Vintage, 2000), 34. This is how the narrator of Faulkner's novel describes the way in which Charlotte Rittenmeyer looks at Harry Wilbourne (her future lover) for the first time. Their ensuing relationship is characterized by violence and love, both integral themes of McCarthy's oeuvre.

42. Pierre Hadot, *The Veil of Isis: An Essay on the History of the Idea of Nature*, trans. Michael Chase (2004; Cambridge, MA: Harvard University Press, 2008), 96.

43. See Cant, *American Exceptionalism*, 196.

44. On the connection between violent content and formal beauty in McCarthy's prose, see Frye, "*Blood Meridian* and the Poetics of Violence," 107–8.

45. Chapter 5 will elaborate on these issues by discussing the logics of containment and extainment, and of antecedence and consequence, vis-à-vis the conceptions of nature that can be found in Schelling, Gilles Châtelet, and Louis Kauffman (Iain Hamilton Grant, "How Nature Came to Be Thought: Schelling's Paradox and the Problem of Location," *Journal of the British Society for Phenomenology* 44, no. 1 [2013]: 40).

46. Emerson, *Prose and Poetry*, 29.

47. Although geocriticism is already an emerging field of cultural inquiry, with many and diverse critical voices, I will focus my critical discussion of it on the work of its founder, Bertrand Westphal. With regard to speculative realism, I will home in on the more nature-philosophical proponents of it, whom I take to be Negarestani, Iain Grant, and Brassier.

48. Land, *Fanged Noumena*, 499.

1. "Trailing the Cord": Literary Descent and the Ethos of Ecology

1. Leo Daugherty, "Gravers False and True: *Blood Meridian* as Gnostic Tragedy," *Southern Quarterly* 30, no. 4 (1992): 124; Petra Mundik, "This Luminosity in Beings So Endarkened: Gnostic Soteriology in *Blood Meridian*," in *They Rode On:* Blood Meridian *and the Tragedy of the American West*, ed. Rick Wallach (Miami: Cormac McCarthy Society, 2013), 214.

2. Edwin T. Arnold, "Naming, Knowing and Nothingness: McCarthy's Moral Parables," *Southern Quarterly* 30, no. 4 (1992): 31; Lydia R. Cooper, *No More Heroes: Narrative Perspective and Morality in Cormac McCarthy* (Baton Rouge: Louisiana State University Press, 2011), 17 and 15.

3. Dana Phillips, "History and the Ugly Facts of Cormac McCarthy's *Blood Meridian*," *American Literature* 68, no. 2 (1996): 450; Vereen M. Bell, *The Achievement of Cormac McCarthy* (Baton Rouge: Louisiana State University Press, 1988), 18.

4. Andrew Keller Estes, *Cormac McCarthy and the Writing of American Spaces* (Amsterdam: Rodopi, 2013), 85. See also K. Wesley Berry, "The Lay of the Land in Cormac McCarthy's Appalachia," in *Comac McCarthy: New Directions*, ed. James D. Lilley (2002; Albuquerque: University of New Mexico Press, 2014), 55.

5. Mundik, "This Luminosity in Beings So Endarkened," 214.

6. Cooper, *No More Heroes*, 65.

7. Bell, *The Achievement of Cormac McCarthy*, 24. See also Phillips, "Ugly Facts," 437–48.

8. This term is modeled after Robert Tally's (*Poe and the Subversion of American Literature: Satire, Fantasy, Critique* [New York: Bloomsbury, 2014]).

9. Bell, *The Achievement of Cormac McCarthy*, 4. In reading McCarthy's work, "we are reminded again that experience is primarily not universal but particular, that we live not in an outline but a place" (ibid.).

10. Berry, "The Lay of the Land," 48.

11. Ibid., 47.

12. This also holds for McCarthy's middle period (see, for example, John Emil Sepich, *Notes on* Blood Meridian [1993; Austin: University of Texas Press, 2011]; Robert L. Jarrett, "Cormac McCarthy's Sense of an Ending: Serialized Narrative and Revision in *Cities of the Plain*," In *Cormac McCarthy: New Directions*, ed. James D. Lilley [2002; Albuquerque: University of New Mexico Press, 2014], 338). Discussing the historical circumstances of the publication of McCarthy's later work, Pierre Lagayette argues that the writer "must also have been influenced by" the realities of the "post-Cold War period" as they shaped American political and cultural consciousness, and that he had to be aware of "the rhetoric of American supremacy which colored world politics for more than four decades" ("The Border Trilogy, *The Road*, and the Cold War," in *The Cambridge Companion to Cormac McCarthy*, ed. Steven Frye [2013; New York: Cambridge University Press, 2014], 80). However, it is always from a distinctly *American* perspective that these parallels between history and fiction are imagined—or, more precisely, from the perspective of American individuals (Jarrett, "Sense of an Ending," 338).

13. On this point, see Christopher Metress, "*Via Negativa*: The Way of Unknowing in Cormac McCarthy's *Outer Dark*," *Southern Review* 37, no. 1 (2001): 149.

14. See Christopher J. Walsh, *In the Wake of the Sun: Navigating the Southern Works of Cormac McCarthy* (Knoxville, TN: Newfound Press, 2009), 22.

15. Tally, *Poe and the Subversion of American Literature*, 1.

16. Ibid.

17. See Bell's suggestion that the protagonist of *Suttree* "detranscends, so to speak, in order to discover a meaningful form of transcendence" (*The Achievement of Cormac McCarthy*, 73).

18. Tally, *Poe and the Subversion of American Literature*, 2, 1, and 2.

19. Certainly, the anecdote one of the unnamed country folks tells about a sheriff of Sevier County named "Fate" is just that—a story about when the sheriff asked to see the license of an old man who was in his car with a girl "up on the Frog mountain" (*COG*, 43). Yet the three short sentences with which McCarthy begins this one-page-long episode seem to cover a lot of what his novels have to say on the topic of fate in general. For instance, they suggest the stoicism with which fate (that is, indifference) is met also by major characters in McCarthy's work, such as Llewelyn Moss in *No Country for Old Men*. The Appalachian country folk say: "Fate's all right. He's plainspoken but I like him. I've rode with him a lot of times" (*COG*, 43).

20. John Cant, *Cormac McCarthy and the Myth of American Exceptionalism* (New York: Routledge, 2008), 276.

21. In this sense, his method is in line with Nick Land's cautionary remark vis-à-vis the aspirations of philosophical authority, which would, therefore, extend all the way to those of literature: "Let us not forget that philoso-

phy is also primate psychology; that our loftiest speculations are merely picking through a minuscule region of the variegated slime encrusting a speck of dust" (Nick Land, *Fanged Noumena: Collected Writings 1987–2007* [Falmouth, UK: Urbanomic, 2012], 178).

22. On the topic of McCarthy's interests in a plethora of fields of knowledge:, see Lydia R. Cooper, "Cormac McCarthy's *The Road* as Apocalyptic Grail Narrative," *Studies in the Novel* 43, no. 2 (2011): 219; Richard B. Woodward, "McCarthy's Venomous Fiction," *New York Times Magazine*, April 19, 1992, accessed March 14, 2015, http://www.nytimes.com/1992/04/19/magazine/cormac-mccarthy-s-venomous-fiction.html?pagewanted=all. In 2012, Alison Flood, a writer for the *Guardian*, revealed that McCarthy has copy edited scientific books like Lisa Randall's *Knocking on Heaven's Door: How Physics and Scientific Thinking Illuminate the Universe and the Modern World* (2011) and Lawrence M. Krauss's *Quantum Man: Richard Feynman's Life in Science* (2011). In the paperback edition Krauss acknowledged McCarthy's involvement by writing on the title page under the subtitle, "with corrections by Cormac McCarthy" (paperback ed., New York: W. W. Norton and Company, 2012). Furthermore, Flood quotes Chris Wood, a neuroscientist at the Santa Fe Institute, as saying that McCarthy's "knowledge of physics and math exceeds that of many professionals in the field" ("Cormac McCarthy's parallel career revealed—as a scientific copy editor!," *Guardian*, February 21, 2012, accessed November 21, 2017, https://www.theguardian.com/books/2012/feb/21/cormac-mccarthy-scientific-copy-editor).

23. On Emerson's regionalist tendencies, see Branka Arsić, *On Leaving: A Reading in Emerson* (Cambridge, MA: Harvard University Press, 2010), 249. Although Arsić mentions the widely held view of Emerson as an ideologue "of the elect nation in early American, Puritan New England" (ibid.), she sides with other scholars in modifying and questioning this view. I do not draw as sharp a line as Arsić does between regionalism and exceptionalism—in fact, in this context, I do not see these terms as opposed to each other. This book argues that there is a convergence of regionalist and nationalist literature, since regionalism in McCarthy's work becomes a starting point in terms of content, while exceptionalism becomes a matter of perspective in terms of form.

24. It should be noted that although Emerson is counted among the leaders of what F. O. Matthiessen has called the "American Renaissance," or the founding of a national literary and philosophical culture, he nevertheless was well versed in European thought (see Lawrence Buell, *Emerson* [Cambridge, MA: Harvard University Press, 2004], 12).

25. Ralph Waldo Emerson, *Emerson's Prose and Poetry: Authoritative Texts, Contexts, Criticism*, , selected and edited by Joel Porte and Saundra Morris (New York: W. W. Norton and Company, 2001), 27.

26. Ibid.

27. To be consistent with the original phrasing in Emerson's works (as well as those of McCarthy, Friedrich Schelling, or Lorenz Oken) I will use the word "man" synonymously with "human." Whenever I mention humanity without elaborating on a quoted passage, I will refer to it as such rather than as "mankind." The use of "mankind" and "humankind" is solely a matter of consistency with the source material. I do not condone the gendered implications of the former terminology in any way whatsoever.

28. Emerson, *Prose and Poetry*, 27.

29. Ibid.

30. Ibid., 53.

31. Ibid., 29.

32. On this point, see Emerson's maxim in his essay "Self-Reliance" (1841): "Insist on yourself; never imitate. Your own gift you can present every moment with the cumulative force of a whole life's cultivation; but of the adopted talent of another, you have only an extemporaneous, half possession" (ibid., 134).

33. Ibid., 92.

34. In a discussion of Emerson's essay

"Man the Reformer" (1841), David Reynolds writes that it explicates what virtually "all of Emerson's essays say implicitly: man as reformer must not only be subversive ('a renouncer of lies') but also reconstructive ('a restorer of truth and good'), and his reconstructive powers should be recognized as organically linked to the ever-renewing powers of nature" (*Beneath the American Renaissance: The Subversive Imagination in the Age of Emerson and Melville* [New York: Alfred A. Knopf, 1988], 97).

35. On Emerson vis-à-vis the theory of nature expressed McCarthy's fifth novel, *Blood Meridian*, see Joseph D. Haske, "Transcendental Musings on *Blood Meridian*'s Western Wastelands," in *They Rode On:* Blood Meridian *and the Tragedy of the American West*, ed. Rick Wallach (Miami: Cormac McCarthy Society, 2013), 191.

36. Woodward, "McCarthy's Venomous Fiction."

37. Emerson, *Prose and Poetry*, 27.

38. Ibid.

39. Thoreau, *Walden* (1854; Oxford: Oxford University Press, 2008), 275 and 269.

40. Ibid., 268.

41. Lawrence Buell, *The Environmental Imagination: Thoreau, Nature Writing, and the Formation of American Culture* (Cambridge, MA: Belknap Press of Harvard University Press, 1995), 248.

42. As Bell puts it, "McCarthy's language is exact, and the metaphors therefore seem so inevitable that the effect is more one of the world's speaking through the writer than of the writer's speaking of the world" (*The Achievement of Cormac McCarthy*, 18). Incidentally, Bell's phrasing here ("the world's speaking through the writer") clearly resonates with Emerson's statement that "nature is already, in its forms and tendencies, describing its own design" (*Prose and Poetry*, 27).

43. On Thoreau and regionalism, see David Mazel, "Regionalism and Ecology," in *A Companion to the Regional Literatures of America*, ed. Charles L. Crow (Malden, MA: Blackwell Publishing, 2003), 130–31.

44. On McCarthy and "regional dialogue," see Natalie Grant, "The Landscape of the Soul: Man and the Natural World in *The Orchard Keeper*," in *Sacred Violence: A Reader's Companion to Cormac McCarthy*, ed. Wade Hall and Rick Wallach (El Paso: Texas Western Press, 1995), 66. On McCarthy and Twain, see Robert L. Jarrett, *Cormac McCarthy* (New York: Twayne, 1997), viii; Leslie Harper Worthington, *Cormac McCarthy and the Ghost of Huck Finn* (Jefferson, NC: McFarland and Company, 2012), 68; Bryan Vescio, "Strangers in Everydayland: Suttree, Huckleberry Finn, and Tragic Humanism," in *You Would Not Believe What Watches*,ed. Rick Wallach, 2nd ed. (Miami: Cormac McCarthy Society, 2014).

45. While in *Huckleberry Finn* it is the characters and the narrator who speak of "niggers" (Mark Twain, *Adventures of Huckleberry Finn* [Mineola, NY: Dover Thrift, 1994], 20 and 179) multiple times, McCarthy mostly lets his characters use that word, while his narrators usually use the word "Negro" (*TOK*, 3) as on the first page of *The Orchard Keeper*. On the different negotiations of violence in McCarthy and Twain, see Tim Parrish, "The Killer Wears the Halo: Cormac McCarthy, Flannery O'Connor, and the American Religion," in *Sacred Violence: A Reader's Companion to Cormac McCarthy*, ed. Wade Hall and Rick Wallach (El Paso: Texas Western Press, 1995), 33–34.

46. Steven Frye, "Yeats' 'Sailing to Byzantium' and McCarthy's *No Country for Old Men*: Art and Artifice in the New Novel," *Cormac McCarthy Journal* 5, no. 1 (2005): 18.

47. Jay Ellis, *No Place for Home: Spatial Constraint and Character Flight in the Novels of Cormac McCarthy* (New York: Routledge, 2006), 63; Erik Hage, *Cormac McCarthy: A Literary Companion* (Jefferson, NC: McFarland and Company, 2010), 117.

48. Georg Guillemin observes: "The fence encloses the local cemetery—as we learn on the novel's last page—so that the falling tree has figuratively breached the boundary be-

tween the dead and the living" (*The Pastoral Vision of Cormac McCarthy* [College Station: Texas A&M University Press, 2004], 23).

49. See Jeremy Dunham, Iain Hamilton Grant, and Sean Watson, *Idealism: The History of a Philosophy* (Montreal: McGill-Queen's University Press, 2011), 4.

50. For instance, in *The Achievement of Cormac McCarthy*, Bell includes both materialist and spiritualist tendencies in his approach to McCarthy: he both endorses a reading of McCarthy as a regionalist and nihilist and is interested in the metaphysical and existential aspects of McCarthy's first five novels. Similarly, Dianne Luce places equal emphasis on the historical and the metaphysical. She expounds the regionalism of McCarthy's work, but she makes an exception in the case of *Outer Dark*, which "does not map a specific locale in East Tennessee" (*Reading the World: Cormac McCarthy's Tennessee Period* (2009; Columbia: University of South Carolina Press, 2010), 124). Luce goes on to analyze McCarthy's realist representations of local sceneries, which seem necessary in juxtaposition with "situations that are 'surreal' or paradoxical in reality" (ibid., 125). For comparable statements, see John M. Grammer, "A Thing against Which Time Will Not Prevail: Pastoral and History in Cormac McCarthy's South," *Southern Quarterly* 30, no. 4 (1992): 25. To me, this is good evidence of the existence of two tendencies in McCarthy scholarship with regard to the issue of particularity and the regional, and the relationship of this issue to the philosophical underpinnings of McCarthy's fiction.

51. Grammer's essay was published at the same time as Daugherty's and also mentioned the McCarthy's relation to gnosticism (Grammer, "Pastoral and History," 27). However, Daugherty's article was more about the gnostic dimension in McCarthy's first Western, rather than in *Child of God*, for instance.

52. Daugherty, "Gravers False and True," 122.

53. Ibid., 124.

54. Ibid.

55. Ibid., 123.

56. Ibid.

57. Shane Schimpf, *A Reader's Guide to* Blood Meridian (2006; Seattle: BonMot Publishing, 2011), 57. Petra Mundik writes: "Knowledge of the true state of the cosmos and of the nature of the alien God is referred to as *gnosis* and those who possess such knowledge refer to themselves as the *pneumatics*. The possession of gnosis enables the spirit, or pneuma, to become aware of its divine origins, escape from the created world, and reunite with the transcendent God—much as the state of Enlightenment enables the attainment of *Nirvana* in Buddhist thought" ("'Striking the Fire Out of the Rock': Gnostic Theology in Cormac McCarthy's *Blood Meridian*," *South Central Review* 26, no. 3 [2009]: 74).

58. Daugherty, "Gravers False and True," 125.

59. The insights with respect to McCarthy's narrative gnosis come at the price of disregarding the rootedness of his novels in the regions in which they are set. Daugherty slightly neglects this rootedness in his otherwise suggestive reading of Holden's persona as archon. Mundik ("'Striking the Fire Out of the Rock'") presents a convincing reading that shows the novel's connection to the mystical and esoteric currents of thought, yet like Daugherty, she disregards the site- and time-specificity of the novel that other interpretations of McCarthy's work in general consider more important.

60. Luce, *Reading the World*, 233.

61. Ibid., emphasis added.

62. Phillips, "Ugly Facts," 448.

63. Ciarán Dowd, "'A Novel in Dramatic Form': Metaphysical Tension in *The Sunset Limited*," in *Intertextual and Interdisciplinary Approaches to Cormac McCarthy: Borders and Crossings*, ed. Nicholas Monk (New York: Routledge, 2012), 117.

64. This is supported by the work of Bell, Luce, and Frye, who have respectively pointed to McCarthy's regionalism and to the notion of transcendence in *Suttree* (Bell, *The*

Achievement of Cormac McCarthy, 4 and 69); combined archival research with investigations into the gnostic dimension of McCarthy's early fictions (Luce, *Reading the World*, 138–144 and 62–75); and noticed both the importance of local color and the religious overtones in *No Country for Old Men* (Frye, "Byzantium," 18–20).

65. The definition of materialism is a paraphrase of Iain Grant's characterization of that philosophical standpoint ("Does Nature Stay What-It-Is? Dynamics and the Antecedence Criterion," in *The Speculative Turn: Continental Materialism and Realism*, ed. Levi Bryant, Nick Srnicek, and Graham Harman [Melbourne: re.press, 2011], 69–70). The definition of spiritualism refers to the description of the pneuma in gnosticism, which Daugherty equates to the notion of a "spirit within" ("Gravers False and True," 123). Although this definition of the spiritual is rooted in the legacy of gnosis, it also applies to the readings that have highlighted the religious and moral aspects of McCarthy's work.

66. See, respectively, Allen Josephs, "The Quest for God in *The Road*," in *The Cambridge Companion to Cormac McCarthy*, ed. Steven Frye (2013; New York: Cambridge University Press, 2014), 133–45; and Markus Wierschem, "The Other End of *The Road*: Re-Reading McCarthy in Light of Thermodynamics and Information Theory," *Cormac McCarthy Journal* 11, no. 1 (2013): 1–22.

67. Luce, *Reading the World*, 138–46.

68. Emerson, *Prose and Poetry*, 27.

69. Quoted in Woodward, "McCarthy's Venomous Fiction."

70. Luce's assessment is much franker: "Novelist Cormac McCarthy is a philosopher and a poet. One of the most fundamental observations to be made about him is that his deepest engagement with the world is represented *obliquely and yet concretely* in his fiction" (*Reading the World*, vi, emphasis added). On McCarthy's knowledge of Platonism, see Garry Wallace, "Meeting McCarthy," *Southern Quarterly* 30, no. 4 (1992): 135.

71. Tally, *Poe and the Subversion of American Literature*, 1.

72. Cooper, *No More Heroes*, 65.

73. Thomas D. Young Jr. also evokes the image of the "formless macule of plasm" (*S*, 430), yet for him this phrase is an allusion not to McCarthy's descendentalism, which I read in conjunction with German *Naturphilosophie*, but to "life" as the ultimate subject of affirmation: "This sense of [Cornelius's] own origins, as opposed to genealogical or theological models, restores *the wonder of his life* and validates the sacramental communion with pure experience as one's highest priority" ("The Imprisonment of Sensibility: *Suttree*," *Southern Quarterly* 30, no. 4 [1992]: 90, emphasis added).

74. Steven Frye, "*Blood Meridian* and the Poetics of Violence," in *The Cambridge Companion to Cormac McCarthy*, ed. Steven Frye (2013; New York: Cambridge University Press, 2014), 107.

75. Vince Brewton, "The Changing Landscape of Violence in Cormac McCarthy's Early Novels and the Border Trilogy," *Southern Literary Journal* 37, no. 1 (2004): 121.

76. Ibid. A later essay by Erika B. Spoden relates the long cultural aftermath of Vietnam to McCarthy's *No Country for Old Men* (see "Let There Be Blood: The Vein of Vietnam in *No Country for Old Men*," *Cormac McCarthy Journal* 10, no. 1 [2012]: 76).

77. Fredric Jameson, *The Political Unconscious: Narrative as a Socially Symbolic Act* (1981; London: Routledge, 2002), ix. To be sure, Jameson's dictate is just one kind of literary historicism. However, it is an exemplary approach that insists on the importance of historical contextualization in investigating cultural artifacts. For a Jamesonian perspective on McCarthy, see David Holloway, "Modernism, Nature, and Utopia: Another Look at 'Optical Democracy' in Cormac McCarthy's Western Quartet," *Southern Quarterly* 38, no. 3 (2000): 198–201.

78. In her discussion of the negative resonances between Emerson's "Nature" and McCarthy's *The Road*, for instance, Nora

Kestermann explicates the contrast between the idealization of nature as divine in nineteenth-century American culture and art and the wasted world in McCarthy's postapocalyptic novel. The ashen world of the novel and the bleak rendering of the struggle of the father and his son to survive in that hostile environment seems antithetical to the notion of a harmonious oneness with the organic realm of nature: "'Nature's Nation' has turned into a stifling landscape of degeneration" (Kestermann, "Ralph Waldo Emerson versus Cormac McCarthy: The Annihilation of Emerson's Values in McCarthy's *The Road*," *Current Objectives of Postgraduate American Studies* 11 [2010], accessed November 15, 2017, https://copas.uni-regensburg.de/article/view/129/153. For a similar reading, see Estes, *American Spaces*, 77. However, Estes rejects the view of the latter work as a degenerate version of the nationalistic ideal of old and argues that McCarthy is even more transcendentalist than Emerson. Some critics have argued that it is Thoreau's writings rather than Emerson's that have influenced McCarthy's poetics, and that if one wants to determine the "transcendentalist McCarthy," one needs to look for his Thoreauvian traits rather than any Emersonian ones (see, for instance, Béatrice Trotignon, "Detailing the Wor(l)d in *Suttree*," in *Myth, Legend, Dust: Critical Responses to Cormac McCarthy*, ed. Rick Wallach [Manchester, UK: Manchester University Press, 2000], 98); Luce, *Reading the World*, 37; William Dow, "Topographical Strides of Thoreau: The Poet and Pioneer in Cormac McCarthy's *Blood Meridian*," *Revue française d'études américaines* 84 [2000]: 91). Certainly after reading *Suttree*, an examination of *Walden* and its ambivalent appraisals of solitary life near the pond are illuminating. Even though Suttree's habitat is the Tennessee River, whereas Thoreau ponders the beauty of a pond, the idealization of aquatic tranquility is strikingly similar. Yet the atmosphere in McCarthy's novel is a little more doomed than it is in Thoreau's reflections. The phenomena of the pond are very different from what McCarthy's protagonist (and—in many instances—alter ego) discovers in the Tennessee River, named "Cloaca Maxima" (*S*, 13) by the narrator. On the first passage in the novel after its enigmatic prologue, we encounter Suttree on his houseboat, fishing in the river, and what we get is an altered picture of tranquility: "With his jaw cradled in the crook of his arm he watched idly surface phenomena, gouts of sewage faintly working, gray clots of nameless waste and yellow condoms roiling slowly out of the murk like some giant form of fluke or tapeworm" (*S*, 7).

79. Scholars like Cooper, Ronja Vieth, Kirk Essary, and Cant, among others, have argued along those lines. The gothic style is clearly evident in McCarthy's novels from *The Orchard Keeper* to *Blood Meridian* (Lydia R. Cooper, "McCarthy, Tennessee, and the Southern Gothic," in *The Cambridge Companion to Cormac McCarthy*, ed. Steven Frye [2013; New York: Cambridge University Press, 2014], 41); they "play on the sublime effects of attraction and repulsion" to shed light on "the unspoken realities of America's unspoken past" (Ronja Vieth, "A Frontier Myth Turns Gothic: *Blood Meridian: Or, the Evening Redness in the West*," *Cormac McCarthy Journal* 8, no. 1 [2010]: 47). Besides McCarthy's penchant for the doppelgänger motif, the "Frontier Gothic" (ibid., 50), and its "western wilderness" imagined in Charles Brockden Brown's *Edgar Huntly* (1799), or the notion evoked in Hawthorne's *The Marble Faun* (1860) that "romance and poetry . . . need Ruin to make them grow" (both quoted in ibid., 49), it is above all Melville who has been recognized as a major influence. On McCarthy's relationship to the American gothic and the genre of horror fiction, see Hage, *A Literary Companion*, 150–52; Michael Madsen, "'A Nameless Wheeling in the Night': Shapes of Evil in Cormac McCarthy's *Blood Meridian* and John Carpenter's *Halloween*," in *Intertextual and Interdisciplinary Approaches to Cormac McCarthy: Borders and Crossings*, ed. Nicholas Monk (New York: Routledge, 2012), 100–111.

80. Steven Frye, *Understanding Cormac McCarthy* (Columbia: University of South Carolina Press, 2009), 119.

81. Ibid.

82. On this point, see Cant, *American Exceptionalism*, 11.

83. Ibid.

84. Woodward stated in 1992, on the occasion of *All the Pretty Horses*: "Each of his five previous novels has been marked by intense natural observation, a kind of *morbid realism*" ("McCarthy's Venomous Fiction," emphasis added). One has to be cautious here, since Woodward's assessment was more of an offhand remark than a sustained argument. Also, it is a "morbid" form of realism, as in the generic term of magical realism. But even in McCarthy's second novel, steeped as it is in the gothic tradition of depicting the ways in which human beings try to live with the consequences of their sins (in this case, incest), scenes like the birth of Culla and Rinthy Holme's child are very much informed by the realist tradition: "*Outer Dark* depicts the physical body with gruesome accuracy" (Katie Owens-Murphy, "The Frontier Ethic behind Cormac McCarthy's Southern Fiction," *Arizona Quarterly* 67, no. 2 [2011]: 161).

85. He does not share the admiration within literary circles for the novels of Henry James, *the* representative of late nineteenth-century fiction who dealt with the interior components of literary characters—or, in James's words, the "consciousness (on the part of the moved and moving creature) subject to fine intensification and wide enlargement" ("Preface to The Princess Casamassima," in *The Theory of Criticism: From Plato to the Present*, ed. Raman Selden [1886; Harlow, UK: Longman, 1988], 503). See also Walsh, *In the Wake of the Sun*, 2–4.

86. On this point, see Frye, *Understanding Cormac McCarthy*, 54–55; Eric Carl Link, "McCarthy and Literary Naturalism," in *The Cambridge Companion to Cormac McCarthy*, ed. Steven Frye (2013; New York: Cambridge University Press, 2014), 155.

87. On McCarthy and naturalism, in addition to Link, "Literary Naturalism,", see Michael T. Clarke, "The New Naturalism: Cormac McCarthy, Frank Norris, and the Question of Postmodernism," *Studies in American Naturalism* 9, no. 1 (2014): 53.

88. Mark Seltzer, *Bodies and Machines* (1992; New York: Routledge, 2014), 19.

89. Link, "Literary Naturalism," 157.

90. Seltzer, *Bodies and Machines*, 19. Yet see also James R. Giles's conceptualization of what he calls a "multilayered determinism" in the narrative ("*Outer Dark* and Romantic Naturalism," in *The Cambridge Companion to Cormac McCarthy*, ed. Steven Frye [New York: Cambridge University Press, 2014], 97). I take this to be a very helpful and suggestive way to account for the connection between Romanticism's obsession with the ineffable and literary naturalism's interest in the history of science.

91. Jonathan Yardley, "Alone, Alone, All, All Alone . . . ," *Washington Post Book World*, January 13, 1974, 1.

92. Most critics of McCarthy have mentioned his indebtedness to Faulkner. For some exemplary readings, see Frye, *Understanding Cormac McCarthy*, 20; Jarrett, "Sense of an Ending," 315; K. E. Wilkerson, "Regions of the Damned: Cormac McCarthy as Regional Writer," *Hudson Valley Regional Review* 11 (1994): 11. For a comparison between McCarthy and O'Connor, see Parrish, "The Killer Wears the Halo," 25. For one between McCarthy and Agee, see Rick Wallach, "Ulysses in Knoxville: Suttree's Ageean Journey," in *You Would Not Believe What Watches*, ed. Rick Wallach, 2nd ed. (Miami: Cormac McCarthy Society, 2014), 78. Joyce's influence is notable here, and not just because of the naming of certain characters in McCarthy's fourth Tennessee novel—namely, Ulysses (the drinking buddy) and Joyce (Suttree's girlfriend). I have elected not to delve further into McCarthy's relation to modernism, largely because of the general consensus of its importance throughout the scholarship on his work.

93. David Holloway's influential *The Late*

Modernism of Cormac McCarthy (Westport, CT: Greenwood Press, 2002) contextualizes the novels between the modern and the postmodern periods. Matthew Guinn also proposes that McCarthy's novels combine a modernist with a postmodernist poetics ("Ruder Forms Survive: Cormac McCarthy's Atavistic Vision," in *Myth, Legend, Dust: Critical Responses to Cormac McCarthy*, ed. Rick Wallach [Manchester, UK: Manchester University Press, 2000], 109 and 112). In a sense, Guinn's proposed periodization of McCarthy's work between the immanence of the indeterminate in postmodern fiction, on the one hand, and the near-transcendent search for order that is so typical of modernist aesthetics, on the other hand, is very similar to Holloway's reading of McCarthy. In contrast to Holloway and Guinn, Arnold notes "the postmodern celebration of McCarthy's exuberant violence" ("Naming, Knowing and Nothingness," 31). To varying degrees, both Metress and Oliver Mort also periodize McCarthy's work within postmodernism, employing a Lyotardian stance (see Metress, "*Via Negativa*," 154; Mort, "'Are We Still the Good Guys?' Cormac McCarthy and the Postmodern Heroic Quest," in *They Rode On:* Blood Meridian *and the Tragedy of the American West*, ed. Rick Wallach [Miami: Cormac McCarthy Society, 2013], 248–49). As will become clear, the present book opposes these kinds of interpretations on the ground of McCarthy's transnational and transhistorical resonance with German idealist philosophies of nature and contemporary speculative realism.

94. See Linda Woodson, "Mapping *The Road* in Post-Postmodernism," *Cormac McCarthy Journal* 6 (2008): 89.

95. Jacques Derrida, *Of Grammatology*, trans. Gayatri Chakravorty Spivak (1967; Baltimore: Johns Hopkins University Press, 1997), 158. See also Bertrand Westphal, foreword to *Geocritical Explorations: Space, Place, and Mapping in Literary and Cultural Studies*, ed. Robert T. Tally Jr. (New York: Palgrave Macmillan, 2011), xii–xiii.

96. On Pynchon's postmodern "subject of the text," see Hanjo Berressem, *Pynchon's Poetics: Interfacing Theory and Text* (Urbana: University of Illinois Press, 1992), 39. For a Lacanian reading of Auster's fiction, see Bernd Herzogenrath, *An Art of Desire: Reading Paul Auster* (Amsterdam: Rodopi, 1999). On the controversy about Derrida's statement concerning textual immanence, see James K. A. Smith, *Jacques Derrida: Live Theory* (New York: Continuum, 2005), 61–62. Regarding McCarthy's contemporaneity with American literary postmodernism, the following statement by Guinn strikes me as very useful, and indeed it prefigures the present interpretation with regard to McCarthy's relation to literary periodization: "even within the postmodern period, [McCarthy] continues *a search for whatever small ontology remains*; in technique and vision he is *unique among contemporary writers*." Guinn consequently holds that "by combining the styles and approaches of both modernist and postmodern fiction, *he has forged a form of his own that promises to transcend his own period*" ("Ruder Forms Survive," 115 [emphasis added]).

97. On McCarthy and postmodernism, see Phillips, "Ugly Facts," 436; Mundik, "'Striking the Fire Out of the Rock,'" 72; Christopher Dacus, "Borderline Insanity: Modernity as a Political Problem in Cormac McCarthy's *Blood Meridian*," in *They Rode On:* Blood Meridian *and the Tragedy of the American West*, ed. Rick Wallach (Miami: Cormac McCarthy Society, 2013), 275. One of the most straightforward statements on this issue comes from Guillemin: "McCarthy can hardly be considered a postmodern writer. Any de-centering intention he may share with postmodernism owes less to the influence of fashionable theory than to the subversive energy of the grotesque" (*Pastoral*, 10).

98. Woodson, "Mapping *The Road* in Post-Postmodernism," 89.

99. Ibid., 94.

100. Ibid., 94 and 95.

101. See Robert L. McLaughlin, "Post-Postmodern Discontent: Contemporary Fiction

and the Social World," *Symploke* 12, nos. 1–2 (2004): 55. More recently, Lucas Thompson has revealed the extent to which McCarthy influenced Wallace's writings (see "'Books Are Made out of Books': David Foster Wallace and Cormac McCarthy," *Cormac McCarthy Journal* 13, no. 1 [2015]: 4).

102. Woodson, "Mapping *The Road* in Post-Postmodernism," 94.

103. "Nature | Geophilosophy | Machinics | Ecosophy," in *Deleuze | Guattari & Ecology*, ed. Bernd Herzogenrath (New York: Palgrave Macmillan, 2009), 1.

104. Nevertheless, the situation is quite different with regard to DeLillo's more recent work, such as *Point Omega* (2010), which falls outside the frame of literary postmodernism (Kate Marshall, "What Are the Novels of the Anthropocene? American Fiction in Geological Time," *American Literary History* 27, no. 3 [2015]: 524).

105. For Derrida's examination of memory's textuality, see his *Writing and Difference*, trans. Alan Bass (1967; Chicago: University of Chicago Press, 1978), 221.

106. Woodward, "McCarthy's Venomous Fiction."

107. John Elder, *Imagining the Earth: Poetry and the Vision of Nature* (1985; Athens: University of Georgia Press, 1996), 207–8.

108. Ibid., 161.

109. Schelling, *SW* VII, 359–60, and *Philosophical Investigations into the Essence of Human Freedom*, trans. Jeff Love and Johannes Schmidt (Albany: State University of New York Press, 2006), 29.

110. Alfred North Whitehead, *Modes of Thought* (New York: Free Press, 1968), 148. As others have noted, Whitehead can be described as one of the chief proponents of twentieth-century Orphism. Consider, for instance, the following passage: "Philosophy is the product of wonder. The effort after the general characterization of the world around us is the romance of human thought" (ibid., 127). Whitehead's magnum opus, *Process and Reality* (1929), is mentioned prominently in the latter part of Elder's book (*Imagining the Earth*, 168). In this context, see, above all, Robert E. Doud, "Orphism in Whitehead and Some Other Poetic Thinkers," *Process Studies* 33, no. 2 (2004): 323.

111. George Monbiot, "Civilisation Ends with a Shutdown of Human Concern. Are We There Already?" *Guardian*, October 29, 2007, accessed November 24, 2017, https://www.theguardian.com/commentisfree/2007/oct/30/comment.books.

112. Buell, *The Environmental Imagination*, 5; Timothy Morton, *The Ecological Thought* (Cambridge, MA: Harvard University Press, 2010), 132.

113. Ursula K. Heise, "The Hitchhiker's Guide to Ecocriticism," *PMLA* 121, no. 2 (2006): and 511, 509, and 511. On deep ecology, see also Alistair Welchman, "Deleuze and Deep Ecology," in *An [Un]likely Alliance: Thinking Environment[s] with Deleuze | Guattari*, ed. Bernd Herzogenrath (Newcastle upon Tyne, UK: Cambridge Scholars Publishing, 2008), 116. On ecofeminism, see Christa Grewe-Volpp, *"Natural Spaces Mapped by Human Minds": Ökokritische und ökofeministische Analysen zeitgenössischer amerikanischer Romane* (Tübingen: Gunter Narr Verlag, 2004), 43–77.

114. Timothy O'Riordan, *Environmentalism* (1976; London: Pion, 1981), 1.

115. Bryan L. Moore, *Ecology and Literature: Ecocentric Personification from Antiquity to the Twenty-First Century* (New York: Palgrave Macmillan, 2008), 5.

116. Ibid., 6.

117. Moore helpfully provides an explanation of the subtle differences between the two terms, but his explanation results not merely in the general alignment of both categories but rather in the supervenience of biocentrism upon ecocentrism as critical frameworks for thinking about the environment. Paraphrasing Max Oelschlaeger, Moore argues: "Ecocentrism . . . is derived from both philosophical and scientific bases, though it is not without challenges on both fronts, as well as others. Biocentrism ('life-centered' ethic), which establishes life in general rather

than the human species in particular as the central verity, arose in the nineteenth century with Darwin and is nearly synonymous with ecocriticism" (ibid., 5).

118. Ibid.

119. O'Riordan, *Environmentalism*, 1.

120. Buell, *The Environmental Imagination*, 425.

121. Leyla Haferkamp, "'The Instructed Third': Processing Ecology with Deleuze," in *An [Un]likely Alliance: Thinking Environment[s] with Deleuze | Guattari*, ed. Bernd Herzogenrath (Newcastle upon Tyne, UK: Cambridge Scholars Publishing, 2008), 53; Astrid Schwarz and Kurt Jax, "Etymology and Original Sources of the Term 'Ecology,'" in *Ecology Revisited: Reflecting on Concepts Advancing Science*, ed. Astrid Schwarz and Kurt Jax (Dordrecht: Springer, 2011), 145.

122. Richard Kerridge points out that "the ecocritic wants to track environmental ideas and representations wherever they appear, to see more clearly a debate which seems to be taking place, often part-concealed, in a great many cultural spaces. Most of all, *ecocriticism seeks to evaluate texts and ideas in terms of their coherence and usefulness as responses to environmental crisis*" (introduction to *Writing the Environment: Ecocriticism & Literature*, ed. Richard Kerridge and Neil Sammels [London: Zed Books Ltd., 1998], 5). To a certain extent, this strong claim regarding ecologically oriented discourses also applies to more recent contributions to the field, including Morton's work, Stacy Alaimo's *Bodily Natures: Science, Environment, and the Material Self* (Bloomington: Indiana University Press, 2010), and Donna Haraway's *Staying with the Trouble: Making Kin in the Chthulucene* (Durham, NC: Duke University Press, 2016).

123. "Ecocriticism," Moore writes, "involves an empathetic view of nature" (*Ecology and Literature*, 196).

124. Cooper, *No More Heroes*, 17 and 65.

125. Moore, *Ecology and Literature*, 196.

126. As I show below, the notion of indifference in McCarthy refers not to the existence of beings in the world but rather to that which does not exist yet which has a certain influence on how these beings behave.

127. Welchman, "Deleuze and Deep Ecology," 116.

128. In Max Oelschlaeger's words, "postmodern environmental ethics, in contrast to modernist ethical theory, is always situated in language, especially attentive to linguistic context, socially dominant forms of narrative (final vocabularies), and the potential for realizing change through alternative discourse" (introduction to *Postmodern Environmental Ethics*, ed. Max Oelschlaeger [Albany: State University of New York Press, 1995], 9). Directly after he draws this parallel to the literary periodization discussed above, he describes the representatives of this postmodern version of ecocentrism as being "interested in what might be called *performativity* generally and *societal transformation* more specifically" (ibid.). Even the relationship between human and nonhuman realities retains a culturally and, above all, linguistically implemented structure in this account.

129. Kate Soper, *What Is Nature?* (1995; Oxford: Blackwell, 2000), 98–112 and 119–30.

130. Ibid., 151.

131. Ibid. Taking up some important points in Soper's account, David Mazel contends that his subject matter—the American environment—is not "the prediscursive origin and cause of environmental discourse but [is instead] an effect of that discourse. The environment is not a simple reflection or projection of human desires and interests, but neither does it transcend those desires and interests" (*American Literary Environmentalism* [Athens: University of Georgia Press, 2000], 19). It is "an idea rather than a presence" and thus "becomes manifest as what Michel Foucault calls a *dispositif*, a category that organizes around itself the heterogeneous disciplines that claim (in this case) the environment as their common object of study and concern" (ibid.). Again, the concept of nature is equated here to the notion of the

environment, a move that shows a restriction on nature's purview qua concept. The characterization of nature as both culturally constructed and "prelogical" cannot hide the fact that nature is still conceived of as an "active entity" (ibid.)—in other words, a substance that becomes problematic when one has to pin down the essential features that make this "entity" what it is.

132. Mazel, *American Literary Environmentalism*, 19, emphasis added.

133. Cheryll Glotfelty, "Introduction: Literary Studies in an Age of Environmental Crisis," in *The Ecocriticism Reader: Landmarks in Literary Ecology*, ed. Cheryll Glotfelty and Harold Fromm (Athens: University of Georgia Press, 1996), xviii.

134. Ibid., xxiii.

135. Robert T. Tally Jr., "Introduction: On Geocriticism," in *Geocritical Explorations: Space, Place, and Mapping in Literary and Cultural Studies*, ed. Robert T. Tally Jr. (New York: Palgrave Macmillan, 2011), 1.

136. Greg Garrard, *Ecocriticism* (2004; New York: Routledge, 2012), 5.

137. Ibid., 4.

138. On Coleridge's conceptual divisions, see Raman Selden, "Wit, Judgement, Fancy and Imagination," in *The Theory of Criticism: From Plato to the Present*, ed. Raman Selden (Harlow, UK: Longman, 1988), 126–28. Regarding environmental criticism's Romanticist heritage, Arne Næss writes: "Deep ecology formulates a program which may have been influenced by my own culture but which is not particularly new in the context of European tradition. . . . The acceptance of so-called 'bioegalitarianism' in principle has been especially rich in British history. Important names: Edward Bancroft, Samuel Taylor Coleridge, William Wordsworth, William Blake, come to mind" ("Is the Deep Ecology Vision a Green Vision or Is It Multicolored Like the Rainbow? An Answer to Nina Witoszek," in *Philosophical Dialogues: Arne Næss and the Progress of Ecophilosophy*, ed. Nina Witoszek and Andrew Brennan [Lanham, MD: Rowman and Littlefield, 1999], 472).

139. Maureen Devine and Christa Grewe-Volpp, introduction to *Words on Water: Literary and Cultural Representations*, ed. Maureen Devine and Christa Grewe-Volpp (Trier: Wissenschaftlicher Verlag Trier, 2008), 1.

140. Timothy Morton's conception of the "mesh" also rejects the divides between nature and culture and between the organic and the inorganic, yet here as elsewhere, the undying basis of this concept is still primarily ethical and not ontological: "The mesh is even more deeply interwoven than biocentric ideas such as the web of life imply, because it does away with boundaries between living and nonliving forms. At the same time, symbiosis ensures that boundaries between lifeforms are never rigid and thin; rather, they are wide and permeable. The concept of the mesh gives rise to an ethics and politics based on (1) the utter singularity and uniqueness of every life-form and (2) the lack of fixed identity anywhere in the system of life-forms" ("The Mesh," in *Environmental Criticism for the Twentieth-First Century*, ed. Stephanie LeMenager, Teresa Shewry, and Ken Hiltner [New York: Routledge, 2011], 22). It is difficult to see how Morton's approach and its emphasis on "the utter singularity and uniqueness of every life-form", as well as his channeling of Derrida in claiming that "*there is no 'outside' of the system of life-forms*" (ibid., 26), differ from biocentrism.

141. Timothy Morton, *Ecology without Nature: Rethinking Environmental Aesthetics* (Cambridge, MA: Harvard University Press, 2007), 1.

142. Garrard, *Ecocriticism*, 4.

143. Morton, *The Ecological Thought*, 132.

144. Morton, *Ecology without Nature*, 3.

145. William Cronon, "The Trouble with Wilderness; or, Getting Back to the Wrong Nature," in *Uncommon Ground: Rethinking the Human Place in Nature*, ed. William Cronon (New York: Norton, 1995), 80. See also Heise, "The Hitchhiker's Guide," 507.

146. This recalls Soper's remark that "ecopolitics must attend to culturalist criticisms of naturalist rhetoric" (*What Is Nature?*, 151).

And the following statement by Morton about the relationship between the concept of nature and the issue of sexual identities is reminiscent of chapter 4 in Soper's *What Is Nature?*: "For about two hundred years, the heavy lifting for homophobic Nature has been organicism, which we've explored in its roles as a bearer of ideas of holism and squishiness. Organicism polices the sprawling, tangled, queer mesh by naturalizing sexual difference" (Morton, *The Ecological Thought*, 84).

147. Morton, *The Ecological Thought*, 15.

148. Ibid., 3.

149. Ibid., 95.

150. McKenzie Wark, *Molecular Red: Theory for the Anthropocene* (London: Verso, 2016), 82. Wark provides a compelling account of nature as a concept and a material reality in the Marxist sense, following theorists like Alexander Bogdanov, Andrey Platonov, Karen Barad, and Haraway. Regrettably, Wark's critique of German idealism does not consider Schellingian *Naturphilosophie* at all.

151. The seeming detour of my argument in the form of a thorough critique of Morton's ecocentric dismissal of "nature" as concept, therefore, is intended as a stand-in for the criticisms that ought to be mounted against McCarthy scholars who defend an ecocentric perspective on his fiction in contrast to a more ontological—that is, nature-philosophical—stance.

152. That move also severs "the study of the relationship between literature and the physical environment" (Glotfelty, "Introduction," xviii) from any consideration of how one could determine the disposition of the latter in the first place—namely, by metaphysical means. Such a conceptual severance implies an inadmissible disconnection between natural sciences like theoretical physics and biology—the total opposite of the idea behind the Santa Fe Institute, where McCarthy has written large portions of his novels (Link, "Literary Naturalism," 155). Link is not alone in connecting McCarthy to Crane's fiction. See also, for example, Ellis, *No Place for Home*, 326.

153. Schelling, *SW* III, 571, and *System of Transcendental Idealism*, trans. Peter Heath (Charlottesville: University Press of Virginia, 1978), 186.

154. Nick Heffernan and David A. Wragg, "Introduction: Culture, Environment and Ecopolitics," in *Culture, Environment and Ecopolitics*, ed. Nick Heffernan and David A. Wragg (Newcastle upon Tyne, UK: Cambridge Scholars Publishing, 2011), 20.

155. I am referring to Hubert Zapf's description of the function of narrative within cultural interaction (*Literatur als kulturelle Ökologie: Zur kulturellen Funktion imaginativer Texte an Beispielen des amerikanischen Romans* [Tübingen: Niemeyer, 2002], 53). For a reading of McCarthy inspired by Zapf's concept, see Sabine Anders, "Literatur als kulturelle Ökologie am Beispiel von Cormac McCarthys *All the Pretty Horses*," in *Kulturökologie und Literatur: Beiträge zu einem transdisziplinären Paradigma der Literaturwissenschaft*, ed. Hubert Zapf (Heidelberg: Winter, 2008), 277.

156. Natalie Grant, "The Landscape of the Soul," 67. Like Grant, Grammer is skeptical about the claim that McCarthy's narratives are ecocentric in the sense of being overly positive about the relationship between humanity and its environment. Grammer's account of McCarthy's early novels seriously calls into question the aspects of some variants of literary ecology, such as, the paradisiacal imagery of the human subject's immersion in nature. Yet his position on McCarthy's pastoralism is ambivalent. In a passage on *Child of God*, Grammer writes: "Lester's cave—which is discovered, with almost allegorical appropriateness, when a plowman's mules fall into it through a sinkhole—is the ultimate, deranged expression of the pastoral will to deny history" ("Pastoral and History," 27). However, into Grammer's opinion, McCarthy's Southern works lean toward the pastoral only in their depiction of the region's traditional, or even ritualistic, denial of historical particularity: "The South, guided by pastoral and republican imperatives, has persistently

attempted to portray itself as a region somehow outside of time and change, a permanent refuge of order in a chaotic world" (ibid., 20). According to Grammer, this viewpoint is precisely what McCarthy subverts and ridicules in his own portrayal of Tennessean necrophiles, drunkards, murderers, and—in the case of Gene Harrogate—sexual deviants with an odd proclivity for watermelons.

157. Holloway, "Modernism, Nature, and Utopia," 192.

158. Ibid.

159. Ibid.

160. I am taking this phrase from the title of an essay Walt Whitman published in 1871, in which he argues that "America needs, and the world needs, a class of bards who will, now and ever, so link and tally the rational physical being of man, with the ensembles of Time and Space, and with this vast and multiform show, Nature, surrounding him, ever tantalizing him, equally a part, and yet not a part of him, as to essentially harmonize, satisfy, and put to rest" (*Democratic Vistas: The Original Edition in Facsimile*, ed. Ed Folsom [1871; Iowa City: University of Iowa Press, 2010], 69). On the resonance between Whitman's *Leaves of Grass* and McCarthy, see Bell, *The Achievement of Cormac McCarthy*, 110; Guillemin, *Pastoral*, 16; Mark Steven, "The Late World of Cormac McCarthy," in *Styles of Extinction: Cormac McCarthy's* The Road, ed. Julian Murphet and Mark Steven (London: Continuum, 2012), 84–85. Note that to emphasize its use as a code word among McCarthy scholars I will henceforth refer to *optical democracy* in italics in the text whenever it is not part as a quotation that does not have it italicized.

161. Edwin T. Arnold, "McCarthy and the Sacred: A Reading of *The Crossing*," in *Cormac McCarthy: New Directions*, ed. James D. Lilley (2002; Albuquerque: University of New Mexico Press, 2014), 221; see also 216.

162. Berry, "The Lay of the Land," 55.

163. Monbiot, "Civilisation Ends with a Shutdown of Human Concern."

164. From an ecocritical point of view—such as that of Berry, who holds that "even readers unimpressed by dirt-choked, bloodred waters and the agrarian critique will recognize McCarthy's ethics of the wild" ("The Lay of the Land," 55)—nature either becomes coterminous with the environment or it is superseded by the latter, since, the argument goes, given climate change and ecocultural exploitation, the ecological part of nature is what is really important. What matters most in all talk about humanity's relationship with the natural world is to keep "domestic peace" within this complex household (*oikos*), to honor "the natural contract," as Michel Serres puts: "Any contract creates a collection of bonds, whose network canonizes relations; today nature is defined by a set of relations whose network unifies the whole Earth. The natural contract connects the second and the first networks into one" (*The Natural Contract*, trans. Elizabeth MacArthur and William Paulson [1990; Ann Arbor: University of Michigan Press, 1995], 46). While all of these sentiments and approaches to literature and culture are commendable, they fall short of McCarthy's concept of nature, which does not so much oppose ecocentrism as integrate it. For more on thinking about nature in the discourse of the Anthropocene, see also Wark, *Molecular Red*, 246.

165. Paul S. Quick affirms this supposed parallelism of social and ecological empathy in his reading of the cemetery scene at the beginning of *The Orchard Keeper* ("An Ecocritical Approach to the Southern Novels of Cormac McCarthy," PhD diss., University of Georgia, 2004, 51).

166. Guillemin, *Pastoral*, 3–4.

167. Ibid., 8.

168. In his chapter on *Blood Meridian*, Guillemin writes: "All of McCarthy's novels are . . . inconclusive, conciliatory in a biocentric sense, and preoccupied with the survival of outsiders in non-heroic ways. The only metaphysical or ideological paradigm the author endorses is wilderness animism" (*Pastoral*, 86). In addition, Guillemin points to the transcendentalist heritage of McCarthy's

work and "the egalitarian tendencies inherent in American pastoralism [that] clearly accommodate the biocentric shift in today's nature writing and prepare for McCarthy's aesthetic of optical democracy" (ibid., 144). It has to be conceded that while Guillemin reads McCarthy from a biocentric angle, he detects an even stronger affinity with "the older idea of mystical immersion in nature. . . . In effect, his mystic animism refers the democratic aspiration that grounds American pastoralism back to a heritage that has at times been ignored, but which has been rehabilitated in the context of the ecocritical debate: the egalitarian cosmology of Native American myth" (ibid., 145).

169. Willard P. Greenwood, *Reading Cormac McCarthy* (Santa Barbara, CA: ABC-Clio, 2009), 94. Luce joins those scholars who emphasize the importance of ecology in McCarthy's work when she writes that "the ecocentric vision that so crucially shapes the Border Trilogy (1992–98) is already manifest in *The Orchard Keeper*" (*Reading the World*, 28). Along the lines of Leo Marx's *The Machine in the Garden*, she remarks in her tracing of the cultural and historical settings of McCarthy's first novel, "The cultural machine imprisons, and this trope extends to human contest at the book's core: the inexorable attempt by aggressive, technology-based culture to contain/detain the more nature-based culture of Red Branch's 'orchard keepers'" (ibid., 36), of which Uncle Ather is the novel's prime representative.

170. Estes, *American Spaces*, 77.

171. Ibid., 26.

172. Ibid.

173. Ibid., 81.

174. Ibid., 85.

175. Ibid., 43.

176. Ibid., 132. For an exemplary study of the different literary renderings of the desert in American literature from an ecocritical perspective, see Catrin Gersdorf, *The Poetics and Politics of the Desert: Landscape and the Construction of America* (New York: Rodopi, 2009).

177. Estes, *American Spaces*, 171.

178. Ibid., 132.

179. Ibid., 54; see also 102.

180. Ibid., 54.

181. With regard to such a conceptual move, see Jane Bennett, *Vibrant Matter: A Political Ecology of Things* (Durham, NC: Duke University Press, 2010), 120.

182. Anthony Paul Smith, *A Non-Philosophical Theory of Nature: Ecologies of Thought* (New York: Palgrave Macmillan, 2013), 5. Admittedly, I am taking Smith's remark slightly out of context, as his argument concerns the nonphilosophy of François Laruelle, not the fiction of McCarthy. Yet the statement is relevant in the context of this book, since McCarthy's conception of natural processes is similarly irreducible to any particular disposition—for example, to be alive or to be part of a functioning ecosystem.

2. *"Shreds of Matter": Physiocentrism and Transnational Speculation*

1. Dana Phillips, "History and the Ugly Facts of Cormac McCarthy's *Blood Meridian*," *American Literature* 68, no. 2 (1996): 446.

2. See Gilles Deleuze's remarks on his own work: "I believe in philosophy as a system, but I dislike the notion of system when people relate it to the coordinates of the Identical, the Similar and the Analogous. . . . The questions of 'overcoming philosophy' or 'the death of philosophy' have never impressed me. I feel I am very classical. The system must not only be in perpetual heterogeneity, it must be in *heterogenesis*, and it seems to me that this has never been tried before" ("Letter-Preface by Gilles Deleuze," in Jean-Clet Martin, *Variations: The Philosophy of Gilles Deleuze*, trans. Constantin V. Boundas and Susan Dyrkton [1990; Edinburgh: Edinburgh University Press, 2010], vii).

3. On this point, see Robert T. Tally Jr. and Christine M. Battista, "Introduction: Ecocritical Geographies, Geocritical Ecologies, and the Spaces of Modernity," in *Ecocriticism and Geocriticism: Overlapping Territories in En-*

vironmental and Spatial Literary Studies, ed. Robert T. Tally Jr. and Christine M. Battista (New York: Palgrave Macmillan, 2016), 1–2.

4. On this point, see Robert T. Tally Jr., "Introduction: On Geocriticism," in *Geocritical Explorations: Space, Place, and Mapping in Literary and Cultural Studies*, ed. Robert T. Tally Jr. (New York: Palgrave Macmillan, 2011), 1; Bertrand Westphal, *Geocriticism: Real and Fictional Spaces*, trans. Robert T. Tally Jr. (2007; Basingstoke: Palgrave Macmillan, 2011), 99.

5. Certainly, it would be possible to point to the difference between space and place (a central topic in environmental criticism as well), yet in Westphal's theory, "space and place are deliberately conflated by me in the concept of 'human space'" (*Geocriticism*, 6).

6. Ibid., 4–5.

7. Ibid., 114.

8. Ibid., 122.

9. Ibid., 2.

10. Ibid., 6. Westphal critically states: "I believe that structuralism's credo might be summed up in Jacques Derrida's laconic formula: *Il n'y a pas de hors-texte*. There is nothing outside the text, and a text is a text is a text. A text may be a Steinian rose, who knows, but anyway a text should have no concrete link with the actual world" (Bertrand Westphal, foreword to *Geocritical Explorations: Space, Place, and Mapping in Literary and Cultural Studies*, ed. Robert T. Tally Jr. [New York: Palgrave Macmillan, 2011], xii). In contrast, he claims that "the era when 'fictitious' narrations can be definitely cut off from the 'real' world is long over" (ibid., xiii).

11. Westphal, *Geocriticism*, 112.

12. Westphal, foreword, xv. To be sure, this characterization reads as if Westphal has been the first to come up with these terms (apart from his mentioning what Deleuze and Félix Guattari call "deterritorialization"). It reads as if he does not acknowledge the developments in literary and cultural analysis of the past twenty-odd years, which have been very much concerned with spatial forms of representation and expression. Yet he immediately adds, "Geocriticism has been theorized, certainly, but it will continue being a work in progress" (ibid.).

13. Andrew Keller Estes, *Cormac McCarthy and the Writing of American Spaces* (Amsterdam: Rodopi, 2013), 77.

14. Westphal, *Geocriticism*, 5–6.

15. Ibid., 6.

16. For the description of geocriticism as a kind of "spatial studies," see Westphal, *Geocriticism*, 111.

17. Thus, the characterization of work by scholars such as Christopher Walsh, Gabe Rikard, or Liana Vrajitoru Andreasen as geocritical simply underlines the advantage of considering McCarthy's fiction from a critical perspective that examines the inter- and intra-action between literary characters, historical persons, regional cultures, and their geographical histories in terms of spatial practice. It could also be said that an investigation of McCarthy's depictions of American spaces is necessary because of this central feature of his work (*In the Wake of the Sun: Navigating the Southern Works of Cormac McCarthy* [Knoxville, TN: Newfound Press, 2009], 62). Gabe Rikard tackles the East Tennessean culture, its spaces, and its narrative depictions by McCarthy from a Foucauldian perspective, navigating the "conduits of power" (*Authority and the Mountaineer in Cormac McCarthy's Appalachia* [Jefferson, NC: McFarland and Company, 2013], 45) in McCarthy's Appalachian sceneries. Liana Vrajitoru Andreasen deals with the question of how "in *Blood Meridian*, the West takes on mythical proportions as a place that transcends its boundaries," observing that McCarthy's fifth novel is "a story that fills and exceeds that space, rendering its inhabitants disposable" ("*Blood Meridian* and the Spatial Metaphysics of the West," in *They Rode On:* Blood Meridian *and the Tragedy of the American West*, ed. Rick Wallach [Miami: Cormac McCarthy Society, 2013], 166). In her careful reading of the novel's "spatial metaphysics" (ibid.), Andreasen remarks on how the judge and the landscape through which his band

of scalp hunters move almost seem to be of one and the same fabric. "The judge has no need for principles," since for him, "there is no other ideal than the one forged by the being that exceeds all beings and assimilates all space" (ibid., 169). The frequent claim that *Blood Meridian* is a demystification of manifest destiny and Western expansionism is thus reformulated in expressly spatial terms.

18. Steven Shaviro, "'The Very Life of the Darkness': A Reading of *Blood Meridian*," *Southern Quarterly* 30, no. 4 (1992): 112.

19. Ibid., 111.

20. Gilles Deleuze and Félix Guattari, *A Thousand Plateaus: Capitalism and Schizophrenia*, trans. Brian Massumi (1980; London: Continuum, 2004), 524.

21. Shaviro, "A Reading of *Blood Meridian*," 113.

22. Deleuze and Guattari, *A Thousand Plateaus*, 524.

23. Westphal, *Geocriticism*, 39.

24. Deleuze and Guattari, *A Thousand Plateaus*, 524.

25. For an exemplary reading of the notion of smooth space, see Paul Patton, *Deleuze and the Political* (London: Routledge, 2000), 114.

26. Deleuze and Guattari, *A Thousand Plateaus*, 529.

27. Westphal, *Geocriticism*, 39.

28. Ibid.

29. Shaviro, "A Reading of *Blood Meridian*," 112.

30. Brian Evenson, "McCarthy's Wanderers: Nomadology, Violence, and Open Country," in *Sacred Violence: A Reader's Companion to Cormac McCarthy*, ed. Wade Hall and Rick Wallach (El Paso: Texas Western Press, 1995), 41.

31. Ibid., 42 and 47.

32. Deleuze and Guattari, *A Thousand Plateaus*, 405.

33. Late in their book, Deleuze and Guattari write: "It was a decisive event when the mathematician Riemann uprooted the multiple from its predicate state and made it a noun, 'multiplicity.' It marked the end of dialectics and the beginning of a typology and topology of multiplicities" (ibid., 533). On this point, see Evan Gottlieb, *Romantic Realities: Speculative Realism and British Romanticism* (Edinburgh: Edinburgh University Press, 2016), 79.

34. Deleuze and Guattari, *A Thousand Plateaus*, 405.

35. Gilles Deleuze, *Difference and Repetition*, trans. Paul Patton (1968; London: Continuum, 2004), 220. On this period in the history of scalp hunting, see Shane Schimpf, "A Short History of Scalping," in *They Rode On:* Blood Meridian *and the Tragedy of the American West*, ed. Rick Wallach (Miami: Cormac McCarthy Society, 2013), 33–37.

36. Deleuze and Guattari, *A Thousand Plateaus*, 389.

37. Westphal, *Geocriticism*, 39.

38. Alan Bourassa, *Deleuze and American Literature: Affect and Virtuality in Faulkner, Wharton, Ellison, and McCarthy* (New York: Palgrave Macmillan, 2009), 89.

39. Ibid., 85.

40. Ibid. Two pages later, Bourassa quotes from Gilles Deleuze's argument that the event "belongs to another dimension than that of denotation, manifestation, or signification. It is essentially pre-individual, non-personal, and a-conceptual" (*The Logic of Sense*, trans. Mark Lester [1969; London: Continuum, 2004], 63).

41. Bourassa, *Deleuze and American Literature*, 76.

42. Deleuze, *The Logic of Sense*, 118, emphasis added. The notions of "actualization" and "the actual" appear again and again throughout Deleuze's oeuvre. For the moment I want to refer to the following exemplary passage from *The Logic of Sense*, because this is Bourassa's primary source text and because the specific passage is arguably Deleuze's clearest rendering of that notion throughout the book: "To be actualized or to actualize oneself means . . . to be incarnated in a body; and to be renewed locally for the sake of limited new actualizations and extensions. . . . To be actualized is also to be *expressed*" (ibid., 127).

43. Bourassa, *Deleuze and American Literature*, 81. On the precise nature of Rinthy's connection to the event of the human, Bourassa writes that her incestuous transgression of filial normativity with Culla "distributes a kind of metaphysical homelessness throughout the space and time of the novel. . . . Rinthy is homeless, and, with her, humanity, the very essence of humanity, is homeless as well" (ibid., 95).

44. Westphal, foreword, xv.

45. Deleuze and Guattari, *A Thousand Plateaus*, 405.

46. Bourassa, *Deleuze and American Literature*, 105.

47. Ibid., 106.

48. See Ray Brassier, *Nihil Unbound: Enlightenment and Extinction* (New York: Palgrave Macmillan, 2007); Iain Hamilton Grant, *Philosophies of Nature after Schelling* (2006. London: Continuum, 2008); Quentin Meillassoux, *After Finitude: An Essay on the Necessity of Contingency*, trans. Ray Brassier (2006; London: Continuum, 2009). Graham Harman is an exception to the rule here, having already been quite prolific. His first book was *Tool-Being: Heidegger and the Metaphysics of Objects* (Chicago: Open Court, 2002). Yet it is his *Guerrilla Metaphysics: Phenomenology and the Carpentry of Things* (Chicago: Open Court, 2005) that can be aligned with Meillassoux's, Grant's, and Brassier's works in the context of the workshop.

49. Ray Brassier, Iain Hamilton Grant, Graham Harman, and Quentin Meillassoux, "Speculative Realism," *Collapse* 3 (2007): n.p.

50. For a similar account of speculative realism's origination, see Grant Hamilton, *The World of Failing Machines: Speculative Realism and Literature* (Winchester, UK: Zero Books, 2016), 1–4.

51. Brassier, Grant, Harman, and Meillassoux, "Speculative Realism," 307. It is crucial to mention other contributors to speculative realism. Interestingly enough, some of them have close ties to the environmental humanities, such as Timothy Morton and Jane Bennett (whose work I have mentioned above), and Levi Bryant, who has been working for years at the intersection of Deleuze studies, ecocentrism, and speculative realism. For instance, see Levi R. Bryant, *Onto-Cartography: An Ontology of Machines and Media* (Edinburgh: Edinburgh University Press, 2014); Brian Willems, *Speculative Realism and Science Fiction* (Edinburgh: Edinburgh University Press, 2017), 1–5. Nonetheless, because of the focus of my argument, I will predominantly use those writings within speculative realism that return to an explicitly nature-philosophical metaphysics and that resonate most strikingly with McCarthy's poetics.

52. Meillassoux, *After Finitude*, 5.

53. Edmund Husserl, *Ideas Pertaining to a Pure Phenomenology and to a Phenomenological Philosophy, First Book*, trans F. Kersten (1913; Dordrecht,: Kluwer Academic Publishers, 1998), 116. For Brassier, this quote is one of the prime examples of continental correlationism (see Ray Brassier, "Alien Theory: The Decline of Materialism in the Name of Matter," PhD diss., University of Warwick, 2001, 16–17, and *Nihil Unbound*, 245).

54. Ashley Kunsa, "'Maps of the World in Its Becoming': Post-Apocalyptic Naming in Cormac McCarthy's *The Road*," *Journal of Modern Literature* 33, no. 1 (2009): 68.

55. In fact, others have noted the thematic convergence of speculative realism and McCarthy's novels. However, these neither account for the whole of McCarthy's oeuvre nor focus on the author's concept of nature. See Sean Braune's essay on *Blood Meridian* and *No Country for Old Men* ("A Chaotic and Dark Vitalism: A Case Study of Cormac McCarthy's Psychopaths amid a Geology of Immorals," *Western American Literature* 50, no. 1 [2015]: 1–24) and Willems's account of *The Road* from a speculative realist point of view (*Speculative Realism and Science Fiction*, 40–59).

56. Although Deleuze worked at the same time as the poststructuralist philosophers who

tried to banish all things metaphysical and anything that might resemble a philosophy of nature (with the exception of Michel Serres and Gilles Simondon, as shown by Alberto Gualandi in "Errancies of the Human: French Philosophies of Nature and the Overturning of the Copernican Revolution," *Collapse* 5 [2012]: 508–9), he was a self-proclaimed metaphysician and had always been interested in conceptualizing nature. In fact, Deleuze and Guattari were very intent on developing a philosophical edifice to support this conceptualization, particularly after their last collaborative work, *What Is Philosophy?* (1991). Gilles Deleuze writes: "Guattari and I want to get back to our joint work and produce a sort of philosophy of Nature, now that any distinction between nature and artifice is becoming blurred" (*Negotiations*, trans. Martin Joughin. [New York: Columbia University Press, 1995], 155). Alain Badiou, who at one time was a colleague of Deleuze and Lyotard, has never accepted the postmodern and poststructuralist dictum that the concept of "truth" is merely historically determined and that it has only secondary value apart from that determination. He has more or less consistently repeated his arguments against the dominant trends in the French philosophy in the 1980s in that throughout his work he opposes the emphases put on the importance of language as well as on the valence of individual human bodies in philosophical reflection. Instead, he promotes a return to the work of Plato, René Descartes, and Georg Wilhelm Friedrich Hegel—philosophers who represented to critical theorists all that is despicable in the intellectual tradition of the West. Additionally, in his *Being and Event* (trans. Oliver Feltham [1988; London: Continuum, 2005]) and subsequent works, he has expressed a renewed commitment to rationalism in general and mathematics in particular as the sole guarantors of truth. McCarthy's interest in the history of mathematics reflects that of Badiou, although the latter's communist politics are diametrically opposed to those of McCarthy. For an exemplary reading of McCarthy's prose inspired by Badiou's philosophy, see Sebastian Huber, *Subject of the Event: Reagency in the American Novel after 2000* (London: Bloomsbury, 2016), 49–88. Finally, Žižek is one of the most influential and popular figures in today's continental thought. He, too, has argued in favor of a return to Hegel and German idealism as a whole—filtered, in his case, through the lens of Lacanian psychoanalysis. This combination of the two can be seen, for instance, in his interpretation of Schelling's account of the "emergence of Evil," a process that is formally presented as "the same as that of the Name-of-the-Father" (Slavoj Žižek, *The Indivisible Remainder: On Schelling and Related Matters* (1996; London: Verso, 2007), 66) in Lacan. Žižek also played an important role in determining the intellectual climate of speculative realism due to the interest in the natural sciences that he shares with Deleuze and Badiou. As John Mullarkey notes (*Post-Continental Philosophy: An Outline* [London: Continuum, 2006], 2), Deleuze and Badiou were interested in biology and mathematics, respectively, while Žižek is interested in quantum physics.

57. See Brassier, *Nihil Unbound*; Badiou, *Being and Event*; Meillassoux, *After Finitude.*

58. In contrast to Braune ("A Chaotic and Dark Vitalism," 3) and in particular Willems (*Speculative Realism and Science Fiction*, 47–49), I have elected to not use Harman's approach in my reading of McCarthy, simply because for McCarthy—as for Schellingian metaphysics—nature is not a thing or an object, but a process.

59. As scholars like Hanjo Berressem and Ronald Bogue have shown, the philosophical stance developed by Deleuze and Guattari is very much in accordance with the work of Maturana, Varela, and other thinkers interested in the topic of self-organization. For instance, Berressem contends that "Guattari relies in many ways on the theory of autopoiesis," even though "he proposes to widen its operational frame beyond that of the biosphere, to which Maturana [and] Varela—at least according to

Guattari—tend to restrict it, toward the more inclusive 'mechanosphere'" (Hanjo Berressem, "Structural Couplings: Radical Constructivism and a Deleuzian Eco*logics*," in *Deleuze | Guattari & Ecology*, ed. Bernd Herzogenrath. [New York: Palgrave Macmillan, 2009], 59–60). Along these lines, Deleuze "ties his philosophy to a theory of the emergence of the subject" and consequently "aligns biophysical registers (the registers of life and production) and psychic registers (the registers of thought and representations)" (ibid., 62), in his first book, *Empiricism and Subjectivity: An Essay on Hume's Theory of Human Nature* (1953). Ronald Bogue argues that "Deleuze and Guattari's valorization of smooth space . . . implies a commitment to a kind of Nietzschean perspectivism (hardly a surprise, given Deleuze's longstanding Nietzschean proclivities) and a rejection of the notion that there is any 'view from nowhere.' In this regard, Deleuze and Guattari's position is consonant with that of Varela and his frequent collaborator Humberto Maturana" ("A Thousand Ecologies," in *Deleuze | Guattari & Ecology*, ed. Bernd Herzogenrath [New York: Palgrave Macmillan, 2009], 51). As will become clear, Brassier's nihilist account of the human subject is concerned precisely with a speculative inquiry into such a "view from nowhere." Above all, see Ray Brassier, "The View from Nowhere," *Identities* 8, no. 2 (2011): 18.

60. The phrase "geology of morals" comes from a chapter title in Deleuze and Guattari's *A Thousand Plateaus*, the full version of which reads: "10,000 B.C.: The Geology of Morals (Who Does the Earth Think It Is?)" (*A Thousand Plateaus*, 44). Despite his critical stance toward Deleuze, Iain Hamilton Grant uses this phrase and others like "planomenon" repeatedly as if they were from the vocabulary of a former mentor (see, for instance, "'Philosophy Become Genetic': The Physics of the World Soul," in *The New Schelling*, ed. Judith Norman and Alistair Welchman [London: Continuum, 2004], 135, 136, and 144).

61. For instance, see Badiou, *Being and Event*, 128 and 140.

62. Iain Hamilton Grant, "The Chemistry of Darkness," *Pli* 9 (2000): 50.

63. Schelling, *SW* III, 258, and *First Outline of a System of the Philosophy of Nature*, trans. Keith Peterson (Albany: State University of New York Press, 2004), 184.

64. I. Grant, *Philosophies of Nature*, ix.

65. I. Grant, "The Chemistry of Darkness," 50.

66. Deleuze, *Difference and Repetition*, 22.

67. Ibid., 15.

68. Ibid., 15 and 243.

69. Quoted in Iain Hamilton Grant, "The 'Eternal and Necessary Bond Between Philosophy and Physics': A Repetition of the Difference Between the Fichtean and Schellingian Systems of Philosophy," *Angelaki* 10, no. 1 (2005): 46.

70. On this point, see Nathan Widder, "Matter as Simulacrum; Thought as Phantasm; Body as Event," in *Deleuze and the Body*, ed. Laura Guillaume and Joe Hughes (Edinburgh: Edinburgh University Press, 2011), 102–3.

71. Bourassa, *Deleuze and American Literature*, 85.

72. Deleuze, *Difference and Repetition*, 220; Deleuze and Guattari, *A Thousand Plateaus*, 50. On the key role of reciprocity as a conceptual figure in Deleuze and Guattari, see Ian Buchanan, *Deleuzism: A Metacommentary* (Edinburgh: Edinburgh University Press, 2000), 122.

73. Deleuze, *Difference and Repetition*, 344 and 345.

74. Gilles Deleuze, "The Actual and the Virtual," in Gilles Deleuze and Claire Parnet, *Dialogues II*, trans. Eliot Ross Albert (New York: Columbia University Press, 2007), 150–51. Gottlieb offers an alternative reading of Deleuze's conceptualization of the actual-virtual relation (*Romantic Realities*, 78–81).

75. Deleuze, *Difference and Repetition*, 316. On the issue of Deleuze's panpsychism, see John Protevi, "Larval Subjects, Autonomous Systems and E. Coli Chemotaxis," in *Deleuze and the Body*, ed. Laura Guillaume

and Joe Hughes (Edinburgh: Edinburgh University Press, 2011), 29–38. In this book, I will differentiate between a "strong" and a "weak" form of panpsychism, a distinction modeled to a certain extent after the one Meillassoux makes between strong and weak correlationism (*After Finitude*, 30). See also Peter Gratton, *Speculative Realism: Problems and Prospects* (London: Bloomsbury, 2014), 53). It is imperative to note that Val Plumwood made a distinction between "strong" and "weak panpsychism" (*Feminism and the Mastery of Nature* [London: Routledge, 1993], 132), the conceptual scaffolding of which is partly compatible with my own.

76. Gilles Deleuze and Félix Guattari, *Anti-Oedipus: Capitalism and Schizophrenia*, trans. Robert Hurley, Mark Seem, and Helen R. Lane (1972; Minneapolis: University of Minnesota Press, 2008), 326–27.

77. Deleuze and Guattari, *A Thousand Plateaus*, 558.

78. Ibid., 45.

79. Ibid., 281.

80. Gilles Deleuze and Félix Guattari, *What Is Philosophy?*, trans. Hugh Tomlinson and Graham Burchell (1991; New York: Columbia University Press, 1994), 38.

81. Deleuze, *Difference and Repetition*, 15.

82. Deleuze and Guattari, *What Is Philosophy?*, 96–97, emphasis added.

83. Ibid., 96.

84. Ibid.

85. I. Grant, "The Chemistry of Darkness," 50.

86. Deleuze and Guattari, *Anti-Oedipus*, 327.

87. I. Grant, "Philosophy Become Genetic," 129–30.

88. On this connection, see Berressem, "Structural Couplings," 66; Bogue, "A Thousand Ecologies," 52; Alistair Welchman, "Deleuze and Deep Ecology," in *An [Un]likely Alliance: Thinking Environment[s] with Deleuze | Guattari*, ed. Bernd Herzogenrath (Newcastle upon Tyne, UK: Cambridge Scholars Publishing, 2008), 124.

89. Iain Hamilton Grant, "Introduction to Schelling's *On the World Soul*," *Collapse* 6 (2012): 63. Recall Olaf Breidbach's comment on Schelling's onception of *Naturphilosophie* as a "science *of* nature [Wissenschaft *der* Natur]" instead of a "science *about* nature [Wissenschaft *von der* Natur]" ("Schelling und die Erfahrungswissenschaft," *Sudhoffs Archiv* 88, no. 2 [2004]: 156).

90. Iain Hamilton Grant, "The Insufficiency of Ground: On Žižek's Schellingianism," in *The Truth of Žižek*, ed. Paul Bowman and Richard Stamp (London: Continuum, 2007), 85.

91. Quoted in I. Grant, "Philosophy Become Genetic," 135.

92. I. Grant, *Philosophies of Nature after Schelling*, 110.

93. I. Grant, "Philosophy Become Genetic," 140 and 144.

94. Iain Hamilton Grant, "Does Nature Stay What-It-Is? Dynamics and the Antecedence Criterion," in *The Speculative Turn: Continental Materialism and Realism*, ed. Levi Bryant, Nick Srnicek, and Graham Harman (Melbourne: re.press, 2011), 69.

95. Deleuze and Guattari, *What Is Philosophy?*, 38.

96. Deleuze and Guattari, *A Thousand Plateaus*, 281.

97. Gilles Deleuze, "Immanence: A Life," in Gilles Deleuze, *Pure Immanence: Essays on A Life*, trans. Anne Boyman (New York: Zone Books, 2001), 29, 27.

98. In an article that discusses the "*identity* of mind and nature," albeit one that "differentiates rather than integrates," Iain Hamilton Grant distances himself from the logic of reciprocity ("The Universe in the Universe: German Idealism and the Natural History of Mind," *Royal Institute of Philosophy Supplement* 72 [2013]: 301 and 313; see also 302).

99. I. Grant, "The 'Eternal and Necessary Bond Between Philosophy and Physics,'" 51.

100. Deleuze and Guattari, *What Is Philosophy?*, 74.

101. On that point, consider Francisco J. Varela's instructive outline of what he calls "the enactive alternative" within the cog-

nitive sciences, by which he means his and Maturana's work on self-organizing systems, steeped in the phenomenological accounts of Martin Heidegger and Maurice Merleau-Ponty ("Whither Perceptual Meaning?," in *Understanding Origins: Contemporary Views on the Origin of Life, Mind, and Society*, ed. Francisco J. Varela and Jean-Pierre Dupuy [Dordrecht: Kluwer Academic Publishers, 1992], 25; see also 251). "The basic notion, then, is that cognitive capacities are inextricably linked to a history that is lived, much like a path that does not exist but is laid down in walking. Consequently, the view of cognition is not that of solving problems through representations, but as a creative bringing forth of a world where the only required condition is that it is effective action: it permits the continued integrity of the system involved" (ibid., 255). In accordance with Berressem's interpretation of Maturana and Varela's connection to ecology ("Structural Couplings," 61), I take it that this "integrity of the system" is precisely what is at stake in any sophisticated rendition of the household of nature, or its homeostasis.

102. Gilles Deleuze, *Expressionism in Philosophy: Spinoza*, trans. Martin Joughin (1968; New York: Zone Books, 1990), 257.

103. Deleuze and Guattari, *What Is Philosophy?*, 96–97.

104. This is not to say that I agree completely with Iain Grant's dismissal of Deleuzian geophilosophy. Rather, his criticism of the latter serves as a model for my rejection of the existing approaches to McCarthy's concept of nature that have gone the furthest toward a delineation of what I call the author's *Naturliteratur*.

105. Deleuze, *The Logic of Sense*, 118.

106. Deleuze, "Immanence," 25.

107. See, above all, John Marks, *Gilles Deleuze: Vitalism and Multiplicity* (London: Pluto Press, 1998), 29.

108. Deleuze and Guattari, *What Is Philosophy?*, 74; Deleuze, "Immanence," 29 and 28.

109. Similarly, Braune uses the Deleuze and Guattari–inspired "version[s] of vitalism" in Land's and Bennett's work, as well as the object-oriented philosophy of Harman, to show that "McCarthy regularly offers a proto-speculative realist philosophy" ("A Chaotic and Dark Vitalism," 3), above all in *Blood Meridian* and *No Country for Old Men*. It is neither the vitalist nor the object-centered aspects of speculative realism that appear to be useful with respect to an analysis of McCarthy's work in general and his concept of nature in particular, but rather the emphasis on a nonvitalist and process-based philosophy of nature (which is, contrary to Braune's rather simplified and brief interpretation, more along the lines of Land's writings than it is of any vitalist postulation).

110. Iain Hamilton Grant, "Movements of the World: The Sources of Transcendental Philosophy," *Analecta Hermeneutica* 3 (2011): 17.

111. See, for instance, Iain Hamilton Grant, "The Chemical Paradigm: Interview with Iain Hamilton Grant," *Collapse* 7 (2011): 60–61.

112. I. Grant, *Philosophies of Nature after Schelling*, 202.

113. Dustin McWerther, "Absolute Naturalism. Review of Iain Hamilton Grant's *Philosophies of Nature after Schelling*," *Radical Philosophy* 144 (2007): 49.

114. I. Grant, *Philosophies of Nature after Schelling*, 202.

115. Deleuze and Guattari, *A Thousand Plateaus*, 281.

116. Ray Brassier, "That Which Is Not: Philosophy as Entwinement of Truth and Negativity," *Stasis* 1 (2013): 177.

117. Ibid., 176.

118. Dianne C. Luce, *Reading the World: Cormac McCarthy's Tennessee Period* (2009; Columbia: University of South Carolina Press, 2010), 158; Carole Juge, "The Road to the Sun They Cannot See: Plato's Allegory of the Cave, Oblivion, and Guidance in Cormac McCarthy's *The Road*," *Cormac McCarthy Journal* 7, no. 1 (2009): 16.

119. I. Grant, "Philosophy Become Genetic," 139.

120. On *The Crossing* and allegory, see in particular Steven Frye, *Understanding Cormac McCarthy* (Columbia: University of South Carolina Press, 2009), 120–21.

121. Bourassa, *Deleuze and American Literature*, 83.

122. Ibid.

123. Reza Negarestani, "The Corpse Bride: Thinking with *Nigredo*," *Collapse* 4 (2008): 142.

124. Deleuze and Guattari, *What Is Philosophy?*, 74; Negarestani, "The Corpse Bride," 137.

125. Shane Schimpf, *A Reader's Guide to* Blood Meridian (2006; Seattle: BonMot Publishing, 2011), 57.

126. I. Grant, "The Chemistry of Darkness," 50.

127. Contrary to Žižek's interpretation in *The Indivisible Remainder*, Iain Grant argues that even the essay on freedom, a fundamental work in Schelling's career, does not make a case that human beings have the exceptional gift of being able to choose between alternatives; rather, it is a crucial contribution to Schelling's earlier project of a philosophy of nature (*Philosophies of Nature after Schelling*, 205). On the question of the continuity of the philosophy of nature in Schelling's oeuvre, see, for instance, Sebastian Schwenzfeuer, *Natur und Subjekt: Die Grundlegung der schellingschen Naturphilosophie* (Freiburg: Verlag Karl Alber, 2012), 155 and 163.

128. Jeremy Dunham, Iain Hamilton Grant, and Sean Watson, *Idealism: The History of a Philosophy* (Montreal: McGill-Queen's University Press, 2011), 129–40.

129. For example, see Wolfgang Wieland, "Die Anfänge der Philosophie Schellings und die Frage nach der Natur," in *Materialien zu Schellings philosophischen Anfängen*, ed. Manfred Frank and Gerhard Kurz (1967; Frankfurt: Suhrkamp, 1975), 237–45. See also Žižek's symptomatic periodization of Schelling's work into three, not five, phases—namely, the philosophy of identity, the philosophy of freedom, and the positive philosophy (*The Indivisible Remainder*, 38–39). This categorization is symptomatic of Žižek's overt reframing of Schelling's thought according to Lacanian psychoanalysis and materialism.

130. Lorenz Oken, *Elements of Physiophilosophy*, trans. Alfred Tulk (1843; London: C. and J. Adlard Printers, 1847). The original work is Lorenz Oken, *Lehrbuch der Naturphilosophie* (1809–11; Zürich: Friedrich Schultheiß, 1843). All of the citations to this work will give first the page number of the German original and then the page number of the English translation. On occasion, I have modified Tulk's translation. For the close relationship between Schelling and Oken, see Michael T. Ghiselin, "Review of F.W.J. Schelling's *First Outline of the Philosophy of Nature* (Translated by Keith R. Peterson)," *History and Philosophy of the Life Sciences* 27, no. 2 (2005): 291; I. Grant, *Philosophies of Nature after Schelling*, 12 and 45. It should be noted that Oken dedicated the first edition of the *Elements* (1809–11) in part to Schelling.

131. Schelling, *SW* VII, 361, and *Philosophical Investigations*, 30.

132. Schelling, *SW*, XI, 486.

133. Schelling, *SW* VIII, 205, and *The Ages of the World*, trans. Frederick de Wolfe Bolman Jr. (New York: Columbia University Press, 1942), 90.

134. I. Grant, "The Insufficiency of Ground," 85.

135. Wolfgang Hogrebe, *Prädikation und Genesis: Metaphysik als Fundamentalheuristik im Ausgang von Schellings Die Weltalter* (Frankfurt: Suhrkamp, 1989), 124.

136. I. Grant, "The Insufficiency of Ground," 85 and 97.

137. Ibid., 93.

138. Robert T. Tally Jr., *Poe and the Subversion of American Literature: Satire, Fantasy, Critique* (New York: Bloomsbury, 2014), 1.

139. I. Grant, "The Insufficiency of Ground," 97–98.

140. Deleuze, *Difference and Repetition*, 80.

141. Oken, *Lehrbuch*, 2; *Elements*, 2.

142. Oken, *Lehrbuch*, 32; *Elements*, 39.

143. Schelling, *SW* VII, 360, and *Philosophical Investigations*, 29.

144. Oken, *Lehrbuch*, 17; *Elements*, 20.

145. Oken, *Lehrbuch*, 17; *Elements*, 21.

146. Oken, *Lehrbuch*, 1; *Elements*, 1.

147. Reza Negarestani, "Notes on the Figure of the Cyclone," in *Leper Creativity: Cyclonopedia Symposium*, ed. Ed Keller, Nicola Masciandaro, and Eugene Thacker (New York: Punctum Books, 2012), 288.

148. Oken, *Lehrbuch*, 11; *Elements*, 14.

149. Cormac McCarthy, notes on "Whales and Men," folder 2, box 97, Cormac McCarthy Papers, Wittliff Collections, Texas State University, San Marcos.

150. Ibid.

151. Ray Brassier, interview by Leon Niemoczynski, *After Nature Blog*, August 26, 2012, accessed November 28, 2015, http://afterxnature.blogspot.de/2012/08/ray-brassier-interviews-with-after_26.html.

152. Richard B. Woodward, "McCarthy's Venomous Fiction," *New York Times Magazine*, April 19, 1992, accessed March 14, 2015, http://www.nytimes.com/1992/04/19/magazine/cormac-mccarthy-s-venomous-fiction.html?pagewanted=all.

153. Sanford E. Marovitz, "Melville's Problematic 'Being,'" in *Herman Melville*, ed. Harold Bloom (New York: Infobase Publishing, 2008), 50.

154. Ibid. See also Schelling, *SW* VII, 360–1, and *Philosophical Inquiries into the Nature of Human Freedom*, trans. James Gutmann (Chicago: Open Court Publishing, 1936), 35. Marovitz uses James Gutmann's older translation of Schelling's text rather than the more recent one that is normally used. In the passage I have left Gutmann's phrasing as cited in Marovitz for the sake of my argument. In the 2006 translation, the passage reads thus: "We must imagine the original yearning as it directs itself to the understanding, though still not recognizing it, just as we in our yearning seek out unknown and nameless good, and as it moves, divining itself, like a wave-wound, whirling sea, akin to Plato's matter, following dark, uncertain law, incapable of constructing for itself anything enduring" (Schelling, *SW* VII, 360–61, and *Philosophical Investigations into the Essence of Human Freedom*, trans. Jeff Love and Johannes Schmidt [Albany: State University of New York Press, 2006], 29–30).

155. Cormac McCarthy, notes on "Whales and Men," 129–30, folder 5, box 97, Cormac McCarthy Papers, Wittliff Collections. Other scholars have previously examined this passage. See Jacqueline Scoones, "The World on Fire: Ethics and Evolution in Cormac McCarthy's Border Trilogy," in *A Cormac McCarthy Companion: The Border Trilogy*, ed. Edwin T. Arnold and Dianne C. Luce (Jackson: University Press of Mississippi, 2001), 159; Michael Lynn Crews, *Books Are Made out of Books: A Guide to Cormac McCarthy's Literary Influences* (Austin: University of Texas Press, 2017), 261–62; Stacey Peebles, *Cormac McCarthy and Performance: Page, Stage, Screen* (Austin: University of Texas Press, 2017), 58. However, these scholars have not related it to Schelling's metaphysics, which in many ways mirror the poetics of *Moby-Dick*. In this context, Jason M. Wirth follows Marovitz in claiming that "*Moby-Dick* can be read as the great American Schellingian novel and that Ahab recasts the tragedy of evil in a specifically New World spacing" (*Schelling's Practice of the Wild: Time, Art, Imagination* [Albany: State University of New York Press, 2015], 167).

156. Wirth, *Schelling's Practice of the Wild*, 171.

157. Christopher Dacus, "The West as Symbol of the Eschaton in Cormac McCarthy," *Cormac McCarthy Journal* 7, no. 1 (2009): 9.

158. On this logic, see Dunham, Grant, and Watson, *Idealism*, 139; Schelling, *SW* VII, 374, and *Philosophical Investigations*, 41.

159. Schelling, *SW* VII, 361, and *Philosophical Investigations*, 30.

160. Shaviro, "A Reading of *Blood Meridian*," 117.

161. On Schelling's anticipation of the theory of *autopoiesis*, see, in particular, Camilla Warnke, "Schellings Idee und Theorie des Organismus und der Paradigmawechsel

der Biologie um die Wende zum 19. Jahrhundert," *Jahrbuch für Geschichte und Theorie der Biologie* 5 (1998): 233.

162. I take this definition of *phusis* from Iain Grant's work on what he calls "Platonic physics," which he finds, above all, in Schelling's *Naturphilosophie* (see "The Chemical Paradigm," 60–61, and *Philosophies of Nature after Schelling*, 6, 30–45, and 111). What is here mentioned as a physiocentric perspective is not congruent with Klaus-Meyer Abich's version of it, which seems to be leaning too much toward the ethico-vitalist tendencies to be found in biocentrism. For a detailed explanation of Abich's stance, see Leena Vilkka, *The Intrinsic Value of Nature* (Amsterdam: Rodopi, 1997), 74.

163. Dunham, Grant, and Watson, *Idealism*, 230–31.

164. Humberto R. Maturana and Francisco J. Varela, *Autopoiesis and Cognition: The Realization of the Living* (Dordrecht: D. Reidel Publishing Company, 1980), 75. The abovementioned essay "Autopoiesis: The Organization of the Living" (1972) is the first part of *Autopoiesis and Cognition*.

165. Ibid., 74.

166. Ibid.

167. Ibid., 232.

168. I. Grant, "Introduction to Schelling's *On the World Soul*," 63.

169. Maturana and Varela, *Autopoiesis and Cognition*, 74.

170. Oken, *Lehrbuch*, 17; *Elements*, 20.

171. Varela, "Whither Perceptual Meaning?," 250.

172. Maturana and Varela, *Autopoiesis and Cognition*, 76.

173. Dunham, Grant, and Watson, *Idealism*, 230.

174. Maturana and Varela, *Autopoiesis and Cognition*, 76, 74, and 121.

175. In accord with the main orientation also of postmodern epistemologies that dismissed any reference to "the absolute" or "the totality," Maturana and Varela state: "The observer . . . always remains in a descriptive domain, that is, in a relative cognitive domain. *No description of an absolute reality is possible.* Such a description would require an interaction with the absolute to be described, but the representation which would arise from such an interaction would necessarily be determined by the autopoietic organization of the observer . . . ; hence, the cognitive reality that it would generate would unavoidably be relative to the knower" (ibid., 121).

176. Cormac McCarthy, notes on "Whales and Men," folder 2, box 97, Cormac McCarthy Papers, Wittliff Collections. For reasons of textual consistency, I have changed underlining to italics.

177. I am here following the logic of Iain Grant: "Since it is only in the process of its genesis that the universe acquires body, physics is not restricted to somatics, as Aristotle and Kant maintain, but must treat also of the generation of bodies, relegating the latter to regionality with respect to matter. As Schelling writes, 'materiality alone is not yet corporeality' [*SW* IX, 424, Grant's translation]" (*Philosophies of Nature after Schelling*, 28).

178. Wirth, *Schelling's Practice of the Wild*, xii and xiii. These rather helpful clarifications are also applicable to Oken's seemingly vitalist orientation in a passage of his *Elements*, where he writes: "There is nothing properly dead in the world; that only is dead which is not, only the nothing. Something can only cease to live, when its motion ceases; this, however, ceases only when deprived of its polarity; the polarity dissolved, however, is zero. Thus individual things retreat into the Absolute, if they cease to live. Everything is endowed with life; the world itself is alive, and continues only, maintains itself, by virtue of its life; just as an organic body maintains itself, only while it is constantly being generated anew by the vital process. . . . Every living thing is twofold in character. It is one persistent in itself, and one immersed in the universe" (Oken, *Lehrbuch*, 22; *Elements*, 23).

179. Maturana and Varela, *Autopoiesis and Cognition*, 74. See, for instance, Robert J. Richards, *The Romantic Conception of Life: Science and Philosophy in the Age of Goethe*

(Chicago: University of Chicago Press, 2002), 157–58.

180. Sean J. McGrath, "Is Schelling's Nature-Philosophy Freudian?," *Analecta Hermeneutica* 3 (2011): 14, emphasis added.

181. Deleuze and Guattari, *A Thousand Plateaus*, 558; Deleuze, "Immanence," 28.

182. Schelling, *SW* II, 566.

183. Elaine P. Miller provides a highly nuanced reading of the ecological implications in Schelling's thought. While my interpretation would reject any wholesale conflation of Schelling's philosophy of nature and ecocentrism, I concede that Miller's argument about a "Schellingian environmental ethics" is compelling, since this ethics "would go beyond the dichotomy of asking whether an ethical relation to nature is mandated purely for the sake of human survival, or whether nature has intrinsic value and we should thus treat it as an entity with rights in and of itself. A Schellingian environmental ethics recognises that *without nature the question of freedom, and thus of ethics, could not even arise*. This generative relationship between nature and freedom reflects the fundamental alterity between nature and human beings" ("'The World Must Be Romanticised . . .': The (Environmental) Ethical Implications of Schelling's Organic Worldview," *Environmental Values* 14, no. 3 [2005]: 310, emphasis added). This is the same way in which I regard McCarthy's idiosyncratic ethics of nature.

184. Schelling, *SW* VII: 359–60, and *Philosophical Investigations*, 29.

185. Schelling, *SW* III, 271, and *First Outline*, 194.

186. I. Grant, *Philosophies of Nature after Schelling*, 11 (quoting Schelling, *SW* IV, 4 [Grant's translation]). Grant also quotes Schelling's 1800 essay on the *General Deduction of the Dynamic Process*, making clear the similarity to later theories of recapitulation vis-à-vis the insufficiency of the organic as a foundational concept, ontologically speaking: "'Since organic nature as such is nothing other than the self-recapitulation of the inorganic at a higher power [*Potenz*], with the categories of the construction of matter in general, those for the construction of the organic product are also given'" (*Philosophies of Nature after Schelling*, 12 [quoting Schelling, *SW* IV, 4 [Grant's translation]).

187. I. Grant, *Philosophies of Nature after Schelling*, 175.

188. Oken, *Lehrbuch*, 6; *Elements*, 8.

189. Oken, *Lehrbuch*, 7; *Elements*, 8.

190. See Dianne C. Luce, "The Road and the Matrix: The World as Tale in *The Crossing*," in *Perspectives on Cormac McCarthy*, ed. Edwin T. Arnold and Dianne C. Luce (Jackson: University Press of Mississippi. 1999), 222. See also Dacus's reading (inspired by Schelling and Arthur Schopenhauer) of McCarthy's Western fiction ("Eschaton in Cormac McCarthy") and Estes's account of Hegelian dialectics in *American Spaces*.

191. Cormac McCarthy, notes on "Whales and Men," folder 2, box 97, Cormac McCarthy Papers, Wittliff Collections.

192. See Georg W. F. Hegel, *Phenomenology of Spirit*, trans. Michael Inwood (1807; Oxford: Oxford University Press, 2018), 13.

193. Frye, *Understanding Cormac McCarthy*, 122.

194. Ibid.

195. Ibid., 124.

196. Miller, "Ethical Implications of Schelling's Organic Worldview," 305.

197. I. Grant, *Philosophies of Nature after Schelling*, 173.

198. Breidbach, "Schelling und die Erfahrungswissenschaft," 172. On Schelling's "physicalist" dialectics, see Werner Hartkopf, *Studien zur Entwicklung der modernen Dialektik: Die Dialektik in Schellings Ansätzen zu einer Naturphilosophie* (Meisenheim: Verlag Anton Hain, 1972), 76.

199. Karsten Kleber, *Der frühe Schelling und Kant: Zur Genese des Identitätssystems aus philosophischer Bewältigung der Natur und Kritik der Transzendentalphilosophie* (Würzburg: Königshausen & Neumann, 2013), 93 and 80.

200. I. Grant, *Philosophies of Nature after Schelling*, 172.

201. Ibid., 175 and 174, emphasis added.

202. McCarthy's pun on the terms "commutativity" and "community" places him firmly in the nineteenth-century Romantic traditions of both the United States and Germany, since both sought to combine art, science, and philosophy in a poetic exegesis of the world's phenomena, along the lines of what Peirce C. Mullen has called "Romantic science" and in accordance with its key objective "to find a non-mechanistic explanation of nature" ("The Romantic as Scientist: Lorenz Oken," *Studies in Romanticism* 16, no. 3 [1977]: 381). Along these lines, in yet another sketch for his unpublished screenplay "Whales and Men," McCarthy writes the following statement, which incidentally concurs with and neatly summarizes the objective of Romantic science in general and Schelling's *Naturphilosophie* in particular: "The claim that life is mechanical is the same as [the claim] that it does not exist" (Cormac McCarthy, notes on "Whales and Men," folder 2, box 97, Cormac McCarthy Papers, Wittliff Collections).

203. Charles P. McKeague, *Beginning Algebra* (Orlando, FL: Academic Press, 1985), 23.

204. I. Grant, *Philosophies of Nature after Schelling*, 174.

205. Woodward, "McCarthy's Venomous Fiction."

206. Ralph Waldo Emerson, *Emerson's Prose and Poetry: Authoritative Texts, Contexts, Criticism*, selected and edited by Joel Porte and Saundra Morris (New York: W. W. Norton and Company, 2001), 27.

207. Schelling, *SW* V, 350, and "On the Science of the Fine Arts," trans. Ella S. Morgan, *Journal of Speculative Philosophy* 15, no. 2 (1881): 156.

208. Schelling, *SW* V, 350, and "On the Science of the Fine Arts," 156. As Edward Allen Beach notes, Schelling opposes "the thesis that myths are but pictorial representations (*Vorstellungen*) of a content that only philosophical reason can adequately grasp" (*The Potencies of God(s): Schelling's Philosophy of Mythology* [Albany: State University of New York Press, 1994], 42).

209. Schelling, *SW* V, 352, and "On the Science of the Fine Arts," 158.

210. Schelling, *SW* III, 349, and *Transcendental Idealism*, 12.

3. *"Cloaca Maxima": Ontological Decay, or the Decomposition of Nature*

1. Iain Hamilton Grant, *Philosophies of Nature after Schelling* (2006. London: Continuum, 2008), 202.

2. Cormac McCarthy, notes on "Whales and Men," folder 2, box 97, Cormac McCarthy Papers, Wittliff Collections.

3. Schelling, *SW* IX, 195–96, and *Historical-Critical Introduction to the Philosophy of Mythology*, trans. Mason Richey and Markus Zisselsberger (Albany: State University of New York Press, 2007), 136.

4. Edward Allen Beach, *The Potencies of God(s): Schelling's Philosophy of Mythology* (Albany: State University of New York Press, 1994), 37–38. This is the passage where Schelling glosses his use of the term: "Because mythology is not something that emerged artificially, but is rather something that emerged naturally—indeed, under the given presupposition, with necessity—*form* and *content*, *matter* and *outer appearance*, cannot be differentiated in it. The ideas are not first present in another form, but rather they emerge only in, and thus also at the same time with, this form. . . . Because consciousness chooses or invents neither the ideas themselves nor their expressions, mythology emerges immediately *as such* and in no other sense than in which it articulates itself . . .—that is, everything in it is thus to be understood as mythology expresses it, not as something else were thought, something else said. Mythology is not *allegorical*; it is *tautegorical*. To mythology the gods are actually existing essences, gods that are not something *else*, do not *mean* something else, but rather *mean* only what they are" (*SW* IX, 195–96, and *Historical-Critical Introduction*, 136).

5. See also Daniel Whistler, *Schelling's Theory of Symbolic Language: Forming the System of Identity* (Oxford: Oxford University Press, 2013), 38–40. Compare this to Jean-François Lyotard's perspective on tautegory in the adjectival use of the term as "the tautegorical" (*Lessons on the Analytic of the Sublime*, trans. Elizabeth Rottenberg [1991; Stanford, CA: Stanford University Press, 1994], 35).

6. John Elder, *Imagining the Earth: Poetry and the Vision of Nature* (1985; Athens: University of Georgia Press, 1996), 30. In his 1965 review of *The Orchard Keeper*, Walter Sullivan discusses what I have characterized as McCarthy's cross-fertilization of style that amounts to a performance of his concept of nature. However, on Sullivan's reading, this concept is still made in the image of humanity and its deliverance. Sullivan writes: "McCarthy is like nobody so much as he is like all the writers who have gone before him and had sense enough to see in the land a source of human salvation. He is a kind of anachronism who celebrates the traditional values in the traditional way" ("Worlds Past and Future: A Christian and Several from the South," *Sewanee Review* 73, no. 4 [1965]: 721).

7. Andrew Keller Estes, *Cormac McCarthy and the Writing of American Spaces* (Amsterdam: Rodopi, 2013), 131; Bryan L. Moore, *Ecology and Literature: Ecocentric Personification from Antiquity to the Twenty-First Century* (New York: Palgrave Macmillan, 2008), 196.

8. Elder, *Imagining the Earth*, 207.

9. Ibid., 30 and 207.

10. I am following M. H. Abrams's canonical definition of "allegory" as "a narrative in which the agents and action, and sometimes the setting as well, are contrived not only to make sense in themselves, but also to signify a second, correlated order of persons, things, concepts, or events" (*A Glossary of Literary Terms* [New York: Holt, Rinehart and Winston, 1971], 4). To a certain degree, the speculative realist challenge I outline in this book lets allegory appear to be the chief correlationist expression among literary forms. The incorporation of allegory within a tautegorical framework vis-à-vis McCarthy, however, does not accept the wholesale dismissal of allegorical literature as too correlationist.

11. In a different context, Claudia Costa Pederson has hinted at the conceptual parallelism between *allegoresis* and *allopoiesis* ("Autopoiesis in Contemporary Bio-Arts in Mexico and Colombia," *Review: Literature and Arts of the Americas* 48, no. 1 [2015]: 26). Note also that the terms "allegorical" and "*allopoietic*" have the same Greek root ἄλλος (*allos*), meaning "other."

12. For exemplary allegorical readings, see John M. Grammer, "A Thing against Which Time Will Not Prevail: Pastoral and History in Cormac McCarthy's South," *Southern Quarterly* 30, no. 4 (1992): 27; Dianne C. Luce, "The Cave of Oblivion: Platonic Mythology in *Child of God*," in *Cormac McCarthy: New Directions*, ed. James D. Lilley (2002; Albuquerque: University of New Mexico Press, 2014), 174; Georg Guillemin, *The Pastoral Vision of Cormac McCarthy* (College Station: Texas A&M University Press, 2004), 3; Lydia R. Cooper, "McCarthy, Tennessee, and the Southern Gothic," in *The Cambridge Companion to Cormac McCarthy*, ed. Steven Frye (2013; New York: Cambridge University Press, 2014), 41.

13. Fredric Jameson, *Fables of Aggression: Wyndham Lewis, the Modernist as Fascist* (1979; Berkeley: University of California Press, 2008), 93–94.

14. Whistler, *Schelling's Theory of Symbolic Language*, 38.

15. Schelling, *SW* VII, 361, and *Philosophical Investigations into the Essence of Human Freedom*, trans. Jeff Love and Johannes Schmidt (Albany: State University of New York Press, 2006), 30.

16. Beach, *The Potencies of God(s)*, 35.

17. Schelling, *SW* III, 258, and *First Outline of a System of the Philosophy of Nature*, trans. Keith Peterson (Albany: State University of New York Press, 2004), 184.

18. Eugene Thacker, *After Life* (Chicago: University of Chicago Press, 2010), 255.

19. Lydia R. Cooper, *No More Heroes: Narrative Perspective and Morality in Cormac McCarthy* (Baton Rouge: Louisiana State University Press, 2011), 17.

20. Schelling, *SW* II, 349, and "World-Soul," 69.

21. Graham Harman, "On Vicarious Causation," *Collapse* 2 (2007): 192. On this point, see also Sean Braune, "A Chaotic and Dark Vitalism: A Case Study of Cormac McCarthy's Psychopaths amid a Geology of Immorals," *Western American Literature* 50, no. 1 (2015): 2–3.

22. Paul S. Quick, "An Ecocritical Approach to the Southern Novels of Cormac McCarthy," PhD diss., University of Georgia, 2004, 51.

23. Cathy Caruth, "Recapturing the Past: Introduction," in *Trauma: Explorations in Memory*, ed. Cathy Caruth (Baltimore: Johns Hopkins University Press, 1995), 151. From the standpoint of *Naturphilosophie*, the question of whether the experience of the inorganic can be "fully owned" cannot be decided at this point, because the solution depends on what is meant by the ownership of an organism's cause (that is, the inorganic). What can be affirmed, though, is the fundamentally traumatic condition of possibility of the forms and phenomena in McCarthy's literary worlds, simply given the way the narrators depict them.

24. See, for instance, Quick, "An Ecocritical Approach," 51.

25. Consider, for example, the passage that has the narrator of *All the Pretty Horses* depict the death of the assassin who was set to kill John Grady Cole in the Saltillo prison: "The cuchillero . . . took hold of John Grady by the hair and forced his head back to cut his throat. As he did so John Grady brought his knife up from the floor and sank it into the cuchillero's heart. He sank it into his heart and snapped the handle *sideways* and broke the blade off in him" (*PH*, 201, emphasis added).

26. Elder, *Imagining the Earth*, 207.

27. To be sure, William Faulkner's work is again a crucial reference here. Generally, I am relying very heavily on Willard Greenwood's contextualization of McCarthy within the Southern gothic genre and its "trope of the imbecile": "In addition to thematic conventions, the dissolution of society in Southern gothic novels is embodied by a cast of violent and disturbed characters who struggle to find their place throughout the narrative. The futility of this struggle is personified by the trope of the imbecile, which is another common feature of the Southern gothic tradition. The imbecile is a character born in a corrupted state, who often engages in corrupting behavior, and who is doomed to an inescapable fate, despite yearning for freedom from the corrupting elements of society" (*Reading Cormac McCarthy*, [Santa Barbara, CA: ABC-Clio, 2009], 17–18). See also Erik Hage, *Cormac McCarthy: A Literary Companion* (Jefferson, NC: McFarland and Company, 2010), 19.

28. Cooper, "McCarthy, Tennessee, and the Southern Gothic," 41.

29. Robert T. Tally Jr., *Poe and the Subversion of American Literature: Satire, Fantasy, Critique* (New York: Bloomsbury, 2014), 2.

30. Nick Land, *Fanged Noumena*, 496; K. Wesley Berry, "The Lay of the Land in Cormac McCarthy's Appalachia," in *Cormac McCarthy: New Directions*, ed. James D. Lilley (2002; Albuquerque: University of New Mexico Press, 2014), 55.

31. Berry, "The Lay of the Land," 55.

32. Caruth, "Recapturing the Past," 151.

33. Land, *Fanged Noumena*, 335 and 499. This is also why the concept of trauma delineated in the present text is profoundly at odds with the Lacanian version of it, irrespective of Slavoj Žižek's Lacan-inspired reading (or better, recasting) of Schelling (*The Indivisible Remainder: On Schelling and Related Matters* [1996; London: Verso, 2007]). As Sean J. McGrath notes, for Žižek, Schelling is "a Lacanian *avant la lettre*" ("Is Schelling's Nature-Philosophy Freudian?," *Analecta Hermeneutica* 3 (2011): 2): the "indivisible remainder" becomes synonymous with Lacan's concept of "the Real" (Žižek, *The Indivisible*

Remainder, 52)—that is, with "a material substrate underlying the imaginary and the symbolic" (Dylan Evans, *An Introductory Dictionary of Lacanian Psychoanalysis* [1996; London: Routledge, 2010], 160). Conversely, Land's notion of geotrauma, which I read in accordance with Schelling's ontological conception of nature's "productivity" qua "unrecoverable ground" (I. Grant, *Philosophies of Nature after Schelling*, 168), is premised on an altogether different notion of materiality and consequently of nature: it is because nature is a continuous process that its material disposition prevents it from being a finite substrate rather than an infinite form of motion.

34. Jean Laplanche and Jean-Bertrand Pontalis, *The Language of Psycho-Analysis*, trans. Donald Nicholson-Smith (1967; London: Karnac Books, 2006), 333.

35. McGrath, "Is Schelling's Nature-Philosophy Freudian?," 15. I do not agree with McGrath's identification of a proto-Bergsonian "élan vital" in Schelling's understanding of the indeterminate "*qualitas occulta*" (ibid., 19 and 15). This is because, in line with Iain Grant's reconstruction of Schellingianism, that identification is yet again a determining and, therefore, regionalizing measure to relegate the givenness of formlessness "to the higher end of life itself" (ibid., 15).

36. Land, *Fanged Noumena*, 498. In literature, such a descent is commonly depicted as a *katabasis*, the exploration of subterranean spaces—both physical and psychological—such as the Appalachian caves in McCarthy's early work. See Bent Sørensen, "Katabasis in Cormac McCarthy's *Blood Meridian*," *Orbis Litterarum* 60, no. 1 (2005): 16–25. One of the most helpful explanations of *katabasis* in connection to the Southern gothic is provided by Joseph R. Millichap, who writes about "the interplay between outward and inward journeys on the part of both Southern writers and their recreated personae. In Classical terms this connection often is expressed by the concepts of anabasis and katabasis, both etymologically derived from the Greek root *banein*, 'to go,' combined with modifiers for 'up' and 'down.' These roots determine their initial meanings in sea-girt Greece as journeys from coast to mountains and back again. . . . Most important, katabasis also came to mean the descent into the underworld so integral to ancient myth and epic" (*A Backward Glance: The Southern Renascence, the Autobiographical Epic, and the Classical Legacy* [Knoxville: University of Tennessee Press, 2009], 5–6).

37. Even though it is unrelated to McCarthy, a similar phrasing can be seen in Karen Barad's insightful work in the interstices of quantum physics, feminism, and the philosophy of nature. See her central concept of "intra-activity," for instance, in "Posthumanist Performativity: Toward an Understanding of How Matter Comes to Matter," *Signs* 28, no. 3 (2003): 824.

38. Iain Hamilton Grant, "'World' in Middle Schelling: Why Nature Transcendentalises," *Pli* 26 (2014): 108.

39. According to that reading, Alan Bourassa's statement that *The Orchard Keeper* is "not a human narrative, but rather the story of the becoming nonhuman of the human" (*Deleuze and American Literature: Affect and Virtuality in Faulkner, Wharton, Ellison, and McCarthy* [New York: Palgrave Macmillan, 2009] 106) might be altered by substituting the terms "organic" and "inorganic," respectively, for the terms "human" and "nonhuman": *The Orchard Keeper* is "not [an organic] narrative," in the sense of the Romantic, transcendentalist, and ecocentric castings of the organism as an entity endowed with life, "but rather the story of the becoming [inorganic] of the [organic]."

40. Cormac McCarthy, notes on "Whales and Men," folder 2, box 97, Cormac McCarthy Papers, Wittliff Collections.

41. Grammer, "Pastoral and History," 22.

42. I. Grant, "'World' in Middle Schelling," 108.

43. See Matthew L. Potts, *Cormac McCarthy and the Signs of Sacrament: Literature, Theology, and the Moral of Stories* (London: Bloomsbury, 2015), 117.

44. Schelling, *SW* VIII, 200, and *The Ages*

of the World, trans. Frederick de Wolfe Bolman Jr. (New York: Columbia University Press, 1942), 84. Certainly, Bolman's more literal translation, "co-knowledge," is also valid. Yet I am opting for Iain Grant's reinterpretation of Schelling's concept of *Mitwissenschaft*, simply because it sheds more light on the way in which human morality is the consequence of physical genesis (*Philosophies of Nature after Schelling*, 26). Consider the context in which Schelling argues this: "A principle which is outside and above the world must be conceded to man. For how could he alone of all creatures retrace the long course of developments from the present back into the deepest night of the past, he alone ascend to the beginning of the ages, if there were not in him a principle of the beginning of the ages? Drawn from the source of things and akin to it, the human soul has a [co-science (*Mitwissenschaft*)] of creation. In the soul lies the highest clarity of all things, and the soul is not so much knowing as itself knowledge [*Wissenschaft*]" (*SW* VIII, 200, and *The Ages of the World*, 84).

45. According to Sebastian Schwenzfeuer, the concept of the "point of indifference" (*Indifferenzpunkt*) usually refers to the inseparability of subject and object in Schelling's philosophy (*Natur und Subjekt: Die Grundlegung der schellingschen Naturphilosophie* [Freiburg: Verlag Karl Alber, 2012], 196). As Lara Ostaric has recently put it, this concept also delineates a key aspect in Schelling's schema of the dynamic process of nature, whereby the *Indifferenzpunkt* is a crucial (albeit "temporary") state "and is upset in the productivity of the organism, namely, its reproduction" ("The Concept of Life in Early Schelling," in *Interpreting Schelling: Critical Essays*, ed. Lara Ostaric [Cambridge: Cambridge University Press, 2014], 68–69). The manner in which I am using it here, though, concerns the point of indifference between the diverse practices of commentary qua co-science: science, art, ethics, and religious belief all partake in the physical genesis of forms, both corporeal and incorporeal.

46. I. Grant, *Philosophies of Nature after Schelling*, 26.

47. On the geocentric understanding of the notion of commentary, see, in particular, Nicola Masciandaro, "Becoming Spice: Commentary as Geophilosophy," *Collapse* 6 (2012): 35–40.

48. See also Rob Nixon, *Slow Violence and the Environmentalism of the Poor* (Cambridge, MA: Harvard University Press, 2011).

49. The following two statements by Schelling that I am paraphrasing here arguably represent a core tenet of the metaphysics of nature that underlies McCarthy's fiction. The first statement is: "For what we want is not that Nature should coincide with the laws of our mind *by chance* (as if through some third intermediary) but that *she herself*, necessarily and originally, should not only express, but even *realize*, the laws of our mind, and that she is, and is called, Nature only insofar as she does so" (Schelling, *SW* II, 55–56, and *Ideas for a Philosophy of Nature*, trans. Errol E. Harris and Peter Heath [Cambridge: Cambridge University Press, 1988], 41–42). The second one is from the *Philosophy of Revelation*, part of which has been translated by Bruce Matthews: "For it is not because there is thinking that there is being, but rather because there is being that there is thinking," (Schelling *SW* XIII, 161, and *The Grounding of Positive Philosophy: The Berlin Lectures*, trans. Bruce Matthews. [Albany: State University of New York Press, 2007], 203). These two statements not only mark a significant aspect of Schelling's idea of nature's self-analysis that is independent of, or indifferent to, the human souls that conduct that analysis, but the two quotes also evoke the nature-philosophical aspect of McCarthy's poetics in just a few words.

50. Certainly, at first glance, it would also be possible to read this passage in terms of the Deleuzian notion of "pre-individual singularities" (Gilles Deleuze, *Difference and Repetition*, trans. Paul Patton [1968; London: Continuum, 2004], 320), rather than the Landian concept of geotrauma or the

Schellingian notion of evil as a prerequisite for the emergence of human freedom within nature. However, in that case, it would not be "the pitch of supplication" that is voiced by Rattner but perhaps that of animality, since the notion of the supplicant is arguably too religious in the Christian sense for Deleuze. With respect to Rattner's threatening appearance, see also Dianne C. Luce, *Reading the World: Cormac McCarthy's Tennessee Period* (2009; Columbia: University of South Carolina Press, 2010), 53.

51. Berry, "The Lay of the Land," 55.

52. See also David Paul Ragan, "Values and Structure in *The Orchard Keeper*," *Southern Quarterly* 30, no. 4 (1992): 10.

53. Cooper, *No More Heroes*, 65; I. Grant, "'World' in Middle Schelling," 108.

54. Hage, *A Literary Companion*, 126.

55. See Béatrice Trotignon, "Detailing the Wor(l)d in *Suttree*," in *Myth, Legend, Dust: Critical Responses to Cormac McCarthy*, ed. Rick Wallach [Manchester, UK: Manchester University Press, 2000], 99

56. Sullivan writes about this part of the novel that Ownby "does not know whose remains he tends. Certainly, he has no inclination to report their existence to the authorities. But out of his humanity, he tends what was once human, periodically dropping in a fresh evergreen to cover the skull: willingly he serves a *memento mori*" ("Worlds Past and Future," 722). Conversely, I argue with regard to *Child of God* that McCarthy is less interested in the Romanticism of *memento mori* than in what Negarestani conceptualizes as the point of putrefaction or the melting point of the organic—perhaps the descendental procedure par excellence.

57. Lorenz Oken, *Lehrbuch der Naturphilosophie* (1809–11; Zürich: Friedrich Schultheiß, 1843), 32, and *Elements of Physiophilosophy*, trans. Alfred Tulk, (1843; London: C. and J. Adlard Printers, 1847), 39.

58. On the relationship between Mark Twain's work and this scene in McCarthy's first novel, see Leslie Harper Worthington, *Cormac McCarthy and the Ghost of Huck Finn* (Jefferson, NC: McFarland and Company, 2012), 40.

59. Tally, *Poe and the Subversion of American Literature*, 1.

60. Iain Hamilton Grant, "'Philosophy Become Genetic': The Physics of the World Soul," in *The New Schelling*, ed. Judith Norman and Alistair Welchman (London: Continuum, 2004), 139.

61. Consider Gilles Deleuze and Félix Guattari's fascinating account of this notion: "The conceptual persona is not the philosopher's representative but, rather, the reverse: the philosopher is only the envelope of his principal conceptual persona and of all the other personae who are the intercessors [*intercesseurs*], the real subjects of his philosophy. Conceptual personae are the philosopher's 'heteronyms,' and the philosopher's name is the simple pseudonym of his personae" (*What Is Philosophy?*, trans. Hugh Tomlinson and Graham Burchell [1991; New York: Columbia University Press, 1994], 64). See also Ronald Bogue, *Deleuze on Music, Painting and the Arts* (2003; London: Routledge, 2013), 171–75.

62. Daniel Whistler, "Schelling's Doctrine of Abstraction," *Pli* 26 (2014): 77.

63. Ibid.

64. Schelling, *SW* II, 395, and "On the World Soul," trans. Iain Hamilton Grant *Collapse* 6 [2012]): 92, emphasis added.

65. Schelling, *SW* II, 389, and "On the World Soul," 84.

66. On this point, see Guillemin, *Pastoral*, 50.

67. See Edwin Arnold's statement that "in his growing madness, Lester has no hold on his own identity. He begins to wear the clothing of his victims, and later he will wear their hair as a wig, anticipating the scalp hunting in *Blood Meridian*. After losing everything else, he begins to lose himself" ("Naming, Knowing and Nothingness: McCarthy's Moral Parables." *Southern Quarterly* 30, no. 4 [1992]: 39).

68. Guillemin, *Pastoral*, 50.

69. Willard P. Greenwood, *Reading Cor-*

mac McCarthy (Santa Barbara, CA: ABC-Clio, 2009), 39–41, emphasis added.

70. Hillary Gamblin, "Discovering the Romantic in a Necrophiliac: The Question of Misogyny in *Child of God*," *Cormac McCarthy Journal* 9, no. 1 (2011): 28.

71. On this and related points, see John Mullarkey, *Post-Continental Philosophy: An Outline* (London: Continuum, 2006), 19.

72. Schelling, *SW* XIII, 161, and *The Grounding of Positive Philosophy*, 203.

73. Luce, *Reading the World*, vii.

74. I. Grant, *Philosophies of Nature after Schelling*, 149 and 148.

75. Schelling, *SW* II, 348, and "On the World Soul," 68.

76. I. Grant, *Philosophies of Nature after Schelling*, 149.

77. Reza Negarestani, "Undercover Softness: An Introduction to the Architecture and Politics of Decay," *Collapse* 6 (2012): 398. For consistency, from now on I will lowercase and italicize that term, as I have done with McCarthy's *optical democracy*.

78. Concerning McCarthy's melancholy narratives, see Guillemin, *Pastoral*, 112.

79. Schelling, *SW* III, 258, and *First Outline*, 184, emphasis added.

80. Reza Negarestani, "The Corpse Bride: Thinking with *Nigredo*," *Collapse* 4 (2008): 142 and 140. While Negarestani traces his theory to Aristotle and Neo-Platonism, rather than to the Plato of the *Timaeus*, the dialectic between subtraction and construction (that is, between remaining and becoming) is still in accordance with the nature-philosophical synthesis presented here. See also Negarestani's discussion of this point in ibid., 132.

81. See Lawrence Buell, *Writing for an Endangered World: Literature, Culture, and Environment in the U.S. and Beyond* (Cambridge, MA: Belknap Press of Harvard University Press, 2001).

82. Ray Brassier, "That Which Is Not: Philosophy as Entwinement of Truth and Negativity," *Stasis* 1 (2013): 177.

83. Negarestani, "Undercover Softness," 399.

84. Note that Reza Negarestani's *Cyclonopedia: Complicity with Anonymous Materials* (Melbourne: re.press, 2008), can be seen as a fictional, metafictional, and metaphysical piece of writing. On this topic, see in particular, Kate Marshall, "*Cyclonopedia* as Novel (A Meditation on Complicity as Inauthenticity)," in *Leper Creativity: Cyclonopedia Symposium*, ed. Ed Keller, Nicola Masciandaro, and Eugene Thacker (New York: Punctum Books, 2012), 147–57; Benjamin Woodard, "The Untimely (and Unshapely) Decomposition of Onto-Epistemological Solidity: Negarestani's *Cyclonopedia* as Metaphysics," In *Leper Creativity: Cyclonopedia Symposium*, ed. Ed Keller, Nicola Masciandaro, and Eugene Thacker (New York: Punctum Books, 2012), 213–23.

85. Negarestani, "The Corpse Bride," 138.

86. Ibid., 142.

87. Negarestani, "Undercover Softness," 384.

88. Carl G. Jung, *Mysterium Coniunctionis: Untersuchung über die Trennung und Zusammensetzung der seelischen Gegensätze in der Alchemie* (Zurich: Rascher Verlag, 1955–57), 2:218.

89. For a Jungian account of *Blood Meridian*, see John Emil Sepich, *Notes on* Blood Meridian (1993; Austin: University of Texas Press, 2011), 141–52.

90. Consider how Negarestani himself links *katabasis*—which is so essential to McCarthy's literary explorations of underground cave systems in his major works, including *The Orchard Keeper* and *Child of God* as well as *The Road*—with *nigredo*: "*Katabasis* is a depthwise and pro-ground (*profundus*) movement; for that reason, in scholastic alchemy, it is often associated with *nigredo* or depthwise and intensive decay" (Negarestani, "The Corpse Bride," 149).

91. Bertrand Mathieu, *Orpheus in Brooklyn: Orphism, Rimbaud, and Henry Miller* (the Hague: Mouton, 1976), 50. What Mathieu argues with respect to the importance of sexual acts in Henry Miller's prose is arguably even more appropriate to the

dark forms of copulation in McCarthy's third novel.

92. Dana Phillips, "History and the Ugly Facts of Cormac McCarthy's *Blood Meridian*," *American Literature* 68, no. 2 (1996): 450.

93. Negarestani, "The Corpse Bride," 142.

94. Negarestani, *Cyclonopedia*, 184, emphasis added.

95. McCarthy also employs nearly the same phrasing in *Suttree* and the second volume of the Border Trilogy, *The Crossing*. In the last pages of the novel, while Suttree is delirious with typhoid fever, he imagines that "he was going again in a corridor through rooms that never ceased, by formless walls unordered unadorned and slightly moist and warm and through soft doors with valved and dripping architraves and regions wet and bluish like *the inward parts of some enormous living thing*. A small soul's going" (*S*, 461, emphasis added). In *The Crossing*, the narrator refers to a situation in which Billy and Boyd Parham and their father are gathering Mr. Echols's wolf traps: "There in the dusty light from the one small window on shelves of roughsawed pine stood a collection of fruitjars and bottles with ground glass stoppers and old apothecary jars all bearing antique octagon labels edged in red upon which in Echols' neat script were listed contents and dates. In the jars dark liquids. Dried viscera. Liver, gall, kidneys. *The inward parts of a beast* who dreams of man and has so dreamt in running dreams a hundred thousand years and more. Dreams of that malignant lesser god come pale and naked and alien to slaughter all his clan and kin and rout them from their house. A god insatiable whom no ceding could appease nor any measure of blood. The jars stood webbed in dust and the light among them made of the little room with its chemic glass a strange basilica dedicated to a practices soon to be extinct among the trades of men as the beast to whom it owed its being" (*TC*, 17). While much could be said about the relationship between these passages, for the moment their stylistic alignment merely serves to further substantiate the thesis of McCarthy's narrative continuity.

96. Negarestani, *Cyclonopedia*, 184.

97. Tally, *Poe and the Subversion of American Literature*, 1–2.

98. Negarestani, "Undercover Softness," 407.

99. Negarestani, "The Corpse Bride," 131.

100. Schelling, *SW* VIII, 200, and *The Ages of the World*, 84.

101. I am relying heavily here on Christian Iber's suggestion that Schelling derives his concept of "co-science" (*Mitwissenschaft*) from the German word "Mitwisserschaft" (*Das Andere der Vernunft als ihr Prinzip: Grundzüge der philosophischen Entwicklung Schellings mit einem Ausblick auf die nachidealistischen Philosophiekonzeptionen Heideggers und Adornos* [Berlin: Walter de Gruyter, 1994], 204). For Iber, Schelling's concept indicates that human beings are "*witnesses* of the most ancient events of history [*Zeugen* des ältesten Geschehens]" (ibid., emphasis added).

102. Negarestani, "The Corpse Bride," 131.

103. On this particular aspect, see Thomas D. Young Jr., "The Imprisonment of Sensibility: *Suttree*," *Southern Quarterly* 30, no. 4 (1992): 72.

104. Deleuze and Guattari, *What Is Philosophy?*, 64.

105. Bertrand Westphal, *Geocriticism: Real and Fictional Spaces*, trans. Robert T. Tally Jr. (2007; Basingstoke: Palgrave Macmillan, 2011), 6.

106. Schelling, *SW* III, 571, and *Transcendental Idealism*, 186.

107. Schelling, *SW* III, 349, and *Transcendental Idealism*, 12.

108. For an excellent account of Suttree's delirious states in McCarthy's fourth novel, see Anthony Uhlmann, "*Suttree*, Joyce, and Flaubert," in *Cormac McCarthy's Borders and Landscapes*, ed. Louise Jillett (New York: Bloomsbury, 2016), 163–73.

109. Émile Zola, "The Experimental Novel," trans. Belle Sherman, in *The Theory of Criticism: From Plato to the Present*, ed.

Raman Selden (1880; Harlow, UK: Longman, 1988), 51. On Zola and McCarthy, see John Cant, *Cormac McCarthy and the Myth of American Exceptionalism* (New York: Routledge, 2008), 91.

110. Cormac McCarthy, notes on "Whales and Men," 144, folder 2, box 97, Cormac McCarthy Papers, Wittliff Collections, emphasis added. The first set of square brackets indicate that the sentence was handwritten.

111. The following anecdote is noteworthy at this point in my argument because it illuminates the author's understanding of his relationship to his fictional world: "Anne DeLisle [his second wife] speaks about McCarthy's penchant for showering after writing. It was during their time together in Tennessee that McCarthy wrote *Child of God.* She claims that it was as though McCarthy had to 'wash' all of this horrible stuff off of him" (Greenwood, *Reading Cormac McCarthy*, 40).

112. Zola, "The Experimental Novel," 51.

113. Note that the narrator tends to depict Joyce in in a style that is somewhat reminiscent of Henry Miller's poetics. In one of the sexual encounters between the protagonist and Joyce, for instance, "Suttree [is] gradually going awash in the sheer outrageous sentience of her. . . . Her hot spiced tongue fat in his mouth and her hands all over him like the very witch of fuck" (*S*, 393). On the connection between Miller and McCarthy, see Peter Josyph, *Adventures in Reading Cormac McCarthy* (Lanham, MD: Scarecrow Press, 2010), 12.

114. Millichap, *A Backward Glance*, 215.

115. Bernadette Bensaude-Vincent and Isabelle Stengers, *A History of Chemistry*, trans. Deborah van Dam (Cambridge, MA: Harvard University Press, 1996), 13, quoted in Iain Hamilton Grant, "The Chemistry of Darkness," *Pli* 9 (2000): 38. Unsurprisingly, as Grant's rhetoric of "the imperceptible" discloses, "The Chemistry of Darkness" is centrally concerned with Deleuze and Guattari's geophilosophy, which in turn is related to the question of alchemy's practice of metallurgy, for instance, in a passage that showcases the authors' somaticist form of vitalism and even criticizes Jung's alchemical recasting of psychoanalysis in his late work: "What metal and metallurgy bring to light is a life proper to matter, a vital state of matter as such, *a material vitalism* . . . . The prodigious idea of *Nonorganic Life* . . . was the invention, the intuition of metallurgy. Metal is neither a thing nor an organism, but a *body* without organs. . . . The relation between metallurgy and alchemy reposes not, as Jung believed, on the symbolic value of metal and its correspondence with an organic soul but on *the immanent power of corporeality in all matter*, and on *the esprit de corps* accompanying it" (Gilles Deleuze and Félix Guattari, *A Thousand Plateaus: Capitalism and Schizophrenia*, trans. Brian Massumi [1980; London: Continuum, 2004], 454, emphasis added).

116. Bensaude-Vincent and Stengers, *A History of Chemistry*, 13.

117. I. Grant, "The Chemistry of Darkness," 39.

118. Grant, "The Chemical Paradigm: Interview with Iain Hamilton Grant." *Collapse* 7 (2011): 41.

119. Rick Wallach, "Ulysses in Knoxville: Suttree's Ageean Journey," in *You Would Not Believe What Watches*, ed. Rick Wallach, 2nd ed. (Miami: Cormac McCarthy Society, 2014), 79. Of the prologue of *Suttree*, with its description of Knoxville and its spaces, Young remarks: "This primitive structure is a living record of that elemental and highly ambiguous activity of human 'settlement' which is essentially the subject of all McCarthy's fiction. *Suttree* . . . is an account of the rise of this 'western world' of human culture as observed in *dramatically ontogenetic terms*" ("The Imprisonment of Sensibility," 72–73, emphasis added).

120. I. Grant, "The Chemical Paradigm," 65.

121. Ibid., 40.

122. Bensaude-Vincent and Stengers, *A History of Chemistry*, 13, emphasis added.

123. Ibid.

124. I. Grant, "The Chemical Paradigm," 41.

125. Bensaude-Vincent and Stengers, *A History of Chemistry*, 13.

126. Ibid.

127. See also the episode in which Suttree travels through the Smoky Mountains where, at one point, he begins to hallucinate various "*alchemical* game" in the forest, "chimeras and cacodemons" (*S*, 287, emphasis added).

128. Young, "The Imprisonment of Sensibility," 73.

129. Ibid., 75.

130. Ibid., emphasis added. Along these lines, Grammer notes about a scene in which Suttree visits an old plantation of his family: "While thus exploring he recalls a scene from childhood: he and an old man have watched a racehorse run on a track; the old man gestures with his stopwatch and declares that they have seen a wonder, 'a thing against which time would not prevail.' Something to remember, he means, but young Suttree, already given to morbid speculation, thinks only of mortality and time's inevitable way with all of us: he 'had already begun to sicken at the slow seeping of life' [*S* 136]" ("Pastoral and History," 19).

131. Schelling, *SW* II, 395, and "On the World Soul," 92.

132. Jung notes: '"Sal terrae est anima' (the soul is the salt of the earth). This significant proposition . . . contains the entire ambiguity of alchemy" (*Mysterium Coniunctionis* 1, 263 [my translation]). Furthermore, he writes that "apart from its conserving effect, salt mainly alludes to the notion of *sapientia*" (ibid., 1:269 [my translation]).

133. In Suttree's search for Harrogate in the underground caves of Knoxville we can see a kind of brotherly care and sense of social responsibility in the protagonist, but also a tendency that is congruent with his own existential search for meaningfulness in human existence. On this point, see Young, "The Imprisonment of Sensibility," 85.

134. However, a drunken Suttree wonders earlier in the novel: "Do shades nurture? As I have seen my image twinned and blown in the smoked glass of a blind man's spectacles I am, I am" (*S*, 80).

135. On *katabasis* in *Suttree*, see, in particular, Millichap, *A Backward Glance*, 215.

136. Trotignon perceptively remarks, "The encroachment of nature over man may be felt in the way a lot of McCarthy's sentences conclude in landscape descriptions" ("Detailing the Wor(l)d in *Suttree*," 91). And I take it that in McCarthy's fiction, the description of landscapes applies to sceneries both above and under the ground—that is, ungrounded spaces. After all, "as above, so it is below," as Suttree tells J-Bone at one of their gatherings (*S*, 23). Furthermore, what Trotignon beautifully terms "*the slow encroachment of the world's sheer materiality*" ("Detailing the Wor(l)d in *Suttree*," 91) is certainly one of the most appropriate phrases to describe what I have conceptualized as the trauma of the earth in McCarthy's Southern fiction.

137. I. Grant, "The Chemical Paradigm," 40.

4. *"Another Kind of Clay": Physiophilosophy and War*

1. I am using Steven Frye's observation concerning McCarthy and Herman Melville's weaver-god (*Understanding Cormac McCarthy* [Columbia: University of South Carolina Press, 2009], 128). Frye also states that the "generic framework" of the novel, in which "Billy emerges as . . . the young hero of the traditional bildungsroman, the mythic frontier American in the making, [or] the outcast cowboy" in fact "exists primarily to allow for the exploration of philosophical issues, and [that] it is the act of storytelling, the rearticulation of life in the form of narrative, that gives shape and meaning to these considerations" (ibid., 121, 120–21).

2. Richard B. Woodward, "McCarthy's Venomous Fiction," *New York Times Magazine*, April 19, 1992, accessed March 14, 2015, http://www.nytimes.com/1992/04/19/magazine/cormac-mccarthy-s-venomous-fic

tion.html?pagewanted=all." See also Kirk Essary, "'We Languish in Obscurity': The Silence of God as Atavistic Calvinism in Cormac McCarthy's Fiction," *Sounding* 97, no. 3 (2014): 278.

3. Steven Shaviro, "'The Very Life of the Darkness': A Reading of *Blood Meridian*," *Southern Quarterly* 30, no. 4 (1992): 115.

4. Belden C. Lane, *Landscapes of the Sacred: Geography and Narrative in American Spirituality* (1988; Baltimore: Johns Hopkins University Press, 2002), 85, emphasis added.

5. Bryan James Gordon, "Antitopic and Afterthought: Givenness and Grammar in Ponca and Omaha," *Kansas Working Papers in Linguistics* 30 (2008): 74 and 78. What I have italicized (for the sake of consistency) is underlined in Gordon's paper.

6. These notes are to be found in Cormac McCarthy, folder 4, box 35, Cormac McCarthy Papers, Wittliff Collections.

7. Lorenz Oken, *Lehrbuch der Naturphilosophie* (1809–11; Zürich: Friedrich Schultheiß, 1843), iii, and *Elements of Physiophilosophy*, trans. Alfred Tulk (1843; London: C. and J. Adlard Printers, 1847), xi.

8. Oken's concept appeared for the first time in *Die Zeugung*, as he mentions (*Lehrbuch*, iii; *Elements*, xi), but he develops the notion of *Ur-Schleim* fully in his *Elements*. In this earlier work, in which he also cites Schelling's *First Outline of a System of the Philosophy of Nature* on the topic of epigenesis (Lorenz Oken, *Die Zeugung* [Bamberg: Joseph Anton Goebhardt, 1805], 106–7), Oken's Platonism is apparent: "Mathematical propositions are eternally invariant and equally certain, since what are they but tautologies of one and the same . . . positing? Mathematics is the form of materiality that floats above it; it is itself the spiritualized materiality, in all its aspects" (ibid., 23 [my translation]).

9. Oken, *Lehrbuch*, 7; *Elements*, 9.

10. Jay Ellis, "'What Happens to Country' in *Blood Meridian*," *Rocky Mountain Review of Language and Literature* 60, no. 1 (2006): 85.

11. Andrew Keller Estes, *Cormac McCarthy and the Writing of American Spaces* (Amsterdam: Rodopi, 2013), 107.

12. For a representative analysis of McCarthy's work that homes in on its linguistic intricacies, see Phillip A. Snyder and Delys W. Snyder, "Modernism, Postmodernism, and Language: McCarthy's Style," in *The Cambridge Companion to Cormac McCarthy*, ed. Steven Frye (2013; New York: Cambridge University Press, 2014), 31 and 36.

13. Georg Guillemin, *The Pastoral Vision of Cormac McCarthy* (College Station: Texas A&M University Press, 2004), 87; Estes, *American Spaces*, 123.

14. Guillemin, *Pastoral*, 79.

15. Estes, *American Spaces*, 131.

16. Ibid.

17. On that point, note McCarthy's recent and highly unusual foray into the field of linguistics, in the form of his article "The Kekulé Problem," in which he ominously asks the question: "Where did language come from?" (*KP*, 22). While (unsurprisingly) he does not offer a straightforward answer, he does articulate a commitment to the natural sciences in his search for clarification regarding the connection between the nature of linguistic articulation and the dynamics of the unconscious. "Problems," he says, "are often well posed in terms of language and language remains a handy tool for explaining them. But the actual process of thinking—in any discipline—is largely an unconscious affair" (25). What is the unconscious, for McCarthy; what exactly is this "actual process of thinking"? According to him, "the unconscious is a biological system *before* it is anything else" (25, emphasis added). Even though there is much more that could be said about these reflections, in the context of my argument it is safe to say that the author's late turn to nonfiction confirms the entwinement of logocentrism and biocentrism in the thematic setting of his 1985 Western fiction, among other works.

18. Oken, *Lehrbuch*, 19 and 20; *Elements*, 24 and 25.

19. See, for instance, Ciarán Dowd, "The Hum of Mystery: Parataxis, Analepsis, and

Geophysiology in *The Road*," *Cormac McCarthy Journal* 11, no. 1 (2013): 23–43; Markus Wierschem, "The Other End of *The Road*: Re-Reading McCarthy in Light of Thermodynamics and Information Theory," *Cormac McCarthy Journal* 11, no. 1 (2013): 1–22.

20. See, for example, Estes, *American Spaces*, 115; Johanna Skibsrud, "'A History of the Present': Knowledge as Violence in Cormac McCarthy's *Blood Meridian*," *Dandelion* 5, no. 1 (2014): 3 and 4; Sara L. Spurgeon, "Foundations of Empire: The Sacred Hunter and the Eucharist of the Wilderness in Cormac McCarthy's *Blood Meridian*," in *Cormac McCarthy*, ed. Harold Bloom (New York: Infobase Publishing, 2009), 85.

21. Spurgeon, "Foundations of Empire," 85–86.

22. Oken, *Lehrbuch*, iii; *Elements*, xi.

23. Boehme provided the central epigraph that prefigures the plot: "It is not to be thought that the life of darkness is sunk in misery and lost as if in sorrowing. There is no sorrowing. For sorrow is a thing that is swallowed up in death, and death and dying are the very life of the darkness" (quoted in *BM*, n.p.). In McCarthy's first Western and novels like *The Crossing* and *Outer Dark*, as I will show, Boehme (whose writings have reportedly influenced McCarthy's work) can be seen as a missing link between Schelling's and Oken's philosophical delineations of the dynamic process and McCarthy's narrative depiction of nature. On McCarthy and Boehme, see, above all, Edwin T. Arnold, "McCarthy and the Sacred: A Reading of *The Crossing*," in *Cormac McCarthy: New Directions*, ed. James D. Lilley (2002; Albuquerque: University of New Mexico Press, 2014), 223. On Boehme's influence on Schelling, see, for instance, Marie-Elise Zovko, *Natur und Gott: Das wirkungsgeschichtliche Verhältnis Schellings und Baaders* (Würzburg: Königshausen & Neumann, 1996), 80–81; Edward Allen Beach , *The Potencies of God(s): Schelling's Philosophy of Mythology* (Albany: State University of New York Press, 1994), 36–37 and 69–75.

24. Shane Schimpf, *A Reader's Guide to* Blood Meridian (2006; Seattle: BonMot Publishing, 2011), 57.

25. Ibid., 58.

26. See chapter 1 for a discussion of the gnostic readings of *Blood Meridian* in particular and of McCarthy in general.

27. René Wellek, "The Minor Transcendentalists and German Philosophy," *New England Quarterly* 15, no. 4 (1942): 663; Oken, *Lehrbuch*, iii; *Elements*, xi.

28. Schelling, *SW* VII, 378 and 360, and *Philosophical Investigations into the Essence of Human Freedom*, trans. Jeff Love and Johannes Schmidt (Albany: State University of New York Press, 2006), 44 and 29; Peirce C. Mullen, "The Romantic as Scientist: Lorenz Oken," *Studies in Romanticism* 16, no. 3 [1977]: 381.

29. Oken, *Lehrbuch*, iv and 19; *Elements* xii and 24.

30. Oken, *Lehrbuch*, iv; *Elements*, xii.

31. Oken, *Lehrbuch*, 3; *Elements*, 4.

32. I. Grant, *Philosophies of Nature*, 144. Oken, *Lehrbuch*, 11; *Elements*, 14.

33. Oken, *Lehrbuch*, 7; *Elements*, 9.

34. Gilles Deleuze and Félix Guattari, *A Thousand Plateaus: Capitalism and Schizophrenia*, trans. Brian Massumi (1980; London: Continuum, 2004), 405.

35. In this regard, the apparent philosophical alignment of the ideas of Oken and Holden contradicts Brian Evenson's claim that "we might call the judge a nomadologist" ("McCarthy's Wanderers: Nomadology, Violence, and Open Country," in *Sacred Violence: A Reader's Companion to Cormac McCarthy*, ed. Wade Hall and Rick Wallach [El Paso: Texas Western Press, 1995]," 47).

36. Oken, *Lehrbuch*, 7; *Elements*, 9, second emphasis added and translation modified. Tulk translates the phrase "*aus dem Ewigen oder dem Natur-Nichts hervorgegangen*" in the last sentence of this passage as "emerged from the Eternal or nothing of Nature"—that is, in the same way as he translates "*Nichts* der Natur" as "*nothing* of Nature" in the previous sentence. In the con-

text of the present argument, it seems more in accordance with Oken's understanding of the generative zero (namely, that it is part of nature, not its negation) to translate literally instead and write "emerged from the Eternal or the *Nature-Nothing*," in keeping with the philosopher's neologism. Of course, it is impossible to say which option is more faithful to what Oken intended when he wrote this passage.

37. Iain Hamilton Grant, *Philosophies of Nature after Schelling* (2006; London: Continuum, 2008), 94.

38. Ibid.

39. Iain Grant has pointed out today's revival of Oken's generative zero in the work of Alain Badiou ("Being and Slime: The Mathematics of Protoplasm in Lorenz Oken's 'Physio-Philosophy,'" *Collapse* 4 [2008]: 314). What separates the accounts of Badiou and Oken is that for Badiou the concept of nature has no philosophical meaning (ibid., 318). As he writes in *Being and Event* (trans. Oliver Feltham [1988; London: Continuum, 2005], 128), which elaborates a new ontology according to the principles and axioms of set theory, "Naturalness is [simply] the intrinsic normality of a situation." "Nature," for Badiou in fact "has no sayable being" (ibid., 140). Note also, in terms of the connection between Cantorian set theory and nineteenth-century forms of biology, Fernando Zalamea's remark that "Cantor himself is [well] situated in terms of a general *organicism* (with considerable and surprising hopes that his *alephs* would help us understand both the living realm and the world around us), where analytic and synthetic considerations relate to one another" (*Synthetic Philosophy of Contemporary Mathematics*, trans. Zachary Luke Fraser [2009; Falmouth, UK: Urbanomic, 2012], 121).

40. Incidentally, this is also the way in which I read McCarthy's statement that "books are made out of books," that "the novel depends for its life on the novels that have been written" (Woodward, "McCarthy's Venomous Fiction"). There is, in other words, a parallel between the cross-fertilization of literary styles (as I discussed in chapter 1) and the recapitulation of zero in every number.

41. I. Grant, *Philosophies of Nature after Schelling*, 129.

42. Ibid., 120. The origin of the recapitulation thesis is, of course, debatable. Iain Grant believes that the naturalist Carl Friedrich Kielmeyer was the source of "the first proposal of the Me[c]kel-Serres law" in 1793 ("The Chemical Paradigm: Interview with Iain Hamilton Grant." *Collapse* 7 [2011]: 49). For a succinct reiteration of the law's history as conceived by the German *Naturphilosophen*, see Stephen Jay Gould, *Ontogeny and Phylogeny* (Cambridge, MA: Harvard University Press, 1977), 35–47; Robert J. Richards, *The Romantic Conception of Life: Science and Philosophy in the Age of Goethe* (Chicago: University of Chicago Press, 2002), 493–94; Knox Peden, "Alkaline Recapitulation: Haeckel's Hypothesis and the Afterlife of a Concept," *Republics of Letters* 4, no. 1 (2014), accessed March 27, 2015, http://arcade.stanford.edu/rofl/alkaline-recapitulation-haeckels-hypothesis-and-afterlife-concept.

43. Compare this with Zalamea's taxonomy of eidal, quiddital, and archeal mathematics: "We will call movements of ascent eidal (from *eidos* [idea]), movements of descent quiddital (from *quidditas* [what there is]), and the search for conceptual variants in the various forms of transit archeal (from *arkhê* [principal])" (*Synthetic Philosophy of Contemporary Mathematics*, 174).

44. Richards, *The Romantic Conception of Life*, 493.

45. Oken, *Lehrbuch*, 2; *Elements*, 2.

46. Oken, *Lehrbuch*, 7; *Elements*, 9.

47. I. Grant, "Being and Slime," 315.

48. Oken, *Lehrbuch* 19; *Elements* 24.

49. Oken, *Lehrbuch*, 2; *Elements*, 2.

50. Reza Negarestani, "Notes on the Figure of the Cyclone," in *Leper Creativity: Cyclonopedia Symposium*, ed. Ed Keller, Nicola Masciandaro, and Eugene Thacker (New York: Punctum Books, 2012), 295–96. See

also Richards's account of Oken's earlier treatise *Die Zeugung* (*The Romantic Conception of Life*, 493).

51. Iain Hamilton Grant, "Does Nature Stay What-It-Is? Dynamics and the Antecedence Criterion," in *The Speculative Turn: Continental Materialism and Realism*, ed. Levi Bryant, Nick Srnicek, and Graham Harman (Melbourne: re.press, 2011), 69.

52. Ibid.

53. Christopher Dacus, "The West as Symbol of the Eschaton in Cormac McCarthy," *Cormac McCarthy Journal* 7, no. 1 (2009): 11.

54. Oken, *Lehrbuch*, 19–20; *Elements*, 24–25.

55. Oken, *Lehrbuch*, 19, 9, and 13; *Elements*, 24, 11, 16, and 15.

56. Oken, *Lehrbuch*, 523; *Elements*, 665.

57. Oken, *Lehrbuch*, 523; *Elements*, 665.

58. I. Grant, "Being and Slime," 321.

59. See Tim Parrish's argument that this passage from *Blood Meridian* has connections to Ralph Waldo Emerson's essay "Self-Reliance" ("The Killer Wears the Halo: Cormac McCarthy, Flannery O'Connor, and the American Religion," in *Sacred Violence: A Reader's Companion to Cormac McCarthy*, ed. Wade Hall and Rick Wallach [El Paso: Texas Western Press, 1995], 25). Although Emerson knew of Oken's philosophy and even writes about him, as Réne Wellek notes ("Emerson and German Philosophy," *New England Quarterly* 16, no. 1 [1943]: 53–55), I argue that Emerson's tendency to view the natural as a divine realm is not entirely compatible with Oken's ontology—which, on the whole, is much darker in content and more systematically deductive in form, compared to Emerson's free-flowing prose. Wellek, too, is skeptical about their full alignment, even though he argues that their metaphysical standpoints are quite similar: "In defining Emerson's position in relation to the history of German thought, everything points to his affinity with Schelling and Oken, even though it is impossible to ignore the personal and national differences: Emerson's deeper religious roots, his stronger individualism, his finer artistry, his preoccupation with practical morality" (ibid., 54–55). In connection with this, see Douglas Anderson's claim that "Emerson simply moved into the spirit of Schelling's transcendental idealism. Some of the specific Emersonian ideas attributable to Schelling's influence are the 'Over-Soul,' natural divinity, fate, and nature as a living organism" ("Emerson's Schellingian Natures: Origins of and Possibilities for American Environmental Thought," *Cognitio* 8, no. 1 [2007]: 14). Yet as I demonstrated above, one's view of the relationship between Emerson, Schelling, and Oken depends on what importance one accords to Schelling's emphasis on the organic realm of nature, or how one interprets Schelling's notion of the organism. Thus, I side with Wellek instead of Anderson, because in contrast to Iain Grant, Anderson holds that the ideas promoted by the supposedly "Schellingian" Emerson are precursors to "Lamarckian evolution and Bergson's vital force" (ibid., 17).

60. Oken, *Lehrbuch*, 13; *Elements*, 16.

61. Oken, *Lehrbuch*, 13; *Elements*, 16.

62. The novel's concern about one of the chief problems in German philosophy after Kant (namely, the rift between the two realms of nature and freedom) is detectable in the preoccupation of *Blood Meridian* with the dialectical relationship between (nonhuman) fate and (human) agency. Whether or not nature and freedom are to be thought of as irreconcilably separate is one of the key questions that troubled the likes of Johann Gottlieb Fichte, Schelling, and Georg W. F. Hegel (on this and related points, see Iain Hamilton Grant, "'Philosophy Become Genetic': The Physics of the World Soul," in *The New Schelling*, ed. Judith Norman and Alistair Welchman [London: Continuum, 2004], 129–30, and *Philosophies of Nature after Schelling*, 199).

63. Oken, *Lehrbuch*, 13; *Elements*, 16.

64. Iain Hamilton Grant, "The 'Eternal and Necessary Bond Between Philosophy and Physics': A Repetition of the Difference Be-

tween the Fichtean and Schellingian Systems of Philosophy," *Angelaki* 10, no. 1 (2005): 51.

65. Ibid., 57.

66. Oken, *Lehrbuch*, 7; *Elements*, 9.

67. Ellis, "'What Happens to Country' in *Blood Meridian*," 92.

68. Ibid., 91.

69. German Romantic philosophers of nature generally tend "to encourage the employment of a priori speculations in attempts to deduce the order of nature from assumed general ideas" (S. J. Holmes, "Von Baer's Perplexities over Evolution," *Isis* 37, nos. 1&2 [1947]: 8).

70. Manuel DeLanda, *A Thousand Years of Nonlinear History* (Cambridge, MA: MIT Press, 1997), 27. While it is true that DeLanda's more recent work argues that "the concept of Nature . . . suggests a fixed object of study in which everything is given" (*Philosophical Chemistry: Genealogy of a Scientific Field* [London: Bloomsbury, 2015], xi)—similar to Timothy Morton's ecocentric philosophy—his simultaneous rejection of positivism and cultural constructivism is precisely what is needed for any contemporary *Naturphilosophie* (ibid., 136–40). For a view that in part corresponds with Morton's and DeLanda's respective approaches to the concept of "nature—in the singular," see Bruno Latour, *Politics of Nature: How to Bring the Sciences into Democracy*, trans. Catherine Porter (1999; Cambridge, MA: Harvard University Press, 2004), 10.

71. Woodward, "McCarthy's Venomous Fiction." For a recent assessment of the connection between Melville and McCarthy, see Cassie Polasek, "'Books Are Made out of Books': Herman Melville's Moby Dick and Cormac McCarthy's Judge Holden," in *They Rode On: Blood Meridian and the Tragedy of the American West*, ed. Rick Wallach (Miami: Cormac McCarthy Society, 2013), 82–94. Like McCarthy's, Melville's work can be linked to the history of alchemy, as in fact Jed Rasula has done. He writes that in Melville, "the lost world is unrecoverable, and this entails the difficult realization of the alchemical nigredo: the fertilizing dark of the white whale's plummet in *Moby-Dick*, or the dissolution of entire cultures—extinction implicated in the larger creative adventure" (*This Compost: Ecological Imperatives in American Poetry* [2002; Athens: University of Georgia Press, 2012], 51).

72. Jill Barnum, "Melville, Lorenz Oken, and Biology: Engaging the 'Long Now,'" *Leviathan* 7, no. 2 (2005): 44.

73. Ibid. For the original in Oken, see his *Lehrbuch*, 152; *Elements*, 186. A few sentences before this section, Oken writes that "the primary mucus [*Urschleim*], out of [which] every thing organic has been created, is the sea-mucus [*Meerschleim*]" (*Lehrbuch*, 151; *Elements*, 185). For a discussion of this passage, see, in particular, Barnum, "Melville, Lorenz Oken, and Biology," 44.

74. Barnum, "Melville, Lorenz Oken, and Biology," 44.

75. Ibid., 45. Here is the passage in which Ishmael tries to describe the skull of the "Sperm Whale": "But if from the comparative dimensions of the whale's proper brain, you deem it incapable of being adequately charted, then I have another idea for you. If you attentively regard almost any quadruped's spine, you will be struck with the resemblance of its vertebræ to a strung necklace of dwarfed skulls, all bearing rudimental resemblance to the skull proper. It is a German conceit, that the vertebræ are absolutely undeveloped skulls" (Herman Melville, *Moby-Dick; or, The Whale* [New York: Penguin Classics, 2003], 381).

76. On the Vietnam War as a theme in *Blood Meridian*, see, above all, Vince Brewton, "The Changing Landscape of Violence in Cormac McCarthy's Early Novels and the Border Trilogy," *Southern Literary Journal* 37, no. 1 (2004): 129–32. On the motif of the human ear necklace as indicative of the practical perversities of manifest destiny, Spurgeon states: "Indeed the native people to whom those ears belonged are viewed by the scalphunters more as natural resources than human beings, just another part of an in-

finitely exploitable landscape" ("Foundations of Empire," 94). Regarding the connection of the practice of collecting human ears in Vietnam to McCarthy's work, see Peter Josyph's comparison of passages from Michael Herr's *Dispatches* (1977) with *Blood Meridian* (*Cormac McCarthy's House: Reading McCarthy without Walls* [Austin: University of Texas Press, 2013], 258).

77. Cormac McCarthy, notes on "Whales and Men," 95, folder 5, box 97, Cormac McCarthy Papers, Wittliff Collections. Incidentally, this passage bears a strong resemblance to a section in *Suttree*, where the protagonist describes his own birth and that of his twin brother, "Antisuttree," in a hallucinating stream of consciousness passage: "I followed him into the world, me. A breech birth. *Hind end fore in common with whales* and bats, life forms meant for other mediums than the earth and having no affinity for it" (*S*, 14, emphasis added).

78. See, for instance, John C. Malone's eulogy for Quine ("Ontology Recapitulates Philology: Willard Quine, Pragmatism, and Radical Behaviorism," *Behavior and Philosophy* 29 [2001]: 63 and 67).

79. In terms of the present argument and its partial reliance on McCarthy's allusion to the biogenetic law in his "Whales and Men," it must be conceded that McCarthy might have very well not have been thinking of Oken when he writing the dialogue cited above. Instead, he could have been alluding to other philosophers of nature from the same period, or even to Haeckel—which is even more likely, since the latter is the best known of the naturalists who conceived of recapitulation in biological terms). However, the many instances in which *Blood Meridian*, *Moby-Dick*, and the *Elements of Physiophilosophy* resonate in striking ways support the argument that Oken's work was the basis of McCarthy's understanding of the recapitulation thesis.

80. Oken, *Lehrbuch*, 151; *Elements*, 185.

81. DeLanda, *A Thousand Years*, 27.

82. Oken, *Lehrbuch*, 523; *Elements*, 665.

83. Ellis, "'What Happens to Country' in *Blood Meridian*," 85.

84. Indeed, the Okenian reading in the present chapter is to an extent compatible with Nietzsche-inspired approaches of a certain kind, a very popular perspective in the scholarship of *Blood Meridian*. In this regard, Christian J. Emden's *Nietzsche's Naturalism: Philosophy and the Life Sciences in the Nineteenth Century* [Cambridge: Cambridge University Press, 2014], 45) is of particular interest, as it demonstrates Nietzsche's commitment to a view that sees human reason and living nature in a single continuum. Furthermore, Emden notes, "Oken's publications appear on Nietzsche's reading lists during the 1860s" (ibid., 46).

85. John Emil Sepich, *Notes on* Blood Meridian (1993; Austin: University of Texas Press, 2011), 111.

86. Although Lydia Cooper states that "*The Crossing* . . . stylistically resembles *Blood Meridian*" (*No More Heroes: Narrative Perspective and Morality in Cormac McCarthy* [Baton Rouge: Louisiana State University Press, 2011], 83), this is arguably an overstatement, given the engaged and affect-laden passages that describe the relationship between the two brothers in the 1994 novel.

87. As I did above, in the case of *optical democracy*, from this point on I refer to the notion of *the void* in italics—whenever it is not part of a quotation, that is—for the sake of stylistic consistency.

88. Frye, *Understanding Cormac McCarthy*, 4.

89. Dianne C. Luce, "The Road and the Matrix: The World as Tale in *The Crossing*," in *Perspectives on Cormac McCarthy*, ed. Edwin T. Arnold and Dianne C. Luce (Jackson: University Press of Mississippi. 1999), 208, emphasis added.

90. Arnold, "McCarthy and the Sacred," 221.

91. See Erik Hage, *Cormac McCarthy: A Literary Companion* (Jefferson, NC: McFarland and Company, 2010) 88.

92. For a wholly different approach to this particular passage, see Nicholas Monk, "Versions of the *Seeleroman*: Cormac McCarthy and Leslie Silko," in *Intertextual and Interdisciplinary Approaches to Cormac McCarthy: Borders and Crossings*, ed. Nicholas Monk (New York: Routledge, 2012), 180–81.

93. Arnold, "McCarthy and the Sacred," 216.

94. Ibid., 221.

95. Ibid., 216.

96. On the philosophical thesis of panpsychism, one version of which holds that mind is a property that belongs to all beings in the world, not just to human beings (or better, all processes in the world), see David Skrbina, *Panpsychism in the West* (Cambridge, MA: MIT Press, 2005). Note also that Steven Shaviro has not only written on McCarthy's *Blood Meridian* but has also published *The Universe Of Things: On Speculative Realism* (Minneapolis: University of Minnesota Press, 2014), in which he proposes a comparable panpsychist metaphysics modeled after the work of Alfred North Whitehead.

97. Friedrich W. J. Schelling, "*Timaeus*" (Stuttgart–Bad Cannstatt: Frommann-Holzbog, 1994), 28 (translation modified). I am partially modifying, yet still relying upon, Iain Grant's translation of this passage in Schelling's commentary (quoted in *Philosophies of Nature after Schelling*, 41), which romanizes the two Greek terms in Schelling's text.

98. Arnold, "McCarthy and the Sacred," 216.

99. I. Grant, "Philosophy Become Genetic," 133.

100. Schelling, *SW* VII, 370, and *Philosophical Investigations*, 38.

101. See Schelling, "*Timaeus*," 32.

102. I. Grant, *Philosophies of Nature after Schelling*, 41.

103. Cormac McCarthy, notes on "Whales and Men," folder 2, box 97, Cormac McCarthy Papers, Wittliff Collections, emphasis added. Note the way the narrator ascribes a certain intelligence to the she-wolf that successfully avoids the traps laid out for it: "She circled the set for the better part of an hour sorting and indexing the various scents and ordering their sequences in an effort to reconstruct the events that had taken place there" (*TC*, 26). Arnold writes about this passage that "the wolf, in its natural world, 'reads' its environment by engaging it in an intimacy unknown to or forgotten by man," an engagement on the part of the animal that "suggests a deeper knowledge" ("McCarthy and the Sacred," 219). But consider also McCarthy's early reflections on the issue of panpsychism in *Blood Meridian*, where the narrator assumes a very similar form of "thought" to the one expressed in the notes for "Whales and Men": "Under the hooves of the horses the alabaster sand shaped itself in whorls strangely symmetric like iron filings in a field and these shapes flared and drew back again, resonating upon that harmonic ground and then turning to swirl away over the playa. As if the very sediment of things contained yet *some residue of sentience*. As if in the transit of those riders were a thing so profoundly terrible as to register even to the uttermost granulation of reality" (*TC*, 247).

104. Note how the notion of the "alcahest" (or "alkahest") once again establishes a thematic bridge between the Border Trilogy and the motifs of decomposition and alchemical practices in McCarthy's earlier work. Paulo A. Porto explains the origin of this archaic sounding term this way: "The word *alkahest* seems to have been coined by Paracelsus, but the concept was fully developed only later. . . . Sometimes it is mentioned under other names—as, for instance, *universale solvens, dissolvens immutabile, ignis aqua, ignis gehennae, summus atque felicissimus salium, liquor unicus*, and *liquor exiguus*. The contexts in which these names appear allow us to conclude that they apply to the same concept. According to van Helmont [a Belgian alchemist who lived from 1579 until 1644, according to Porto], the alkahest was a liquor capable of dissolving any material substance without leaving residues. In this process, it would not undergo change either in quality

or in quantity, while the substance to be dissolved would be reduced to its *primum ens* (first being)—a state in which it would retain its specific virtues (e.g., its medicinal properties) and would be free of any impurities. . . . The possibility of obtaining a universal solvent is one of the traditional alchemical themes that van Helmont assimilated and reworked. The 'dissolution' of a substance to its 'primary matter' was generally recognized as one of the steps in alchemical work" ("'*Summus atque felicissimus salium*': The Medical Relevance of the *Liquor alkahest*," *Bulletin of the History of Medicine* 76, no. 1 [2002]: 5 and 8). Perhaps the "blood's alcahest" (*TC*, 73) in the case of Suttree is alcohol, the "universal solvent" that both disentangles his life and purifies it, so he can leave Knoxville at the ending of the novel.

105. I. Grant, "Antecedence Criterion," 69.

106. I am using S. K. Robisch's translation of the *brujo*'s Spanish here ("The Trapper Mystic: Werewolves in The Crossing," in *Myth, Legend, Dust: Critical Responses to Cormac McCarthy*, ed. Rick Wallach [Manchester, UK: Manchester University Press, 2000], 291).

107. Schelling, *SW* VII, 370, and *Philosophical Investigations*, 38.

108. Oken, *Lehrbuch*, 13; *Elements*, 16.

109. Oken, *Lehrbuch*, 38; *Elements*, 47, emphasis added.

110. Arnold, "McCarthy and the Sacred," 224.

111. Cormac McCarthy, notes on "Whales and Men," folder 2, box 97, Cormac McCarthy Papers, Wittliff Collections.

112. Nick Land, *Fanged Noumena: Collected Writings 1987–2007* (Falmouth, UK: Urbanomic, 2012), 496.

113. Frye, *Understanding Cormac McCarthy*, 121.

114. Ibid., 127. This is the full passage from *Moby-Dick*: "It was a wondrous sight. The wood was green as mosses of the Icy Glen; the trees stood high and haughty, feeling their living sap; the industrious earth beneath was as a weaver's loom, with a gorgeous carpet on it, whereof the ground-vine tendrils formed the warp and woof, and the living flowers the figures. All the trees, with all their laden branches; all the shrubs, and ferns, and grasses; the message-carrying air; all these unceasingly were active. Through the lacings of the leaves, the great sun seemed a flying shuttle weaving the unwearied verdure" (Melville, *Moby-Dick*, 489–90).

115. Melville, *Moby-Dick*, 490, emphasis added.

116. Consider a passage in *The Crossing*, when the atmosphere in a bar has become very tense after a few Mexican soldiers require Billy to drink mescal with them: "He looked across the table at the youngest man who sat slightly apart with his hat down over his forehead and his full glass in both hands before him like an offering. Who'd so far said no word at all. The whole room had begun to *hum* very slightly" (*TC*, 359, emphasis added). Consider also how the narrator of *Cities of the Plain* describes Magdalena's body when she has one of her epileptic fits: "[Eduardo] felt the tremor of her like the *hum* of a current running in her bones" (*CP*, 183, emphasis added). And in another example, after John Grady has seen Magdalena's corpse with her throat slit by Tiburcio, the narrator describes her lover riding through the night: "it was dark and windy and starless and cold and the sacaton grass along the creek thrashed in the wind and the small bare trees he passed *hummed* like wires" (ibid., 233, emphasis added).

117. Frye, *Understanding Cormac McCarthy*, 128.

118. Ibid.

119. Oken, *Lehrbuch*, 7; *Elements*, 9.

120. Oken, *Lehrbuch*, 13; *Elements*, 16. As I mentioned above, in my distinction between a strong and a weak form of panpsychism, I am chiefly inspired by Quentin Meillassoux's separation of "strong" and "weak correlationism" (*After Finitude: An Essay on the Necessity of Contingency*, trans. Ray Brassier [2006; London: Continuum, 2009],

30). For a related version of this distinction among various forms of panpsychism, see Val Plumwood, *Feminism and the Mastery of Nature* (London: Routledge, 1993), 132 and 209.

121. Arnold, "McCarthy and the Sacred," 224.

122. Cormac McCarthy, notes on "Whales and Men," folder 2, box 97, Cormac McCarthy Papers, Wittliff Collections.

123. Concerning the centrality of the first interpolated tale, Frye writes: "The interchange between the priest and the [heretic] pensioner, told to Billy, functions as one of the novel's thematic lynch-pins, making *The Crossing* itself an act of witness encompassing all the individual acts of its characters" (*Understanding Cormac McCarthy*, 124).

124. Oken, *Lehrbuch*, 13; *Elements*, 16.

125. Frye, *Understanding Cormac McCarthy*, 124.

126. Ibid.

127. I do not use the term "speculative fiction" in the generic sense of the term here, so I have marked it accordingly.

128. According to this view, thought is ultimately reducible to its neurophysiological production, regardless of the latter's importance for any material assessment of the former: "Schelling perhaps saw more clearly: he knew that thought was not always encapsulated within the brain, that it could be everywhere . . . outside . . . in the morning dew" (Gilles Châtelet, *Figuring Space: Philosophy, Mathematics, and Physics* [Dordrecht: Kluwer Academic Publishers, 2000], 14).

129. See James R. Giles, "*Outer Dark* and Romantic Naturalism," in *The Cambridge Companion to Cormac McCarthy*, ed. Steven Frye (New York: Cambridge University Press, 2014), 95.

130. The Spanish translations are from Jim Campbell, "A Translation of Spanish Passages in *The Crossing*," accessed November 29, 2017, http://www.cormacmccarthy.com/wp-content/uploads/CrossingTrans.pdf.

131. Richards, *The Romantic Conception of Life*, 305.

5. "Malignant Life": Indifference, Identity, and Narrative Extainment

1. Bertrand Westphal, foreword to *Geocritical Explorations: Space, Place, and Mapping in Literary and Cultural Studies*, ed. Robert T. Tally Jr. (New York: Palgrave Macmillan, 2011), xii.

2. Bernd Herzogenrath, "Nature | Geophilosophy | Machinics | Ecosophy," in *Deleuze | Guattari & Ecology*, ed. Bernd Herzogenrath (New York: Palgrave Macmillan, 2009), 1.

3. Bertrand Westphal, *Geocriticism: Real and Fictional Spaces*, trans. Robert T. Tally Jr. (2007; Basingstoke: Palgrave Macmillan, 2011), 169.

4. Schelling, *SW* XIII, 161, and *The Grounding of Positive Philosophy: The Berlin Lectures*, trans. Bruce Matthews. (Albany: State University of New York Press, 2007), 203.

5. Andrew Bowie writes: "The date of the Lectures has not been finally established. . . . The probable date is 1833–34, but there is also evidence to suggest 1836–7" ("Translator's Introduction," in Friedrich W. J. Schelling, *On the History of Modern Philosophy*, trans. Andrew Bowie [Cambridge: Cambridge University Press, 1994], 1).

6. Schelling, *SW* X, 143–44, and *On the History of Modern Philosophy*, trans. Andrew Bowie (Cambridge: Cambridge University Press, 1994), 147.

7. Westphal, *Geocriticism*, 86.

8. Iain Hamilton Grant, "How Nature Came to Be Thought: Schelling's Paradox and the Problem of Location," *Journal of the British Society for Phenomenology* 44, no. 1 (2013): 30 and 40–41.

9. Ibid., 28.

10. Ibid., 31 and 32.

11. Ibid., 40.

12. Iain Hamilton Grant, "Everything," *Monist* 98, no. 2 (2015): 166.

13. Westphal, *Geocriticism*, 85, emphasis added.

14. Cormac McCarthy, notes on "Whales and Men," folder 2, box 97, Cormac McCarthy Papers, Wittliff Collections.

15. I. Grant, "How Nature Came to Be Thought," 30.

16. Westphal, *Geocriticism*, 169.

17. I. Grant, "How Nature Came to Be Thought," 27.

18. Here is the full passage from Grant's discussion of Schelling's remark from *On the History of Modern Philosophy*, in which he clarifies why, paradoxically, the iteration of "the 'whole world" is always "*less than* the world," already hinting at the critical insight that any appeal to the absolute (including the divine) is always firmly grounded in natural process: "The difficulty here is clearly expressed: it is the *whole* world (WW) that reason captures and there is more than reason in the world (W). But if W contains 'more' than WW, then either reason, being part of W, does not for that reason contain WW and the statement simply contradicts itself, or the wholeness of the world is an artefact of the reason that contains it, so that the 'whole world' is *less than* the world, an abstraction from it, perhaps" (ibid.).

19. I. Grant, "Everything," 166.

20. Schelling, *SW* X, 143–44, and *On the History of Modern Philosophy*, 147.

21. Schelling, *SW* II, 55–56, and *Ideas for a Philosophy of Nature*, trans. Errol E. Harris and Peter Heath (Cambridge: Cambridge University Press, 1988), 41–42.

22. Katie Owens-Murphy, "The Frontier Ethic behind Cormac McCarthy's Southern Fiction," *Arizona Quarterly* 67, no. 2 (2011): 161.

23. James R. Giles, "*Outer Dark* and Romantic Naturalism," in *The Cambridge Companion to Cormac McCarthy*, ed. Steven Frye (New York: Cambridge University Press, 2014), 97.

24. Christopher Metress, "*Via Negativa*: The Way of Unknowing in Cormac McCarthy's *Outer Dark*," *Southern Review* 37, no. 1 (2001): 154.

25. Oliver Mort, "'Are We Still the Good Guys?' Cormac McCarthy and the Postmodern Heroic Quest," in *They Rode On:* Blood Meridian *and the Tragedy of the American West*, ed. Rick Wallach (Miami: Cormac McCarthy Society, 2013), 248.

26. Metress, "*Via Negativa*," 154.

27. Edwin T. Arnold, "Naming, Knowing and Nothingness: McCarthy's Moral Parables." *Southern Quarterly* 30, no. 4 (1992): 32. See also William J. Schafer, "Cormac McCarthy: The Hard Wages of Original Sin," *Appalachian Journal* 4, no. 2 (1977): 112.

28. Cormac McCarthy, notes on *Blood Meridian*, folder 6, box 35, Cormac McCarthy Papers, Wittliff Collections.

29. Martin Erickson, *Beautiful Mathematics* (Washington: Mathematical Association of America, 2011), 1.

30. Certainly, what Steven Frye has stated with regard to *Blood Meridian* can also be applied to *Outer Dark*, as well as most of McCarthy's other novels: "Although McCarthy's interest in violence may be in part political, it is in a deeper sense *ontological*" ("*Blood Meridian* and the Poetics of Violence," in *The Cambridge Companion to Cormac McCarthy*, ed. Steven Frye (2013; New York: Cambridge University Press, 2014), 109, emphasis added.

31. See Marie-Elise Zovko, *Natur und Gott: Das wirkungsgeschichtliche Verhältnis Schellings und Baaders* (Würzburg: Königshausen & Neumann, 1996), 80–81; Edward Allen Beach , *The Potencies of God(s): Schelling's Philosophy of Mythology* (Albany: State University of New York Press, 1994), 36–37 and 69–75.

32. Schelling, *SW* VII, 360, and *Philosophical Investigations into the Essence of Human Freedom*, trans. Jeff Love and Johannes Schmidt (Albany: State University of New York Press, 2006), 29.

33. Schelling, *SW* VII, 360, and *Philosophical Investigations*, 29.

34. Arnold, "Naming, Knowing and Nothingness," 32.

35. Schelling, *SW* VII, 360, and *Philosophical Investigations*, 29.

36. Devin Zane Shaw, *Freedom and Nature in Schelling's Philosophy of Art* (London : Continuum, 2010), 76. Shaw helpfully

glosses this notion thus: "Aesthetic intuition produces from the identity of subject and object, of conscious (free) and unconscious (natural) activity; it is 'intellectual intuition become objective' [*SW* III, 625, and *Transcendental Idealism*, 229] through the work of art" (Shaw, *Freedom and Nature*, 65–66).

37. On allegory in *Outer Dark*, see Vereen M. Bell, *The Achievement of Cormac McCarthy* (Baton Rouge: Louisiana State University Press, 1988), 33; Russell M. Hillier, "'In a Dark Parody' of John Bunyan's *The Pilgrim's Progress*: The Presence of Subversive Allegory in Cormac McCarthy's *Outer Dark*," *ANQ* 19, no. 4 (2006): 53.

38. Cormac McCarthy, notes on *Outer Dark*, 14, folder 1, box 9, Cormac McCarthy Papers, Wittliff Collections. Interestingly, McCarthy included the following passage in an even earlier version of *Outer Dark*, emphasizing Culla's awkward religiosity in a monologue that was omitted from the final manuscript of the novel: "God, he said, I am sorry for what I done. Still faceupward in the fine rain. Then he said, no, I aint sorry neither. I'm sorry for what happent is all. You know what I aim to do. So they aint no need in. . . . Hep me, he said. For her is the only reason I ast it. She dont know no better. Hep me for her. He lowered his face and looked about him. Then he looked up again and said, quite softly, Amen" (notes on *Outer Dark*, folder 1, box 8, Cormac McCarthy Papers, Wittliff Collections).

39. On this point, see Alan Richardson, "Rethinking Romantic Incest: Human Universals, Literary Representation, and the Biology of the Mind," *New Literary History* 31, no. 3 (2000): 553.

40. Cormac McCarthy, notes on *Outer Dark*, folder 1, box 9, Cormac McCarthy Papers, Wittliff Collections.

41. Lorenz Oken, *Lehrbuch der Naturphilosophie* (1809–11; Zürich: Friedrich Schultheiß, 1843), 7, and *Elements of Physiophilosophy*, trans. Alfred Tulk (1843; London: C. and J. Adlard Printers, 1847), 9.

42. Schelling, *SW* III, 312, and *First Outline of a System of the Philosophy of Nature*, trans. Keith Peterson (Albany: State University of New York Press, 2004), 222.

43. Schelling, *SW* III, 309; and *First Outline of a System of the Philosophy of Nature*, 219. It is important to note that directly after this characterization of the nature of difference, Schelling specifies his viewpoint by saying that "the difference [of contraries] must not be looked upon as a difference at all, and is nothing for intuition, except through a third that sustains it—to which change itself adheres" (*SW* III, 309; and *First Outline of a System of the Philosophy of Nature*, 219–20).

44. Dianne C. Luce, *Reading the World: Cormac McCarthy's Tennessee Period* (2009; Columbia: University of South Carolina Press, 2010), 97.

45. Ibid., 97–98, emphasis added.

46. See Markus Wierschem's ingenious interpretation of the squire's name in the same context that most scholars so far have used to read the novel's title,—namely, the book of Matthew. Wierschem writes: "The squire self-righteously asserts that 'shiftlessness is a sin' and espouses working 'daybreak to backbreak for a Godgiven dollar' [*OD*, 48], even as he himself exploits both Culla and his black servants. . . . As elsewhere in the novel, names are significant here: divorced from the core virtue of charity, *Salter* is a prime example of another of Jesus's famous metaphors, the 'salt of the earth' (Matt. 5:13) mentioned in the beatitudes, which, gone stale is 'cast out' and trodden under foot not unlike the unprofitable servant. Furthermore, his name evokes the musical poems and prayers of the Book of Psalms, the *Psalter*" ("'Some Witless Paraclete Beleaguered with All Limbo's Clamor': On Violent Contagion and Apocalyptic Logic in Cormac McCarthy's *Outer Dark*," *Contagion* 22 [2015]: 192).

47. Tim Parrish, "The Killer Wears the Halo: Cormac McCarthy, Flannery O'Connor, and the American Religion," in *Sacred Violence: A Reader's Companion to Cormac McCarthy*, ed. Wade Hall and Rick Wallach (El Paso: Texas Western Press, 1995), 39.

48. John M. Grammer, "A Thing against Which Time Will Not Prevail: Pastoral and History in Cormac McCarthy's South," *Southern Quarterly* 30, no. 4 (1992): 24.

49. Ibid.

50. Ibid.

51. On the link between Culla and the triune, see also Arnold, "Naming, Knowing and Nothingness," 44; Georg Guillemin, *The Pastoral Vision of Cormac McCarthy* (College Station: Texas A&M University Press, 2004), 68.

52. Cormac McCarthy, notes on *Outer Dark*, 187, folder 1, box 9, Cormac McCarthy Papers, Wittliff Collections.

53. Cormac McCarthy, notes on *Outer Dark*, folder 1, box 8, Cormac McCarthy Papers, Wittliff Collections. On the distorted image of the Holy Trinity in the form of the triune in *Outer Dark*, see Hillier, "The Presence of Subversive Allegory in Cormac McCarthy's *Outer Dark*," 56–57.

54. Friedrich W. J. Schelling, "*Timaeus*" (Stuttgart–Bad Cannstatt: Frommann-Holzbog, 1994), 28 (translation modified).

55. See Guillemin's statement that "the fact that Culla's complicity with the triune calls these sub-characters into being does not imply his consent to, or even awareness of, the triune's genesis; no pact is signed. The complicity is inscribed by the narrator who creates the characters, the pastoral world, and the terrorism in the image of his own psyche" (*Pastoral*, 68).

56. Schelling, *SW* VII, 370, and *Philosophical Investigations*, 38.

57. Schelling, *SW* VIII, 200, and *The Ages of the World*, trans. Frederick de Wolfe Bolman Jr. (New York: Columbia University Press, 1942), 84. Needless to say, the century in which McCarthy started writing his novels and dramatic texts is replete with examples of just such behavior.

58. Schelling, *SW* VIII, 200, and *The Ages of the World*, 84.

59. Note also the similarity in diction between this scene and the one describing the disintegration of the Green Fly Inn's porch, which I examined in my reading of *The Orchard Keeper* in chapter 3: of the three murderers it is the "mute one" (*OD*, 244) who devours Culla's child in this subverted pose of the supplicant, while the "attitudes" of the men descending into the pile of glass and dirt, together with the porch, is named "mute supplication" (*TOK*, 25) by the narrator of McCarthy's first novel.

60. Lydia R. Cooper, *No More Heroes: Narrative Perspective and Morality in Cormac McCarthy* [Baton Rouge: Louisiana State University Press, 2011], 37.

61. Ibid., 37–38.

62. Schelling, *SW* III, 309, and *First Outline*, 219.

63. Ann Fisher-Wirth, "Abjection and 'the Feminine' in *Outer Dark*," in *Cormac McCarthy: New Directions*, ed. James D. Lilley (2002; Albuquerque: University of New Mexico Press, 2014), 136.

64. Ibid., 137.

65. See Shaw, *Freedom and Nature*, 3.

66. Steven Frye argues that "*Cities of the Plain* involves a single plot with at least two thematic emphases, each centering on a character," with Grady representing the side of "heroic pursuits, . . . romance and nostalgia," and Billy representing "one of McCarthy's basic concerns; that is, the tension between the ideal and the real, the interiors of human conception and the concrete fundamentals of the world, in essence, between dreams and their alternative in the tactile present" (*Understanding Cormac McCarthy* [Columbia: University of South Carolina Press, 2009], 133). Even though Frye has a point when he writes that the two "mythic heroes" embody "romantic" and "realist" (ibid., 132) types, respectively, I would argue that the kind of narrative extainment that is at stake in the first and second volumes of the Border Trilogy from the standpoint of John Grady deals as much with the question of the nature of "the tension between the ideal and the real, the interiors of human conception," as Billy's narrative does, albeit from a different angle—namely, the extainment of nature's identity

via the generation of ethics as a free expression of nature.

67. I am excluding the novel's epilogue from this chapter's argument, since this later part of the novel merely describes Billy's life after John Grady's death and is, therefore, less interesting in terms of the type of narrative extainment I want to focus on.

68. Arnold emphasizes the unusually hopeful atmosphere that permeates McCarthy's 1992 novel ("Naming, Knowing and Nothingness," 47).

69. This is how the narrator depicts the intimate scene, in which John Grady speaks to God while "[holding] his bloodied claw of a hand over the severed wall of his stomach. Holding himself close that he not escape from himself for he felt it over and over, that lightness that he took for his soul and which stood so tentatively at the door of his corporeal self. Like some light-footed animal that stood testing the air at the open door of a cage. . . . Help me, he said. If you think I'm worth it. Amen" (*CP*, 256–57).

70. Iain Hamilton Grant, "'World' in Middle Schelling: Why Nature Transcendentalises," *Pli* 26 (2014): 108.

71. Cooper, *No More Heroes*, 65.

72. E. Douka Kabitoglou, *Plato and the English Romantics* (1990; New York: Routledge, 2013), 207.

73. Iain Hamilton Grant, *Philosophies of Nature after Schelling*, (2006. London: Continuum, 2008), 16.

74. Schelling, *SW* III, 309, and *First Outline*, 219, emphasis added.

75. Herman Melville, *Moby-Dick; or, The Whale* (New York: Penguin Classics, 2003), 382.

76. For a recent example of such a reading, see David Gugin, "The Blood of a Nomad: Environmental Stylistics and *All the Pretty Horses*," in *Cormac McCarthy's Borders and Landscapes*, ed. Louise Jillett (New York: Bloomsbury, 2016), 92.

77. Arnold, "Naming, Knowing and Nothingness," 47.

78. The Romanticism evoked by this passage is substantiated a few pages later, when the narrator describes John Grady falling asleep "as he lay in his cot" at Don Héctor's ranch: "as he was drifting to sleep his thoughts were of horses and of the open country and of horses. Horses still wild on the mesa who'd never seen a man afoot and who knew nothing of him or his life yet in whose souls he would come to reside forever" (*PH*, 117–18).

79. Cooper, *No More Heroes*, 65.

80. Jane Bennett, *Vibrant Matter: A Political Ecology of Things* (Durham, NC: Duke University Press, 2010), 63 and 10.

81. Cormac McCarthy, notes on *Outer Dark*, folder 2, box 9, Cormac McCarthy Papers, Wittliff Collections.

82. Iain Hamilton Grant, "The Universe in the Universe: German Idealism and the Natural History of Mind," *Royal Institute of Philosophy Supplement* 72 (2013): 309.

83. For another reading of this passage, see Petra Mundik, *A Bloody and Barbarous God: The Metaphysics of Cormac McCarthy* (Albuquerque: University of New Mexico Press, 2016), 110.

84. To remind the reader, here is the passage: "In the spring or warmer weather when the snow thaws in the woods the tracks of winter reappear on slender pedestals and the snow reveals *in palimpsest* old buried wanderings, struggles, scenes of death. Tales of winter brought to light again like time turned back upon itself" (*COG*, 130. emphasis added).

85. I. Grant, "How Nature Came to Be Thought," 40.

86. Schelling, *SW* VIII, 200, and *The Ages of the World*, 84.

87. Megan Riley McGilchrist, *The Western Landscape in Cormac McCarthy and Wallace Stegner: Myths of the Frontier* (New York: Routledge, 2010), 127.

88. Frye, *Understanding Cormac McCarthy*, 136.

89. Schelling, *SW* VIII, 200, and *The Ages of the World*, 84 (translation modified).

90. I. Grant, "How Nature Came to Be Thought," 40.

6. "The Ashes of Its Ruin": Writing Nature between Orphism and Prometheanism

1. Pierre Hadot, *The Veil of Isis: An Essay on the History of the Idea of Nature*, trans. Michael Chase (2004; Cambridge, MA: Harvard University Press, 2008), 98.

2. Richard Powers, *Orfeo* (New York: W. W. Norton, 2014; *Prometheus*. DVD. Directed by Ridley Scott. Burbank, CA: Twentieth Century Fox, 2012.) See also, for instance, Carl Kerényi's classic study (1959), *Prometheus: Archetypal Image of Human Existence* (trans. Ralph Manheim [Princeton, NJ: Princeton University Press, 1991]).

3. On the figure of Prometheus in *Blood Meridian*, see, in particular, Harold Bloom, *Novelists and Novels* (Philadelphia, PA: Chelsea House, 2005), 583. On McCarthy's allusion to the legend of Orpheus and his wife, Eurydice, see Kenneth Lincoln, *Cormac McCarthy: American Canticles* (New York: Palgrave Macmillan, 2009), 132).

4. Hadot, *The Veil of Isis*, 1.

5. Ibid.

6. Ibid., 155.

7. In my recounting of the myth I am relying heavily on Carol Dougherty, *Prometheus* (London: Routledge, 2006), 35–37. For an excellent discussion of this myth and its persisting impact on contemporary culture, see Christopher John Müller, *Prometheanism: Technology, Digital Culture and Human Obsolescence* (Lanham, MD: Rowman and Littlefield, 2016).

8. Scott D. Yarbrough, "Tricksters and Lightbringers in McCarthy's Post-Appalachian Novels," *Cormac McCarthy Journal* 10, no. 1 (2012): 48.

9. Ray Brassier, "Prometheanism and Its Critics," in *#Accelerate: The Accelerationist Reader*, ed. Robin Mackay and Armen Avanessian (Falmouth, UK: Urbanomic, 2014), 469. In addition to being one of the four initiators of speculative realism, Brassier is also a forthright promoter of the "Promethean attitude" (ibid.).

10. Dougherty, *Prometheus*, 34. It is true that, as Dougherty writes, "for all their cleverness and wit, tricksters are also often portrayed as dull-witted, responsible for disorder and chaos. In the trickster narrative, cunning and stupidity go together, each one illuminating the other." Following Kerényi, she adds that "the positive and negative qualities of the traditional trickster figure are expressed in the Greek tradition through the two brothers Prometheus and Epimetheus" (ibid.), the former being the clever one and the other being "dull-witted." Even though there are many dull-witted characters in McCarthy's fiction, and it would be promising to read these vis-à-vis the figure of Epimetheus, for reasons of my argument here I emphasize the role of Prometheus and his contrapuntal position with regard to Orpheus, along the lines of Hadot's *The Veil of Isis*. For a contemporary interpretation of the myth of the "dull-witted" brother of Prometheus from a philosophical point of view, see Bernard Stiegler's magisterial *Technics and Time*, vol. 1, *The Fault of Epimetheus* (trans. Richard Beardsworth and George Collins (1994; Stanford, CA: Stanford University Press, 1998).

11. Brassier, "Prometheanism and Its Critics," 470.

12. Dougherty, *Prometheus*, 17.

13. Ridley Scott, "Interview," in "Prometheus Crew: On a Mission Collision," 2011, accessed January 27, 2015, http://pop.inquirer.net/?s=prometheus.

14. My mention of Scott's movie is not arbitrary: merely a year after *Prometheus*, the filmmaker directed *The Counselor*, a movie for which McCarthy wrote the screenplay.

15. Schelling, *SW* XIII, 427.

16. I am drawing here on Judith E. Bernstock, *Under the Spell of Orpheus: The Persistence of a Myth in Twentieth-Century Art* (Carbondale: Southern Illinois University Press, 1991), xvii; and Bertrand Mathieu, *Orpheus in Brooklyn: Orphism, Rimbaud, and Henry Miller* (the Hague: Mouton, 1976), 48. On Orpheus and literature, see also Maurice Blanchot, *The Space of Literature*, trans. Ann Smock (1955; Lincoln: University of Nebraska Press, 1982), 171–76.

17. Brassier, "Prometheanism and Its Critics," 478.

18. Hadot, *The Veil of Isis*, 96.

19. Schelling, *SW* VII, 60, and *Philosophical Investigations into the Essence of Human Freedom*, trans. Jeff Love and Johannes Schmidt (Albany: State University of New York Press, 2006), 29.

20. Hadot, *The Veil of Isis*, 98.

21. Along these lines, Mathieu suggests that "Rimbaud, Hart Crane, and Henry Miller" are also "writers who taught themselves how to revindicate the role of the poet in the face of modern horrors by tactically combining the stance of Prometheus and Orpheus, the defiant firestealer and the resourceful singer" (*Orpheus in Brooklyn*, 12). The connection to Miller seems especially important, as McCarthy was reportedly influenced by Miller (Peter Josyph, *Adventures in Reading Cormac McCarthy* [Lanham, MD: Scarecrow Press, 2010], 12).

22. Yarbrough, "Tricksters and Lightbringers," 47.

23. Andy DuMont, "Luminous Deceptions: Contingent Community and Aesthetic Form in Cormac McCarthy's *The Road*," *Cormac McCarthy Journal* 10, no. 1 (2012): 62.

24. Jack London, *To Build a Fire and Other Favorite Stories* (Mineola, NY: Dover Publications, 2008), 7.

25. DuMont, "Luminous Deceptions," 62.

26. Steven Frye, "*Blood Meridian* and the Poetics of Violence," in *The Cambridge Companion to Cormac McCarthy*, ed. Steven Frye (2013; New York: Cambridge University Press, 2014), 107.

27. See Hadot's listing of "five possible translations of the enigmatic saying—which shows how difficult it is to understand Heraclitus: [1] The constitution of each thing tends to hide (i.e., is hard to know). [2] The constitution of each thing wants to be hidden (i.e., does not want to be revealed). [3] The origin tends to hide itself (i.e., the origin of things is hard to know). [4] What causes things to appear tends to make then disappear (i.e., what causes birth tends to cause death). [5] Form (or appearance) tends to disappear (i.e., what is born wants to die)" (*The Veil of Isis*, 9–10). Hadot argues that "the last two translations are probably closest to what Heraclitus meant, since they have the antithetical character that is typical of his thought" (ibid., 10). While this interpretation makes a lot of sense in general and in terms of McCarthy's poetics, I would add that the third translation is equally aligned with McCarthy's concept of nature, since the term "origin" and its stated unknowability recalls the gnostic phrasing of the "No thing," which Edwin T. Arnold has linked to the mysticism of Jacob Boehme in his reading of *The Crossing* ("McCarthy and the Sacred: A Reading of *The Crossing*," in *Cormac McCarthy: New Directions*, ed. James D. Lilley [2002; Albuquerque: University of New Mexico Press, 2014], 224).

28. Iain Hamilton Grant, "Everything," *Monist* 98, no. 2 (2015): 166.

29. Jason M. Wirth, *The Conspiracy of Life: Meditations on Schelling and His Time* (Albany: State University of New York Press, 2003), 204. It is more than noteworthy, especially in the present context, that Wirth continues: "By 'thought' Schelling did not mean a determination, as if the limitless could simply be delimited. One who attempts to locate freedom within a specific domain is like the Orpheus who loses Eurydice because he demands to see her" (ibid.). On a different level, this is also why for McCarthy, as well as for Schelling, nature cannot be regionalized on an ontological level—regardless of the claim that it is, indeed, material through and through, thereby affirming its constant mobility and remoldability.

30. Mathieu, *Orpheus in Brooklyn*, 40 and 41.

31. Lorenz Oken, *Lehrbuch der Naturphilosophie* (1809–11; Zürich: Friedrich Schultheiß, 1843), 523, and *Elements of Physiophilosophy*, trans. Alfred Tulk (1843; London: C. and J. Adlard Printers, 1847), 665.

32. Yarbrough, "Tricksters and Lightbringers," 50.

33. Willard P. Greenwood, *Reading Cor-*

mac McCarthy (Santa Barbara, CA: ABC-Clio, 2009), 104.

34. On the topic of chance in *No Country for Old Men*, see Sean Braune, "A Chaotic and Dark Vitalism: A Case Study of Cormac McCarthy's Psychopaths amid a Geology of Immorals," *Western American Literature* 50, no. 1 (2015): 5; Jay Ellis, *No Place for Home: Spatial Constraint and Character Flight in the Novels of Cormac McCarthy* (New York: Routledge, 2006), 229.

35. As with the earlier passage about the world's tale that is reflected in John Grady's first steps from the hospital bed after the fight with the *cuchillero*, this last sentence recalls an earlier sentence from McCarthy's oeuvre—namely, one from McCarthy's 1979 novel in which the narrator describes a scene in which a known drunkard and friend of Suttree is just about to get shot by a bouncer, after he has stolen some of the guests' wallets: "*In the act is wedded the interior man and the man as seen*" (*S*, 375, emphasis added).

36. Cormac McCarthy, notes on "Whales and Men," folder 2, box 97, Cormac McCarthy Papers, Wittliff Collections.

37. This is also arguably the most crucial difference between him and Sheriff Bell.

38. On the connection of the jeremiad narrative to *No Country for Old Men*, see Ellis, *No Place for Home*, 227. *No Country for Old Men* can be regarded as a narrative in which the American jeremiad is recast in accordance with *Naturphilosophie* insofar as moral decay is not a phenomenon outside of nature but a symptom of its complex dynamics. What this means, however, is not that moral (or social) decay is to be viewed negatively in terms of a deviation from the order of things. Instead it means that it is false to argue that such a phenomenon is a somehow "unnatural" instance of an ostensibly orderly and harmonious nature—that is, the homeostasis underlying the ethos of ecocriticism.

39. Wirth, *The Conspiracy of Life*, 204.

40. Iain Hamilton Grant, "'Philosophy Become Genetic': The Physics of the World Soul," in *The New Schelling*, ed. Judith Norman and Alistair Welchman (London: Continuum, 2004), 129–30.

41. Schelling quoted in ibid., 135.

42. According to Ellis, McCarthy regards the realm of normativity (what Ellis calls "our evolved systems of morality") as separate from the natural realm: these systems "exist precariously situated above an animal world aligned more closely to the mute sensibilities of rocks and stones and trees than to our sufferings. . . . But that does not mean that morality in McCarthy's worldview never existed, any more than the inevitable failure of dreams to be realized means that their force did not create life against that inevitable darkness. It is simply the case that such force remains the imaginative provenance of humans, and that it cannot be confirmed by the natural world, or some god, or by chance. It can only be confirmed in the imaginative attempt that will inevitably fail" (*No Place for Home*, 268). What I want to draw attention to here is that while the last sentence's affirmation of the imaginative seems applicable to McCarthy's use of the myth of unveiling nature, I strongly disagree with Ellis's claim that in these novels human forms of normative practice and discourse are somehow not part of "the natural world." This is because, according to McCarthy's poetics, nonhuman nature is antecedent and human normativity is consequent.

43. Erika B. Spoden, "Let There Be Blood: The Vein of Vietnam in *No Country for Old Men*," *Cormac McCarthy Journal* 10, no. 1 (2012): 81. See *NC*, 155–6. See also the phrasing McCarthy employs when describing the thunderstorm Jimmy Blevins is trying to escape when the three boys are riding through northern Mexico: "The storm front towered above them and the wind was cool on their sweating faces. They slumped bleary-eyed in their saddles and looked at one another. Shrouded in the black thunderheads the distant lighting glowed mutely *like welding* seen through foundry smoke. As if repairs were under way at some flawed place in the iron dark of the world" (*PH*, 67, emphasis added).

44. Schelling, *SW* VII, 360, and *Philosophical Investigations*, 29.

45. Another crucial distinction between Chigurh and Bell is the latter's conviction of the importance of intact social relations. Talking about his community work as a county sheriff, Bell mentions "*cemetery cleanins*," at which he would be present many times. As an aside, he notes that apart from this service being good for the families involved, there is another reason why he had always thought it would be good to be part of these gatherings: "*It is community and it is respect, of course, but the dead have more claims on you than what you might want to admit or even what you might know about and them claims can be very strong indeed. Very strong indeed. You get the feeling they just dont want to turn loose. So any little thing helps, in that respect*" (*NC*, 124).

46. See Steven Frye, *Understanding Cormac McCarthy* (Columbia: University of South Carolina Press, 2009), 101.

47. For an account of nihilism in McCarthy, see Vereen M. Bell, "The Ambiguous Nihilism of Cormac McCarthy," *Southern Literary Journal* 15, no. 2 (1983): 32–33.

48. Paul Patton, "McCarthy's Fire," in *Styles of Extinction: Cormac McCarthy's* The Road, ed. Julian Murphet and Mark Steven (London: Continuum, 2012), 131.

49. Greenwood, *Reading Cormac McCarthy*, 95.

50. Daniel Luttrull, "Prometheus Hits *The Road*: Revising the Myth," *Cormac McCarthy Journal* 8, no. 1 (2010): 21.

51. Cormac McCarthy, notes on *The Road*, folder 6, box 87, Cormac McCarthy Papers, Wittliff Collections.

52. Ibid.

53. As I mentioned above, *The Sunset Limited* was conceived of as a play before it was refigured as a novel, which was also the case for *No Country for Old Men*. See Stacey Peebles, "McCarthy and Film," in *The Cambridge Companion to Cormac McCarthy*, ed. Steven Frye (2013; New York: Cambridge University Press, 2014), 167 and 171.

54. Markus Wierschem, "'It's More True but It Aint as Good': Searching for Truth in the Death-Deferring Dialogue of McCarthy's *The Sunset Limited*," in *Imaginary Dialogues in America*, ed. Till Kinzel and Jarmila Mildorf (Heidelberg: Winter, 2014), 328.

55. Ray Brassier is routinely mentioned in tandem with philosophers and writers such as the antinatalist David Benatar and the horror fiction writer Thomas Ligotti. Even though crucial passages in Brassier's *Nihil Unbound* connect his ethical standpoint to the philosophical traditions of pessimism and, above all, nihilism, his is an "ambiguous nihilism," to use Vereen Bell's comment about McCarthy's early fiction. The nihilist stance, Brassier argues, is not defeatist in character but emancipatory by nature: "Nihilism is not an existential quandary but a speculative opportunity" (*Nihil Unbound: Enlightenment and Extinction* [New York: Palgrave Macmillan, 2007], xi).

56. On a related point, E. Ann Kaplan develops an interesting notion of "pretrauma" in her discussion of a number of recent movies, including John Hillcoat's 2010 adaptation of *The Road* (*Climate Trauma: Foreseeing the Future in Dystopian Film and Fiction* [New Brunswick, NJ: Rutgers University Press, 2016], 18). Arguably, the Promethean stance, which is certainly a substantial part of the novel's (and its adaptation's) underlying epistemology, can also be useful in connection to this concept, in that the novel not only negotiates "the collapse of the natural world and the disintegration of the social contract," as Kaplan states (ibid.), but also the traumatic event of humankind's eventually self-effectuated transformation on the level of the concept. This line of reasoning, it has to be noted, runs counter to Greenwood's view that "McCarthy's [later] work reflects humanity's hostility toward rationalism" (*Reading Cormac McCarthy*, 95).

57. Alfred North Whitehead, *Modes of Thought* (New York: Free Press, 1968), 148.

58. Brassier, "Prometheanism and Its Critics," 487.

59. Christopher Dacus, "The West as Sym-

bol of the Eschaton in Cormac McCarthy," *Cormac McCarthy Journal* 7, no. 1 (2009): 9.

60. Brassier, "Prometheanism and Its Critics," 486, emphasis added.

61. Oken, *Lehrbuch* 2; *Elements*, 2.

62. Brassier, *Nihil Unbound*, 48.

63. Richard B. Woodward, "McCarthy's Venomous Fiction," *New York Times Magazine*, April 19, 1992, accessed March 14, 2015, http://www.nytimes.com/1992/04/19/magazine/cormac-mccarthy-s-venomous-fiction.html?pagewanted=all.

64. Brassier, *Nihil Unbound*, 228.

65. Brassier, "Prometheanism and Its Critics," 478.

66. Shelly L. Rambo, "Beyond Redemption? Reading Cormac McCarthy's *The Road* after the End of the World," *Studies in the Literary Imagination* 41, no. 2 (2008): 115.

67. Ibid.

68. Andrew Keller Estes, *Cormac McCarthy and the Writing of American Spaces* (Amsterdam: Rodopi, 2013), 132.

69. Herman Melville, *Moby-Dick; or, The Whale* (New York: Penguin Classics, 2003), 489–90, emphasis added.

70. Schelling, *SW* III, 628, and *First Outline of a System of the Philosophy of Nature*, trans. Keith Peterson (Albany: State University of New York Press, 2004), 232.

Conclusion. Naturphilosophie and the Literature of Nature

1. Vereen M. Bell, *The Achievement of Cormac McCarthy* (Baton Rouge: Louisiana State University Press, 1988), xiii.

2. Ibid.

3. Quoted in Pierre Hadot, *The Veil of Isis: An Essay on the History of the Idea of Nature*, trans. Michael Chase (2004; Cambridge, MA: Harvard University Press, 2008), 1.

4. Bell, *The Achievement of Cormac McCarthy*, xiii.

5. Cormac McCarthy, folder 2, box 97, Cormac McCarthy Papers, Wittliff Collections.

BIBLIOGRAPHY

Abrams, M. H. *A Glossary of Literary Terms*. New York: Holt, Rinehart and Winston, 1971.

Alaimo, Stacy. *Bodily Natures: Science, Environment, and the Material Self*. Bloomington: Indiana University Press, 2010.

Anders, Sabine. "Literatur als kulturelle Ökologie am Beispiel von Cormac McCarthys *All the Pretty Horses*." In *Kulturökologie und Literatur: Beiträge zu einem transdisziplinären Paradigma der Literaturwissenschaft*, edited by Hubert Zapf, 277–92. Heidelberg: Winter, 2008.

Anderson, Douglas. "Emerson's Schellingian Natures: Origins of and Possibilities for American Environmental Thought." *Cognitio* 8, no. 1 (2007): 13–22.

Andreasen, Liana Vrajitoru. "*Blood Meridian* and the Spatial Metaphysics of the West." In *They Rode On:* Blood Meridian *and the Tragedy of the American West*, edited by Rick Wallach, 166–76. Miami: Cormac McCarthy Society, 2013.

Arnold, Edwin T. "McCarthy and the Sacred: A Reading of *The Crossing*." In *Cormac McCarthy: New Directions*, edited by James D. Lilley, 215–38. 2002. Albuquerque: University of New Mexico Press, 2014.

———. "Naming, Knowing and Nothingness: McCarthy's Moral Parables." *Southern Quarterly* 30, no. 4 (1992): 31–50.

Arsić, Branka. *On Leaving: A Reading in Emerson*. Cambridge, MA: Harvard University Press, 2010.

Badiou, Alain. *Being and Event*. Translated by Oliver Feltham. 1988. London: Continuum, 2005.

Barad, Karen. "Posthumanist Performativity: Toward an Understanding of How Matter Comes to Matter." *Signs* 28, no. 3 (2003): 801–31.

Barnum, Jill. "Melville, Lorenz Oken, and Biology: Engaging the 'Long Now.'" *Leviathan* 7, no. 2 (2005): 41–46.

Beach, Edward Allen. *The Potencies of God(s): Schelling's Philosophy of Mythology*. Albany: State University of New York Press, 1994.

Bell, Vereen M. *The Achievement of Cormac McCarthy*. Baton Rouge: Louisiana State University Press, 1988.

———. "The Ambiguous Nihilism of Cormac McCarthy." *Southern Literary Journal* 15, no. 2 (1983): 31–41.

Bennett, Jane. *Vibrant Matter: A Political Ecology of Things*. Durham, NC: Duke University Press, 2010.

Bensaude-Vincent, Bernadette, and Isabelle Stengers. *A History of Chemistry*. Translated by Deborah van Dam. Cambridge, MA: Harvard University Press, 1996.

Bernstock, Judith E. *Under the Spell of Orpheus: The Persistence of a Myth in Twentieth-Century Art*. Carbondale: Southern Illinois University Press, 1991.

Berressem, Hanjo. *Pynchon's Poetics: Interfacing Theory and Text*. Urbana: University of Illinois Press, 1992.

———. "Structural Couplings: Radical Constructivism and a Deleuzian Eco*logics*." In *Deleuze | Guattari & Ecology*, edited by Bernd Herzogenrath, 57–101. New York: Palgrave Macmillan, 2009.

Berry, K. Wesley. "The Lay of the Land in Cormac McCarthy's Appalachia." In *Cormac McCarthy: New Directions*, edited by James D. Lilley, 47–73. 2002. Albuquerque: University of New Mexico Press, 2014.

Blanchot, Maurice. *The Space of Literature*. Translated by Ann Smock. 1955. Lincoln: University of Nebraska Press, 1982.

Bloom, Harold. *Novelists and Novels*. Philadelphia, PA: Chelsea House. 2005.

Bogue, Ronald. *Deleuze on Music, Painting and the Arts*. 2003. London: Routledge, 2013.

———. "A Thousand Ecologies." In *Deleuze | Guattari & Ecology*, edited by Bernd Herzogenrath, 42–56. New York: Palgrave Macmillan, 2009.

Bourassa, Alan. *Deleuze and American Literature: Affect and Virtuality in Faulkner, Wharton, Ellison, and McCarthy*. New York: Palgrave Macmillan, 2009.

Bowie, Andrew. "Translator's Introduction." In Friedrich W. J. Schelling. *On the History of Modern Philosophy*. Translated by Andrew Bowie, 1–40. Cambridge: Cambridge University Press, 1994.

Brassier, Ray. "Alien Theory: The Decline of Materialism in the Name of Matter." PhD diss., University of Warwick, 2001.

———. Interview by Leon Niemoczynski. *After Nature Blog*, August 26, 2012. Accessed November 28, 2015. http://afterxnature.blogspot.de/2012/08/ray-brassier-interviews-with-after_26.html.

———. *Nihil Unbound: Enlightenment and Extinction*. New York: Palgrave Macmillan, 2007.

———. "Prometheanism and Its Critics." In *#Accelerate: The Accelerationist Reader*, edited by Robin Mackay and Armen Avanessian, 467–87. Falmouth, UK: Urbanomic, 2014.

———. "That Which Is Not: Philosophy as Entwinement of Truth and Negativity." *Stasis* 1 (2013): 174–86.

———. "The View from Nowhere." *Identities* 8, no. 2 (2011): 7–23.

Brassier, Ray, Iain Hamilton Grant, Graham Harman, and Quentin Meillassoux. "Speculative Realism." *Collapse* 3 (2007): 307–449.

Braune, Sean. "A Chaotic and Dark Vitalism: A Case Study of Cormac McCarthy's Psychopaths amid a Geology of Immorals." *Western American Literature* 50, no. 1 (2015): 1–24.

Breidbach, Olaf. "Schelling und die Erfahrungswissenschaft." *Sudhoffs Archiv* 88, no. 2 (2004): 158–174.

Brewton, Vince. "The Changing Landscape of Violence in Cormac McCarthy's Early Novels and the Border Trilogy." *Southern Literary Journal* 37, no. 1 (2004): 121–43.

Bryant, Levi R. *Onto-Cartography: An Ontology of Machines and Media*. Edinburgh: Edinburgh University Press, 2014.

Buchanan, Ian. *Deleuzism: A Metacommentary*. Edinburgh: Edinburgh University Press, 2000.

Buell, Lawrence. *Emerson*. 2003. Cambridge, MA: Harvard University Press, 2004.

———. *The Environmental Imagination: Thoreau, Nature Writing, and the Formation of American Culture*. Cambridge, MA: Belknap Press of Harvard University Press, 1995.

———. *Writing for an Endangered World: Literature, Culture, and Environment in the U.S. and Beyond*. Cambridge, MA: Belknap Press of Harvard University Press, 2001.

Campbell, Jim. "A Translation of Spanish Passages in *The Crossing*." Accessed November 29, 2017. http://www.cormacmccarthy.com/wp-content/uploads/CrossingTrans.pdf.

Canfield, J. Douglas. "The Dawning of the Age of Aquarius: Abjection, Identity, and the Carnivalesque in Cormac McCarthy's *Suttree*." *Contemporary Literature* 44, no. 4 (2003): 664–96.

Cant, John. *Cormac McCarthy and the Myth of American Exceptionalism*. New York: Routledge, 2008.

Caruth, Cathy. "Recapturing the Past: Introduction." In *Trauma: Explorations in Memory*, edited by Cathy Caruth, 151–57. Baltimore: Johns Hopkins University Press, 1995.

Châtelet, Gilles. *Figuring Space: Philosophy, Mathematics, and Physics*. Dordrecht: Kluwer Academic Publishers, 2000.

Clarke, Michael T. "The New Naturalism: Cormac McCarthy, Frank Norris, and the Question of Postmodernism." *Studies in American Naturalism* 9, no. 1 (2014): 52–78.

Cooper, Lydia R. "Cormac McCarthy's *The Road* as Apocalyptic Grail Narrative." *Studies in the Novel* 43, no. 2 (2011): 218–36.

———. "McCarthy, Tennessee, and the Southern Gothic." In *The Cambridge Companion to Cormac McCarthy*, edited by Steven Frye, 41–53. 2013. New York: Cambridge University Press, 2014.

———. *No More Heroes: Narrative Perspective and Morality in Cormac McCarthy*. Baton Rouge: Louisiana State University Press, 2011.

Crews, Michael Lynn. *Books Are Made out of Books: A Guide to Cormac McCarthy's Literary Influences*. Austin: University of Texas Press, 2017.

Cronon, William. "The Trouble with Wilderness; or, Getting Back to the Wrong Nature." In *Uncommon Ground: Rethinking the Human Place in Nature*, edited by William Cronon, 69–90. New York: Norton, 1995.

Dacus, Christopher. "Borderline Insanity: Modernity as a Political Problem in Cormac McCarthy's *Blood Meridian*." In *They Rode On:* Blood Meridian *and the Tragedy of the American West*, edited by Rick Wallach, 273–81. Miami: Cormac McCarthy Society, 2013.

———. "The West as Symbol of the Eschaton in Cormac McCarthy." *Cormac McCarthy Journal* 7, no. 1 (2009): 7–15.

Daugherty, Leo. "Gravers False and True: *Blood Meridian* as Gnostic Tragedy." *Southern Quarterly* 30, no. 4 (1992): 122–33.

DeLanda, Manuel. *Philosophical Chemistry: Genealogy of a Scientific Field*. London: Bloomsbury, 2015.

———. *A Thousand Years of Nonlinear History*. Cambridge, MA: MIT Press, 1997.

Deleuze, Gilles. "The Actual and the Virtual." Translated by Eliot Ross Albert. In Gilles Deleuze and Claire Parnet, *Dialogues II*, 148–52. 1995. New York: Columbia University Press, 2007.

———. *Difference and Repetition*. Translated by Paul Patton. 1968. London: Continuum, 2004.

———. *Expressionism in Philosophy: Spinoza*. Translated by Martin Joughin. 1968. New York: Zone Books, 1990.

———. "Immanence: A Life." In Gilles Deleuze, *Pure Immanence: Essays on A Life*, translated by Anne Boyman, 25–33. New York: Zone Books, 2001.

———. "Letter-Preface by Gilles Deleuze." In Jean-Clet Martin, *Variations: The Philosophy of Gilles Deleuze*, translated by Constantin V. Boundas and Susan Dyrkton, vii–viii. 1990. Edinburgh: Edinburgh University Press, 2010.

———. *The Logic of Sense*. Translated by Mark Lester. 1969. London: Continuum, 2004.

———. *Negotiations*. Translated by Martin Joughin. New York: Columbia University Press, 1995.

Deleuze, Gilles, and Félix Guattari. *Anti-Oedipus: Capitalism and Schizophrenia*. Translated by Robert Hurley, Mark Seem, and Helen R. Lane. 1972. Minneapolis: University of Minnesota Press, 2008.

———. *A Thousand Plateaus: Capitalism and Schizophrenia*. Translated by Brian Massumi. 1980. London: Continuum, 2004.

———. *What Is Philosophy?* Translated by Hugh Tomlinson and Graham Burchell. 1991. New York: Columbia University Press, 1994.

Derrida, Jacques. *Of Grammatology*. Translated by Gayatri Chakravorty Spivak. 1967. Baltimore: Johns Hopkins University Press, 1997.

———. *Writing and Difference*. Translated by Alan Bass. 1967. Chicago: University of Chicago Press, 1978.

Devine, Maureen, and Christa Grewe-Volpp. Introduction to *Words on Water: Literary and Cultural Representations*, edited by Maureen Devine and Christa Grewe-Volpp, 1–8. Trier: Wissenschaftlicher Verlag Trier, 2008.

Doud, Robert E. "Orphism in Whitehead and Some Other Poetic Thinkers." *Process Studies* 33, no. 2 (2004): 323–38.

Dougherty, Carol. *Prometheus*. London: Routledge, 2006.

Dow, William. "Topographical Strides of Thoreau: The Poet and Pioneer in Cormac McCarthy's *Blood Meridian*." *Revue française d'études américaines* 84 (2000): 89–105.

Dowd, Ciarán. "The Hum of Mystery: Parataxis, Analepsis, and Geophysiology in *The Road*." *Cormac McCarthy Journal* 11, no. 1 (2013): 23–43.

———. "'A Novel in Dramatic Form': Metaphysical Tension in *The Sunset Limited*." In *Intertextual and Interdisciplinary Approaches to Cormac McCarthy: Borders and Crossings*, edited by Nicholas Monk, 112–120. New York: Routledge, 2012.

DuMont, Andy. "Luminous Deceptions: Contingent Community and Aesthetic Form in Cormac McCarthy's *The Road*." *Cormac McCarthy Journal* 10, no. 1 (2012): 56–75.

Dunham, Jeremy, Iain Hamilton Grant, and Sean Watson. *Idealism: The History of a Philosophy*. Montreal: McGill-Queen's University Press, 2011.

Elder, John. *Imagining the Earth: Poetry and the Vision of Nature*. 1985. Athens: University of Georgia Press, 1996.

Ellis, Jay. *No Place for Home: Spatial Constraint and Character Flight in the Novels of Cormac McCarthy*. New York: Routledge, 2006.

———. "'What Happens to Country' in *Blood Meridian*." *Rocky Mountain Review of Language and Literature* 60, no. 1 (2006): 85–97.

Emden, Christian J. *Nietzsche's Naturalism: Philosophy and the Life Sciences in the Nineteenth Century*. Cambridge: Cambridge University Press, 2014.

Emerson, Ralph Waldo. *Emerson's Prose and Poetry: Authoritative Texts, Contexts, Criticism*. Selected and edited by Joel Porte and Saundra Morris. New York: W. W. Norton and Company, 2001.

Erickson, Martin. *Beautiful Mathematics*. Washington: Mathematical Association of America, 2011.

Essary, Kirk. "'We Languish in Obscurity': The Silence of God as Atavistic Calvinism in Cormac McCarthy's Fiction." *Soundings* 97, no. 3 (2014): 265–96.

Estes, Andrew Keller. *Cormac McCarthy and the Writing of American Spaces*. Amsterdam: Rodopi, 2013.

Evans, Dylan. *An Introductory Dictionary of Lacanian Psychoanalysis*. 1996. London: Routledge, 2010.

Evenson, Brian. "McCarthy's Wanderers: Nomadology, Violence, and Open Country." In *Sacred Violence: A Reader's Companion to Cormac McCarthy*, edited by Wade Hall and Rick Wallach, 41–48. El Paso: Texas Western Press, 1995.

Faulkner, William. *Wild Palms*. 1939. London: Vintage, 2000.

Fisher-Wirth, Ann. "Abjection and 'the Feminine' in *Outer Dark*." In *Cormac McCarthy: New Directions*, edited by James D. Lilley, 2002, 125–40. Albuquerque: University of New Mexico Press, 2014.

Flood, Alison. "Cormac McCarthy's Parallel Career Revealed—As a Scientific Copy Editor!" *Guardian*. February 21, 2012. Accessed November 21, 2017. https://www.theguardian.com/books/2012/feb/21/cormac-mccarthy-scientific-copy-editor.

Frye, Steven. "*Blood Meridian* and the Poetics of Violence." In *The Cambridge Companion to Cormac McCarthy*, edited by Steven Frye, 107–20. 2013. New York: Cambridge University Press, 2014.

———. *Understanding Cormac McCarthy*. Columbia: University of South Carolina Press, 2009.

———. "Yeats' 'Sailing to Byzantium' and McCarthy's *No Country for Old Men*: Art and Artifice in the New Novel." *Cormac McCarthy Journal* 5, no. 1 (2005): 14–20.

Furey, Rachel. "Sentence Fragments, Sound, and Setting in *Suttree* and *The Road*." *Cormac McCarthy Journal* 9, no. 1 (2011): 51–65.

Gamblin, Hillary. "Discovering the Romantic in a Necrophiliac: The Question of Misogyny in *Child of God*." *Cormac McCarthy Journal* 9, no. 1 (2011): 28–37.

Garrard, Greg. *Ecocriticism*. 2004. New York: Routledge, 2012.

Gersdorf, Catrin. *The Poetics and Politics of the Desert: Landscape and the Construction of America*. New York: Rodopi, 2009.

Ghiselin, Michael T. "Review of F.W.J. Schelling's *First Outline of the Philosophy of Nature* (Translated by Keith R. Peterson)." *History and Philosophy of the Life Sciences* 27, no. 2 (2005): 291.

Giles, James R. "*Outer Dark* and Romantic Naturalism." In *The Cambridge Companion* to *Cormac McCarthy*, edited by Steven Frye, 95–106. 2013. New York: Cambridge University Press, 2014.

Glotfelty, Cheryll. "Introduction: Literary Studies in an Age of Environmental Crisis." In *The Ecocriticism Reader: Landmarks in Literary Ecology*, edited by Cheryll Glotfelty and Harold Fromm, xv–xxxvii. Athens: University of Georgia Press, 1996.

Gordon, Bryan James. "Antitopic and Afterthought: Givenness and Grammar in Ponca and Omaha." *Kansas Working Papers in Linguistics* 30 (2008): 74–87.

Gottlieb, Evan. *Romantic Realities: Speculative Realism and British Romanticism.* Edinburgh: Edinburgh University Press, 2016.

Gould, Stephen Jay. *Ontogeny and Phylogeny*. Cambridge, MA: Harvard University Press, 1977.

Grammer, John M. "A Thing against Which Time Will Not Prevail: Pastoral and History in Cormac McCarthy's South." *Southern Quarterly* 30, no. 4 (1992): 19–30.

Grant, Iain Hamilton. "Being and Slime: The Mathematics of Protoplasm in Lorenz Oken's 'Physio-Philosophy.'" *Collapse* 4 (2008): 287–321.

———. "The Chemical Paradigm: Interview with Iain Hamilton Grant." *Collapse* 7 (2011): 39–82.

———. "The Chemistry of Darkness." *Pli* 9 (2000): 36–52.

———. "Does Nature Stay What-It-Is? Dynamics and the Antecedence Criterion." In *The Speculative Turn: Continental Materialism and Realism*, edited by Levi Bryant, Nick Srnicek, and Graham Harman, 66–83. Melbourne: re.press, 2011.

———. "The 'Eternal and Necessary Bond Between Philosophy and Physics': A Repetition of the Difference Between the Fichtean and Schellingian Systems of Philosophy." *Angelaki* 10, no. 1 (2005): 43–59.

———. "Everything." *Monist* 98, no. 2 (2015): 156–67.

———. "How Nature Came to Be Thought: Schelling's Paradox and the Problem of Location." *Journal of the British Society for Phenomenology* 44, no. 1 (2013): 24–43.

———. "The Insufficiency of Ground: On Žižek's Schellingianism." In *The Truth of Žižek*, edited by Paul Bowman and Richard Stamp, 82–98. London: Continuum, 2007.

———. "Introduction to Schelling's *On the World Soul*," *Collapse* 6 (2012): 59–65.

———. "Movements of the World: The Sources of Transcendental Philosophy." *Analecta Hermeneutica* 3 (2011): 1–17.

———. *Philosophies of Nature after Schelling*. 2006. London: Continuum, 2008.

———. "'Philosophy Become Genetic': The Physics of the World Soul." In *The New Schelling*, edited by Judith Norman and Alistair Welchman, 128–50. London: Continuum, 2004.

———. "The Universe in the Universe: German Idealism and the Natural History of Mind." *Royal Institute of Philosophy Supplement* 72 (2013): 297–316.

———. "'World' in Middle Schelling: Why Nature Transcendentalises." *Pli* 26 (2014): 82–108.

Grant, Natalie. "The Landscape of the Soul: Man and the Natural World in *The Orchard Keeper*." In *Sacred Violence: A Reader's Companion to Cormac McCarthy*, edited by Wade Hall and Rick Wallach, 61–68. El Paso: Texas Western Press, 1995.

Gratton, Peter. *Speculative Realism: Problems and Prospects*. London: Bloomsbury, 2014.

Greenwood, Willard P. *Reading Cormac McCarthy*. Santa Barbara, CA: ABC-Clio, 2009.

Grewe-Volpp, Christa. *"Natural Spaces Mapped by Human Minds": Ökokritische und ökofeministische Analysen zeitgenössischer amerikanischer Romane*. Tübingen: Gunter Narr Verlag, 2004.

Gualandi, Alberto. "Errancies of the Human: French Philosophies of Nature and the Overturning of the Copernican Revolution." *Collapse* 5 (2012): 501–48.

Gugin, David. "The Blood of a Nomad: Environmental Stylistics and *All the Pretty Horses*." In *Cormac McCarthy's Borders and Landscapes*, edited by Louise Jillett, 83–94. New York: Bloomsbury, 2016.

Guillemin, Georg. *The Pastoral Vision of Cormac McCarthy*. College Station: Texas A&M University Press, 2004.

Guinn, Matthew. "Ruder Forms Survive: Cormac McCarthy's Atavistic Vision." In *Myth, Legend, Dust: Critical Responses to Cormac McCarthy*, edited by Rick Wallach, 108–15. Manchester, UK: Manchester University Press, 2000.

Hadot, Pierre. *The Veil of Isis: An Essay on the History of the Idea of Nature*. Translated by Michael Chase. 2004. Cambridge, MA: Harvard University Press, 2008.

Haferkamp, Leyla. "'The Instructed Third': Processing Ecology with Deleuze." In *An [Un]likely Alliance: Thinking Environment[s] with Deleuze | Guattari*, edited by Bernd Herzogenrath, 52–65. Newcastle upon Tyne, UK: Cambridge Scholars Publishing, 2008.

Hage, Erik. *Cormac McCarthy: A Literary Companion*. Jefferson, NC: McFarland and Company, 2010.

Hamilton, Grant. *The World of Failing Machines: Speculative Realism and Literature*. Winchester, UK: Zero Books, 2016.

Haraway, Donna. *Staying with the Trouble: Making Kin in the Chthulucene*. Durham, NC: Duke University Press, 2016.

Harman, Graham. *Guerrilla Metaphysics: Phenomenology and the Carpentry of Things*. Chicago: Open Court, 2005.

———. "On Vicarious Causation." *Collapse* 2 (2007): 187–221.

———. *Tool-Being: Heidegger and the Metaphysics of Objects*. Chicago: Open Court, 2002.

Hartkopf, Werner. *Studien zur Entwicklung der modernen Dialektik: Die Dialektik in Schellings Ansätzen zu einer Naturphilosophie*. Meisenheim: Verlag Anton Hain, 1972.

Haske, Joseph D. "Transcendental Musings on *Blood Meridian*'s Western Wasteland." In *They Rode On:* Blood Meridian *and the Tragedy of the American West*, edited by Rick Wallach, 191–95. Miami: Cormac McCarthy Society, 2013.

Hawthorne, Nathaniel. *The Marble Faun*. 1860. Oxford: Oxford University Press, 2002.

Heffernan, Nick, and David A. Wragg. "Introduction: Culture, Environment and Ecopolitics." In *Culture, Environment and Ecopolitics*, edited by Nick Heffernan and David A. Wragg, 1–31. Newcastle upon Tyne, UK: Cambridge Scholars Publishing, 2011.

Hegel, Georg W. F. *Phenomenology of Spirit*. Translated by Michael Inwood. 1807. Oxford: Oxford University Press, 2018.

Heise, Ursula K. "The Hitchhiker's Guide to Ecocriticism." *PMLA* 121, no. 2 (2006): 503–16.

Herzogenrath, Bernd. *An Art of Desire: Reading Paul Auster*. Amsterdam: Rodopi, 1999.

———. "Nature | Geophilosophy | Machinics | Ecosophy." In *Deleuze | Guattari & Ecology*, edited by Bernd Herzogenrath, 1–22. New York: Palgrave Macmillan, 2009.

Hillier, Russell M. "'In a Dark Parody' of John Bunyan's *The Pilgrim's Progress*: The Presence of Subversive Allegory in Cormac McCarthy's *Outer Dark*." *ANQ* 19, no. 4 (2006): 52–59.

Hogrebe, Wolfgang. *Prädikation und Genesis: Metaphysik als Fundamentalheuristik im Ausgang von Schellings* Die Weltalter. Frankfurt: Suhrkamp, 1989.

Holloway, David. *The Late Modernism of Cormac McCarthy*. Westport, CT: Greenwood Press, 2002.

———. "Modernism, Nature, and Utopia: Another Look at 'Optical Democracy' in Cormac McCarthy's Western Quartet." *Southern Quarterly* 38, no. 3 (2000): 186–205.

Holmes, S. J. "Von Baer's Perplexities over Evolution." *Isis* 37, nos. 1 and 2 (1947): 7–14.

Huber, Sebastian. *Subject of the Event: Reagency in the American Novel after 2000*. London: Bloomsbury, 2016.

Husserl, Edmund. *Ideas Pertaining to a Pure Phenomenology and to a Phenomenological Philosophy, First Book*. Translated by F. Kersten. 1913. Dordrecht: Kluwer Academic Publishers, 1998.

Iber, Christian. *Das Andere der Vernunft als ihr Prinzip: Grundzüge der philosophischen Entwicklung Schellings mit einem Ausblick auf die nachidealistischen Philosophiekonzeptionen Heideggers und Adornos*. Berlin: Walter de Gruyter, 1994.

James, Henry. "Preface to *The Princess Casamassima*." In *The Theory of Criticism: From Plato to the Present*, edited by Raman Selden. 502–3. 1886. Harlow, UK: Longman, 1988.

Jameson, Fredric. *Fables of Aggression: Wyndham Lewis, the Modernist as Fascist*. 1979. Berkeley: University of California Press, 2008.

———. *The Political Unconscious: Narrative as a Socially Symbolic Act*. 1981. London: Routledge, 2002.

Jarrett, Robert L. *Cormac McCarthy*. New York: Twayne, 1997.

———. "Cormac McCarthy's Sense of an Ending: Serialized Narrative and Revision in *Cities of the Plain*." In *Cormac McCarthy: New Directions*, edited by James D. Lilley, 313–42. 2002. Albuquerque: University of New Mexico Press, 2014.

Josephs, Allen. "The Quest for God in *The Road*." In *The Cambridge Companion to Cormac McCarthy*, edited by Steven Frye, 133–45. 2013. New York: Cambridge University Press, 2014. 133–45.

Josyph, Peter. *Adventures in Reading Cormac McCarthy*. Lanham, MD: Scarecrow Press, 2010.

———. *Cormac McCarthy's House: Reading McCarthy without Walls*. Austin: University of Texas Press, 2013.

Juge, Carole. "The Road to the Sun They Cannot See: Plato's Allegory of the Cave,

Oblivion, and Guidance in Cormac McCarthy's *The Road*." *Cormac McCarthy Journal* 7, no. 1 (2009): 16–30.

Jung, Carl G. *Mysterium Coniunctionis: Untersuchung über die Trennung und Zusammensetzung der seelischen Gegensätze in der Alchemie*. 3 vols. Zurich: Rascher Verlag, 1955–57.

Kabitoglou, E. Douka. *Plato and the English Romantics*. 1990. New York: Routledge, 2013.

Kaplan, E. Ann. *Climate Trauma: Foreseeing the Future in Dystopian Film and Fiction*. New Brunswick, NJ: Rutgers University Press, 2016.

Kenner, Hugh. *The Pound Era*. Berkeley: University of California Press, 1971.

Kerényi, Carl. *Prometheus: Archetypal Image of Human Existence*. Translated by Ralph Manheim. Princeton, NJ: Princeton University Press, 1991.

Kerridge, Richard. Introduction to *Writing the Environment: Ecocriticism & Literature*, edited by Richard Kerridge and Neil Sammels, 1–10. London: Zed Books Ltd., 1998.

Kestermann, Nora. "Ralph Waldo Emerson versus Cormac McCarthy: The Annihilation of Emerson's Values in McCarthy's *The Road*." *Current Objectives of Postgraduate American Studies* 11 (2010). Accessed November 15, 2017. https://copas.uni-regensburg.de/article/view/129/153.

Kleber, Karsten. *Der frühe Schelling und Kant: Zur Genese des Identitätssystems aus philosophischer Bewältigung der Natur und Kritik der Transzendentalphilosophie*. Würzburg: Königshausen & Neumann, 2013.

Krauss, Lawrence M. *Quantum Man: Richard Feynman's Life in Science*. Paperback ed.. New York: W. W. Norton and Company, 2012.

Kristeva, Julia. *Powers of Horror: An Essay on Abjection*. Translated by Leon S. Roudiez. 1980. New York: Columbia University Press, 1982.

Kunsa, Ashley. "'Maps of the World in Its Becoming': Post-Apocalyptic Naming in Cormac McCarthy's *The Road*." *Journal of Modern Literature* 33, no. 1 (2009): 57–74.

Lagayette, Pierre. "The Border Trilogy, *The Road*, and the Cold War." In *The Cambridge Companion to Cormac McCarthy*, edited by Steven Frye, 79–91. 2013. New York: Cambridge University Press, 2014.

Land, Nick. *Fanged Noumena: Collected Writings 1987–2007*. Falmouth, UK: Urbanomic, 2012.

———. "Philosophy in a War-Zone." *Dissolution*. Accessed May 1, 2018. www.larsholdhus.com/Dissolution.pdf.

Lane, Belden C. *Landscapes of the Sacred: Geography and Narrative in American Spirituality*. 1988. Baltimore: Johns Hopkins University Press, 2002.

Laplanche, Jean, and Jean-Bertrand Pontalis. *The Language of Psycho-Analysis*. Translated by Donald Nicholson-Smith. 1967. London: Karnac Books, 2006.

Latour, Bruno. *Politics of Nature: How to Bring the Sciences into Democracy*. Translated by Catherine Porter. 1999. Cambridge, MA: Harvard University Press, 2004.

Lincoln, Kenneth. *Cormac McCarthy: American Canticles*. New York: Palgrave Macmillan, 2009.

Link, Eric Carl. "McCarthy and Literary Naturalism." In *The Cambridge Companion to Cormac McCarthy*, edited by Steven Frye, 149–61. 2013. New York: Cambridge University Press, 2014.

London, Jack. *To Build a Fire and Other Favorite Stories.* Mineola, NY: Dover Publications, 2008.

Luce, Dianne C. "The Cave of Oblivion: Platonic Mythology in *Child of God.*" In *Cormac McCarthy: New Directions*, edited by James D. Lilley, 171–98. 2002. Albuquerque: University of New Mexico Press, 2014.

———. *Reading the World: Cormac McCarthy's Tennessee Period.* 2009. Columbia: University of South Carolina Press, 2010.

———. "The Road and the Matrix: The World as Tale in *The Crossing.*" In *Perspectives on Cormac McCarthy*, edited by Edwin T. Arnold and Dianne C. Luce, 195–220. Jackson: University Press of Mississippi, 1999.

Luttrull, Daniel. "Prometheus Hits *The Road*: Revising the Myth." *Cormac McCarthy Journal* 8, no.1 (2010): 17–28.

Lyotard, Jean-François. *Lessons on the Analytic of the Sublime.* Translated by Elizabeth Rottenberg. 1991. Stanford, CA: Stanford University Press, 1994.

Madsen, Michael. "'A Nameless Wheeling in the Night': Shapes of Evil in Cormac McCarthy's *Blood Meridian* and John Carpenter's *Halloween.*" In *Intertextual and Interdisciplinary Approaches to Cormac McCarthy: Borders and Crossings*, edited by Nicholas Monk, 100–111. New York: Routledge, 2012.

Malone, John C. "Ontology Recapitulates Philology: Willard Quine, Pragmatism, and Radical Behaviorism." *Behavior and Philosophy* 29 (2001): 63–74.

Marks, John. *Gilles Deleuze: Vitalism and Multiplicity.* London: Pluto Press, 1998.

Marovitz, Sanford E. "Melville's Problematic 'Being.'" In *Herman Melville*, edited by Harold Bloom, 39–56. New York: Infobase Publishing, 2008.

Marshall, Kate. "*Cyclonopedia* as Novel (A Meditation on Complicity as Inauthenticity)." In *Leper Creativity: Cyclonopedia Symposium*, edited by Ed Keller, Nicola Masciandaro, and Eugene Thacker, 147–57. New York: Punctum Books, 2012.

———. "What Are the Novels of the Anthropocene? American Fiction in Geological Time." *American Literary History* 27, no. 3 (2015): 523–38.

Marx, Leo. *The Machine in the Garden: Technology and the Pastoral Ideal in America.* 1964. Oxford: Oxford University Press, 1967.

Masciandaro, Nicola. "Becoming Spice: Commentary as Geophilosophy," 2010. *Collapse* 6 (2012): 21–56.

Matthiessen, F. O. *American Renaissance: Art and Expression in the Age of Emerson and Whitman.* 1941. Whitefish, MT: Kessinger, 2007.

Mathieu, Bertrand. *Orpheus in Brooklyn: Orphism, Rimbaud, and Henry Miller.* The Hague: Mouton, 1976.

Maturana, Humberto R., and Francisco J. Varela. *Autopoiesis and Cognition: The Realization of the Living.* Dordrecht: D. Reidel Publishing Company, 1980.

Mazel, David. *American Literary Environmentalism.* Athens: University of Georgia Press, 2000.

———. "Regionalism and Ecology." In *A Companion to the Regional Literatures of America*, edited by Charles L. Crow, 129–36. Malden, MA: Blackwell Publishing, 2003.

McCarthy, Cormac. *All the Pretty Horses.* New York: Alfred A. Knopf. 1992.

———. *Blood Meridian, Or the Evening Redness in the West.* 1985. New York: Vintage Books, 1992.

———. *Child of God.* 1973. London: Picador, 2010.

———. *Cities of the Plain*. New York: Alfred A. Knopf, 1998.
———. *The Crossing*. 1994. New York: Vintage Books, 1995.
———. "The Kekulé Problem." *Nautilus* 19 (2017): 22–31.
———. *No Country for Old Men*. 2005. London: Picador, 2007.
———. *The Orchard Keeper*. 1965. New York: Vintage Books, 1993.
———. *Outer Dark*. 1968. London: Picador, 2011.
———. *The Sunset Limited: A Novel in Dramatic Form*. 2006. London: Picador, 2011.
———. *Suttree*. 1979. London: Picador, 1989.
McGilchrist, Megan Riley. *The Western Landscape in Cormac McCarthy and Wallace Stegner: Myths of the Frontier*. New York: Routledge, 2010.
McGrath, Sean J. "Is Schelling's Nature-Philosophy Freudian?" *Analecta Hermeneutica* 3 (2011): 1–20.
McKeague, Charles P. *Beginning Algebra*. Orlando, FL: Academic Press, Inc. 1985.
McLaughlin, Robert L. "Post-Postmodern Discontent: Contemporary Fiction and the Social World." *Symploke* 12, nos. 1–2 (2004): 53–68.
McWerther, Dustin. "Absolute Naturalism. Review of Iain Hamilton Grant's *Philosophies of Nature after Schelling*." *Radical Philosophy* 144 (2007): 49–52.
Meillassoux, Quentin. *After Finitude: An Essay on the Necessity of Contingency*. Translated by Ray Brassier. 2006. London: Continuum, 2009.
Melville, Herman. *Moby-Dick; or, The Whale*. New York: Penguin Classics, 2003.
Metress, Christopher. "*Via Negativa*: The Way of Unknowing in Cormac McCarthy's *Outer Dark*." *Southern Review* 37, no. 1 (2001): 147–54.
Miller, Elaine P. "'The World Must Be Romanticised . . .': The (Environmental) Ethical Implications of Schelling's Organic Worldview." *Environmental Values* 14, no. 3 (2005): 295–316.
Millichap, Joseph R. *A Backward Glance: The Southern Renascence, the Autobiographical Epic, and the Classical Legacy*. Knoxville: University of Tennessee Press, 2009.
Monbiot, George. "Civilisation Ends with a Shutdown of Human Concern. Are We There Already?" *Guardian*. October 29, 2007. Accessed November 24, 2017. https://www.theguardian.com/commentisfree/2007/oct/30/comment.books.
Monk, Nicholas. "Versions of the *Seeleroman*: Cormac McCarthy and Leslie Silko." In *Intertextual and Interdisciplinary Approaches to Cormac McCarthy: Borders and Crossings*, edited by Nicholas Monk, 168–183. New York: Routledge, 2012.
Moore, Bryan L. *Ecology and Literature: Ecocentric Personification from Antiquity to the Twenty-First Century*. New York: Palgrave Macmillan, 2008.
Mort, Oliver. "'Are We Still the Good Guys?' Cormac McCarthy and the Postmodern Heroic Quest." In *They Rode On:* Blood Meridian *and the Tragedy of the American West*, edited by Rick Wallach, 246–55. Miami: Cormac McCarthy Society, 2013.
Morton, Timothy. *The Ecological Thought*. Cambridge, MA: Harvard University Press, 2010.
———. *Ecology without Nature: Rethinking Environmental Aesthetics*. Cambridge, MA: Harvard University Press, 2007.
———. "The Mesh." In *Environmental Criticism for the Twentieth-First Century*, edited by Stephanie LeMenager, Teresa Shewry, and Ken Hiltner, 19–30. New York: Routledge, 2011.

Mullarkey, John. *Post-Continental Philosophy: An Outline*. London: Continuum, 2006.

Mullen, Peirce C. "The Romantic as Scientist: Lorenz Oken." *Studies in Romanticism* 16, no. 3 (1977): 381–99.

Müller, Christopher John. *Prometheanism: Technology, Digital Culture and Human Obsolescence*. Lanham, MD: Rowman and Littlefield, 2016.

Mundik, Petra. *A Bloody and Barbarous God: The Metaphysics of Cormac McCarthy*. Albuquerque: University of New Mexico Press, 2016.

———. "'Striking the Fire Out of the Rock': Gnostic Theology in Cormac McCarthy's *Blood Meridian*." *South Central Review* 26, no. 3 (2009): 72–97.

———. "This Luminosity in Beings So Endarkened: Gnostic Soteriology in *Blood Meridian*." In *They Rode On:* Blood Meridian *and the Tragedy of the American West*, edited by Rick Wallach, 196–223. Miami: Cormac McCarthy Society, 2013.

Næss, Arne. "Is the Deep Ecology Vision a Green Vision or Is It Multicolored Like the Rainbow? An Answer to Nina Witoszek." In *Philosophical Dialogues: Arne Næss and the Progress of Ecophilosophy*, edited by Nina Witoszek and Andrew Brennan, 466–72. Lanham, MD: Rowman and Littlefield, 1999.

Negarestani, Reza. "The Corpse Bride: Thinking with *Nigredo*." *Collapse* 4 (2008): 129–61.

———. *Cyclonopedia: Complicity with Anonymous Materials*. Melbourne: re.press, 2008.

———. "Notes on the Figure of the Cyclone." In *Leper Creativity: Cyclonopedia Symposium*, edited by Ed Keller, Nicola Masciandaro, and Eugene Thacker, 287–97. New York: Punctum Books, 2012.

———. "Undercover Softness: An Introduction to the Architecture and Politics of Decay," 2010. *Collapse* 6 (2012): 379–430.

Nixon, Rob. *Slow Violence and the Environmentalism of the Poor*. Cambridge, MA: Harvard University Press, 2011.

Oelschlaeger, Max. Introduction to *Postmodern Environmental Ethics*, edited by Max Oelschlaeger, 1–20. Albany: State University of New York Press, 1995.

Oken, Lorenz. *Die Zeugung*. Bamberg: Joseph Anton Goebhardt, 1805.

———. *Elements of Physiophilosophy*. Translated by Alfred Tulk. 1843. London: C. and J. Adlard Printers, 1847.

———. *Lehrbuch der Naturphilosophie*. 1809–11. Zurich: Friedrich Schultheiß, 1843.

O'Riordan, Timothy. *Environmentalism*. 1976. London: Pion, 1981.

Ostaric, Lara. "The Concept of Life in Early Schelling." In *Interpreting Schelling: Critical Essays*, edited by Lara Ostaric, 48–70. Cambridge: Cambridge University Press, 2014.

Owens-Murphy, Katie. "The Frontier Ethic behind Cormac McCarthy's Southern Fiction." *Arizona Quarterly* 67, no. 2 (2011): 155–78.

Parrish, Tim. "The Killer Wears the Halo: Cormac McCarthy, Flannery O'Connor, and the American Religion." In *Sacred Violence: A Reader's Companion to Cormac McCarthy*, edited by Wade Hall and Rick Wallach, 25–39. El Paso: Texas Western Press, 1995.

Patton, Paul. *Deleuze and the Political*. London: Routledge, 2000.

———. "McCarthy's Fire." In *Styles of Extinction: Cormac McCarthy's* The Road, edited by Julian Murphet and Mark Steven, 131–43. London: Continuum, 2012.

Peden, Knox. "Alkaline Recapitulation: Haeckel's Hypothesis and the Afterlife of a Concept." *Republics of Letters* 4, no. 1 (2014). Accessed March 27, 2015. http://arcade.stanford.edu/rofl/alkaline-recapitulation-haeckels-hypothesis-and-afterlife-concept.

Pederson, Claudia Costa. "Autopoiesis in Contemporary Bio-Arts in Mexico and Colombia." *Review: Literature and Arts of the Americas* 48, no. 1 (2015): 22–30.

Peebles, Stacey. *Cormac McCarthy and Performance: Page, Stage, Screen.* Austin: University of Texas Press, 2017.

———. "McCarthy and Film." In *The Cambridge Companion to Cormac McCarthy*, edited by Steven Frye, 162–74. 2013. New York: Cambridge University Press, 2014.

Phillips, Dana. "History and the Ugly Facts of Cormac McCarthy's *Blood Meridian*." *American Literature* 68, no. 2 (1996): 433–60.

Plumwood, Val. *Feminism and the Mastery of Nature*. London: Routledge, 1993.

Polasek, Cassie. "'Books Are Made out of Books': Herman Melville's Moby Dick and Cormac McCarthy's Judge Holden." In *They Rode On:* Blood Meridian *and the Tragedy of the American West*, edited by Rick Wallach, 82–94. Miami: Cormac McCarthy Society, 2013.

Porto, Paolo A. "'*Summus atque felicissimus salium*': The Medical Relevance of the *Liquor alkahest*." *Bulletin of the History of Medicine* 76, no. 1 (2002): 1–29.

Potts, Matthew L. *Cormac McCarthy and the Signs of Sacrament: Literature, Theology, and the Moral of Stories*. London: Bloomsbury, 2015.

Powers, Richard. *Orfeo*. New York: W. W. Norton, 2014.

Protevi, John. "Larval Subjects, Autonomous Systems and E. Coli Chemotaxis." In *Deleuze and the Body*, edited by Laura Guillaume and Joe Hughes, 29–52. Edinburgh: Edinburgh University Press, 2011.

Quick, Paul S. "An Ecocritical Approach to the Southern Novels of Cormac McCarthy." PhD diss., University of Georgia, 2004.

Ragan, David Paul. "Values and Structure in *The Orchard Keeper*." *Southern Quarterly* 30, no. 4 (1992): 10–18.

Rambo, Shelly L. "Beyond Redemption? Reading Cormac McCarthy's *The Road* after the End of the World." *Studies in the Literary Imagination* 41, no. 2 (2008): 99–120.

Rasula, Jed. *This Compost: Ecological Imperatives in American Poetry*. 2002. Athens: University of Georgia Press, 2012.

Reynolds, David S. *Beneath the American Renaissance: The Subversive Imagination in the Age of Emerson and Melville*. New York: Alfred A. Knopf, 1988.

Richards, Robert J. *The Romantic Conception of Life: Science and Philosophy in the Age of Goethe*. Chicago: University of Chicago Press, 2002.

Richardson, Alan. "Rethinking Romantic Incest: Human Universals, Literary Representation, and the Biology of the Mind." *New Literary History* 31, no. 3 (2000): 553–572.

Rikard, Gabe. *Authority and the Mountaineer in Cormac McCarthy's Appalachia*. Jefferson, NC: McFarland and Company, 2013.

Robisch, S. K. "The Trapper Mystic: Werewolves in *The Crossing*." In *Myth, Legend, Dust: Critical Responses to Cormac McCarthy*, edited by Rick Wallach, 288–92. Manchester, UK: Manchester University Press, 2000.

Schafer, William J. "Cormac McCarthy: The Hard Wages of Original Sin." *Appalachian Journal* 4, no. 2 (1977): 105–19.

Schelling, Friedrich W. J. *The Ages of the World*. Translated by Frederick de Wolfe Bolman Jr. New York: Columbia University Press, 1942.

———. *First Outline of a System of the Philosophy of Nature*. Translated by Keith Peterson. Albany: State University of New York Press, 2004.

———. *The Grounding of Positive Philosophy: The Berlin Lectures*. Translated by Bruce Matthews. Albany: State University of New York Press, 2007.

———. *Historical-Critical Introduction to the Philosophy of Mythology*. Translated by Mason Richey and Markus Zisselsberger. Albany: State University of New York Press, 2007.

———. *Ideas for a Philosophy of Nature*. Translated by Errol E. Harris and Peter Heath. Cambridge: Cambridge University Press, 1988.

———. *On the History of Modern Philosophy*. Translated by Andrew Bowie. Cambridge: Cambridge University Press, 1994.

———. "On the Science of the Fine Arts." Translated by Ella S. Morgan. *Journal of Speculative Philosophy* 15, no. 2 (1881): 152–58.

———. "On the World Soul." Translated by Iain Hamilton Grant. *Collapse* 6 (2012): 67–95.

———. *Philosophical Inquiries into the Nature of Human Freedom*. Translated by James Gutmann. Chicago: Open Court Publishing, 1936.

———. *Philosophical Investigations into the Essence of Human Freedom*. Translated by Jeff Love and Johannes Schmidt. Albany: State University of New York Press, 2006.

———. *Schellings sämmtliche Werke*, edited by Karl Friedrich August Schelling. 14 vols. Stuttgart: J. G. Cotta'scher Verlag, 1856–61.

———. *System of Transcendental Idealism*. Translated by Peter Heath. Charlottesville: University Press of Virginia, 1978.

———. "*Timaeus*." Stuttgart-Bad Cannstatt: Frommann-Holzbog, 1994.

Schimpf, Shane. *A Reader's Guide to* Blood Meridian. 2006. Seattle: BonMot Publishing, 2011.

———. "A Short History of Scalping." In *They Rode On:* Blood Meridian *and the Tragedy of the American West*, edited by Rick Wallach, 25–37. Miami: Cormac McCarthy Society, 2013.

Schwarz, Astrid, and Kurt Jax. "Etymology and Original Sources of the Term 'Ecology.'" In *Ecology Revisited: Reflecting on Concepts Advancing Science*, edited by Astrid Schwarz and Kurt Jax, 145–47. Dordrecht: Springer, 2011.

Schwenzfeuer, Sebastian. *Natur und Subjekt: Die Grundlegung der schellingschen Naturphilosophie*. Freiburg: Verlag Karl Alber, 2012.

Scoones, Jacqueline. "The World on Fire: Ethics and Evolution in Cormac McCarthy's Border Trilogy." In *A Cormac McCarthy Companion: The Border Trilogy*, edited by Edwin T. Arnold and Dianne C. Luce, 131–60. Jackson: University Press of Mississippi, 2001.

Scott, Ridley. "Interview." In "*Prometheus* Crew: On a Mission Collision." 2011. Accessed January 27, 2015. http://pop.inquirer.net/?s=prometheus.

———, dir. *Prometheus*. Burbank, CA: Twentieth Century Fox, 2012. DVD.

Selden, Raman. "Wit, Judgement, Fancy and Imagination." In *The Theory of Criticism: From Plato to the Present*, edited by Raman Selden, 125–29. Harlow, UK: Longman, 1988.

Seltzer, Mark. *Bodies and Machines*. 1992. New York: Routledge, 2014.

Sepich, John Emil. *Notes on* Blood Meridian. 1993. Austin: University of Texas Press, 2011.

Serres, Michel. *The Natural Contract*. Translated by Elizabeth MacArthur and William Paulson. 1990. Ann Arbor: University of Michigan Press, 1995.

Shaviro, Steven. *The Universe of Things: On Speculative Realism*. Minneapolis: University of Minnesota Press, 2014.

———. "'The Very Life of the Darkness': A Reading of *Blood Meridian*." *Southern Quarterly* 30, no. 4 (1992): 111–121.

Shaw, Devin Zane. *Freedom and Nature in Schelling's Philosophy of Art*. London: Continuum, 2010.

Skibsrud, Johanna. "'A History of the Present': Knowledge as Violence in Cormac McCarthy's *Blood Meridian*." *Dandelion* 5, no. 1 (2014): 1–10.

Skrbina, David. *Panpsychism in the West*. Cambridge, MA: MIT Press, 2005.

Smith, Anthony Paul. *A Non-Philosophical Theory of Nature: Ecologies of Thought*. New York: Palgrave Macmillan, 2013.

Smith, James K. A. *Jacques Derrida: Live Theory*. New York: Continuum, 2005.

Snyder, Phillip A., and Delys W. Snyder. "Modernism, Postmodernism, and Language: McCarthy's Style." In *The Cambridge Companion to Cormac McCarthy*, edited by Steven Frye, 2013, 27–38. 2013. New York: Cambridge University Press, 2014.

Soper, Kate. *What Is Nature?* 1995. Oxford: Blackwell, 2000.

Sørensen, Bent. "Katabasis in Cormac McCarthy's *Blood Meridian*." *Orbis Litterarum* 60, no. 1 (2005): 16–25.

Spoden, Erika B. "Let There Be Blood: The Vein of Vietnam in *No Country for Old Men*." *Cormac McCarthy Journal* 10, no. 1 (2012): 76–92.

Spurgeon, Sara L. "Foundations of Empire: The Sacred Hunter and the Eucharist of the Wilderness in Cormac McCarthy's *Blood Meridian*." In *Cormac McCarthy*, edited by Harold Bloom, 85–105. New York: Infobase Publishing, 2009.

Steven, Mark. "The Late World of Cormac McCarthy." In *Styles of Extinction: Cormac McCarthy's* The Road, edited by Julian Murphet and Mark Steven, 63–87. London: Continuum, 2012.

Stiegler, Bernard. *Technics and Time*. Vol. 1, *The Fault of Epimetheus*. Translated by Richard Beardsworth and George Collins. 1994. Stanford, CA: Stanford University Press, 1998.

Sullivan, Walter. "Worlds Past and Future: A Christian and Several from the South." *Sewanee Review* 73, no. 4 (1965): 719–26.

Tally, Robert T., Jr. "Introduction: On Geocriticism." In *Geocritical Explorations: Space, Place, and Mapping in Literary and Cultural Studies*, edited by Robert T. Tally Jr., 1–9. New York: Palgrave Macmillan, 2011.

———. *Poe and the Subversion of American Literature: Satire, Fantasy, Critique*. New York: Bloomsbury, 2014.

Tally, Robert T., Jr., and Christine M. Battista. "Introduction: Ecocritical Geographies, Geocritical Ecologies, and the Spaces of Modernity." In *Ecocriticism and Geocriticism: Overlapping Territories in Environmental and Spatial Literary Studies*, edited by Robert T. Tally Jr. and Christine M. Battista, 1–18. New York: Palgrave Macmillan, 2016.

Thacker, Eugene. *After Life*. Chicago: University of Chicago Press, 2010.

Thompson, Lucas. "'Books Are Made out of Books': David Foster Wallace and Cormac McCarthy." *Cormac McCarthy Journal* 13, no. 1 (2015): 3–26.

Thoreau, Henry D. *Walden*. 1854. Oxford: Oxford University Press, 2008.

Trotignon, Béatrice. "Detailing the Wor(l)d in *Suttree*." In *Myth, Legend, Dust: Critical Responses to Cormac McCarthy*, edited by Rick Wallach, 89–99. Manchester, UK: Manchester University Press, 2000.

Twain, Mark. *Adventures of Huckleberry Finn*. Mineola, NY: Dover Thrift, 1994.

Uhlmann, Anthony. "*Suttree*, Joyce, and Flaubert." In *Cormac McCarthy's Borders and Landscapes*, edited by Louise Jillett, 163–73. New York: Bloomsbury, 2016.

Varela, Francisco J. "Whither Perceptual Meaning?" In *Understanding Origins: Contemporary Views on the Origin of Life, Mind, and Society*, edited by Francisco J. Varela and Jean-Pierre Dupuy, 235–63. Dordrecht: Kluwer Academic Publishers, 1992.

Vescio, Bryan. "Strangers in Everydayland: Suttree, Huckleberry Finn, and Tragic Humanism." In *You Would Not Believe What Watches*, edited by Rick Wallach, 108–115. 2nd ed. Miami: Cormac McCarthy Society, 2014.

Vieth, Ronja. "A Frontier Myth Turns Gothic: *Blood Meridian: Or, the Evening Redness in the West*." *Cormac McCarthy Journal* 8, no. 1 (2010): 47–62.

Vilkka, Leena. *The Intrinsic Value of Nature*. Amsterdam: Rodopi, 1997.

Wallace, Garry. "Meeting McCarthy." *Southern Quarterly* 30, no. 4 (1992): 134–39.

Wallach, Rick. "Ulysses in Knoxville: Suttree's Ageean Journey." In *You Would Not Believe What Watches*, edited by Rick Wallach, 78–86. 2nd ed. Miami: Cormac McCarthy Society, 2014.

Walsh, Christopher J. *In the Wake of the Sun: Navigating the Southern Works of Cormac McCarthy*. Knoxville, TN: Newfound Press, 2009.

Wark, McKenzie. *Molecular Red: Theory for the Anthropocene*. London: Verso, 2016.

Warnke, Camilla. "Schellings Idee und Theorie des Organismus und der Paradigmawechsel der Biologie um die Wende zum 19. Jahrhundert." *Jahrbuch für Geschichte und Theorie der Biologie* 5 (1998): 187–234.

Welchman, Alistair. "Deleuze and Deep Ecology." In *An [Un]likely Alliance: Thinking Environment[s] with Deleuze | Guattari*, edited by Bernd Herzogenrath, 116–38. Newcastle upon Tyne, UK: Cambridge Scholars Publishing, 2008.

Wellek, René. "Emerson and German Philosophy." *New England Quarterly* 16, no. 1 (1943): 41–62.

———. "The Minor Transcendentalists and German Philosophy." *New England Quarterly* 15, no. 4 (1942): 652–80.

Westphal, Bertrand. Foreword to *Geocritical Explorations: Space, Place, and Mapping in Literary and Cultural Studies*, edited by Robert T. Tally Jr., ix–xv. New York: Palgrave Macmillan, 2011.

———. *Geocriticism: Real and Fictional Spaces*. Translated by Robert T. Tally Jr. 2007. Basingstoke: Palgrave Macmillan, 2011.

Whistler, Daniel. "Schelling's Doctrine of Abstraction." *Pli* 26 (2014): 58–81.

———. *Schelling's Theory of Symbolic Language: Forming the System of Identity*. Oxford: Oxford University Press, 2013.

Whitehead, Alfred North. *Modes of Thought*. New York: Free Press, 1968.

Whitman, Walt. *Democratic Vistas: The Original Edition in Facsimile*. Edited by Ed Folsom. 1871. Iowa City: University of Iowa Press, 2010.

Widder, Nathan. "Matter as Simulacrum; Thought as Phantasm; Body as Event." In *Deleuze and the Body*, edited by Laura Guillaume and Joe Hughes, 96–114. Edinburgh: Edinburgh University Press, 2011.

Wieland, Wolfgang. "Die Anfänge der Philosophie Schellings und die Frage nach der Natur." In *Materialien zu Schellings philosophischen Anfängen*, edited by Manfred Frank and Gerhard Kurz, 237–279. 1967. Frankfurt: Suhrkamp, 1975.

Wierschem, Markus. "'It's More True but It Aint as Good': Searching for Truth in the Death-Deferring Dialogue of McCarthy's *The Sunset Limited*." In *Imaginary Dialogues in America*, edited by Till Kinzel and Jarmila Mildorf, 327–347. Heidelberg: Winter, 2014.

———. "The Other End of *The Road*: Re-Reading McCarthy in Light of Thermodynamics and Information Theory." *Cormac McCarthy Journal* 11, no. 1 (2013): 1–22.

———. "'Some Witless Paraclete Beleaguered with All Limbo's Clamor': On Violent Contagion and Apocalyptic Logic in Cormac McCarthy's *Outer Dark*." *Contagion* 22 (2015): 185–202.

Wilkerson, K. E. "Regions of the Damned: Cormac McCarthy as Regional Writer." *Hudson Valley Regional Review* 11 (1994): 11–29.

Willems, Brian. *Speculative Realism and Science Fiction*. Edinburgh: Edinburgh University Press, 2017.

Williams, Raymond. *Marxism and Literature*. 1977. Oxford: Oxford University Press, 2009.

Wirth, Jason M. *The Conspiracy of Life: Meditations on Schelling and His Time*. Albany: State University of New York Press, 2003.

———. *Schelling's Practice of the Wild: Time, Art, Imagination*. Albany: State University of New York Press, 2015.

Witek, Terri. "Reeds and Hides: Cormac McCarthy's Domestic Spaces." In *Cormac McCarthy*, edited by Harold Bloom, 23–29. New York: Infobase Publishing, 2009.

Woodard, Benjamin. "The Untimely (and Unshapely) Decomposition of Onto-Epistemological Solidity: Negarestani's *Cyclonopedia* as Metaphysics." In *Leper Creativity: Cyclonopedia Symposium*, edited by Ed Keller, Nicola Masciandaro, and Eugene Thacker, 213–23. New York: Punctum Books, 2012.

Woodson, Linda. "Mapping *The Road* in Post-Postmodernism." *Cormac McCarthy Journal* 6 (2008): 87–97.

Woodward, Richard B. "McCarthy's Venomous Fiction." *New York Times Magazine*, April 19, 1992. Accessed March 14, 2015. http://www.nytimes.com/1992/04/19/magazine/cormac-mccarthy-s-venomous-fiction.html?pagewanted=all.

Worthington, Leslie Harper. *Cormac McCarthy and the Ghost of Huck Finn*. Jefferson, NC: McFarland and Company, 2012.

Yarbrough, Scott D. "Tricksters and Lightbringers in McCarthy's Post-Appalachian Novels." *Cormac McCarthy Journal* 10, no. 1 (2012): 46–55.

Yardley, Jonathan. "Alone, Alone, All, All Alone . . ." *Washington Post Book World*, January 13, 1974, 1.

Young, Thomas D., Jr. "The Imprisonment of Sensibility: *Suttree*." *Southern Quarterly* 30, no. 4 (1992): 72–92.

Zalamea, Fernando. *Synthetic Philosophy of Contemporary Mathematics*. Translated by Zachary Luke Fraser. 2009. Falmouth, UK: Urbanomic, 2012.

Zapf, Hubert. *Literatur als kulturelle Ökologie: Zur kulturellen Funktion imaginativer Texte an Beispielen des amerikanischen Romans*. Tübingen: Niemeyer, 2002.

Žižek, Slavoj. *The Indivisible Remainder: On Schelling and Related Matters*. 1996. London: Verso, 2007.

Zola, Émile. "The Experimental Novel." Translated by Belle Sherman. In *The Theory of Criticism: From Plato to the Present*, edited by Raman Selden, 51–54. 1880. Harlow, UK: Longman, 1988.

Zovko, Marie-Elise. *Natur und Gott: Das wirkungsgeschichtliche Verhältnis Schellings und Baaders*. Würzburg: Königshausen & Neumann, 1996.

INDEX